Shaping the Future Through Standardization

Kai Jakobs
RWTH Aachen University, Germany

A volume in the Advances in
Standardization Research (ASR)
Book Series

IGI Global
DISSEMINATOR OF KNOWLEDGE

Published in the United States of America by
    IGI Global
    Engineering Science Reference (an imprint of IGI Global)
    701 E. Chocolate Avenue
    Hershey PA, USA 17033
    Tel: 717-533-8845
    Fax: 717-533-8661
    E-mail: cust@igi-global.com
    Web site: http://www.igi-global.com

Library of Congress Cataloging-in-Publication Data

Names: Jakobs, Kai, 1957- editor.
Title: Shaping the future through standardization / Kai Jakobs, editor.
Description: Hershey : Engineering Science Reference, 2019. | Includes
  bibliographical references and index. | Summary: "This book examines
  quality and standardization within diverse organizations globally with a
  special focus on future perspectives, including how standards and
  standardization may shape the future"-- Provided by publisher.
Identifiers: LCCN 2019037693 (print) | LCCN 2019037694 (ebook) | ISBN
  9781799821816 (hardcover) | ISBN 9781799821823 (paperback) | ISBN
  9781799821830 (ebook)
Subjects: LCSH: Standardization.
Classification: LCC T59 .S48 2019 (print) | LCC T59 (ebook) | DDC
  389/.6--dc23
LC record available at https://lccn.loc.gov/2019037693
LC ebook record available at https://lccn.loc.gov/2019037694

This book is published in the IGI Global book series Advances in Standardization Research (ASR) (ISSN: 2472-7296; eISSN: 2472-730X)

British Cataloguing in Publication Data
A Cataloguing in Publication record for this book is available from the British Library.

All work contributed to this book is new, previously-unpublished material.
The views expressed in this book are those of the authors, but not necessarily of the publisher.

For electronic access to this publication, please contact: eresources@igi-global.com.

Advances in Standardization Research (ASR) Book Series

ISSN:2472-7296
EISSN:2472-730X

Editor-in-Chief: Kai Jakobs, RWTH Aachen University, Germany

MISSION

Today, the technical, economic and regulatory importance of standards is no longer questioned. Standards allow complex technical systems to interoperate, they extend or even create markets and have been an important tool in the establishment of the European single market. The underlying standardization process provides a platform for pre-competitive co-operation and can support open innovation.

The **Advances in Standardization Research (ASR) Book Series** seeks to advance the available literature on the development, characteristics, deployment and value of standards. Highly multi-disciplinary standardization research provides deeper insight into the ways standards shape the environment within which they function and how, in turn, their development is shaped by the respective institutional and procedural environment. The series thus helps to better utilize standards for the improvement of organizational processes in both the private and the public sector. It also contributes to a better understanding of standardization processes and should thus enable a more effective and efficient development of more useful standards.

COVERAGE

- Descriptive Theory of Standardization
- Technological innovation and standardization
- Open source and standardization
- Standards for information infrastructures
- National, regional, international, and corporate standards strategies
- Multinational and Transnational Perspectives and Impacts
- Standards in the Private Sector
- Standards Research and Education Activities
- Conformity assessment

IGI Global is currently accepting manuscripts for publication within this series. To submit a proposal for a volume in this series, please contact our Acquisition Editors at Acquisitions@igi-global.com or visit: http://www.igi-global.com/publish/.

Titles in this Series

For a list of additional titles in this series, please visit:
http://www.igi-global.com/book-series/advances-standardization-research/154747

Critical Theory and Transformative Learning

Victor X. Wang (Grand Canyon University, USA)
Information Science Reference • © 2018 • 333pp • H/C (ISBN: 9781522560869) • US $185.00

Innovations in Measuring and Evaluating Scientific Information

J. John Jeyasekar (Tamil Nadu State Forensic Sciences Department, India) and P. Saravanan (Lekshmipuram College of Arts and Science, India)
Information Science Reference • © 2018 • 298pp • H/C (ISBN: 9781522534570) • US $195.00

For an entire list of titles in this series, please visit:
http://www.igi-global.com/book-series/advances-standardization-research/154747

701 East Chocolate Avenue, Hershey, PA 17033, USA
Tel: 717-533-8845 x100 • Fax: 717-533-8661
E-Mail: cust@igi-global.com • www.igi-global.com

Editorial Advisory Board

Table of Contents

Section 1
The Development of Standards

Jeff Mangers, University of Luxembourg, Luxembourg
Christof Oberhausen, Paul Wurth Geprolux S.A., Luxembourg
Meysam Minoufekr, University of Luxembourg, Luxembourg
Peter Plapper, University of Luxembourg, Luxembourg

Sylvain Maechler, University of Lausanne, Switzerland
Jean-Christophe Graz, University of Lausanne, Switzerland

Sabrina Petersohn, German Centre for Higher Education Research and
Science Studies (DZHW), Germany
Sophie Biesenbender, German Centre for Higher Education Research
and Science Studies (DZHW), Germany
Christoph Thiedig, German Centre for Higher Education Research and
Science Studies (DZHW), Germany

Section 5
The Practitioners' Corner

Detailed Table of Contents

Section 1
The Development of Standards

Chapter 1
Creation of an ISO Standard at the Example of Value Stream Management
Method 1
> *Jeff Mangers, University of Luxembourg, Luxembourg*
> *Christof Oberhausen, Paul Wurth Geprolux S.A., Luxembourg*
> *Meysam Minoufekr, University of Luxembourg, Luxembourg*
> *Peter Plapper, University of Luxembourg, Luxembourg*

The main objectives of this chapter are to elucidate the necessity of a standardized value stream management (VSM) and to clarify how this standard can effectively increase corporate performance within cross-enterprise supply chain networks (SCNs). VSM is an effective tool to collect, evaluate, and continuously improve product and information flows within companies in a common and standardized manner. The findings of this chapter are not only valid for consistent product and information flows but are representative for the relevance of standards in general. In a globalized economy, standards need to be generally accepted and valid for all countries. Thus, corporate or national standards only have limited impact. The International Standardization Organization (ISO) provides the means to develop, negotiate and communicate standards, which are globally binding. This chapter shares the experience of ISO 22468 standard development within ISO/TC 154 WG7 and proves its applicability by an administrative use case.

Chapter 2

The global ecological crisis has prompted the development of tools that try to redefine relations between business and nature, among them, natural capital accounting methodologies. The International Organization for Standardization (ISO) recently set standards on which these methodologies are based. Other actors, including the Big Four audit and accounting firms, developed their own methodologies outside the scope of ISO. This chapter examines why and how ISO developed natural capital accounting standards that are likely to compete with other methodologies. From the assumption that standards are not just technical, but also political instruments, it argues that they shape the future by creating power relations between actors within and outside ISO. The chapter suggests that these ISO standards aims at competing with first-movers' methodologies, in particular on the power implications resulting from transparency. It builds the argument on international political economy approaches to emphasise the link between technical specifications and power relations in contemporary capitalism.

Chapter 3

The following contribution asks which role standards for research information play in practices of responsible research evaluation. The authors develop the notion of assessment standards against the background of functional standard classifications. The development of semantic and procedural assessment standards in the national research evaluation exercises of the Netherlands, Great Britain, and Italy are investigated using a qualitative case study design. A central finding of the study is that assessment standards incorporate conflicting values. A continuous tradeoff between the transparency of evaluation procedures and provided information as well as the variety of research outputs is being counterbalanced in all countries by compensating a higher level of semantic standardization with lower degrees of procedural standardization.

Section 2
Participation in Standards Setting

Chapter 4

Since standardization is essential and additionally has organizational effects, studying motivation for participating in the standardization processes is important. A phenomenological study of descriptions made by individual participants in project teams for geographical information at the Swedish Standards Institute, SIS, was conducted 2016-2017. The study indicated that participants were motivated, but there were different motivators depending on the participants' differing contexts. For most participants, the main personal meaningful goal was to be at the forefront of development. For participants employed by organizations with frequent interactions with stakeholders, the main personal meaningful goal was to satisfy the stakeholders' needs. This study also showed that several members felt that they do not have sufficient time for working with standardization asks due to the fact that their daily work in their organizations often has higher priority in relation to standardization work. This may slow down the development of standards and other publications due to lack of resources.

Chapter 5

This chapter explores patterns and recent trends in meeting attendance at four standard development organizations (SDO): 3GPP, IETF, IEEE 802.11, and One M2M. Average meeting attendance has slightly increased over the last two decades. It is rare for individuals to attend meetings in different SDOs. IETF has the least attendee overlap with other SDOs and the lowest attendee affiliation concentration. Nevertheless, 3GPP attendance has become more diverse and IETF attendance more concentrated. The affiliations of attendees of 3GPP and IETF have become more similar over time while OneM2M attendance has become more distinct from other SDOs. IEEE 802.11 attendance has become significantly less diverse since 2007. Until 2014, there was a significant convergence with 3GPP. Since 2014, this trend has reversed, and attendance at IEEE 802.11 has become more similar to IETF. The author explores implications of the described evidence for differences between telecommunications and internet standardization, companies' standardization strategies, and consequences of the patent policy change at IEEE.

Section 3
Shedding Some More Light on ISO9001

Chapter 6

Vasileios Mavroeidis, Hellenic Open University, Greece
Petros E. Maravelakis, Department of Business Administration,
*   University of Piraeus, Greece*
Katarzyna Tarnawska, European Commission, Belgium

Existing literature states that standardization and certification are not only crucial
for enterprises, but they have a positive impact on productivity, international trade,
innovation, and competition as well. This research employs data derived by the
European Innovation Union Scoreboard and the International Standardization
Organization from 2005 to 2014 to investigate the relation between innovation and
certified quality management systems according to ISO 9001. Using suitable panel
data analysis, the authors analyse the data gathered form a panel accounting for the
different countries and different years. The main result of this study is that we are
able to provide evidence to policymakers, academics, and entrepreneurs that there
is a statistically significant relationship between innovation and certified quality
management systems. The originality of this chapter stems from the fact that up to
now, to the authors' knowledge, the impact of ISO 9001 on innovation has not been
examined in the European context.

Chapter 7

Hiam Serhan, AgroParisTech, France
Doudja Saïdi-Kabeche, AgroParisTech, France

In a connected society and organizations working with digitized business models,
standards will have more important roles than ever in shaping activity systems content,
structure, and governance. While the standardization conformity/innovation duality
has received great attention in literature, little research has been done on the role of
managers in managing the tensions of knowledge codification required during ISO
9001 standard implementation. By utilizing Danone's Networking Attitude experience
as a case study, the authors address this gap by exploring how managerial skills
and practices were used to overcome the cognitive and emotional tensions related
to internal knowledge codification, transfer, and use. The main contribution is to
elucidate the role of managers in resolving these paradoxes and creating innovation
capabilities. Further, they demonstrate the mutually beneficial relationship between
knowledge codification and innovation if knowledge management is approached
more as an evolving pragmatic knowing than a technical means that may create
rigidity and resistance.

Section 4
Legal and Regulatory Aspects

Chapter 8

Harshvardhan Jitendra Pandit, Trinity College Dublin, Ireland
Christophe Debruyne, Trinity College Dublin, Ireland
Declan O'Sullivan, Trinity College Dublin, Ireland
Dave Lewis, Trinity College Dublin, Ireland

The General Data Protection Regulation (GDPR) has changed the ecosystem of services involving personal data and information. It emphasises several obligations and rights, amongst which the Right to Data Portability requires providing a copy of the given personal data in a commonly used, structured, and machine-readable format – for interoperability. The GDPR thus explicitly motivates the use and adoption of data interoperability concerning information. This chapter explores the entities and their interactions in the context of the GDPR to provide an information model for the development of interoperable services. The model categorises information and exchanges and explores existing standards and efforts towards use for interoperable interactions. The chapter concludes with an argument for the use and adoption of structured metadata to enable more expressive services through semantic interoperability.

Chapter 9

Marta Orviska, Faculty of Economics, Matej Bel University in Banska
    Bystrica, Slovakia
Jan Hunady, Faculty of Economics, Matej Bel University in Banska
    Bystrica, Slovakia

E-commerce has several advantages for customers and improves firm productivity. The research aims to examine factors determining the usage of e-commerce within the EU with the focus on problems related to standards. This includes especially a lack of interoperability and labelling problems. Firstly, the authors found rising popularity of online purchases in recent years. Despite the increase, Visegrad countries are still lagging behind the EU average. A similar increase is also evident in e-commerce engagement as well as in turnover from e-commerce. Furthermore, they also estimated logit regressions to find factors affecting the probability of firm engagement in e-commerce. Interoperability problems, when selling online, are more frequently reported by wholesale firms as well as those in the information and communication sector. The majority of firms in our sample stated that common rules of e-commerce within the EU could be beneficial. This is particularly important for those reporting problems with interoperability and different labelling.

Section 5
The Practitioners' Corner

Chapter 10

Christophe Sene, CEN/TC-276, France

Standardization is one source of informal rules that regulate the public realm: standards are not legally-binding, but, as soft law instruments, they influence the governance, ethics, and conduct of companies. Standardization brings unique benefits to companies in term of knowledge, credibility, and risk reduction by bringing accountability and predictability. To foster active participation of companies in standardization, higher and continuous education in standardization is essential to build mutual understanding between companies and the standardization world since decision making in the former is a relatively quick top-down hierarchical process while in the latter time-consuming consensus-building is the norm. The concept of Student Standardization Societies (SSS) is introduced as the best way to promote standardization in the long term, and advice is given for the practical implementation of SSS and their relationship with Official Standardization Organizations.

Chapter 11

Hans Teichmann, Independent Researcher, Switzerland

For the economic growth in least developed countries (LDCs), the transfer of technical and scientific know-how is an uncontested necessity. Poverty and underdevelopment in LDCs are interrelated features. Technology transfers may fail, however, unless varied constraints are taken into account. The focus of this study is on obstacles to an efficient technology transfer to LDCs, and on the major role which global, bilingual standards can play in this process. The global standards setting organizations International Organization for Standardization (ISO) and International Electrotechnical Commission (IEC) have recognized the need for a general, comprehensive, and effective support of the LDCs' bodies for national quality infrastructure (NQI). Standardization is not only a vital socio-economic function in itself, but standards represent part of much wider, essential infrastructures. Three stakeholder groups are particularly concerned: the users of the global standards in LDCs, the global standards setting organizations, and the individual National Quality Infrastructure bodies.

Preface

Today's standards are tomorrow's technology. This holds particularly, but by no means exclusively, for Information and Communication Technologies (ICT). Perhaps most notably these days, however, it holds for the development of smart systems.

As it happens, I have already discussed smart systems in the preface to 'Corporate and Global Standardization Initiatives in Contemporary Society'. Therefore, in the following I will only provide a recap. This (extended) recap will form the preliminary canter for the main discussion topic – Responsible Standardisation. I will argue that this is urgently needed for the standardisation of smart systems

'Smartness' is injected into rather more 'traditional' technologies by the integration of Information and Communication Technologies (ICT). This way, transport systems, for example, become Intelligent Transport Systems (ITS), manufacturing is turned into Smart Manufacturing (aka 'Industry 4.0) and power supply into the Smart Grid. Together with similar developments in other sectors (e.g. smart buildings, e-health, ambient assisted living or autonomous driving) these smart applications represent cornerstones of Smart Cities, which may thus more or less be considered as a superset of smart technologies. Among others, a smart city will comprise smart buildings, utilise the smart grid, provide smart transport facilities and e-health services and incorporate smart production sites (Jakobs, 2018a). Figure 1 visualises this and depicts a simple 3-layer-model of a smart city. It shows a hierarchy of technologies and policies; all of which will eventually be based on (international) standards. At the topmost level, standards for 'smart policies and objectives' provide guidance to city leadership for the development of an overall smart city strategy, the identification of priorities, the development of a practical implementation roadmap, and for an effective approach to monitoring and evaluating progress. Today, standards setting still very much focuses on the bottom level, i.e. on communication systems and protocols. With respect to the upper levels standardisation is mostly limited to (high-level) requirements for smart applications and performance indicators for the objectives and policies[1].

This newly gained smartness also extends to the underlying infrastructure. Its main components include Cyber-Physical Systems (CPSs) and the Internet of Things

Figure 1. Smart city model

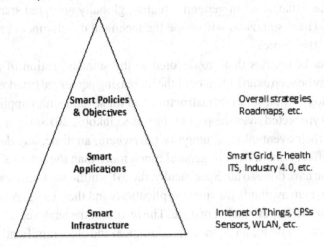

Smart Policies & Objectives	Overall strategies, Roadmaps, etc.
Smart Applications	Smart Grid, E-health ITS, Industry 4.0, etc.
Smart Infrastructure	Internet of Things, CPSs Sensors, WLAN, etc.

(IoT). Forecasts indicate anything between 20 and 50 billion IoT devices for the year 2020[2]. With these numbers it appears safe to say that the IoT will eventually add the 'anything' dimension to the frequently claimed 'anyplace' and 'anytime' characteristics of today's Internet. In any case, a smart communication infrastructure is the necessary pre-requisite for smart applications.

Standards for a smart communication infrastructure have mostly been developed for the field of (power-)constrained devices. Relevant activities in this field are ongoing in e.g. oneM2M, where standards for a common M2M (Machine-to-Machine) Service Layer are being developed. Within the European Telecommunications Standards Institute (ETSI), the 'Smart M2M Communications' committee works on the interface between the service layer and the application layer. Other ETSI Technical Committees (TCs) as well as groups of the Institute of Electrical and Electronics Engineers (IEEE), the International Telecommunication Union (ITU) and several other Standards Setting Organisations (SSOs) work on wireless applications. Within the Internet Engineering Task Force (IETF), several Working Groups (WGs) focus on constrained devices.

According to an unpublished document by the International Organization for Standardization (ISO), there were more than 900 IoT-related standards late 2016 (ISO, 2016). Of those, around 140 come from the IEEE, 200 from ITU and 300 from the joint committee for ICT standardisation of the ISO and the International Electrotechnical Committee (IEC; ISO/IEC JTC1). However, most of these are rather more generic standards in the field of wireless communication systems that were not necessarily developed specifically for the IoT but may well be deployed by it as well.

Interoperability is the key requirement for all smart systems. To achieve interoperability between an extremely broad spectrum of devices and applications, to guarantee the privacy of data and the security of the communication system and indeed to make 'smartness' in general a reality, globally accepted standards are a sine-qua-non. These standards will shape the technical development and thus, to a certain extent, the future.

The number of entities that are devoted to the standardisation of a particular technology may be seen as an indicator of the increasing perceived (market) relevance of this technology. For a smart infrastructure and for several smart applications this number has skyrocketed over the past eight years (Jakobs, 2018a).

Thanks to their eventual true[3] ubiquity (anywhere, anytime, any device) smart systems will affect human lives in general much more than the Internet and mobile communication have done so far. Specifically, the IoT's billions of sensors will collect data and make them available for smart applications and their users. A considerable part of this data will be personal or private. The results of the analyses of this massive amount of data will have major economic, ecological and other ramifications and will directly impact governments, citizens and businesses alike. To adequately deal with this will represent a major challenge for policy makers and for society as a whole. Accordingly, potentially severe non-technical issues will need to be addressed in the context of smart applications, specifically during standardisation.

Many smart applications will have hard and very specific requirements on the underlying communication infrastructure. Perhaps most notably, guaranteed levels of e.g. reliability and predictability will become increasingly important. As a consequence, application design, communication technology, operating systems and control loops will need to be extremely closely coupled – loosely coupled systems will hardly be able to meet these requirements. In fact, these close interrelations between infrastructure elements and applications almost mandate joint standardisation, i.e. that smart applications should be standardised in conjunction with the infrastructure (v.d.Brink et al., 2019). This means that the 'usual suspects' who typically populate standardisation WGs, i.e. computer scientists and telecommunication engineers at the infrastructure side, will need to co-operate with technical experts from numerous other disciplines who work on the respective application side.

Moreover, the true ubiquity of smart systems and their unclear ramifications for various fields of society imply that 'exotics' (in the world of ICT standardisation) like e.g. citizens, NGOs and unions[4] will need to be involved in the standards setting process. The same may in many cases also hold for politicians, sociologists and even philosophers (if ethical issues are to be discussed); they will also need to have a say in one way or another. Generally, societal issues, including sustainability, need to play an adequate role already during standards development.

For instance, when thinking about the IoT or Smart Cities, the thought 'Big Brother' comes to mind all too easily (see, e.g., Allam & Newman, 2018 or Lööw et al., 2019). After all, parts of the technology (like sensors and Big Data analytics) are readily available and are being implemented while this is being written. Adequate measures will need to be taken early on in order to make smart applications widely acceptable despite such justified concerns.

One such measure, perhaps the least complex one, would be to make sure that adequate mechanisms and provisions are in place to guarantee data security and privacy. These mechanisms would have a technical as well as a legal dimension. Dedicated standards will be required to cover the former; given the resource-constrainedness of most 'smart' devices (like sensors and actuators) existing standards will not normally be directly implementable[5]. Issues relating to the latter will differ between regions; for Europe and the European General Data Protection Regulation (GDPR; see, e.g., Stuurman, 2017 or Wachter, 2018).

Along entirely different lines, another measure would be to motivate as many groups of stakeholders as possible to contribute to the standardisation of smart applications (perhaps less so for the infrastructure). This holds specifically for those groups that are not normally represented in standards setting but nevertheless stand to be heavily affected by smart applications (see above). This would serve two purposes. For one, basing standards for smart applications on technical expertise alone will not do adequate justice to the complexity of the problem (with its numerous decidedly non-technical facets). Accordingly, non-technical expertise will need to be incorporated into the standards in order to eventually develop a technology that is not just technically sound but benefits the economy and, ultimately, society as a whole. In addition, basing standards (and thus technology) on the broadest possible consensus by involving a wide range of stakeholder groups will foster its wider acceptance.

Yet another measure, which is also the focus of this Preface, would be to incorporate ethical aspects from the earliest development stages onward[6]. As Williams and Edge (1996) note, "The shaping process (of a technology) begins with the earliest stages of research and development" (p. 874). Specifically, this includes the standardisation stage.

To this end, 'Responsible Standardisation' (RS) might well be a suitable approach (see Figure 2). The idea of RS is closely linked to (and indeed borrowed from) Responsible Research and Innovation (RRI). To paraphrase (European Commission, 2013), RRI is a comprehensive approach to research and innovation that allows all stakeholders at an early stage to obtain relevant knowledge on the consequences of the outcomes of their actions and to evaluate these outcomes (and those of any potential options) in terms of societal needs and moral values. In the context of standards setting such guidelines could ensure that standardisation initiatives take into account internationally agreed non-technical aspects to be associated with a certain technology.

Figure 2. The need for responsible standardisation

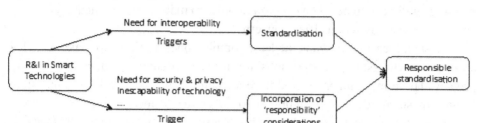

That is, RS could help ensure that standardisation takes into account not just technical and economic, but also e.g. ethical, environmental and privacy aspects. To this end, privacy-by-design principles (Danezis et al., 2014) could be adapted to integrate these aspects into the process ('ethics by design'; see e.g. (European Commission, 2015) for a discussion of related aspects in the IoT context). Moreover, technology assessment could be applied (see, e.g., Grunwald, 2015), as could be principles of the social shaping of technology (see, e.g., Williams & Edge, 1996), in order to detect potentially undesired outcomes of the standardisation and deployment processes and to take appropriate counter-measures as early as possible. This holds particularly for new and hardly understood technologies for which standards could also serve as a socio-ethical framework.

The world of standards setting itself will also be affected by these developments. Perhaps most notably, the multi-disciplinary nature of smart systems will pose extra problems for the traditionally rather more 'mono-disciplinary' standardisation process. It will require co-operation between standardisation entities and – perhaps even more important and difficult – between individuals with very different cultures, from equally different backgrounds and with a wide range of expertise.

Whether or not all this can be achieved by 'traditional' SSOs within the framework of the current standardisation environment remains an open question. Nevertheless, a recent study (Jakobs, 2018b) found that experts working on research into and standardisation of smart systems quite unanimously opposed the idea of any new SSO (which might cater for the specific characteristics of smart system standardisation). And their argument that the number of SSOs is large enough as it is carries weight; a new entity may well increase the existing complexity without adding much value.

However, smart systems' eventual true ubiquity and the associated major societal ramifications warrant extra efforts to make sure that the best possible system will be designed. And despite the experts' views this may well be best achieved most effectively and efficiently through dedicated, centralised efforts. Whether or not this is a realistic proposition remains to be seen, though. After all, co-operation and co-ordination between SSOs still leave a lot to be desired after around four decades (this holds particularly for consortia). It is hard to believe that this is going to change any time soon.

Still, a dedicated 'Smart Systems SSO', perhaps not unlike ISO/IEC's JTC1 but sponsored by a range of SSOs, could lead, co-ordinate, align and at least partly perform relevant standardisation activities. Such an entity would probably not solve all co-ordination problems, but if it were sponsored by at least the major SSOs in the field their combined expertise and 'market power' should be a unique selling point and attract the big corporate players.

In addition, given the number and diversity of smart systems' stakeholders, this entity would need to adopt a process that caters to this variety. For instance, it might be helpful to adopt a two-tier process, where the technical issues and the socio-economic/societal/ethical ones are considered separately by different groups and where the latter informs the former. As already mentioned, 'ethics by design' should be a guiding principle here. Last but not least, it will probably be necessary to provide (government) money to ensure participation of societal stakeholders.

Smart systems standardisation is still at a comparably early stage, so it should not be too late to devise an environment that adequately caters for the standardisation of a technology which has the potential to dramatically change out lives – for better or worse.

Over to the papers. Taken together, they represent a nice cross section of the varied current efforts in standardisation research, with a view towards the future.

Possibly following a phase of research and development, a standard's life typically begins with its formal development. Accordingly, the first section of this book relates to 'The Development of Standards' and addresses this aspect from three very different angles. The first chapter looks at the rationale behind, and the first steps of, the development of a sample ISO standard. It is entitled 'Creation of an ISO Standard at the example of Value Stream Management method' and was co-authored by Jeff Mangers, Christof Oberhausen, Meysam Minoufekr and Peter Plapper. This chapter motivates why a VSM standard is needed and how this standard can increase corporate performance. For Industry 4.0, for instance, and against the background of an increasing globalisation, the importance of a standardised communication between internal actors as well as with the outside world become more and more important. VSM is a powerful and at the same time easy-to-use tool, which is used to analyse efficiency of product and information flows. The VSM method, as defined in ISO 22468, may be used by an individual station, a complete plant and even for a manufacturing network, comprising several companies.

The second chapter, by Sylvain Maechler and Jean-Christophe Graz, looks at a very recent development, 'The standardisation of natural capital accounting methodologies'. Standardisation in this field has been pushed by ISO on the one hand and large firms active in accounting and auditing ('the Big Four') on the other.

The latter, who started first, could not establish their proprietary specifications as a (global) standard and had no interest in making proprietary knowledge available for the common good; they did not participate in the ISO activities. The whole process was highly political, raising power relation issues both within outside ISO. It also revealed the diverging views between different stakeholder communities, specifically between life-cycle assessment experts and environmental economists.

In some way, chapter three is linked to this as both chapters look at issues relating to 'responsibility'; one on the way of dealing with natural resources, the other on how to perform research evaluation. Entitled 'Investigating Assessment Standards in the Netherlands, Italy and the United Kingdom: Challenges for Responsible Research Evaluation' the chapter was written by Sabrina Petersohn, Sophie Biesenbender and Christoph Thiedig. It discusses the role standards for research information play in the context of responsible research evaluation. Semantic and procedural assessment standards developed and deployed in the Netherlands, Great Britain and Italy are analysed via qualitative case studies. A central finding is that these standards incorporate conflicting values: A high level of specification of semantic and procedural standards leads to increased transparency regarding the assessed content and the procedures to be followed. This, however, leads to a decreasing diversity of the information provided and of related evaluation practices.

The variety of stakeholders (corporate, societal, etc.) is an important characteristic of a standardisation process. The same holds for the actual individuals that populate the SSOs' working groups, a fact that is frequently ignored. After all, at the end of the day it is them who define the standard. Accordingly, it is crucial to understand the motivations that drive these people and the influence they exert in a working group or committee. Section two, entitled 'Participation in Standards Setting', addresses these questions.

Specifically, chapter four discusses 'The individuals' participation in standards setting: Role, Influence and Motivation'; it was written by Jonas Lundsten and Jesper Mayntz Paasch. This study focuses on individuals' motives for participation in the formal standardisation of geographic information To this end, a number of chaipersons and members of Technical Committees at the Swedish Standards Institute were interviewed. The majority of interviewees expressed a strong personal motivation in their standardisation work. In general, though, motivation corresponds to the interest of the respective employer; e.g., inadequate time allocated for participation may reduce motivation. This seems to happen quite frequently, although it may well be in contrast with employers' interests

Covering both individuals and their affiliations, chapter five, by Justus Alexander Baron, discusses 'Participation in the Standards Organizations Developing the Internet of Things: Recent Trends and Implications'. It looks at attendance patterns and recent trends in some SDOs that are active in IoT standardisation. Over the past few decades, many SDO characteristics have been remarkably stable. Yet, there have also been relevant changes, 'institutional convergence' being one of them: affiliations of IETF and 3GPP attendees have become more similar over time. In contrast, co-attendance declined rather quickly and significantly over time for OneM2M and 3GPP. Along slightly different lines, changes in the participation patterns in IEEE 802.11 suggest a different source of influence – the introduction of IEEE's new patent policy in 2015.

Let us now look at specific standards. The ISO 9000 series of standards series has been – and will continue to be – highly influential (and also much hyped). It dates back to the year 2000. But even after 19 years it is still a popular subject for research and we continue to learn more and more about the various and varied aspects, issues and impacts surrounding the standards of this series including, perhaps most notably, its relation to innovation. The discussion of the link between standardisation and innovation has been with us for quite some time now, yet the exact nature of this link still remains a matter of debate. The two chapters of section three, 'Shedding Some More Light on ISO 9001', highlight the diversity of facets to be analysed as well as the range of methods deployed to study it. Chapter six, co-authored by Vasileios Mavroeidis, Petros E. Maravelakis and Katarzyna Tarnawska, asks the question 'Does innovation flourish by the implementation of certified management systems? A study in European context'. Based on data from the European Innovation Union Scoreboard and from ISO that cover the years 2005 to 2014, the chapter analyses the relation between innovation and ISO 9001 certified quality management systems. It finds a statistically significant relation between innovation and such systems. This is the first attempt at analysing the impact of ISO 9001 on innovation has not been examined in the European context.

Chapter 7 is entitled 'Managing the Standardization Knowledge Codification Paradox: Creative Experience and Expansive Learning' and was written by Hiam Serhan and Doudja Saidi-Kabèche. They study discusses the role of managers in dealing with the tensions associated with knowledge codification required during any ISO 9001 implementation. To this end, a case study of Danone's 'Networking Attitude' system reveals the value of paradoxes as a strategy to address organisational tensions and to unearth innovation capabilities during the implementation of quality management practices. The chapter also demonstrates a mutually beneficial relationship between knowledge codification and organisational learning and innovation.

The legal dimension of standards must not be overlooked. Unfortunately, legal scholars do not necessarily consider standards and standardisation as part of their field of research (neither do economists, social scientists or engineers, though). Given the relevance that standards themselves actually do have for legislation and regulation (certainly in Europe), not to mention the importance that (standards essential) patents have for standards, potential implementers and, of course, the patent holders, this is a bit astonishing. Thus, section four addresses some 'Legal and Regulatory Aspects'.

Regarding the former, chapter eight, by Harshvardhan Jitendra Pandit, Christophe Debruyne, Declan O'Sullivan and Dave Lewis, looks at a comparably recent European development, the General Data Protection Regulation (GDPR) and its relation to data interoperability, perhaps the one single most important field for standardisation these days. It is entitled 'Data Interoperability & GDPR'. Interoperability is the overriding requirement for most ICT services. The chapter explores entities and their interactions in the context of the GDPR to provide an information model to enable the development of such interoperable services that comply with the GDPR. The model categorises information and analyses existing standards with respect to their deployability towards interoperability, taking into account based the requirements on legal compliance imposed by the GDPR and other legislation.

Looking more at the regulatory side, chapter nine discusses 'E-commerce in the EU – the Role of Common Standards and Regulations'. The chapter authors are Marta Orviska and Jan Hunady. They examine standards related factors that influence the usage of e-commerce within the EU. Lack of interoperability and labelling problems feature quite prominently. The former problems are frequently reported by wholesalers and firms from the ICT sector. In general, the majority of firms under study stated that EU-wide common rules of e-commerce would be beneficial.

Finally, section five is handed over to the practitioners. Frequently, it is (implicitly) assumed that information flows primarily from research to practice. And this is indeed typically the case. In fact, I am absolutely convinced that most research activities, certainly those of the type compiled in this book, should not be performed inside the proverbial ivory tower. Rather, they should serve to help, for example, individuals, businesses and policy makers to make better informed decisions[7]. Yet, information should also flow in the reverse direction. And this information, from practice for research, should help 'ground' research and drag it out of said tower. Once again, this clearly holds for the research described in this book.

In 'The Practitioners' Corner', Christophe Sene, chairman of CEN TC 276 (Surface active agents) has authored an invited paper that aims at 'Fostering The Participation Of Companies In Standardization, A Soft Law Instrument To Reduce Risks', which also discusses 'The Concept Of Student Standardization Societies' in chapter 10. With standardisation rarely being a topic of secondary or tertiary education, well-educated standards setters are set to become an all too rare breed in the not-too-distant future. Most likely, this will eventually have a visible negative impact on all of us.

Also with a view towards the future, chapter 11, written by Hans Teichmann, a former IEC officer who is now retired, addresses the problem of 'Technology

Transfer to Least Developed Countries through Global Standards'. To be sustainable, future standardisation activities will need to take into account requirements of and the reality of life in these countries much more than they do today.

I do hope that reading this book will motivate at least some of you to think about how to help Shaping the Future Through Standardisation.

REFERENCES

Allam, Z., & Newman, P. (2018). Redefining the smart city: Culture, metabolism and governance. *Smart Cities*, *1*(1), 4–25. doi:10.3390martcities1010002

Ammar, M., Russello, G., & Crispo, B. (2018). Internet of Things: A survey on the security of IoT frameworks. *Journal of Information Security and Applications*, *38*, 8–27. doi:10.1016/j.jisa.2017.11.002

Danezis, G. (2015). *Privacy and Data Protection by Design – from policy to engineering*. Retrieved from https://arxiv.org/pdf/1501.03726

European Commission. (Ed.). (2013). *Options for Strengthening Responsible Research and Innovation*. Report of the Expert Group on the State of Art in Europe on Responsible Research and Innovation. Retrieved from https://ec.europa.eu/research/science-society/document_library/pdf_06/options-for-strengthening_en.pdf

European Commission. (Ed.). (2015). *Internet of Things – IoT Governance, Privacy and Security Issues*. Retrieved from https://www.researchgate.net/profile/Christine_Hennebert/publication/275540220_IoT_Governance_Privacy_and_Security_Issues/links/553f4f390cf24c6a05d1fd2a/IoT-Governance-Privacy-and-Security-Issues.pdf

European Parliament. (Ed.). (2016). *Ethical Aspects of Cyber-Physical Systems – Scientific Foresight study*. Retrieved from http://www.europarl.europa.eu/RegData/etudes/STUD/2016/563501/EPRS_STU(2016)563501_EN.pdf

Grunwald, A. (2015). Technology assessment. In *Encyclopaedia of Information Science and Technology* (3rd ed.; pp. 3998–4006). IGI Global. doi:10.4018/978-1-4666-5888-2.ch394

IEEE. (Ed.). (2019). *The IEEE Global Initiative on Ethics of Autonomous and Intelligent Systems. Ethically Aligned Design: A Vision for Prioritizing Human Well-being with Autonomous and Intelligent Systems, First Edition*. IEEE. Retrieved from https://standards.ieee.org/content/ieee-standards/en/industry-connections/ec/autonomous-systems.html

ISO. (Ed.). (2016). Standards related to the Internet of Things. Unpublished ISO document.

Jakobs, K. (2005). The Role of the 'Third Estate' in ICT Standardisation. In S. Bolin (Ed.), *The Standards Edge: Future Generation*. The Bolin Group.

Jakobs, K. (2018a). Jakobs, K. (2018). On Standardizing the Internet of Things and Its Applications. In *Internet of Things A to Z: Technologies and Applications* (pp. 191–218). IEEE. doi:10.1002/9781119456735.ch7

Jakobs, K. (2018b). *'Smart' Standardisation*. Presented at the 82nd IEC General Meeting.

Khan, M. A., & Salah, K. (2018). IoT security: Review, blockchain solutions, and open challenges. *Future Generation Computer Systems*, *82*, 395–411. doi:10.1016/j.future.2017.11.022

Lööw, J., Abrahamsson, L., & Johansson, J. (2019). Mining 4.0—The Impact of New Technology from a Work Place Perspective. Mining. *Metallurgy & Exploration*, *36*(4), 701–707. doi:10.100742461-019-00104-9

Stuurman, K. (2017). The Digitisation Driven Impact of Data Protection Regulation on the Standardisation Process. In *Digitalisation: Challenge and Opportunity for Standardisation. Proc. 22nd EURAS Annual Standardisation Conference*. Mainz Publishers.

Brink, L., Folmer, E., & Jakobs, K. (2019). Coping with Multi-Disciplinarity in Standardisation. In *Proc. 24th EURAS Annual Standardisation Conference – Standards for a Bio-Based Economy* (pp. 453-466). Mainz Publishers.

Wachter, S. (2018). The GDPR and the Internet of Things: A three-step transparency model. Law. *Innovation and Technology*, *10*(2), 266–294.

Williams, R., & Edge, D. (1996). The Social Shaping of Technology. *Research Policy*, *25*(6), 856–899. doi:10.1016/0048-7333(96)00885-2

ENDNOTES

[1]   See e.g. https://www.itu.int/ITU-T/recommendations/index_sg.aspx?sg=20 (accessed 2 October 2019).

[2]   20 billion: http://www.gartner.com/newsroom/id/3598917 (accessed 2 October 2019). 50 billion: http://www.electronicproducts.com/Internet_of_Things/Research/The_Internet_of_Things_forecast_of_50_billion_connected_

devices_by_2020_is_grossly_over_estimated_and_entirely_misleading.aspx (accessed 2 October 2019).

3   As opposed to the frequently claimed ubiquity oft he Internet, which refers only to its accessibility, really (which is not truly ubiquitous either).

4   The 'Third Estate'; see (Jakobs, 2005).

5   See e.g. (Khan & Salah, 2018) and (Ammar, 2018) for much more information on this crucial topic.

6   See also e.g. (European Parliament, 2016) and (IEEE, 2019).

7   This is not to say that research may not just be an end in itself, aiming to increase knowledge and understanding without any (immediate) practical implications and relevance. But this should not become the norm.

Acknowledgment

I would like to thank Ms. Josie Dadeboe, of IGI Global, for her crucial contribution to the (more or less timely) completion of this book. Her persistence helped a lot indeed. Thanks a lot.

Section 1
The Development of Standards

Chapter 1
Creation of an ISO Standard at the Example of Value Stream Management Method

Jeff Mangers
University of Luxembourg, Luxembourg

Christof Oberhausen
Paul Wurth Geprolux S.A., Luxembourg

Meysam Minoufekr
University of Luxembourg, Luxembourg

Peter Plapper
ⓘD https://orcid.org/0000-0003-3507-1397
University of Luxembourg, Luxembourg

ABSTRACT

The main objectives of this chapter are to elucidate the necessity of a standardized value stream management (VSM) and to clarify how this standard can effectively increase corporate performance within cross-enterprise supply chain networks (SCNs). VSM is an effective tool to collect, evaluate, and continuously improve product and information flows within companies in a common and standardized manner. The findings of this chapter are not only valid for consistent product and information flows but are representative for the relevance of standards in general. In a globalized economy, standards need to be generally accepted and valid for all countries. Thus, corporate or national standards only have limited impact. The International Standardization Organization (ISO) provides the means to develop, negotiate and communicate standards, which are globally binding. This chapter shares the experience of ISO 22468 standard development within ISO/TC 154 WG7 and proves its applicability by an administrative use case.
DOI: 10.4018/978-1-7998-2181-6.ch001

INTRODUCTION

Standards are taking a more and more important role in our daily life. They help to provide consumers with confidence that their products and services are safe, reliable and of appropriate quality. Today, thousands of standards organizations around the world exist, which often endorse each other, build upon each other or compete with each other (Bartleson, 2013). Standards are mainly developed to achieve interoperability referred to technology or information and communication issues (Blind, Pohlisch, Zi, 2018). One standardization organization, which is valid on national and international level, is the standardization body ISO. This is an independent, non-governmental international organization, which associates experts from all over the world. Thus, it is possible to combine and share the global knowledge to develop international standards that support innovation and provide solutions for global challenges (ISO, 2019-1).

The idea of standardization started with obvious things like measures and weights. Nowadays, standards can be found in nearly every component or part of our daily life. Standards on road, toy, workplace, and transportation safety the same as for credit cards, paper sizes, currencies and secure medical packaging are just a few relevant standards in today's world. Regulators and governances count on standards to foster better regulations, by knowing that globally established experts have created the sound basis (ISO, 2019-1). ISO technical committees (TCs), which are groups of experts from different fields and various backgrounds carry out the preparation of international standards and thus ensure a significant quality.

In this chapter, the standardization of VSM is used to elucidate the relevance and necessity of standards nowadays and in the future. An international standard is the highest level of standard in view of effort quality, and impact.

The VSM method was made popular by Rother and Shook (Rother & Shook, 1999) and was used for many years by academia and practitioners to assess manufacturing operations and to distinguish waste from value-adding processes, in order to minimize waste and shorten lead time (Plapper, 2011), (Keyte & Locher, 2004), (Klevers, 2007), (Erlach, 2013), (Brown, Amundson, Badurdeen, 2014). However, over the years a large variety of VSM methods has evolved, tailored to the alleged slightly different use cases of every operation. Most companies operate in Business-to-Business (B2B) supply chain networks, which spreads the value creation across many firms. Often VSM is applied within the plant or inside the company, but the application of this lean tool across company borders is restricted due to different corporate standards. This limits to create a value stream map across the entire SCN, mainly due to problems at the interfaces.

A common standard, which is accepted internationally, would eliminate this type of multiple documentation of the VSM. This common standard represents an important milestone in the elimination of inefficiencies between different actors of a supply chain. By predefining a common language, the cross-enterprise communication is significantly facilitated. Furthermore, this common standard represents an important preliminary-work for future research, since a common understanding or communication language is the cornerstone of a consistent and collaborating supply chain. Mainly with regard to Industry 4.0 and further promoted digitalization in the future, a prescribed standard is of major importance. It specifies the importance of standards in today's world, the same as in the future, to avoid inefficiencies and rework.

The following sections of this chapter are structured as follow: First, the current challenges of SCNs are stated and accordingly a problem definition for VSM is defined. This part concludes with putting up three research questions for this chapter. Secondly, the state of the art is shown and gaps in the currently used value stream methods are derived. The third part describes what was needed to develop a new VSM standard, followed by the benefits of this new standard, mainly referred to its future usage. Before concluding this chapter, an administrative use case validates the applicability of VSM in unconventional areas. By following this guideline, the questions why standards are needed and how they can effectively increase future corporate performance are answered and exemplified by the VSM standardization.

Problem Definition And Research Questions

A main problem in today's world and probably even more accurate in the future, are communication issues caused by a more and more interconnected world. These communication issues lead to misunderstandings, which create collaboration challenges between departments and even more between enterprises. These result from ambiguous information, insufficient transparency or conflicting targets related to the value creation process. The result is, that important information is scattered within organizations or supply chain networks. In addition, frequent customer changes lead to deviations of required materials, components and associated processes. Throughout the whole supply chain, this enhance the need of a consistent and uniform communication (Oberhausen, Minoufekr, Plapper, 2017-1).

Another frequent problem of SCNs is the amount of shared information within the supply chain. By shared information, the following groups of parameters are meant: resources, inventory, production, transport, demand. Most companies are not willing to share the complete and needed amount of information with other participants of the SCN, even if this is vital for an effective supply chain (Sitek, Nielsen, Wikarek, 2014). However, a complex SCN can only work if all the participants are willing to share a certain amount of internal information with the rest of their supply chain.

3

Figure 1. Example of a cross-enterprise supply chain

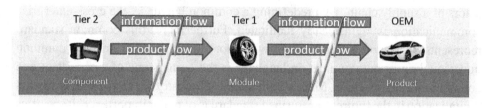

Figure 1 visualizes the information flow of B2B orders and the product flow towards the end customer, with obstacles at the interfaces between the companies that inhibit an effective supply chain cooperation. The product flow proceeds from the different suppliers until the customer and the information flow runs in the opposite direction. Both flows are dependent on a consistent and comprehensive communication.

Especially in case of internal or supply chain audits, when the overall process flow needs to be mapped, analyzed and discussed beyond departmental or organizational boundaries, complications and misunderstandings arise i.e. from notational differences that result in rework and finally in a waste of resources. The value stream method is an established technique, which is used to analyze and design information and process flows within organizations (Plapper & André, 2011). Until now, the recording of a value stream map is considered a paper-based method (Rother& Shook, 1999) and therefore no uniform and consistent method existed or was needed. However, with an increasing globalization and the need to depict the information and process flow of entire supply chains, the communication and collaboration between the interacting partners becomes more important. To overcome these communication and collaboration difficulties in supply chain networks, mainly referred to process and information flows, a standardized method to analyze and design value streams within and across companies is needed (Oberhausen, Minoufekr, Plapper, 2017-1).

The information transparency further decreases while considering different types of VSM patents and applying a variety of VSM software solutions. Thus, this diversity concerning the use of VSM creates a need for standardization. Based on a comparison of existing VSM approaches, a standardization of VSM in four different categories is proposed (cf. (Oberhausen & Plapper, 2015)):

- **VSM symbols:** Catalogue with around 50 standardized VSM symbols for the visual presentation of process workflows.
- **VSM data boxes and VSM parameters:** Selection of value stream relevant process variables for the gathering and analysis of value stream.

- **VSM parameters and calculation:** Unification of value stream relevant parameters and calculations procedures to ensure an uniform calculation of value streams (e.g. lead time).
- **VSM visualization:** Consistent form of presentation of value streams to enable a universal understanding throughout different economic sectors.

These four standardized categories ensure a common understanding and application of value streams and are the basis for the new VSM standard. In this context, the following assumption can be formulated:

A standardized VSM method will facilitate the communication and collaboration in complex SCNs, based on a common understanding and accessibility of value stream data. This will avoid repetitive work and decrease dependencies of tier 1 and tier 2 suppliers contrary to their respective OEMs. This will be advantageous for ever participants of the SCN.

To verify this key assumption, following three research questions need to be further investigated:

1. How does communication in cross-enterprise value streams can be established?
2. What are the key elements for a Value Stream Management within cross-enterprise value networks?
3. How standardization of Value Stream Management can effectively increase corporate performance in the future? And, to what extent does Value Stream Management can be used?

STATE OF THE ART

The state of the art section focuses on available VSM literature and answers research question number one, how communication can be established in cross-enterprise value streams.

In the context of globalization and digitized cooperation, there is a trend towards collaborative manufacturing associated with make or buy decisions across multiple companies (Oberhausen, Minoufekr, Plapper, 2017-1). This leads to complex SCNs, with numerous cross-enterprise transactions, often including cross-border communication. Especially the interfaces of supply chain networks are prone to inefficiencies, misunderstandings and delays due to a lack of standardized B2B transactions. This leads to waste in form of rework, errors and mistakes due to misunderstandings (Oberhausen, Minoufekr, Plapper, 2018). To overcome the inefficiencies between the different actors of the supply chain and to reduce unnecessary costs, it is important to mobilize all suppliers and customers of the supply chain to co-operate (Naude, Badenhorst-Weiss, 2011).

To resolve supply chain issues as stated by (Wang, Heng, & Chau, 2007)), a standardized cross-enterprise VSM method is sought (Oberhausen & Plapper, 2016). According to previous publications about the standardization of methods and processes, the process complexity and sectoral differences need to be taken into account (Schäfermeyer & Rosenkranz, 2011), (Schmitz & Leukel, 2005). In line with the advancement of cloud technology, where "standardization for interoperability" is required, as stated by (Gao, 2015), a common VSM methodology in consideration of existing VSM approaches, patents and software solutions will enhance the collaboration and communication in interconnected value networks. This will enable an improved coordination of the total SCN.

In the following, the state of the art of currently used VSM approaches, patents in the field of VSM and VSM software will be discussed briefly. Further details can be retrieved from (Oberhausen, Minoufekr, Plapper, 2017-1). Afterwards, the four different value stream levels that are used to visualize, analyze and subsequently design value streams are mentioned. Here, further details can be found in (Oberhausen, 2018).

A)   VSM approaches:

Numerous different VSM approaches (Hines, 1999), (Rother& Shook, 1999), (Keyte & Locher, 2004), (Klevers, 2007), (Bevilacqua, Ciarapica, Giacchetta, 2008), (Stich, Schmidt, Meier, Cuber, Kompa, 2011), (Erlach & Brown, 2013), (Kuhlang, Hempen, Edtmayr, Deuse, Sihn, 2013), (Brown, Amundson, Badurdeen, 2014) exist and moreover, (Womack & Jones, 2011) developed a VSM extension for supply chains. To handle this variety of different approaches, a detailed comparison of existing VSM methodologies has been performed to enable a generic and accurate use of VSM.

B)   Patents in the field of VSM:

To gain a comprehensive overview of existing VSM concepts and solutions and for the subsequent definition of a standardized VSM method, a patent review has been conducted, which can be found in Appendix 1. As part of the ISO standard development, it needs to be clarified which of these patents are competing or complementary. In case of competing patents, fair, reasonable, and non-discriminatory terms (FRAND) are suitable to support a mutually beneficial cooperation.

C)   VSM Software:

Numerous IT solutions are available on the market for the analysis, simulation and design of value streams. These software solutions can be classified in three different categories, VSM Templates or Add-Ons, VSM Drawing Applications and VSM Stand-Alone Simulation Software (Oberhausen, 2018).

(Oberhausen, 2018) includes an exhaustive list of literature about VSM. It is structured in four groups:

- Conventional VSM methods and literature studies,
- VSM with reference to industrial engineering, and key performance indicators (KPI),
- Further refinement and extended applications of VSM,
- Transfer of VSM to B2B interactions and SCN.

The existing VSM approaches, patents and software reveals an inconsistent conception that leads to a divergent understanding of VSM. This is particularly problematic for the collaboration and communication of organizations within cross-enterprise SCNs (Oberhausen, Minoufekr, Plapper, 2017-1).

To visualize, analyze and subsequently design value stream networks, four different value stream levels exist. These four different levels enable a structured collection of value stream relevant data and a consistent presentation of value streams on several levels. Through this, it is possible to either analyze a whole value creation network, cross-enterprise value streams, value streams of individual plants or value streams of one single process. The four levels are the following (Oberhausen, 2018):

1) Macro-level:

At this level, an overview over the whole value creation network, from the customer order until the delivery to the end customer, is described. This involves a cross-enterprise VSM.

2) Meso-level:

At this level, the transport logistics as well as the information logistics links of the different actors are depicted. This involves a cross-enterprise VSM.

3) Micro-level:

At this level, an individual location or plant is considered with an analysis and continuous improvement by means of a classical and internal value stream. Here, mainly material and information flows of internal process flows are illustrated.

4)   Nano-level:

At this level, a detailed analysis and design of an individual process can be performed. Here, the process sequence of one individual process is outlined.

VSM STANDARD DEVELOPMENT

The state of the art shows that there is a variety of VSM approaches, patents and software solutions. However, there is a lack of integration with regard to available VSM methodologies and IT solutions. Research question number two, what the key elements of VSM within a cross-enterprise value network are, will be discussed in this section. The key elements of the VSM standardization are divided into four categories (Oberhausen, Minoufekr, Plapper, 2017-1):

1)   VSM symbols and terminology:

Based on a set of standard symbols, which shall be used commonly, there is a clear and concise definition of VSM notation, especially for specific processes or use cases. This will avoid the use of similar, adapted or adjusted symbols and terminology, and thus prevent misunderstandings or deviations.

2)   VSM data boxes and VSM parameters:

To achieve a uniform size and structure of VSM data boxes as well as a consistent use of parameters, a recommendation for common VSM parameters that are suited for different process types is beneficial (cf. (Oberhausen & Plapper, 2017)). The consideration of process-related and industry-specific differences in terms of VSM parameters helps to find a generic classification for VSM data boxes depending on defined process types (cf. (Oberhausen & Plapper, 2015));

3)   VSM calculation procedure:

To quantitatively analyze value streams and to gain more detailed information about the performance of individual sections of the overall process chain, a consistent calculation procedure is envisaged. In total, 17 connected calculation procedures were developed.

4)   VSM visualization:

Figure 2. Value stream map as a typical visualization (Source: Oberhausen, Minoufekr, Plapper, 2017-1)

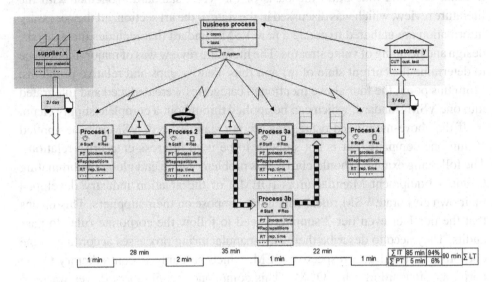

Concerning the visualization of value stream data, there is a variety of available approaches, e.g.:

a.   Pipeline map
b.   Swimlane diagram
c.   Flow chart
d.   Variety or flexibility funnel
e.   Value stream map

The pipeline map, which has been introduced by Scott and Westbrook (Scott & Westbrook, 1991), visualizes the overall lead time as a time bar consisting of horizontal lines that represent process time and vertical lines related to idle time. Swimlane diagrams are commonly used for the visualization of business processes, associated responsibilities as well as linkages of different departments or organizations. Flow charts consisting of nodes and edges in combination with techniques from Operations Research are suited for the visualization of process flows. To visualize the changing number of product variants within a process, a variety or flexibility funnel is helpful. A common visualization of value streams, which is recommended for standardization, is the value stream map (cf. Figure 2).

This diagram typically comprises the product and information flow from the supplier to the customer as well as a bottom line for a detailed analysis of the overall lead time, divided into process and idle time.

Together, these four categories enable a common understanding of value stream relevant data and thus build the basis of the VSM standard. Together with the literature review, which was discussed in the state of the art section, all the necessary information are gathered to create a new VSM standard that includes the analysis, design and planning of value streams. The literature review was of major importance to determine the current state of art and thus identify gaps and relative problems. From this point, the four above mentioned categories were deduced and integrated into one VSM standard, which can be applied throughout a complete supply chain.

If the above-mentioned categories are not standardized, VSM can be applied within one company, but is not suitable to be used in cross-enterprise relations. The following example should clarify this problem. Large and globally dominating Original Equipment Manufacturers (OEMs) of the aviation industry developed their own corporate VSM rules, which they impose on their suppliers. This means that the tier 1 or even tier 2 suppliers need to follow the corporate rules to pass audits. They need to describe their own manufacturing processes according to the corporate standard of a respective OEM, which probably is contradictory to the corporate standard of other OEMs. This compliance requirement drives waste of rework, especially reformatting of the documentation by the supplier (Oberhausen, Minoufekr, Plapper, 2017-1). This cross-enterprise VSM example reinforces the need for a common method. This can be analyzed only with one common method. A common VSM method is a major pre-requisite to optimize the entire SCN, because B2B information transparency is only possible by means of a standardized method.

BENEFITS OF A STANDARDIZED VSM

This section tries to solve the first part of research question number three by explaining how a VSM standard can effectively increase corporate performance, mainly with regard to the future.

The main identified problem of SCNs in a global market is communication between different departments and mainly between different actors within the SCN (Oberhausen, Minoufekr, Plapper, 2017-1). To ensure a smooth communication, the first requirement, which need to be in place, is a common understanding of the topic. In this case, it means a common understanding of key symbols, data boxes and parameters, calculation procedures and of the value stream visualization. It means to use a common language, the same as is valid to speak with other people. In a professional world, where different actors from all over the world want to collaborate with each other, this is only possibly by referring to standards. Regarding to SCNs and mainly value streams, no standard method existed (Oberhausen, Minoufekr, Plapper, 2017-1). Through generating the standard as an ISO standard, it is furthermore ensured that this common method is not only used on a national level, but directly on an international level. Therefore, the first benefit of this newly developed standard is to have a universal and common communication and understanding of value streams.

A second identified problem is avoidable rework and relating thereto waste of time and resources. This is mainly caused by different guidelines from OEMs towards their supplier. If a tier 1 producer needs to follow different guidelines from different OEMs in order to pass their audits, this means an additional investment of time and resources for the tier 1 producer. Consequently, the second benefit of the new VSM standard and of standards in general is that they protect smaller actors within a business network. Standards ensure that every participant employs the exact same method and no one can specify which methods need to be applied. This can as well be beneficial for an OEM, since the procedure is already defined in advance. This way, it is easier for an OEM to conduct audits since all his suppliers are using the same method. Through this, unnecessary work on both sides can be prevented.

A last benefit of a standardized VSM is that the tool itself obtains a greater prominence and reputation. This will be beneficial for all companies who did not applied the VSM tool before. This way, the new VSM standard is not only useful for cross-enterprise relations, but also beneficial for internal usage. The basic VSM procedure, which is defined within the new standard, explains precisely how to complete a value stream analysis, design and planning in order to collect, evaluate and continuously improve internal product and information flows. With a supplementary guideline on how to use and apply VSM, companies can easily start to apply this lean tool on their own and thus eliminate internal waste.

This section clearly states the benefits, which will arise out of the VSM standardization. The initial goal was to initiate a more consistent and universal communication between different partners of a SCN, but it was shown that even individual companies benefit from this new standard.

The next section explains the ISO standardization process with expert knowledge from ISO 22468. The extensive applicability of VSM and mainly of the value stream map is proved by exemplifying the ISO standardization process.

ADMINISTRATIVE USE CASE of VSM

To prove that the proposed VSM method (Oberhausen, 2018) is suited as international standard, the suggested procedure needs to demonstrate its general applicability. It was already validated to analyze a versatility of value creation processes, like material-, energy- or data-related value streams in previous works (Oberhausen, Weber, Plapper, 2015), (Oberhausen & Plapper, 2015), (Oberhausen & Plapper, 2017), (Oberhausen, Minoufekr, Plapper, 2017-1), (Oberhausen, Minoufekr, Plapper,

2017-2), (Oberhausen, Minoufekr, Plapper, 2018). To prove the applicability of VSM within different fields, the standardization process will be used as administrative use case and will be illustrated by a Value Stream Map with a closer look to its individual processes (different development stages). This was never done before and should prove the applicability of the Value Stream Map outside of industrial applications and at the same time answer the second part of the research question number three. Complementary information from ISO are added to better understand the standardization development.

Based on the pull principle (pull systems authorize releases based on information from inside the system, this means it authorizes parts to be processed in response to actual demand arrival (Khojasteh, 2016)), any lean value stream starts with the customer. In this specific case, the general public (figure 3, upper right corner), industrial partners and literature study were indicating to the authors the pressing need for a common, globally applicable VSM standard. The development of the standard was based on existing knowledge, which was collected from patents, scientific publications, industrial companies and experts (figure 3, upper left part). The first two steps were performed with support of Luxembourgish ILNAS and the following steps with support of ISO. Stage 30 and stage 50 may be skipped, depending on TC decision, which is illustrated by bypass flows. The standardization process will finish as soon as the standard is released to the general public (figure 3, upper right part). Beneath, the timelines show the process-, idle- and lead time. Each of the value-adding steps (editing the standard) requires approximately 6 months and represent the process time. The voting process takes approximately 3 months, during which the P-members reassure the vote with their national norming institutions and is considered idle time The overall lead time is estimated to be approximately 10 years with a value adding share of 66,5%.

ISO sponsors the development of the standard. The national standardization body, the " Institut Luxembourgeois de la Normalisation, de l'Accréditation, de la Sécurité et qualité des produits et services" (ILNAS) delegates the authors as experts to the Technical Committee 154.

Figure 3 shows a Value Stream Map of the ISO standardization process with its respective stages.

The following section describes briefly, what the different ISO stages require and how the different stages were undergone for ISO 22468.

Before starting with the elaboration of an ISO standard, it is common to conduct a preliminary stage, mainly for projects, which are not yet sufficiently mature to proceed to further stages. This optional stage allows a workgroup to invest some preparatory work into the project like detecting the need of a new standard and the creation of a plan. The committee shall evaluate the market relevance and resources required for the project (ISO/IEC, 2019). In the case of ISO 22468, the main reason was to create a globally accepted and applied standard to apply VSM, which will simplify cross-enterprise cooperation later on. ISO 22468 was appointed to TC 154 (Processes, data elements and documents in commerce, industry and administration) WG 7, which deals with electronic data exchange. With support of national standardization body, the first documentation was authored during the preliminary stage.

The matter of the first step is to confirm that a new International Standard in the subject area is really needed (ISO, 2019-2), whereas the matter of the second step is to introduce a new standard to the ISO expert teams as New Work Item Proposal (NWIP). Every NWIP needs to be submitted for vote using a specific form (Form 4), which is available at the ISO website (ISO, 2019-3). For the voting, the electronic balloting portal shall be used and for a positive result, two requirements need to be fulfilled. First, the work item needs to be approved by a two-thirds majority of P-members and second, at least 4 P-members (5 P-members in committees with 17 or more P-members) need to be nominated as technical experts and participate actively in the development of the project (ISO/IEC, 2019). They will represent the later WG. The authors of the future standard must be aware that at this point in time, they are forced to transfer copyright and ownership and commercial exploitation rights to ISO (ISO, 2019-2). For ISO 22468, the proposal for a new project was registered on the 5th February 2017 and thereby the proposal stage 10 was inchoate. During the ballot, a two-thirds majority was reached and technical experts from China, Germany, Republic of Korea, Netherlands and Luxembourg were nominated. This was an important step, since the fundamentals to develop the standard were set, by having set up an international team of experts to create a VSM standard.

Figure 3. Value stream map – ISO standardization process

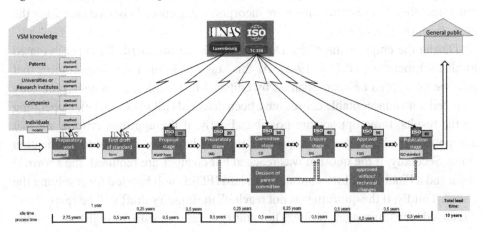

During the preparatory stage, the preparation of a Working Draft (WD) is done by a working group, which is set up by the parent committee. The WG is led by a convener (usually the project leader) and composed of experts, which were nominated previously by the P-members. Together, they will author the future international standard (ISO, 2019-2). It exists two possibilities for the preparatory stage to end. Firstly, it can end when a working draft is available for circulation to the members of the TC or SC as a first Committee Draft (CD). In this case, it is necessary to undergo stage 30 as well. Secondly, the committee can chose to skip stage 30, the CD. In this case, the preparatory stage ends when the enquiry draft (DIS) is available for circulation (stage 40) (ISO/IEC, 2019). For ISO 22468, further development of the draft, the same as patent and software research was done during the preparatory stage. This was mainly done to avoid any copyright issues and to create a valid foundation for the later standard.

If the committee stage is conducted, it can be seen as the principal stage, at which comments from national bodies are taken into consideration. The Committee Draft (CD) shall be circulated to all P-members and O-members of the TC, to comment on the current work and receive further input. After the closing for submission of replies, the secretariat has to prepare a compilation of comments and indicate its proposal to continue with the project. Three possibilities exists, firstly to discuss the CD and comments at the next meeting, secondly circulate a revised CD for consideration and thirdly to register the CD for enquiry stage. Committees are required to respond to every comment received. The goal is to reach consensus on the technical content and thus subsequent CDs can be circulated until consensus (general agreement) is reached on the technical content. The committee stage ends when all technical issues have been resolved and the committee draft is accepted for circulation as an enquiry draft (ISO/IEC, 2019). In the case of VSM, it was decided to undergo stage 30 as well and the committee draft was approved by a two-thirds majority (16th September 2018) of P-members vote, with additional comments from one P-member. These comments were incorporated accurately before launching the next stage, the enquiry stage.

During the enquiry stage, the Draft International Standard (DIS) is circulated to all ISO members (ISO 2019-2). At this stage, it is of major importance, that positive votes (can be accompanied by editorial or technical comments) are only assigned if no unacceptable causes have been detected (ISO/IEC, 2019). Depending on the results, three options are possible. Firstly, if the approval criteria are met and no technical changes are requested, the standard goes straight to publication stage. Secondly, if the quorum was reached but changes are required, the approval stage and a Final Draft International Standard (FDIS) will be used for resolving the issues. Thirdly, if the quorum was not reached, the enquiry draft will be revised and circulated for a subsequent voting. The enquiry stage ends with the registration of the text for circulation as a FDIS or publication as an international standard (ISO/IEC, 2019). In the case of VSM, further adjustments were implemented during the DIS stage, prior to launch the DIS-ballot (40) on the 26th June 2019, which ended with a positive result (8 in favor votes and 0 negative votes) on the 18th September 2019. Additionally, the current version was translated into French. At this well-advanced development status, it is crucial to receive further feedback from affected experts, to refine the standard further.

The approval stage is required only in case that the approval criteria of the DIS-ballot were met but technical changes are required. In this case, the FDIS is circulated to all ISO members for a voting, with the same approval criteria like for the DIS voting (ISO, 2019-2). If the FDIS has been approved in accordance to the voting requirements, it shall proceed to the publication stage. However, if the requirements are not achieved, further rework is needed. In this case, four different possibilities exist. Firstly, a modified draft is submitted as a CD, DIS or FDIS, secondly, a technical specification is submitted, thirdly, a publicly available specification is published or fourthly the project is cancelled (ISO/IEC, 2019). The approval stage ends with the circulation of the voting report, stating that the FDIS has been approved for publication as an international standard, with the publication of a technical specification, or with the document being remit to the committee (ISO/IEC, 2019). In the case of ISO 22468, some technical changes were required from the secretariat prior to publish the new VSM standard.

After positive voting, a period of 6 weeks is granted to the office of the CEO to correct editorial corrections (ISO/IEC, 2019). Committee secretaries and project leaders get a two-week sign-off period before the standard is published by the ISO/CS as international standard (ISO, 2019-2). The publication stage ends with the publication of the international standard (ISO/IEC, 2019). In the case of ISO 22468, the final stage was not reached yet, prior to the publication of this chapter.

After publishing an international standard, it needs to be ensured that the standard remains up to date and relevant. Therefore, ISO developed a process through which it guarantees that ISO deliverables remain contemporary. During this so-called "systematic review", committee members play an important role, which is described within (ISO/IEC, 2019, subclause 2.9).

Table 1 summarizes the different standardization stages with its associated documents and the information if it is obligatory or optional to undergo the respective stage.

Further, more detailed information about the different stages and the processes of standard elaboration can be found in (Hallström, 1996), (Hallström, 2005) and (Cargill, 2011).

To complete this chapter, first, a short discussion about what has been done, the advantages and the limitations of the new VSM standard will be detained. Following

Table 1. Project stages and associated documents (ISO/IEC, 2019)

Project stage	Associated document
Preliminary stage (00) - optional	Preliminary work item (PWI)
Proposal stage (10) - obligatory	New work item proposal (NWIP)
Preparatory stage (20) – optional	Working draft(s) (WD)
Committee stage (30) - optional	Committee draft(s) (CD)
Enquiry stage (40) - obligatory	Enquiry draft (ISO/DIS)
Approval stage (50) - optional	Final draft international standard (FDIS)
Publication stage (60) - obligatory	International standard (ISO)

the discussion, future research directions will be stated before a final conclusion will be given.

DISCUSSION

By developing a VSM standard, a first important step to overcome communication issues within cross-enterprise networks has been done through defining a common language for all supply chain participants. This VSM standard categorizes four categories:

- symbols and terminology,
- data boxes and parameters,
- calculation procedure and
- visualization.

Together, they combine the key elements of VSM.

This standard will mainly be beneficial for cross-enterprise communication, since it specifies a clear guideline for VSM. Furthermore, companies can as well benefit from this standard internally, because of the VSM procedure and the VSM guideline which explains how to perform a value stream analysis.

However, still many important limitations exist, which should be addressed briefly. A major issue that need to be solved is how companies can share their information with other participants in a SCN. This standard only defines the presentation of the information (gives a framework for a unified design of the information), not how participants of a cross-enterprise SCN can safely share their internal information. This limitation and issue needs to be treated in future researches.

Some further research directions and ideas will be mentioned in the following section.

FUTURE RESEARCH DIRECTIONS

The main future activity will be the continuation of the standardization activities as member of the ISO committee, leading to a comprehensive, universal VSM standard. This is an important task, considering the global need for a standardized VSM. Furthermore, after having published the standard, the authors need to make sure that the standard remains current and relevant.

Besides this, a supplementary guideline how to use the VSM standard will be developed in a future project. On the one hand, this will help to better teach the employment of the new VSM standard and on the other hand enable the possibility to apply the VSM method independently. This new guideline is crucial to ensure a correct employment and understanding of the VSM method.

Further research will concentrate on applying VSM in closed cycles, mainly to improve cross-enterprise usage and to digitize VSM. Within closed cycles, the idea is to visualize different value streams within the circular economy and thus overcome problems at supply chain interfaces. To be able to share up-to-date data with other actors of the supply chain, a digitization of value streams is envisaged. Both are very interesting and promising topics for the future and are based on the standardized VSM. Without the preliminary work of defining a common VSM, these future researches would not be possible. One missing component to simplify cross-enterprise collaboration is how to share the information of value streams. This means for example, how an OEM can retrieves a certain amount of information from supplier one and two of his supply chain, without seeing production information concerning another OEM.

CONCLUSION

This chapter focuses mainly on why a VSM standard is needed and how this standard can effectively increase corporate performance. Even if this is based on VSM, the ideas and output are the same for standardization in general. The chapter clearly states why standards are important in today's world and maybe even more in the future. With regard to Industry 4.0 and an expanding globalization, the importance of a standardized communication between internal actors and cross-enterprise actors will become more and more important. If machines should be able to talk to each other in the future, it is important that they all communicate in the same language. The same applies for a well-interconnected SCN.

While operating in complex B2B networks, collaboration and communication issues arise for most global organizations. Originating from lean production, VSM is a powerful and at the same time easy-to-use tool, which is used to analyze efficiency of product and information flows. However, state-of-the-art showed a diversity of different VSM variants, patents and commercially available VSM software. To provide the experts with a uniform understanding of value stream data, four different aspects of VSM were communized. ISO/ TC 154/ WG 7 hosts the development of the related VSM standard. This chapter describes the standardization process of ISO, which proves the applicability of the common method to visualize and analyze information-based administrative value streams.

An international standard approved by ISO has significant implications and enables further efficiencies. The VSM method, as defined in ISO 22468, is applicable to all process flows, which create value output. It enables to distinguish value-adding tasks from non-value-adding tasks (waste) and is a prerequisite to minimize the latter. The main goal of VSM is to first depict the current state, second identify improvement potentials, and last implement an improved state.

The relevant value streams range from physical products, which are fabricated in manual operations one by one, to semi-automated manufacturing plants, up to fully automated, agile production systems. This method refers to low-volume, serial production and to mass production value chains. In addition, this standard is capable to analyze non-tangible processes or information-based value streams, like virtual, data-based processes, services and administrative processes. As example, a value stream map of the standardization process was illustrated prior.

Using the VSM standard for further developments will provide experts with additional opportunities. The ISO 22468 is validated for an individual station, for a complete plant, and even for a manufacturing network, composed of several companies, which form a SCN. Now, with the availability of an international common standard, the complete SCN, composed of many plants or several companies, who each create their individual share of value of the final product, can be analyzed and evaluated with this method to focus value creation to the end customer, rather than only the intermediate client.

Still, it has to be stated once again, that this standard alone does not solve all the problem within complex SCNs. Further research, mainly on how to share crucial information with other participants of a SCN, needs to be conducted. The VSM sets the framework for sharing information within a SCN.

ACKNOWLEDGMENT

The authors are grateful to the following supporters of this research:

- Interreg NWE, project Di-Plast – Digital Circular Economy for the Plastics Industry

- "Institut Luxembourgeois de la Normalisation, de l'Accréditation, de la Sécurité et qualité des produits et services" (ILNAS) for coaching us as convener of WG 7 in ISO/TC 154

- Fonds National de la Recherche (FNR) Luxembourg, for financing of a previous, preparatory research project

- Tier 1 supplier, for ongoing support of the development of the norm with industrial requirements

REFERENCES

Bartleson, K. (2013). *10 Standards Organizations That Affect You (Whether You Know It Or Not)*. Retrieved from https://www.electronicdesign.com/communications/10-standards-organizations-affect-you-whether-you-know-it-or-not

Bevilacqua, M., Ciarapica, F. E., & Giacchetta, G. (2008). Value Stream Mapping in Project Management: A Case Study. *Project Management Journal, 39*(3), 110–124. doi:10.1002/pmj.20069

Blind, K., Pohlisch, J., & Zi, A. (2018). Publishing, patenting and standardization: Motives and barriers of scientists. *Research Policy, 4*(7), 1185–1197. doi:10.1016/j.respol.2018.03.011

Brown, A., Amundson, J., & Badurdeen, F. (2014). Sustainable value stream mapping (Sus-VSM) in different manufacturing system configurations: Application case studies. *Journal of Cleaner Production, 85*, 164–179. doi:10.1016/j.jclepro.2014.05.101

Cargill, C. F. (2011). Why Standardization Efforts Fail. *The Journal of Electronic Publishing: JEP, 14*(1). doi:10.3998/3336451.0014.103

Erlach, K. (2013). *Value Stream Design*. Springer Berlin Heidelberg. doi:10.1007/978-3-642-12569-0

FlexSim Software Products Inc. (2017). *FlexSimVSM*. Retrieved January 26, 2017, from https://www.flexsim.com/value-stream-mapping/

Gao, R., Wang, L., Teti, R., Dornfeld, D., Kumara, S., Mori, M., & Helu, M. (2015). Cloud-enabled prognosis for manufacturing. *CIRP Annals - Manufacturing Technology, 64*(2), 749–772.

Hallström, K. T. (1996). The Production of Management Standards. Revue d'économie industrielle, 61-76.

Hallström, K. T. (2005). *Organizing the process of standardization. In A world of standards* (2nd ed.; pp. 85–99). Oxford University Press.

Hines, P., Rich, N., Bicheno, J., Brunt, D., Taylor, D., Butterworth, C., & Sullivan, J. (1998). Value Stream Management. *International Journal of Logistics Management, 9*(1), 25–42. doi:10.1108/09574099810805726

ISO 2018. ISO in brief - Great things happen when the world agrees. (n.d.). Retrieved from https://www.iso.org/files/live/sites/isoorg/files/store/en/PUB100007.pdf

ISO 2019-1. Benefits of ISO standards. (n.d.). Retrieved July 10, 2019, from https://www.iso.org/benefits-of-standards.html

ISO 2019-2. Developing ISO standards. (n.d.). Retrieved July 10, 2019, from https://www.iso.org/stages-and-resources-for-standards-development.html

ISO 2019-3. ISO forms, model agendas, standard letters. (n.d.). Retrieved July 10, 2019, from https://www.iso.org/iso-forms-model-agendas-standard-letters.html

ISO 2019-4. All about ISO. (n.d.). Retrieved July 10, 2019, from https://www.iso.org/about-us.html https://www.iso.org/about-us.html

ISO 2019-5. International harmonized stage codes. (n.d.). Retrieved July 10, 2019, from https://www.iso.org/members.html

ISO 2019-6. Who develops standards? (n.d.). Retrieved July 10, 2019, from https://www.iso.org/who-develops-standards.html

ISO/IEC 2015. ISO membership manual. (n.d.). Retrieved from https://www.iso.org/files/live/sites/isoorg/files/archive/pdf/en/iso_membership_manual.pdf

ISO/IEC 2019. Directives, Part 1 Consolidated ISO Supplement — Procedures specific to ISO. (n.d.). Retrieved from https://www.iso.org/sites/directives/current/consolidated/index.xhtml

Keyte, B., & Locher, D. A. (2004). *The Complete Lean Enterprise: Value Stream Mapping for Administrative and Office Processes.* CRC Press. doi:10.1201/b16650

Khojasteh, Y. (2016). *Production Control Systems - A Guide to Enhance Performance of Pull Systems*. Springer.

Klevers, T. (2007). *Wertstrom-Mapping und Wertstrom-Design*. mi-Fachverlag.

Kuhlang, P., Hempen, S., Edtmayr, T., Deuse, J., & Sihn, W. (2013). Systematic and Continuous Improvement of Value Streams. *7th IFAC Conference on Manufacturing Modelling, Management, and Control* 10.3182/20130619-3-RU-3018.00257

LEANPILOT GmbH. (2017). *LEANPILOT*. Retrieved January 26, 2017, from http://www.leanpilot.com/index.html

Naude, M., & Badenhorst-Weiss, J. (2011). The effect of problems on supply chain wide efficiency. *Journal of Transport and Supply Chain*, *5*, 278–298.

Oberhausen, C. (2018). *Standardisierte Unternehmensübergreifende Wertstrommethode (StreaM)* (Dissertation). Université du Luxembourg.

Oberhausen, C., Minoufekr, M., & Plapper, P. (2017a). Standardized Value Stream Management Method to Visualize, Analyze and Optimize Cross-Enterprise Value Stream Data. *International Journal of Standardization Research*, *15*.

Oberhausen, C., Minoufekr, M., Plapper, P. (2018). Application of Value Stream Management to enhance Product and Information Flows in Supply Chain Networks-Based on the example of Web-Based Automotive Retail Business. *Management and Production Engineering Review*, *9*.

Oberhausen, C., Minoufekr, M., Plapper, P. (2017b). Continuous Improvement of Complex Process Flows by Means of Stream as the "Standardized Cross-Enterprise Value Stream Management Method". *IEEE IEEM*.

Oberhausen, C., & Plapper, P. (2015). Value Stream Management in the "Lean Manufacturing Laboratory." *CIRP Conference on Learning Factories*. 10.1016/j.procir.2015.02.087

Oberhausen, C., & Plapper, P. (2016). A Standardized Value Stream Management Method for Supply Chain Networks. In D. Dimitrov & T. Oosthuizen (Eds.), *Proceedings of COMA'16 International Conference on Competitive Manufacturing* (pp. 428–433). COMA'16.

Oberhausen, C., & Plapper, P. (2017). Cross-Enterprise Value Stream Assessment. *Journal of Advances in Management Research*, *14*(2), 182–193. doi:10.1108/JAMR-05-2016-0038

Oberhausen, C., Weber, D., & Plapper, P. (2015). Value Stream Management in high variability production systems. *SSRG Int. J. Ind. Eng*, *2*(1), 1–4.

Plapper, P., & André, C. (2011). Wertstrommethode – Value Stream Mapping. In Der Qualitätsmanagement-Berater (10th ed.; pp. 1–27). Academic Press.

Profit Surge Consulting. (2017). *Profit Surge VSM Software*. Retrieved January 26, 2017, from http://profit-surge.com/ProfitSurgeVSM.html

Rother, M., & Shook, J. (1999). *Learning to see: value-stream mapping to create value and eliminate muda (1.2)*. Lean Enterprise Institute.

Schäfermeyer, M., & Rosenkranz, C. (2011). To Standardize or not to Standardize? - Understanding the Effect of Business Process Complexity on Business Process Standardization. *ECIS 2011 Proceedings*.

Schmitz, V., & Leukel, J. (2005). Findings and Recommendations from a Pan-European Research Project: Comparative Analysis of E-Catalog Standards. *International Journal of IT Standards and Standardization Research*, *3*(2), 51–65. doi:10.4018/jitsr.2005070105

Scott, C., & Westbrook, R. (1991). New Strategic Tools for Supply Chain Management. *International Journal of Physical Distribution & Logistics Management*, *21*(1), 23–33. doi:10.1108/09600039110002225

Siemens PLM Software Inc. (2017). *Tecnomatix*. Retrieved January 26, 2017, from https://www.plm.automation.siemens.com/en_us/products/tecnomatix/manufacturing-simulation/material-flow/plant-simulation.shtml

Sitek, P., Nielsen, I. E., & Wikarek, J. (2014). A hybrid multi-agent approach to the solving supply chain problems. *Procedia Computer Science*, *35*, 1557–1566. doi:10.1016/j.procs.2014.08.239

Stich, V., Schmidt, C., Meier, C., Cuber, S., & Kompa, S. (2011). Cross-company coordination in Built-to-Order Production Networks in Machinery and Equipment Industry. *4th Int. Conf. Chang. Agil. Reconfigurable Virtual Prod.*, 563-568.

The eVSM Group. (2017). *eVSM*. Retrieved January 26, 2017, from https://evsm.com/

Wang, W. Y. C., Heng, M. S. H., & Chau, P. Y. K. (2007). *Supply Chain Management : Issues in the New Era of Collaboration and Competition*. Retrieved from http://www.loc.gov/catdir/toc/ecip0611/2006010099.html

Womack, J. P., & Jones, D. T. (2011). *Seeing the Whole Value Stream* (2nd ed.). Lean Enterprise Institute.

KEY TERMS AND DEFINITIONS

Business-to-Business (B2B): Business relationship between two or more companies, a situation where one business makes a commercial transaction with another business.

Central Secretariat (CS): Acts as secretariat within the Technical Committee and coordinates the development of standards.

Institut Luxembourgeoise de la Normalisation, de l´Accréditation, de la Sécurité et qualité des produits et services (ILNAS): Public administration, which is the national norming institution of Luxembourg and represents Luxembourg within ISO.

International Organization for Standardization (ISO): Independent, non-governmental international organization that brings together experts from all over the world to develop international standards.

Lead Time (LT): Time period from the date of order receipt to the transfer of the product to the end customer, so the total of the process time and idle time.

Standard: Technical document that provides requirements, specifications, guidelines or characteristics to ensure that materials, products, processes and services are suitable and uniform for their purpose.

Supply Chain Network (SCN): Complex structure of supply chains with a higher level of interdependence and connectivity between multiple organizations.

Technical Committee (TC)/Sub-Committee (SC): Group of experts that represents a specific sector and works together on ISO standards within one field.

Value Stream Management (VSM): Effective tool for the collection, evaluation and continuous improvement of product and information flows within organizations.

Working Group (WG): Subdivision of a Technical Committee to focus on a specific task during the development of an ISO standard, members of a working group actively participate in a concerned project.

APPENDIX 1: PATENT REVIEW

Table 2. List of VSM patents (source: Oberhausen, Minoufekr, Plapper, 2017-1)

No.	Patent	Applicant	Country/ Region
WO2014138271	Cloud-based real-time value stream mapping system and method	Whitehead, C.	World
US 20060242005 A1	Comprehensive method to improve manufacturing	Rodrigue, R.P. et al.	USA
US 20070005451 A1	Crop Value Chain Optimization	Iwig, R.C. et al.	USA
WO 2008021400 A2	Dynamic Value Stream Mapping Software	Glenn, J.R. et al.	World
US 20100070425 A1	Ecosystem value stream optimization system, method and device	Cornford, A.B.	USA
US 20140365266 A1	Enterprise Process Evaluation	Sethi, R. & Raghavendra, R.S.	USA
US 7383192 B2	Method for displaying Product Value Chain Flow Diagram and Product Value Chain Data	Sekimoto, S. et al.	USA
US20080077445A1	Method of Healthcare Delivery With Value Stream Mapping	Mecklenburg, R.	USA
US20060080157 A1	Method of improving administrative functions of a business using value streams with display of status	Shuker, T.	USA
US 20060085237 A1	Method of improving information technology processes of a business using Value Stream Management	Shuker, T. & Luckman, J.	USA
WO 2007067892 A2	System and method for dynamically simulating value stream and network maps	Adra, H.I.	World
WO2011075444A1	System and method for Process Improvement and associated products and services	Ansley, R.	World
EP1139251A2, EP1139251A3, US7280973B1, CA2404081A1	Value Chain Optimization System and Method	Hack, S. et al.	Europe, USA, Canada
US 20050154575 A1	Value stream improvement process simulation	Whitman, J.M. & Treiber, K.K.R.	USA
US 20040039625 A1	Value stream process management approach and web-site	Malnack, S.J. et al.	USA
US20090031598 A1	Value Stream Simulation and Display Board	Soni, A. & Malnati, P.A.	USA

APPENDIX 2: WHAT IS ISO?

ISO is an independent, non-governmental international institution with a membership of 163 nations all over the world. One member represents every nation. The idea is to bring together experts who share their knowledge and develop on a voluntary basis, consensus-bases and marked relevant international standards that support innovation and provide solutions to global challenges (ISO, 2019-4).

The initial aim of ISO was to ´facilitate the international coordination and unification of industrial standards´, which came up in 1946 when delegates from 25 countries met at the Institute of Civil Engineers in London to create a new international organization. Around one year later, on 23rd February 1947, ISO officially began its operations. Since that day, 22701 international standards that cover almost all aspects of technology and manufacturing have been published. (ISO, 2019-4).

ISO ensures that products and services are safe, reliable and of good quality and provides a platform for the development. A standard is a document that contains practical information and best practices and often describes an agreed way of doing something or a solution for a global problem. Therefore, ISO standards help to make product compatible, identify safety issues of products and services and share good ideas, solutions, technical expertise and best management practices (ISO, 2018).

APPENDIX 3: ISO-MEMBERSHIP

ISO-membership comes with rights, benefits, good practice and obligations. This means that every member needs to actively take up his rights and benefits, follow good practice and adhere to his obligations, to deliver excellence within the ISO system (ISO, 2015).

ISO is a global network of national standard bodies, where members are mainly standard organizations of their countries and have one member per country. Based on the level of access and influence within the ISO system, three different member categories exist. The first right is to participate in developing ISO standards. The second right is to sell ISO standards and publications, and use copyright, the ISO name and logo. The third right is to participate in developing ISO policy and the fourth right is to participate in governing ISO (ISO, 2015). The first member category are full members or member bodies, who participate and vote in ISO technical and policy meetings and influence the development and strategy of standards. The second member category are correspondent members who attend ISO technical and policy meetings as observer and thus monitor the development and strategy of ISO standards. The last member category are subscriber members who cannot participate actively in ISO´s work but are kept up to date. (ISO, 2019-5). Luxembourg is represented by ILNAS and is a full member within ISO.

Furthermore, ISO full members can choose whether they want to be part of a particular TC and their level of involvement (O-member or P-member). O-members can observe the currently developed standards and offer comments and advice. They may vote, but do not have to. P-members have a voting obligation and need to participate actively by voting on standards at various stages of its development (ISO, 2019-6).

Experts, who develop ISO standards, mostly work in the field and have profound knowledge. They understand and anticipate the challenges of their sector, and take advantage of standardizations to create a levelled playing field that benefits everyone. The participation of developing countries in standardization is supported through the Committee on Developing Country Matters (DEVCO). The knowledge and expertise of international standards can help developing countries realize their potential and by involving them in the development work. It is made sure that their needs are take into account (ISO, 2019-6).

The main actors in the ISO process are members, experts and ISO/Central Secretariat (CS). Experts are writing the standards. ISO members approve standards, represent ISO in their country, enable national experts, propose new standards and help to manage technical committees. The ISO/CS strengthens relationships with partners, facilitates participation in standardization, provide a neutral platform, coordinates the standard development process and makes standards available and it increases awareness around international standards and ISO (ISO, 2018).

Chapter 2
The Standardisation of Natural Capital Accounting Methodologies

Sylvain Maechler

https://orcid.org/0000-0002-4107-2698
University of Lausanne, Switzerland

Jean-Christophe Graz

https://orcid.org/0000-0002-5583-8332
University of Lausanne, Switzerland

ABSTRACT

The global ecological crisis has prompted the development of tools that try to redefine relations between business and nature, among them, natural capital accounting methodologies. The International Organization for Standardization (ISO) recently set standards on which these methodologies are based. Other actors, including the Big Four audit and accounting firms, developed their own methodologies outside the scope of ISO. This chapter examines why and how ISO developed natural capital accounting standards that are likely to compete with other methodologies. From the assumption that standards are not just technical, but also political instruments, it argues that they shape the future by creating power relations between actors within and outside ISO. The chapter suggests that these ISO standards aims at competing with first-movers' methodologies, in particular on the power implications resulting from transparency. It builds the argument on international political economy approaches to emphasise the link between technical specifications and power relations in contemporary capitalism.

DOI: 10.4018/978-1-7998-2181-6.ch002

INTRODUCTION

This chapter explores two of the core topics addressed in this volume: standards as a tool for forecasting or shaping the future and the power relations in which groups of individuals exert their influence in standard-setting processes. To this end, the chapter focuses on the recent development of natural capital accounting methodologies and two new standards developed within the aegis of the International Organization for Standardization (ISO) for such methodologies: ISO 14007 (Environmental management: Determining environmental costs and benefits) and ISO 14008 (Monetary valuation of environmental impacts and related environmental aspects). These two standards aim at putting a price tag on environmental impacts resulting from the economic activities of organisations (ISO 14008) and supporting an environmental cost & benefit analysis to relate such impacts to decision-making processes (ISO 14007). Martin Baxter, Chair of the technical committee 207, subcommittee 1, environmental management systems of ISO recently claimed in an interview that "[t]here is a growing drive towards valuing natural capital, as well as a need to undertake a monetary assessment of an organization's environmental aspects and impacts (…) having a set of standardized, harmonized methods becomes important" (Gould, 2018a). Those two standards are indeed conceived to complement one another by allowing "decision-makers to make informed choices in a way which is more likely to be economically and environmentally sustainable" (Gould, 2018a). While such topic is deeply technical, it also raised political issues both within and outside the working groups set for drafting the standards.

While the drafting process initiated by ISO in 2015 remains landmark, it is worth noting that a number of other bodies had pioneered initiatives on the issue of natural capital accounting before that. For instance, the Natural Capital Coalition and the Big Four audit and accounting firms, Deloitte, Ernst & Young, KPMG and PricewaterhouseCoopers, (the Big Four). The first is a "global public-private partnership" (Andonova, 2017, p. 2) created in 2012 and supported by very large multinational companies (MNCs), non-governmental organisations (NGOs), states, academia and United Nations (UN) bodies. Such initiative aims at developing a "standardised framework for business to identify, measure and value their impacts and dependencies on natural capital" (Natural Capital Coalition, 2018b). To this end, they published in 2016 the Natural Capital Protocol that provides guidelines for natural capital accounting. While the Big Four are key stakeholders within this Coalition, they also have had a prominent role in the sustainability reporting, consulting and assurance market for many years (Villiers & Maroun, 2018). Since 2010, they started to develop their own natural capital accounting methodologies to identify, quantify, value and compare the environmental impacts of MNCs. To this end, the Big Four often directly influence the development of future private regulations and standards (Fransen & LeBaron, 2019). However, they refused to take part in the work of ISO, while representatives of the Natural Capital Coalition have only been passively involved.

As many other concepts or tools developed to face the ecological crisis, natural capital accounting is based on the environmental liberal paradigm of the so-called green economy that aims at making environmental and economic goals compatible (Bernstein, 2002; Bracking, 2015; Dempsey, 2016). Such a way of 'economicising nature' often relies on the 'valuation of ecosystem services', i.e. the valuation of the stocks and, most importantly, flows of benefits provided by nature. A number of techniques in environmental economics allow to put a monetary value on such benefits expected from nature. Ecosystem services valuation as standardised in ISO 14008 is only one component of natural capital accounting. Others are related to the development of environmental indicators and reporting techniques to make financial and environmental data directly comparable, so that a cost and benefit analysis can easily be undertaken. Ecosystem services is now an established and well defined concept (see: Boisvert, Méral, & Froger, 2013; Boyd & Banzhaf, 2007; Costanza et al., 2017). In contrast, natural capital accounting is still a new, vague and ill-defined concept with no agreed and shared definition. While it includes a heterogeneous set of tools and instruments, all of them aim at making financial and environmental data comparable and, therefore, prone to have a price. Natural capital accounting is thus defined as a tool that aims at measuring, valuing, recording, summarising and processing information about nature according to a predefined procedure.[1] It includes monetary valuation (ISO 14008), cost & benefit analysis (ISO 14007), disclosure through environmental reporting (which procedure is included in the two standards), and ideally an environmental action plan (provided by ISO 14001, the core standard of the ISO 14000 series).

The main objective of standards in natural capital accounting is to assess the risks and uncertainties arising directly or indirectly from the ecological crisis. As Maechler and colleagues recently underlined, "understanding, calculating or 'taming' uncertainty has become a matter of great concern of policy makers and scientific research in a world facing global, epochal and complex changes" (2019, p. 6). Against this background, the authors contend that natural capital accounting aims at reducing the complexity of the ecological crisis into objectifiable units of analysis. In other words, it aims at transforming uncertainties – something that is so complex that it is not susceptible to measurement – into quantitative and thus manageable risks. As a forecasting tool, natural capital accounting codifies such processes of uncertainty reduction.

This chapter examines why and how ISO set standards for natural capital accounting methodologies likely to compete with methodologies being developed by other actors and in other arenas. Drawing on scholarship in international political economy

(IPE) that conceptualises the authority of standards and technical specifications in transnational environmental governance, we assume that standards are not just technical, but also political instruments (Graz, 2019; Katz-Rosene & Paterson, 2018; Yates & Murphy, 2019). We argue that the development of standards for natural capital accounting is thus likely to shape the future by transforming power relations within and outside standard-setting arenas. More specifically, these power relations build upon standardised science-based metrics deemed to support private policies in order to account for the past and anticipate the future state of 'nature'. Our findings suggest that the development of ISO 14007 & ISO 14008 aims at competing with first-movers' methodologies, in particular on the power implications resulting from a transparent documentation and reporting.

The method used in this chapter builds on a case study based on qualitative material: semi-structured interviews with four members of the two working groups in charge of setting the standards in ISO including the two convenors of ISO 14007 & ISO 14008, as well as a participant observation of five days within the ISO Working Group 8 developing ISO 14007 in Beirut, Lebanon in March 2019.[2] We also make use of other primary sources: formal documents from ISO including the two standards, informal documents provided by interviewees, and documents produced by the Big Four, the Natural Capital Coalition and other arenas developing such methodologies for natural capital accounting.

The aim of the chapter is to provide the reader with an overview of the issues related to the standard-setting process of tools for natural capital accounting methodologies. The first section of this paper examines the characteristics of standards and used for quantification: their purpose, the actors involved, and their power dimensions. The other three more empirical sections follow the same architecture regarding natural capital accounting and the standard-setting process of ISO 14007 & ISO 14008 (purpose, actors, power). The chapter concludes by summarising the main results.

CHARACTERISTICS OF STANDARDS

Purpose: The Forecasting Dimension of (Quantitative) Standards

The global ecological crisis gave rise to many uncertainties related to the complexity of biophysical systems and unexpected consequences such as so-called 'feedback loops' effects. Economic actors have actively participated in the development of tools to reduce ecological uncertainties, including environmental indicators, models, risk management plans, sustainability assessments, accounting, and reporting. These tools often aim at representing the future state of nature in quantitative terms, in order to reduce undefined uncertainties into quantitative risks. Against this background, scholars have shown the importance of putting numbers on things in order to 'make things the same' (MacKenzie, 2009) or transforming "qualities into quantities, difference into magnitude" (Espeland & Stevens, 1998, p. 315).

Yet, quantifying is not enough. A common way to think is needed such as the metric system so that everyone measures the same thing according to the same procedure. This is why standardisation allows to simplify previously complex things by creating "a vision of a world united" (Yates & Murphy, 2019, p. 2). As Higgins and Larner (2010, p. 11), explain standards govern our everyday life. By shaping the future, they reduce the uncertainties arising from the many complexities of the world. Therefore, standards providing a procedure to quantify 'nature' – such as ISO 14007 & ISO 14008 – are critical technical and political infrastructures to reduce the uncertainties of the ecological crisis.

Such dominant mode of governing the future through uncertainty reduction builds upon a specific instrumental rationality which attempts to respond to the systemic feature of risk in contemporary society (Beck, 1992). Indeed, capitalism has evolved in recent decades in such a way that risk "is now economically 'systemic, enveloping everyone'; and this is perhaps nowhere more apparent than in relation to nature and the risks ascribed to environmental transformation" (Christophers, 2018, pp. 331–332; J. Levy, 2005). Power (2004, pp. 10, 59) justifies the rise of the "risk management of everything" on the assumption that "individuals, organisations and societies have no choice but to organize in the face of uncertainty, to act 'as if' they know the risks they face". Risk management studies claim to provide tools for anticipating uncertainties. With a focus on the ability to control all uncertainties, they explore strategies for "managing the uncontrollable" (Kaplan & Mikes, 2012, p. 11). Building on the example of corporate sustainability management and environmental standardisation, Sardá and Pogutz (2018, p. xxvii) note that "we need to learn not just to manage the possible or the improbable, but also to manage the impossible".

Actors: Privatisation of International Standardisation

The ecological crisis has prompted the rise of transnational private regulations such as environmental standards and certifications. They often provide a framework that shape MNCs' relation with nature. According to Murphy and Yates (2009, p. 2), ISO standards "may have had more impact than any of the UN-sponsored agreement of the 1990s". It has led Mazower (2013, p. 102) to describe ISO as "perhaps the most influential private organization in the contemporary world, with a vast and largely invisible influence over most aspects of how we live". Yet, these standards are often designed by the MNCs themselves, since they are based on 'multistakeholder' model, defined by Mena and Palazzo (2012, p. 528) as "private governance mechanisms involving corporations, civil society organizations, and sometimes other actors, such as governments, academia or unions, to cope with social and environmental challenges across industries and on a global scale".

IPE scholars emphasise the importance of private actors in shaping the rules of global political economy (Cutler, 2010), considering especially MNCs as "an intrinsic part of the fabric of environmental governance, as rule maker, and often rule enforcer" (D. L. Levy & Newell, 2005, p. 330).The authority of private actors rests on an institutionalised form of power that is not exclusively conveyed by government institutions. It includes standards. Such involvement of private actors in the regulation of capitalism is nothing new, as Yates and Murphy recently underlined in a book exploring "the global standard setting since 1880". They point out that "private standardization has come to provide a critical infrastructure for the global economy" (2019, p. 2). In the environmental field, such an approach acknowledging the political role of MNCs is usually preferred by market liberals, since "it shifts the burden of regulation from the State to the firm, which can monitor environmental performance much more efficiently" (Clapp & Dauvergne, 2011, p. 175). Dauvergne (2018) adopts a more critical stance by describing such tools as "eco-business" practices for communication and public relations. In the same vein, Bair and Palpacuer (2015, p. S3) argue that these instruments aim at promoting the ethical image of MNCs, by absorbing and anticipating criticisms, resistances, and contestations.

Power: The Political Dimension of Standards

Voluntary standards have always faced the difficult task of balancing opposing interests of producers and consumers while supporting technological innovations and broader welfare purposes. While consensus-based voluntary standards set procedures addressing such concerns, opposing commercial interests may be so great that so-called standards wars may preclude reaching the level of consensus required to agree on a common standard. Notorious cases in point include colour TV and videotapes, as well as early ISO attempt to define an Open System Interconnection (OSI) for what will later be known as the Internet (Yates & Murphy, 2019). Producers may also align their interests in setting so-called consortia standards outside official arenas such as ISO, seen as too slow, burdensome and bureaucratic to find a timely solution for innovative technologies.

Standards can thus make whole new markets possible through what Egeydi (2000) calls 'gateway technologies' and shape entire business models as they can "become a condition for firms that wish to compete in the global marketplace" (Clapp, 1998, p. 299). According to Busch (2011, p. 13), standards are even part of "the technical, political, social, economic, and ethical infrastructure that constitutes human societies". He points out that international standards "shape not only the physical world around us but our social lives and even our very selves. [… They] are recipes by which we create realities" (2011, p. 2). Therefore, standardisation processes often create winners and losers and even the committee-based model whose procedure is based on the rule of consensus does not, however, prevent the most powerful actors from imposing their views (Yates & Murphy, 2019). It is from this understanding that standards materialise a "non-conventional form of power in the organisation of contemporary capitalism" (2019, p. 8), and that Busch (2011, p. 33) stresses "the importance of power with respect to standards (…) reflected in the fact that the emergence of standards is almost invariably the result of conflict or disagreement".

Finally, standards are produced by a specialised knowledge usually called 'expertise', defined by Littoz-Monnet (2017, p. 2) as "a codified knowledge produced by specialist, and that is generally assumed to require skills and experience not possessed by professional administrators". There are, however, clear interconnections between politics and technical expertise, since the latter integrates scientific knowledge into a political decision-making process (Granjou, 2003). Therefore, standards are both technical and political, and they often blur the boundaries between what is political on the one hand, and what is a-political and purely technical on the other (Porter, 2005). As Mattli and Büthe (2011, p. 11) point out, "standards do not embody some objective truth or undisputed scientific wisdom professed by experts". In contrast, they are made by individual, driven by diverse and varied interests, and thus reflect and materialise power relations in their quest of regulation.

PUROPOSE OF STANDARDS FOR NATURAL CAPITAL ACCOUNTING

Environmental Management Systems Standards

ISO 14007 & ISO 14008 standards are part of the ISO 14000 series, 'environmental management system standards'. They are "formal structured framework of policies, procedures, and practices to manage and reduce an organization's environmental impact" (Sardá & Pogutz, 2018, p. 150), providing MNCs with a framework for the protection of the environment (Neves, Salgado, & Beijo, 2017, p. 253). During the 1980s and 1990s, some MNCs established the first voluntary codes of conduct to define their relation with the environment and improve their environmental performance. It aimed at responding to several environmental catastrophes in the 1980s and to the 1992 Rio Earth Summit, in which industries played a key role by supporting the development of different 'voluntary' or 'best practice' codes (Clapp

& Dauvergne, 2011, p. 175; Sardá & Pogutz, 2018, p. 148). Published in 1996, ISO 14001 was largely based on the British Standard 7750 of 1994. It was revised in 2015, to ensure that "the standards are [still] updated and relevant for the marketplace" (Ciravegna Martins da Fonseca, 2015, p. 43), and adapted to the latest trends in this domain. ISO 14001, the only certifiable standard of the ISO 14000 series, is often portrayed as the "Global Green Standard" (Heras-Saizarbitoria, 2017, p. 4), i.e. the "world's most used standard supporting the development of appropriate environmental policies and ensuring their implementation in all types of organizations" (Sardá & Pogutz, 2018, p. 150). ISO 14001 aims at helping organisations to enhance their environmental performance, fulfil their compliance obligations and achieve their environmental objectives.

While Prakash and Potoski identify a number of framework conditions likely to help ISO 14001 to effectively induce "firms to pollute less and better comply with governmental regulations" (2006, p. xii), others have more doubts regarding the standards' effectiveness besides their use as a tool to compete in the global marketplace (Ciravegna Martins da Fonseca, 2015, p. 43). Whatever that may be, the importance of ISO 14001 in contemporary capitalism should be understood in the wake of the success of management systems standards such as ISO 9000 series first published in 1987. This management systems standard is intrinsically forward-looking, since its main principle is 'continual improvement', which needs to be measured and documented, ideally quantitatively. To achieve this goal, the other standards of the ISO 14000 series provide "practical tools for companies and organisations of all kinds looking to manage their environmental responsibilities" (ISO, 2018a). Thus, in contrast to certifiable standards such as ISO 14001, international standards ISO 14007 & ISO 14008 cannot be used in certified conformity assessment. They remain, however, key tools designed to help organisations effectively identify, measure, describe and monitor their environmental impacts in quantitative terms.

Natural Capital Accounting: an Academic Perspective

As briefly explained in the introduction, natural capital accounting builds on the concept of 'ecosystem services', whose textbook definition is "the benefits human populations derive, directly or indirectly, from ecosystem functions" (Costanza et al., 1997, p. 253), but also on 'environmental accounting', which aims at providing a standardised measure of the sustainability of an organisation. In contrast to natural capital accounting, environmental accounting usually concerns public actors and provides accounts of the "environmental events which arise as a result of, and are intimately tied to, the economic actions of entities" (Bebbington & Thomson, 2007, p. 42).

Natural capital accounting is based on the leitmotiv that "we don't protect what we don't value" (Myers & Reichert, 1997), following a narrative pointing out that "once nature and the service it provides are valued as market goods (...) nature will have a fighting chance" (Ervine, 2018, p. 159). Helm (2016, p. 4) argues that "refusing to price or place an economic value on nature risks environmental meltdown". Therefore, it is often portrayed as making "environmental concerns compatible with economic growth within predominantly capitalist markets and states" (Dempsey, 2016, p. 237). Such a view has been acknowledged by Costanza and his colleagues in a prominent study about the global valuation of ecosystem services, in which they claim that "the environment versus the economy is a false choice" (2014, p. 154). They point out that valuing ecosystem services is ultimately about raising awareness regarding the epochal decline of 'nature'.

But from a critical perspective, it relates to the fabrication of 'nature' as 'natural capital', through the integration of economic theory into environmental issues (Akerman, 2003; Sullivan, 2017). Against this background, Gómez-Baggethun and Ruiz-Pérez (2011) argue that monetary valuation of nature is the first step in a process of commodification of ecosystem services, currently promoted by dominant neoliberal discourses. Some point out that such "standardised science-based measurements" (Turnhout, Neves, & Lijster, 2014, p. 581) subscribe to a depoliticisation of environmental governance and regulations, transforming political concerns into economic and technical solutions, or what Felli (2015, p. 1743) calls "the neoliberal depoliticisation of environmental policy". Market-based instruments for nature thus raise concern within the academic community about the "expansion of market valuation to spheres that were formerly unaffected by commerce" (Gómez-Baggethun & Ruiz-Pérez, 2011, p. 619), and more broadly, about the "neoliberalisation of environmental regulation, management, and governance" (Castree, 2010, p. 1). However, such criticisms often build on an ill-defined or unclear definition of "neoliberalisation" of nature (Levrel & Missemer, 2018), and Boisvert and her colleagues (2013, p. 1123) have underlined the "gap between discourse and practice" about market-based instruments for nature.

Environmental Accounting: Tools Developed by Practitioners

The power play raised by the most recent stage of development in natural accounting methodologies does not comes in a void. Back in 1993, the UN already set a System of Environmental-Economic Accounting, with the objective of becoming an "international statistical standard for environmental-economic accounting" (United Nations, 2014, p. vii). While the latest version of the methodology published in 2012 is viewed as having "the same authority and weight as the System of National Accounts" (Hamilton, 2016, p. 27), its scope remains in the domain of states' accounting systems rather than corporate accounting. At the intergovernmental level, the Organisation for Economic Cooperation and Development (OECD) also published several reports on this topic. The first was released in 2004. Entitled "Measuring Sustainable Development", it discussed the transformation of environmental units into monetary data (OECD, 2004). It was followed in 2006 by another one on "Cost-Benefit Analysis and the Environment" (OECD, 2006), whose main author was David Pearce, also involved in the so-called "Pearce Report". With the official name of "Blueprint for a Green Economy" (Pearce, Markandya, & Barbier, 1989), the report gave rise to one of the first modern forms of environmental accounting and reporting. In 2018, the OECD released a new report providing an in-depth explanation of the latest methods and techniques on environmental accounting, focusing especially on environmental cost and benefit analysis (OECD, 2018).

While natural capital accounting informs decision-makers of the uncertainties that should be considered, there is always a part of such uncertainty that cannot be captured, so that there are clear limits in our capacities to anticipate the future (Maechler et al., 2019). However, this chapter contends that the ultimate aim of natural capital accounting – especially from a business perspective – is to make the future state of nature knowable, comparable and thus governable, by valuing both positive and negative externalities (i.e. 'impacts') of economic activities.[3] The "True Value" methodology document of the audit and accounting firm KPMG points out that:

What executives need is a method to understand and quantify their externalities and the likelihood they will affect their company's earning capability and risk profile in the future (...) to help businesses combine financial earnings data with monetized externality data and quantify the likelihood and potential impact of the latter coming to influence the former. Ultimately, we need a standardized approach to measure societal value creation (KPMG International Cooperative, 2014, p. 5).

KPMG's methodology aims at measuring in monetary terms the "societal value creation", i.e. the environmental but also economic and social externalities. It allows to compare very different data into a common metric: money. This practice is part of the broader project of quantifying the relationships between capitalism – its actors – and the world in which they operate. Focusing only on the environmental side, the PricewaterhouseCoopers methodology aims at the quantification and valuation of the firm's "environmental impacts associated with its operations and entire supply chain" (PricewaterhouseCoopers, 2015). To achieve this goal, their methodology represents nature as a 'liability' or an 'asset' into corporate extra-financial reporting of firms. Against this background, these natural capital accounting methodologies aim at transforming the heterogeneity of nature into objectifiable and commensurable units of analysis in quite the same way as transnational capitalism needs financial accounting standards to support capital accumulation. Since the Big Four are not only powerful actors in the accounting field but also key providers of audit, management consulting, financial and tax services for public and private entities, natural capital accounting could also soon be about the integration of nature into an international tax regime, involving clear implications regarding climate and biodiversity diplomacy and global political economy relations.

What is the Purpose of ISO 14007 & ISO 14008?
The Challenge of Openness and Transparency

As we have seen above, ISO 14007 & ISO 14008 set standards for two key components of natural capital accounting methodologies. ISO 14008 provides a monetarised measure of an organisation's environmental impacts, building on the notion of 'ecosystem services'. ISO 14007 provides a standardised procedure to undertake an environmental cost and benefit analysis.

While ISO recognises a strong trend in monetary assessments (ISO, 2018b), transparency of such procedure is often very low. According to the convenor of ISO 14007, the Big Four are well known to have no interest in sharing their data and methodologies, and therefore leave other stakeholders uninformed on how they came to such or such monetary upshot. Although this behaviour is part of any companies' business model developing new tools to expand their market shares, it raises substantial concerns in a procedure whose underlying objective is precisely the disclosure of (environmental) information. This is all the more the case regarding an issue on which we should all have a say: the global ecological crisis. In this regard, both ISO 14008 and ISO 14007 underline the importance of transparent documentation and reporting during the all process of monetary valuation and cost-benefit analysis. The main purpose of ISO 14008 is indeed to "increase the awareness, comparability and transparency of the monetary valuation of environmental impacts and related environmental aspects. It demonstrates the benefits that monetary valuation methods offer to users. To achieve this purpose, standardised and transparent documentation of the methods, data and assumptions used to derive monetary values is essential" (ISO 14008). On its side, ISO 14007 provides "guidance on determining and documenting (…) environmental costs and benefits in a comprehensive and transparent way". It also helps "organisations disclose and exchange relevant information in a transparent way" (ISO 14007).

ISO 14008 builds on the concept ecosystem services, which is "useful to increase the understanding of natural capital and ecosystem services, their stocks & flows and linkages" (Pandeya et al., 2016, p. 251). ISO 14008 monetary values the flows of ecosystem services, i.e. the environmental impacts. However, ISO 14008 makes a distinction between an environmental impact and aspect. It refers to the distinction

Figure 1. ISO 14007 & ISO 14008 (Inspired by a figure and related explanations provided by one member of the working groups)

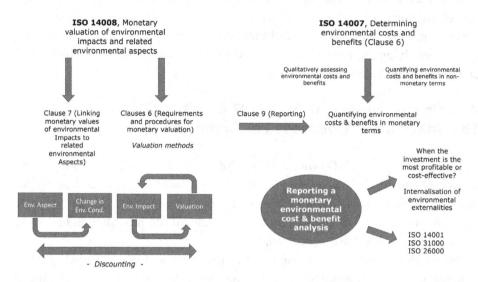

made in ISO 14001, which considers an environmental aspect as an element of the organisation's activities, products or services that can interact with the environment, or the 'interfaces' of the organisation with the environment. Environmental aspect is used as an analytical category to identify where the impact comes from in the operations of an organisation. For instance, an environmental aspect can provoke a change in environmental conditions, such as a change in the concentration of carbon dioxide in the air, which then impacts the natural environment and society. In ISO 14008, these impacts are valued in monetary terms according to clause 6 of the standard, 'requirements and procedures for monetary valuation' (see figure above), which provides different economic methods of valuation. It is also possible to skip these valuations techniques by directly linking valuation and environmental aspects through the so-called 'public averting cost method' based on targets at the administrative level. The value is then calculated according to the "cost of the last (most expensive) averting action to comply with a policy target", i.e. the marginal abatement cost (ISO 14008).

Therefore, ISO 14008 provides a monetary value from an environmental impact or directly from an environmental aspect. The reporting of the monetary valuation (clause 9) allows the further use of ISO 14007. ISO 14007 suggests that the cost and benefit analysis can also be expressed in qualitative way or in quantitative non-monetary term (e.g. number of species loses, number of death/years). However, according to our interviewees, ISO 14007 has clearly been initially developed to be linked with ISO 14008 and thus expressed in quantitative monetary terms. Indeed, one of the objective of ISO 14007 is to clarify "why and how monetary valuation can be used and communicated as part of an existing environmental management approach or system" (ISO, 2019). As seen above, expressing different things in a common unit is the best way to reduce undefined uncertainties into manageable risks. Such possibility of direct comparison of environmental and financial data is in line with the standard itself, which aims at creating "a better understanding of issues such as the financial implications related to the environment of a given site, the organization as a whole, or along the organization's value chain" (ISO 14007).

Through the cost and benefit analysis, ISO 14007 helps to decide how much and especially when firms, states or 'society' as a whole have the greatest financial interest to reduce (or internalise) their environmental impacts (or externalities), so that the investment is the most profitable or cost-effective. Such a way to balance present costs against future benefits is a key issue in the prior phase, i.e. the monetary valuation. ISO 14008 thus provides guidelines to weight the monetary valuation according to different points in time ('discounting'). Discounting the future is a particular feature of uncertainty reduction in environmental economics. Natural capital accounting thus allows to compare future benefits (or costs) against any action that an organisation may take in the present. This means that these future costs and benefits have to be converted into a net present value. The usual assumptions made by 'experts' (in particular environmental economists) is that "the social or shadow price of a unit of consumption in the future is lower than the price of a unit of consumption today" (OECD, 2018, p. 197). ISO 14008 thus points out that "when the monetary values are applied to environmental impacts or aspects that occur at different points in time, discounting shall be performed".

Finally, as any other guidance standards, the first aim of ISO 14007 & ISO 14008 is to objectify standards that require certification, in particular ISO 14001. But they can also be used in relation with other management standards, such as ISO 31000 (Risk management), to objectify environmental risks, or with other guidance standards, in particular ISO 26000 (Social responsibility), to define the relation between an organisation, the society and its environment, increasing the transparency and comparability of corporate social responsibility reporting. ISO 14007 & ISO 14008 thus provide organisations with a 'toolbox' for transparent natural capital accounting.

ACTORS OF NATURAL CAPITAL ACCOUNTING

It is important to remind that ISO does not invent anything new. The convenor of ISO 14007 himself reminds that "ISO is only based on existing practices, follows what already exists".[4] While we have seen above that the UN or the OECD have been involved in the field, their scope remains in the domain of states' environmental accounting systems rather than corporate natural capital accounting. Yet, other stakeholders have been involved in corporate natural capital accounting. Recently, The World Wide Fund for Nature, the World Bank, the World Business Council for Sustainable Development or the International Federation of Accountants all stressed the need to create a standardised procedure to translate environmental data into monetary units of analysis in order to face the global ecological crisis (The Association of Chartered Certified Accountants, Fauna & Flora International, & KPMG International Cooperative, 2012; WBCSD, 2011; WWF International, 2014). Various kinds of consulting firms, such as True Price, Trucost and eCountability, have been recently founded to offer natural capital accounting services to MNCs. As seen above, the Big Four are at the leading edge of the development of such methodology. Several years ago, Ernst & Young already stressed that "it is time for our profession to play a leadership role in accounting for the relationship between the business world and the natural world" (Ernst & Young, International Federation of Accountants, & Natural Capital Coalition, 2014, p. 3). Moreover, many firms have already applied these methodologies, such as Kering, LafargeHolcim, Novo Nordisk or Novartis among others, always with the support of one of the Big Four.

Many of these actors including the Big Four meet within the Natural Capital Coalition – a platform founded in 2012, with its Natural Capital Protocol launched in 2016. This document provides a general guidance on how to measure impacts and dependencies on nature capital (Natural Capital Coalition, 2018b), but is still much too vague to be applied as a standard. According to Barker (2019, p. 70), the Natural Capital Protocol is not "a 'how to' guide for natural capital accounting; instead it is an eclectic mix of different approaches, applied in different ways to varying ends – more a 'take your pick' document than an accounting standard". The concrete activity of the Natural Capital Coalition consists in the promotion of such practices: it unites leading initiatives under "a common vision of a world that conserves and enhances the natural capital" (Natural Capital Coalition, 2018a). For this purpose, they organise presentations and meetings during which companies present their results and promote the usefulness of such an approach for their business.

POWER RELATIONS IN NATURAL CAPITAL ACCOUNTING STANDARDISATION

The Conflicts within ISO

ISO 14007 & ISO 14008 followed the same institutional path and have been developed by the same 'leading experts', raising similar debates, conflicts and disagreements. ISO 14008 was initially submitted to subcommittee 5, which sets standards in the field of life-cycle assessment (LCA). Bengt Steen, a chemical engineer who proposed the new item agenda of ISO 14008 also took part in the development of ISO 14040 on LCA within subcommittee 5 during the 1990s. He pointed out that "the good thing with subcommittee 5 is that it contains a lot of engineers, while other subcommittees contain more people from a management background".[5] However, subcommittee 5 was opposed to monetary valuation practices and refused to host the future standard. In contrast, subcommittee 1 accepted to host it. This subcommittee is constituted of many environmental economists, usually committed to the cause of environmental and monetary valuation. What may seem anecdotal reflects the broader disagreements regarding the monetary valuation of nature between economists and engineers. In this regard, it is interesting to note that ISO 14008 underlines in its first paragraph that "using monetary valuation does not mean that money is the only metric of value" (ISO 14008). As a result of these issues related to the monetisation of the environment, the working groups developing both ISO 14007 & ISO 14008 have been constituted of experts from two distinct disciplinary backgrounds: life-cycle assessment (engineering) and environmental economics. Even though the interviewees underlined that the working groups "agreed 90% of the time"[6], such distinct disciplinary background raised particular debates on the issue of the discount rate: how to value the future in comparison to the present?

Indeed, the discount rate directly shape the future of business relation with nature, since a higher discount rate means that we should not reduce our environmental impacts too quickly on the assumption that "the economic cost to people today will be higher than the benefit of protecting people in the future" (Hickel, 2018). This is for instance what suggests William Nordhaus, laureate of the 2018 Nobel Memorial Prize in Economic Sciences, who hardly criticised the use of a low discount rate of 1.4% in the famous "Stern Review", a report on the economic costs of climate change (Nordhaus, 2007, p. 686; Stern, 2006). Against this background, while LCA uses a constant discount rate of 0%, which means that future and present generations are valued equally (Hickel, 2018), environmental economists usually use a positive figure: they value the present more than the future. Our interviewees underlined that most disagreements within the working group concerned this single issue, which determine how the standard will forecast and anticipate the future management of the ecological crisis. They explained that if a fixed discount rate had been prescribed, no consensus would have been possible. ISO 14008 thus leaves the choice of the discount rate open, but asks for full transparency: "the process of discounting and the discount rates used, including when performed with a zero-discount rate, shall be documented and justified" (ISO 14008). This outcome has significant consequences regarding the implications that such emphasis on transparent documentation and reporting may have to be in conformity with the standard. However, not taking any decision regarding the discount rate to be applied can also be interpreted as a significant failure of ISO in a period in which societies have to make important intergenerational choices.

ISO and the First-Movers

ISO often faces 'first-movers' in its attempt to set a standard. In this regard, ISO tries to impose its own standards thanks to the legitimacy of the institution based on a multistakeholder consensus (Hahn & Weidtmann, 2016). While states, academic scholars, consultants and experts from MNCs such as Veolia and Électricité de France all join in the standard-setting processes of ISO, the Big Four rather opt only for the Natural Capital Coalition. Since 2010, the Big Four published a full range of documents available online in which they describe their methodologies and illustrate them with case-studies that identify and quantify in financial terms MNC's environmental impacts. However, they do not share their full data and methodology because this is part of their business model. In contrast, these documents emphasize the relevance for business of taking account of nature capital and thus encourage the use of such tools. For instance, a document published by Ernst & Young, the International Federation of Accountants and the Natural Capital Coalition called "Accounting for Natural Capital: The elephant in the boardroom" illustrates such 'selling strategy'. It underlines that "natural capital is still largely hidden from view and absent from the corporate narrative. This situation is no longer acceptable if organisation are to become truly sustainable" (Ernst & Young et al., 2014, pp. 1, 3).

While representatives of the Natural Capital Coalition such as the Policy Director joined the working groups developing ISO 14007 and ISO 14008, their participation has remained limited to the firsts meetings. Indeed, they have been marginalised within the working groups. Working groups' members pointed out that representatives of the Natural Capital Coalition were not sufficiently familiar with the work of ISO, which is "democratic and formalised"[7], in contrast to the Coalition's work. Second, they always made proposal to change the text, to bring in the definitions they use in the Natural Capital Protocol. Thus, they were seen by other members of the working groups as "entrepreneurs building their own agenda".[8] According to the convenor of ISO 14007, "they were not involved because ISO was taking away attention by the market on their own things". More generally, he stressed the competition between different initiatives in this domain.[9]

This competition between different methodologies and potential standards resulted in the fact that none of the Big Four took part to the ISO working groups, despite an explicit invitation to do so from the convenor of ISO 14008. Such defect from the Big Four is striking, since a close relation usually exists between the accounting market and official standardisation bodies in the field of traditional accounting standards (Ramirez, 2013). Moreover, the Big Four are members of the national standardisation bodies like the British Standards Institution. Our analysis suggests that the transparency required by the standard is likely to have been a tipping point regarding the non-involvement of the Big Four. According to some views, they are wary of any standard that could modify their 'business model' regarding their own methodology, and they might only use the standards if they are in their favour. The convenor of ISO 14007 pointed out that "they make business with their own methodologies" and "are not interested that new standard are being developed".[10] As briefly discussed above, this is fully understandable from a business perspective. However, transparency remains a core issue for the comparability of the data presented to both internal and external stakeholders. Without sufficient transparency, it is unlikely that natural capital accounting will achieve one of its main publicly recognised objectives: strengthening the 'social license to operate' by reducing the risks and uncertainties of business operations by making standardised information public for internal and external stakeholders alike.

There is thus clear evidence that such topic is not only about the techniques of environmental economics. Standardising natural capital accounting also raises power relations. This is not surprising, since it might also, in a near future, be about its integration into law, allowing authorities to engage ecological tax compliance procedures based on standardised accounting metrics. Against this background, this chapter provided an analysis in the wake of existing studies that ley emphasis on the underlying socio-political dimensions of the growing number of tools designed to integrate nature into an accounting and economic framework (Martinez-Alier, 2002; Purushothaman, Thomas, Abraham, & Dhar, 2013).

CONCLUSION

This chapter has provided an analysis of recent developments on natural capital accounting and related standards likely to shape future relations between MNCs and nature. We saw that private actors and especially MNCs operating in the field are often directly involved in standardisation processes. Yet, this was not so much the case for ISO 14007 & ISO 14008, as the main actors – the Big Four – did not take part in the working groups in charge of setting the standards. This is not surprising, considering the importance of their own methodologies in their business model. The first-movers could not impose their own standard and had no interest in the standard as drafted as it directly competed with their own proprietary methodology. Being opposed to ceding proprietary knowledge for the supposed common good of a standardised natural capital accounting methodology, they rather adopted a damage limitation strategy regarding the key issue threatening their business model – transparency. A similar strategy has been described by Graz and Hauert (2019, p. 179) regarding the largest players of the hospitality industry blocking any move towards labels and classification schemes such as stars.

Therefore, we have seen that standard-setting process is not only technical but also political, raising power relations both within and outside ISO. We have stressed the divergence of views at the level of ISO regarding the monetisation of nature, especially the issue of the discount rate at the level of the working groups. The latter reflects two distinct disciplinary backgrounds: experts of life-cycle assessment excluding the relevance of taking discount rate on-board on the one hand, and environmental economists debating among themselves about the rate of the discount on the other. Ultimately, such debate boils down to whether, and if so, how to value the future in comparison with the present on the balance sheet of a firm. Yet, the outcome of the negotiations leading to the international standard ISO 14008 is a double no, resulting from too much disagreement on the size of the discount rate. Despite what might look as a significant failure, the standard still provides guidance not only on valuation per se, but also on the importance of transparent documentation and reporting. It is especially from this perspective that these standards compete with other arenas, in particular the Natural Capital Coalition and the Big Four.

Finally, the role of natural capital accounting standards and quantitative measurement for shaping the future provide a quantitative procedure against which deciding how much and especially when firms, states or 'society' as a whole have the greatest financial interest to reduce their environmental impacts, so that the investment is the most profitable or cost-effective. This should encourage further research on how natural capital accounting and standards will shape our responses to the ecological crisis.

ACKNOWLEDGMENT

We had the opportunity to present a first draft of this paper at the 24th Conference of the European Academy for Standardisation (EURAS) at LUISS Guido Carli University of Rome. We are grateful to the participants for their questions and feedbacks. We also thank the reviewers for their valuable comments on previous drafts of the chapter.

This research received no specific grant from any funding agency in the public, commercial, or not-for-profit sectors.

REFERENCES

Akerman, M. (2003). What Does 'Natural Capital' Do? The Role of Metaphor in Economic Understanding of the Environment. *Environmental Values*, *12*(4), 431–448. doi:10.3197/096327103129341397

Andonova, L. B. (2017). *Governance entrepreneurs: International organizations and the rise of global public-private partnerships*. Cambridge, UK: Cambridge University Press. doi:10.1017/9781316694015

Bair, J., & Palpacuer, F. (2015). CSR beyond the corporation: Contested governance in global value chains. *Global Networks*, *15*(1), S1–S19. doi:10.1111/glob.12085

Barker, R. (2019). Corporate natural capital accounting. *Oxford Review of Economic Policy*, *35*(1), 68–87. doi:10.1093/oxrep/gry031

Bebbington, J., & Thomson, I. (2007). Social and Environmental Accounting, Auditing, and Reporting: A Potential Source of Organisational Risk Governance? *Environment and Planning. C, Government & Policy*, *25*(1), 38–55. doi:10.1068/c0616j

Beck, U. (1992). *Risk Society: Towards a New Modernity*. London: SAGE.

Bernstein, S. (2002). Liberal Environmentalism and Global Environmental Governance. *Global Environmental Politics*, *2*(3), 1–16. doi:10.1162/152638002320310509

Boisvert, V., Méral, P., & Froger, G. (2013). Market-Based Instruments for Ecosystem Services: Institutional Innovation or Renovation? *Society & Natural Resources*, *26*(10), 1122–1136. doi:10.1080/08941920.2013.820815

Boyd, J., & Banzhaf, S. (2007). What are ecosystem services? The need for standardized environmental accounting units. *Ecological Economics*, *63*(2–3), 616–626. doi:10.1016/j.ecolecon.2007.01.002

Bracking, S. (2015). Performativity in the Green Economy: How far does climate finance create a fictive economy? *Third World Quarterly*, *36*(12), 2337–2357. doi:10.1080/01436597.2015.1086263

Busch, L. (2011). *Standards: Recipes for Reality*. Cambridge, MA: The MIT Press. doi:10.7551/mitpress/8962.001.0001

Castree, N. (2010). Neoliberalism and the biophysical environment: A synthesis and evaluation of the research. *Environment and Society: Advances in Research, 1*(1), 5–45. doi:10.3167/ares.2010.010102

Christophers, B. (2018). Risking value theory in the political economy of finance and nature. *Progress in Human Geography, 42*(3), 330–349. doi:10.1177/0309132516679268

Ciravegna Martins da Fonseca, L. M. (2015). ISO 14001:2015: An improved tool for sustainability. *Journal of Industrial Engineering and Management, 8*(1), 37–50. doi:10.3926/jiem.1298

Clapp, J. (1998). The Privatization of Global Environmental Governance: ISO 14000 and the Developing World. *Global Governance, 4*(3), 295–316. doi:10.1163/19426720-00403004

Clapp, J., & Dauvergne, P. (2011). *Paths to a Green World – The Political Economy of the Global Environment*. Cambridge, MA: MIT Press.

Costanza, R., d'Arge, R., de Groot, R., Farber, S., Grasso, M., Hannon, B., ... van den Belt, M. (1997). The value of the world's ecosystem services and natural capital. *Nature, 387*(6630), 253–260. doi:10.1038/387253a0

Costanza, R., de Groot, R., Braat, L., Kubiszewski, I., Fioramonti, L., Sutton, P., ... Grasso, M. (2017). Twenty years of ecosystem services: How far have we come and how far do we still need to go? *Ecosystem Services, 28*, 1–16. doi:10.1016/j.ecoser.2017.09.008

Costanza, R., de Groot, R., Sutton, P., van der Ploeg, S., Anderson, S. J., Kubiszewski, I., ... Turner, R. K. (2014). Changes in the global value of ecosystem services. *Global Environmental Change, 26*, 152–158. doi:10.1016/j.gloenvcha.2014.04.002

Cutler, A. C. (2010). The legitimacy of private transnational governance: Experts and the transnational market for force. *Socio-economic Review, 8*(1), 157–185. doi:10.1093er/mwp027

Dauvergne, P. (2018). *Will Big Business Destroy Our Planet?* Cambridge, UK: Polity.

de Villiers, C., & Maroun, W. (Eds.). (2018). *Sustainability Accounting and Integrated Reporting*. London: Routledge.

Dempsey, J. (2016). *Enterprising Nature: Economics, Markets, and Finance in Global Biodiversity Politics*. Chichester, UK: Wiley. doi:10.1002/9781118640517

Egyedi, T. M. (2000). The Standardised Container: Gateway Technologies in Cargo Transport. *Homo Oeconomicus, 17*, 231–262.

Ernst & Young, International Federation of Accountants, & Natural Capital Coalition. (2014). *Accounting for Natural Capital – The elephant in the boardroom*. Retrieved from Chartered Institute of Management Accountants website: https://www.ey.com/Publication/vwLUAssets/Accounting-for-natural-capital/$File/EY-Accounting-for-natural-capital.pdf

Ervine, K. (2018). *Carbon*. Cambridge, MA: Polity.

Espeland, W. N., & Stevens, M. L. (1998). Commensuration as a Social Process. *Annual Review of Sociology, 24*(1), 313–343. doi:10.1146/annurev.soc.24.1.313

Felli, R. (2015). Environment, not planning: The neoliberal depoliticisation of environmental policy by means of emissions trading. *Environmental Politics, 24*(5), 641–660. doi:10.1080/09644016.2015.1051323

Fransen, L., & LeBaron, G. (2019). Big audit firms as regulatory intermediaries in transnational labor governance. *Regulation & Governance, 13*(2), 260–279. doi:10.1111/rego.12224

Gómez-Baggethun, E., & Ruiz-Pérez, M. (2011). Economic valuation and the commodification of ecosystem services. *Progress in Physical Geography, 35*(5), 613–628. doi:10.1177/0309133311421708

Gould, R. (2018, May 8). *The secret to unlocking green finance*. Retrieved 16 April 2019, from ISO website: http://www.iso.org/cms/render/live/en/sites/isoorg/contents/news/2018/05/Ref2287.html

Granjou, C. (2003). L'expertise scientifique à destination politique. *Cahiers Internationaux de Sociologie, 1*(114), 175–183. doi:10.3917/cis.114.0175

Graz, J.-C. (2019). *The Power of Standards: Hybrid Authority and the Globalisation of Services*. Cambridge, UK: Cambridge University Press. doi:10.1017/9781108759038

Graz, J.-C., & Hauert, C. (2019). Translating Technical Diplomacy: The Participation of Civil Society Organisations in International Standardisation. *Global Society, 33*(2), 163–183. doi:10.1080/13600826.2019.1567476

Hahn, R., & Weidtmann, C. (2016). Transnational Governance, Deliberative Democracy, and the Legitimacy of ISO 26000: Analyzing the Case of a Global Multistakeholder Process. *Business & Society*, *55*(1), 90–129. doi:10.1177/0007650312462666

Hamilton, K. (2016). Measuring Sustainability in the UN System of Environmental-Economic Accounting. *Environmental and Resource Economics*, *64*(1), 25–36. doi:10.100710640-015-9924-y

Helm, D. (2016). *Natural Capital: Valuing the Planet*. New Haven, CT: Yale University Press.

Heras-Saizarbitoria, I. (Ed.). (2017). *ISO 9001, ISO 14001, and New Management Standards*. New York: Springer.

Hickel, J. (2018). *The Nobel Prize for Climate Catastrophe*. Retrieved from https://foreignpolicy.com/2018/12/06/the-nobel-prize-for-climate-catastrophe/

Higgins, V., & Larner, W. (Eds.). (2010). *Calculating the Social: Standards and the Reconfiguration of Governing*. New York: Palgrave Macmillan. doi:10.1057/9780230289673

International, W. W. F. (2014). *Accounting for Natural Capital in EU Policy Decision-Making: A WWF background paper on policy developments*. Retrieved from http://wwf.panda.org/?uNewsID=222134

ISO. (2018a). *ISO 14000 Environmental management*. Retrieved from ISO website: http://www.iso.org/cms/render/live/en/sites/isoorg/home/standards/popular-standards/iso-14000-environmental-manageme.html

ISO. (2018b). *ISO 14008—Monetary Valuation of environmental impacts and related environmental aspects*. Retrieved from https://committee.iso.org/sites/tc207sc1/home/projects/ongoing/iso-14008.html

ISO. (2019). *ISO 14008:2019 has now been published!* Retrieved from ISO/TC 207/SC 1 website: https://committee.iso.org/sites/tc207sc1/home/news/content-left-area/news-and-updates/iso-140082019-has-now-been-publi.html

Kaplan, R. S., & Mikes, A. (2012). Managing Risks: A New Framework. *Harvard Business Review*.

Katz-Rosene, R., & Paterson, M. (2018). *Thinking Ecologically About the Global Political Economy*. New York: Routledge. doi:10.4324/9781315677835

KPMG International Cooperative. (2014). *A New Vision of Value. Connecting corporate and societal value creation*. Amstelveen: KPMG.

Levrel, H., & Missemer, A. (2018). La mise en économie de la nature, contrepoints historiques et contemporains. *Revue Economique, 69*, 120–146.

Levy, D. L., & Newell, P. (2005). *The Business of Global Environmental Governance*. Cambridge, MA: MIT Press.

Levy, J. (2005). *Freaks of Fortune: The Emerging World of Capitalism and Risk in America*. Cambridge, MA: Harvard University Press.

Littoz-Monnet, A. (2017). Production and uses of expertise by international bureaucracies. In *A. Littoz-Monnet, The Politics of Expertise in International Organizations: How International Bureaucracies Produce and Mobilize Knowledge* (pp. 1–18). New York: Routledge. doi:10.4324/9781315542386-1

MacKenzie, D. (2009). Making things the same: Gases, emission rights and the politics of carbon markets. *Accounting, Organizations and Society, 34*(3), 440–455. doi:10.1016/j.aos.2008.02.004

Maechler, S., Furrer, E., Lunghi, E., Monthoux, M., Yousefzai, C., & Graz, J.-C. (2019). Substituting risk for uncertainty. Where are the limits and how to face them? *Les Cahiers de l'IEP*, (73), 1–28.

Martinez-Alier, J. (2002). *The Environmentalism of the Poor: A Study of Ecological Conflicts and Valuation*. Cheltenham, UK: Edward Elgar Publishing. doi:10.4337/9781843765486

Mattli, W., & Buthe, T. (2011). *The New Global Rulers*. Princeton, NJ: Princeton University Press.

Mazower, M. (2013). *Governing the World: The History of an Idea, 1815 to the Present*. New York: Penguin Books.

Mena, S., & Palazzo, G. (2012). Input and Output Legitimacy of Multi-Stakeholder Initiatives. *Business Ethics Quarterly, 22*(3), 527–556. doi:10.5840/beq201222333

Myers, J. P., & Reichert, J. S. (1997). Perspective in nature's services. In G. Daily (Ed.), *Nature's Services: Societal Dependence on Natural Ecosystems* (pp. xvii–xx). Washington, DC: Island Press.

Natural Capital Coalition. (2018a). *Natural Capital Coalition | Coalition Organizations*. Retrieved from https://naturalcapitalcoalition.org/who/coalition-organizations/

Natural Capital Coalition. (2018b). *Natural Capital Coalition | Protocol.* Retrieved from https://naturalcapitalcoalition.org/protocol/

Neves, F. de O., Salgado, E. G., & Beijo, L. A. (2017). Analysis of the Environmental Management System based on ISO 14001 on the American continent. *Journal of Environmental Management, 199,* 251–262. doi:10.1016/j.jenvman.2017.05.049 PMID:28552409

Nordhaus, W. D. (2007). A Review of the Stern Review on the Economics of Climate Change. *Journal of Economic Literature, 45*(3), 686–702. doi:10.1257/jel.45.3.686 PMID:17626869

OECD. (2004). *Measuring Sustainable Development: Integrated Economic, Environmental and Social Frameworks.* Retrieved from: https://www.oecd-ilibrary. org/environment/measuring-sustainable-development_9789264020139-en

OECD. (2006). *Cost-Benefit Analysis and the Environment: Recent Developments.* Retrieved from http://www.oecd.org/greengrowth/tools-evaluation/cost-benefitana lysisandtheenvironmentrecentdevelopments2006.htm

OECD. (2018). *Cost-Benefit Analysis and the Environment: Further Developments and Policy Use.* Retrieved from https://www.oecd.org/governance/cost-benefit-analysis-and-the-environment-9789264085169-en.htm

Pandeya, B., Buytaert, W., Zulkafli, Z., Karpouzoglou, T., Mao, F., & Hannah, D. M. (2016). A comparative analysis of ecosystem services valuation approaches for application at the local scale and in data scarce regions. *Ecosystem Services, 22,* 250–259. doi:10.1016/j.ecoser.2016.10.015

Pearce, D. W., Markandya, A., & Barbier, E. B. (1989). *Blueprint for a Green Economy.* London: Earthscan.

Porter, T. (2005). Private Authority, Technical Authority, and the Globalization of Accounting Standards. *Business and Politics, 7*(3), 1–30. doi:10.2202/1469-3569.1138

Power, M. (2004). *The Risk Management of Everything.* London: Demos. doi:10.1108/eb023001

Prakash, A., & Potoski, M. (2006). *The Voluntary Environmentalists: Green Clubs, ISO 14001, and Voluntary Environmental Regulations.* Cambridge, UK: Cambridge University Press. doi:10.1017/CBO9780511617683

PricewaterhouseCoopers. (2015). *Valuing corporate environmental impacts.* London: PwC.

Purushothaman, S., Thomas, B., Abraham, R., & Dhar, U. (2013). Beyond money metrics: Alternative approaches to conceptualising and assessing ecosystem services. *Conservation & Society, 11*(4), 321. doi:10.4103/0972-4923.125739

Ramirez, C. (2013). Normalisation des services marchands ou marchandisation des normes. In *J.-C. Graz & N. Niang, Services sans frontières* (pp. 223–252). Paris: Presses de Sciences Po.

Sardá, R., & Pogutz, S. (2018). *Corporate Sustainability in the 21st Century: Increasing the Resilience of Social-Ecological Systems.* New York: Routledge. doi:10.4324/9781315180908

Stern, N. (2006). *Stern Review: The Economics of Climate Change.* London: Stationery Office.

Sullivan, S. (2017). Making nature investable: From legibility to leverageability in fabricating 'nature' as 'natural capital'. *Science & Technology Studies, 20*, 1–30.

The Association of Chartered Certified Accountants, Fauna & Flora International, & KPMG International Cooperative. (2012). *Is natural capital a material issue? Executive summary.* Retrieved from http://www.acca.ee/content/dam/acca/global/PDF-technical/environmental-publications/natural-capital-summary.pdf

Turnhout, E., Neves, K., & de Lijster, E. (2014). 'Measurementality' in Biodiversity Governance: Knowledge, Transparency, and the Intergovernmental Science-Policy Platform on Biodiversity and Ecosystem Services (Ipbes). *Environment and Planning A. Economy and Space, 46*(3), 581–597.

United Nations. (Ed.). (2014). *System of environmental-economic accounting 2012: Central framework.* New York: United Nations.

WBCSD. (2011). Guide to corporate ecosystem valuation: A framework for improving corporate decision-making. Geneva: World Business Council for Sustainable Development (WBCSD).

Yates, J., & Murphy, C. N. (2009). *The International Organization for Standardization.* London: Routledge.

Yates, J., & Murphy, C. N. (2019). *Engineering Rules. Global Standard Setting since 1880.* Baltimore, MD: Johns Hopkins University Press.

KEY TERMS AND DEFINITIONS

Big Four Audit and Accounting Firms: The four largest and most powerful world companies offering accounting but also audit, management consulting, financial or legal services for public and private entities.

Ecological Crisis: The radical, systemic, and complex changes of ecological systems due to human interferences with the biosphere.

Environmental Accounting: A set of rules and categories designed to measure nature in monetary or biophysical units.

International Organization for Standardization (ISO): The non-governmental organisation in charge of setting voluntary international standards with a membership of standardisation bodies from 164 countries.

International Political Economy: A field of study closely related to the discipline of international relations exploring the relations between the political and economic sphere at the global level.

Natural Capital: An extension the economic notion of capital to natural resources and that is supposed to underpin all other forms of capital, i.e. human, technological manufactured and financial capital.

Natural Capital Accounting: A tool that aims at measuring, recording, summarising, and processing information about nature according to a predefined procedure. It includes monetary valuation, environmental reporting, cost and benefit analysis and ideally an environmental action plan or strategy.

Power: The individual or collective ability to influence the outcome of a process, whether voluntarily or not (e.g. the setting of a new standard).

Standard: A voluntary technical specification explicitly documented and published as tools for the organisation of production and exchange of goods and services.

Transnational Private Governance: A form of cooperation between state and non-state across borders in order to establish rules and standards of behaviour.

ENDNOTES

[1]   See also the online recording of the webinar of 'We Value Nature' on "an introduction to natural capital", 3rd October 2019. https://wbcsd.zoom.us/recording/play/ENLNLPhSfAWpNI7cCFc5w3J_7GQXaDVq69s8EIwFyR04gyeDFZ42Qm2DZUEKYHjl?continueMode=true

[2]   ISO/TC 207/SC 1/WG 8 "Guidelines on determining environmental costs and benefits".

[3]   Externalities were defined by Coase as "actions of business firms which have harmful effects on others". See: Coase, R. (1960). The Problem of Social Cost. *The Journal of Law & Economics*, 3, 1–44.

[4]   Interview with the Convenor of ISO 14007, Aarau, Switzerland (22 January, 2019).

[5]   Skype Interview with the Convenor of ISO 14008 (26 November, 2018).

[6]   Interview with a member of the two ISO working groups, Geneva, Switzerland (26 November, 2018).

[7]   Skype Interview with the Convenor of ISO 14008 (26 November 2018).

[8]   Skype Interview with the Convenor of ISO 14008 (26 November 2018).

[9]   Interview with the Convenor of ISO 14007, Aarau, Switzerland (22 January, 2019).

[10]   Interview with the Convenor of ISO 14007, Aarau, Switzerland (22 January, 2019).

Chapter 3
Investigating Assessment Standards in the Netherlands, Italy, and the United Kingdom:
Challenges for Responsible Research Evaluation

Sabrina Petersohn
German Centre for Higher Education Research and Science Studies (DZHW), Germany

Sophie Biesenbender
https://orcid.org/0000-0003-4891-762X
German Centre for Higher Education Research and Science Studies (DZHW), Germany

Christoph Thiedig
German Centre for Higher Education Research and Science Studies (DZHW), Germany

ABSTRACT

The following contribution asks which role standards for research information play in practices of responsible research evaluation. The authors develop the notion of assessment standards against the background of functional standard classifications. The development of semantic and procedural assessment standards in the national research evaluation exercises of the Netherlands, Great Britain, and Italy are investigated using a qualitative case study design. A central finding of the study is that assessment standards incorporate conflicting values. A continuous tradeoff between the transparency of evaluation procedures and provided information as well as the variety of research outputs is being counterbalanced in all countries by compensating a higher level of semantic standardization with lower degrees of procedural standardization.

DOI: 10.4018/978-1-7998-2181-6.ch003

INTRODUCTION

Research organizations, research groups and individual researchers are regularly subject to ex ante and ex post assessments of research quality in multiple contexts, such as the evaluation of grant proposals, scientific publications and in hiring or tenure processes (Butler, 2007). In many countries, institutional funding of research depends on performance-based research funding systems (Hicks, 2012; Lepori, Reale, & Spinello, 2018). Some of these systems make use of comprehensive national evaluation schemes, such as the "Research Excellence Framework" (REF) in the United Kingdom and the "Quality of Research Evaluation" (VQR) in Italy (Rebora & Turri, 2013). In other countries, standardized national evaluation systems are in place that are not tied to resource allocation but used for quality control in a context of organizational learning, as is the case for the Dutch "Standard Evaluation Protocol" (SEP) (van der Meulen, 2007)

Assessment activities comprise the use of qualitative and quantitative methodologies, such as peer review and bibliometric indicators, respectively (Moed & Halevi, 2015). Bibliometrics is "the field of science that deals with the development and application of quantitative measures and indicators for science and technology, based on bibliographic information" (van Leeuwen, 2004, p. 374). A branch of this field, "evaluative bibliometrics" (Narin, 1976), focuses on the evaluation of scientific activities by means of output and impact measurement (van Leeuwen, 2004).

Although peer review is considered to be the most viable method to assessing scientific quality, it has been subject to criticism pertaining to its lack of fairness, reliability and structural conservatism (Hansson, 2010; Reinhart, 2012). In the face of the complexity and scale of national evaluations, bibliometrics are supposed to deliver cost-effective, large-scale and often deemed more objective alternatives to peer review (Butler, 2007; Gläser & Laudel, 2007).

In the wake of the proliferation of quantitative research assessment, prominent initiatives (Cagan, 2013; Hicks, Wouters, Waltman, Rijcke, & Rafols, 2015; Wilsdon et al., 2015) call for an increased focus on practices of responsible research evaluation. These focus on producing research metrics or indicators that adhere to certain principles such as transparency and diversity.

The quality of research metrics notably depends on the quality of information and data that are being used as well as their collection and handling (Biesenbender, 2019). Data about research activity in general are called research information (RI). RI comprises information on a research institution's (scientific) staff and structure, projects, third-party funding, publications, patents etc. Research assessment processes and their outcomes depend not only on the type of information being used but also on the way the information is being processed, aggregated and compared. In the responsible research evaluation discourse, standardization of processes of RI data collection, processing and analysis and their subsequent transformation into metrics are discussed controversially both as a chance to increase stakeholder participation and transparency and as a risk to diversity by producing standardized, uniform metrics (Hicks, Wouters, Waltman, Rijcke, & Rafols, 2015; Ràfols, 2019; Wilsdon et al., 2015).

Whether standards for research information foster transparency or reduce diversity has been treated primarily as a normative question in the discourse about responsible research evaluation. The study takes a more empirically oriented stance on this question. Which values are incorporated into RI standards strongly depends on the different pathways that the promulgation and enforcement of RI standards follow. The following contribution investigates the use and functions of RI standards in the collection and processing of information in research evaluation. It thereby aims to re-assess the role standards can play in practices of responsible research evaluation with a focus on the crucial phases of setting up a suitable information basis and procedural guidelines.

The emergent field of standards research deals with a plethora of existing standards (de Vries et al., 2018). The bulk of studies focus on industry, business and thus overall market related standards. Particularly the technological domain takes centre stage with an increasing number and diversity of ICT standards (Jakobs, 2006). Recently, more attention is being paid to standardization processes in non-market related fields addressing societal issues (Wurster, Egyedi, & Hommels, 2013). The present study focusses on societally relevant standards in the field of quality control and assessment of publicly funded research. This issue has not yet been addressed by standards research.

Theoretical developments in the field provide important cues for our study, such as the functional differentiation of standard types (Egyedi & Ortt, 2017). This chapter contributes to an understanding of functions of standards in the realm of research assessment as a complement to traditional modes of research governance by developing the notion of "assessment standards".

The study finds that assessment standards regulate and guide evaluation processes by providing a consensual, selective information basis and by prescribing actions of the participants and relevant stakeholders. Assessment standards may originate from the national evaluation scheme or from differing policy contexts. The development context for standards is expected to determine its 'fit' for the specific evaluation instrument and constitutes an important criterion from the perspective of responsible research evaluation. Additionally, the relation between semantic and procedural assessment standards as well as the degree of standardization is crucial for resolving the tension between the major principles of responsible research evaluation.

This chapter presents the results of a qualitative case study on the role of assessment standards in the national evaluation systems of the Netherlands, Italy and Great Britain. The study first develops the notion of assessment standards against the background of functional standard classifications. It then presents the research governance and quality control systems of the three science systems under study. Subsequently, semantic and procedural assessment standards and their inner workings are described against the background of the national assessment practices. The concluding section discusses the implications of values incorporated into assessment standards for responsible research evaluation and suggests avenues for future research.

THEORETICAL BACKGROUND

Standards represent a central form of voluntary social regulation by consensus (Brunsson, Rasche, & Seidl, 2012). The International Standards Organization (ISO) defines a standard as a document "established by consensus and approved by a recognized body that provides for common and repeated use, rules, guidelines or characteristics for activities or their results, aimed at the achievement of the optimum degree of order in a given context" (International Organization for Standardization, 2001, p. 9). A standard's primary function is informative: It formalizes negotiated agreements and (expert) knowledge, thereby aiding communication, a common understanding and exchange and providing transparency. Standards also act as focussing and selection devices by reducing the variety of available options (Egyedi & Ortt, 2017, p. 118; Kurihara, 2008). Standards have a number of major secondary functions such as classification or categorization, compatibility or behavioural protocols specifying courses of actions (Egyedi & Ortt, 2017, p. 119).

Several different typologies or classifications of standards exist (de Vries, 2006; Egyedi & Ortt, 2017; Jakobs, 2000). According to a functional differentiation of standard types, semantic or terminological standards as well as product or design standards (Blind & Gauch, 2009; Timmermans & Epstein, 2010, p. 72) have a classificatory function. Compatibility is the main aim of primarily technical interface or adaptability standards (de Vries, 2006; Egyedi & Ortt, 2017). Quality standards as well as process standards prescribe kinds and sequences of actions and activities (Brunsson, Rasche, & Seidl, 2012; de Vries, 2006; Higginbotham, 2017). Performance standards are located between the classification and behavioural protocol function (Brunsson et al., 2012).

A central assumption of this study is that standards increasingly play a role in the governance of research. In many national research systems substantial shifts in the modes of governance can be observed away from hierarchical, state-centered modes of substantive governance to increasing degrees of institutional autonomy and decentralized, procedural governance in combination with increased accountability which requires continuous quality monitoring and ex post performance assessment (Whitley, 2011). The rise of national research evaluation systems as „organised sets of procedures for assessing the merits of research undertaken in publicly-funded organisations that are implemented on a regular basis" (Whitley, 2007, p. 6) is closely related to this shift. These procedures are supposed to provide an indispensable information basis for decisions regarding research priorities and funding allocation on national and institutional level (Gläser, Lange, Laudel, & Schimank, 2010).

The authors argue that standards support this form of procedural governance in a complementary manner. However, in this specific domain, standards have not been systematically studied yet.

The authors define *"assessment standards"* as written procedural guidelines and rules regarding the planning and implementation of national or institutional evaluation processes, established by consensus by recognized stakeholders and approved by the scientific community. Evaluation rests on two fundamental pillars: the collection of relevant information or evidence and the identification of evaluative standards against which the current state is measured and assessed (Picciotto, 2005). The proposed conception of assessment standards focuses on standards pertaining to the collection and processing of evaluative information and to standards regulating evaluation as a procedure. Evaluation standards as criteria of merit, worth or value are not included in this definition.

Assessment standards can be further differentiated into distinct subgroups: First, *terminological or semantic (assessment) standards* which comprise standards regarding the classification and definition of research information. These standards provide a selective information basis and common understanding thereof for evaluation activities. They may not be confused with the semantic or terminology standards that allow for efficient communication in basic research and for knowledge transfer from basic to applied research (Blind & Gauch, 2009).

Second, *procedural (assessment) standards*: They encompass standards regarding the collection, processing and analysis of RI for the purpose of evaluative documentation and reporting. Related to these reporting standards are rules for the general evaluation schedule and defining the scope of evaluation units (along, for example, disciplinary differences). Additionally, procedural (assessment) standards more narrowly prescribe not only the preparation for but the actual evaluation procedures with regard to responsibilities and ways of working of review committees as well as their composition and appointment.

Third and closely related to procedural (assessment) standards are the technically oriented *design standards* defining the properties and features of Current Research Information Systems (CRIS) along with *compatibility standards* that allow for the interoperability of CRIS with different databases such as publication and citation databases, repositories or administrative staff and project databases.

Figure 1. Overview and stages of the research evaluation process

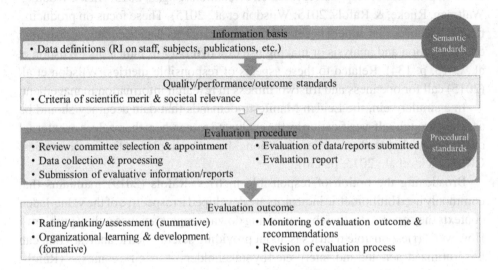

Quality, performance or outcome standards denoting fixed criteria and definitions for research quality or performance are excluded from the conception of assessment standards on the following grounds: As multidimensional constructs, research quality and performance are not (easily) amenable to standardization (Whitley, 2011). Additionally, the authority to define desirable outcomes is restricted: Only peers are deemed feasible to form a quality judgement about the merits of research contributions to their respective scientific community. Peer review has an inherently informal and unstandardized nature (Hansson, 2010). Lastly, quality, outcome or performance standards are seen as a consequence of the implementation of assessment standards, which focus on data collection and processing in evaluation.

The following figure (Figure 1) locates the two assessment standard sub-types forming the analytical focus of this paper within the overall evaluation process.

Standard setting can be conceived as a value-laden process. Standardization research has adapted the concept of responsible innovation to the standard development and implementation process by making use of the notion of value-sensitive design (Friedman, Kahn, & Borning, 2008). It implies the identification and understanding of stakeholder values and the embodiment of these values in standard-setting to increase the acceptance of a standard (van de Kaa, 2013).

Best practices and principles of research evaluation have been discussed in the responsible research evaluation discourse, and standardization features as an important issue in this debate. In the wake of the proliferation of quantitative research assessment prominent initiatives such as the San Francisco Declaration of Research Assessment, the Leiden Manifesto and the 'Metric Tide' report call for an increased focus on practices of responsible research evaluation (Cagan, 2013; Hicks, Wouters, Waltman, Rijcke, & Rafols, 2015; Wilsdon et al., 2015). These focus on producing research metrics that adhere to certain principles such as data accuracy, transparent data collection and analysis or making use of a diversity of indicators (Wilsdon et al., 2015, p. 134). Related to these aspects of responsible metrics, Wilsdon et al. (2015) call for openness and trustworthiness in research information management.

In a similar vein, the Leiden Manifesto demands that data accuracy should be assured through self-verification by the evaluated researchers themselves or external quality control procedures. These functions should be implemented in universities' CRIS (Hicks et al., 2015, p. 430).

Broadening the notion of responsible metrics, Ràfols (2019) maintains that commonly used bibliometric indicators are developed irrespective of the value-laden contexts they operate in, thereby narrowing down complex science policy problems. However, "(r)esponsible metrics is about providing scientometric analyses that can be scrutinized, adapted and, interpreted by stakeholders of specific contexts" (Ràfols, 2019, p. 15). According to Ràfols, CRIS may not be as helpful in contributing to responsible metrics. He cautions against the widespread use of centralized information infrastructures since they potentially foster the production of uniform, non-contextualized research metrics by means of standardization.

The discourse normatively charges the information, classification and selection function of standards. While a selective information basis with defined elements is seen as beneficial for procedural fairness and transparency, it is also considered as potentially restrictive with regard to the recognition of the diversity of research missions and impacts. The present study takes a step back by contributing a functional, empirically grounded perspective to the role of assessment standards in responsible research assessment especially with regard to their contribution to the values of transparency and diversity. The impact of semantic standards on transparency is related to the selection of elements to be included in the information basis, the definition and categorization as well as classification of elements. This ensures that all participants share a common understanding with regard to the data basis of the evaluation. Transparency related to procedural standards also refers to the visibility of procedures (selection, methods of working and reporting of review committees) as evidenced by the scope of the documentation of the assessment. Diversity is largely connected to semantic standardization and also relates to the selection, definition and classification of elements of the information basis. The higher the diversity, the more varied and complex is the information basis with ensuing trade-offs with regard to transparency.

By describing the development and functions of standards for the setting up of an evaluative information basis and procedural guidelines in three different evaluations systems, the authors analyse how assessment standards can be functional or dysfunctional for the establishment of a suitable and responsible information basis and procedures for research assessment. The analysis illustrates that assessment standards cannot be simply infused with values because the establishment of an ideal degree of transparency and diversity is a complex endeavour depending on several context factors such as the aims and scope of the evaluation exercise, the structure of the national science system and factors intrinsic to the information basis of the evaluation, for example subject classifications employed. The determination of the ideal degree of these values as well as the corresponding value-sensitive design of standards is beyond the scope of this paper. However, the contribution points out the multi-faceted impact assessment standards have on the transparency and diversity of the information basis (selection of data, data definitions and classifications) and the procedures (responsibilities, documentation, visibility of adopted approaches and methods) adopted in research assessment, thereby emphasizing the need for further empirical research on this topic.

METHODS AND EMPIRICAL DATA

The study is explorative and qualitative in nature and contains case studies of three countries. The country selection strategy follows a 'diverse cases' design (Seawright & Gerring, 2008): First, the three countries under study exemplify different structures and modes of governance with regard to the science system. Second, the three country cases exemplify different assessment instruments with divergent objectives and mechanisms.

The study combines interview data with analyses of legal and policy documents as well as reviews of secondary literature.

For the Netherlands, the official documentation of the evaluation protocols has been studied in depth. Furthermore, policy papers published by the Royal Netherlands Academy of Arts and Sciences (KNAW), the main funding organization, the Dutch Research Council (NWO), and the Association of Universities Netherlands (VSNU) were collected. Additionally, four semi-standardized expert interviews with representatives from KNAW, the Data Archiving and Networked Services organization (DANS) and two Dutch universities were conducted.

The Italian case was addressed based on nine interviews with representatives of the Italian science system (from the Italian Ministry of Education, Universities and Research–MIUR, the Italian National Agency for the Evaluation of the University and Research Systems–ANVUR), different HEIs and research institutions as well as science scholars. Policy documents include the official documentation of past evaluation exercises (legal documents, official calls, background documentation, reports).

Analysis of the UK case mainly relied on the scholarly literature, practitioner and project reports about the RI and CRIS landscape and its developments. In addition, official documentation of the Research Assessment Exercises (RAE) and the Research Excellence Framework evaluation exercises (REF) was assessed. These findings were contextualized and expanded by nine expert interviews conducted with representatives from various stakeholders of the UK Higher Education and Research sector, among them HEIs and not-for-profit organisations.

All interviews were audio-recorded and partly transcribed. They lasted between 60 and 120 minutes. The semi-structured interview guideline encompasses the following broad topical areas: the science policy context of research information, institutional RI policy, national and institutional reporting contexts, standardization of RI, use of CRIS in the processing of RI, CRIS system features, uses and standards of CRIS and change dynamics of CRIS and RI standards.

The empirical material was analysed with the help of thematic coding (Boyatzis, 1998; Saldaña, 2013). The analytical procedure consisted of an iterative reading of interview transcripts and policy documents as well as secondary literature. The reading was informed by deductive concepts of standardization research such as standard types and functions and by our background knowledge of research governance and policy in the countries studied. The initial deductive selection of themes was complemented by thematic foci emanating from our material. Emergent themes were then grouped for detecting patterns within and differences as well as commonalities across our cases.

CASE DESCRIPTION

The three countries under study represent European science systems of different size, organizational setup, governance and regulation. In addition, the role and significance of the central evaluation instrument varies over the three empirical cases.

In addition to national processes of RI standardization, there are also few international initiatives to further standards in the handling and processing of research information. For instance, the CERIF standard (short for Common European Research Information Format) constitutes a syntactic standard to enhance the exchange of data between different research information systems (Biesenbender & Herwig, 2019). It is hosted and maintained by euroCRIS, a not-for-profit organization that fosters cooperation of RI and CRIS experts. Nowadays a number of institutional CRIS are (partly) based on the CERIF standard as does OpenAIRE, a European open science infrastructure collecting metadata from several data sources, including CRIS (Houssos et al., 2014). Compliance is, however, limited in cases, where national specificities need to be implemented (e.g. national classifications of staff, publications or academic disciplines), which is why the CERIF standard is of limited practical relevance for the design of assessment standards in all three countries as the empirical analysis will illustrate.

In addition, national research evaluation schemes themselves are the topic of initiatives on the European level aiming to foster international cooperation and mutual learning in order to improve national research assessment practices. Due to heterogeneous national research evaluation contexts, the harmonization of research assessment on an international or European level is not deemed realistic at the moment although a convergence on the inclusion of and heightened attention for societal impact assessment can be observed (Jong, Smit, & van Drooge, 2015; Power, 2015; Sivertsen, 2017).

The Netherlands

The Research System in the Netherlands

The Dutch university sector consists of 14 public universities (Westerheijden, de Boer, & Enders, 2009). Basic research is also performed by 19 research institutes operating under the auspices of the KNAW and the NWO (van Steen, 2012).

University funding is divided into three funding streams: Governmental institutional funding, competitive project-based funding from NWO and third party funding from the European Union, government and companies (Jongbloed, 2018).

The research system is governed by the Ministry of Education, Culture and Science (Dutch acronym: OCW) and by the Ministry of Economic Affairs and Climate (Dutch acronym: EZK). The main pillars of science and higher education policy are stipulated in the Higher Education and Research Act (Dutch acronym WHW) issued in 1993 (van Steen, 2012; Westerheijden, de Boer, & Enders, 2009).

Additionally, Dutch research policy is shaped by a dense layer of advisory bodies, sectoral councils and intermediary organizations and characterized by a culture of consensual decision making (van der Meulen & Rip, 1998). Central are the KNAW which acts as one of the major independent advisory councils for basic science, the funding council NWO and the association of Dutch universities (Dutch acronym VSNU) which represents the interests of the universities (van Steen, 2012).

The WHW codified the retreat from the strong state-centered mode of governance of the higher education sector from the 1980s in favor of a decentralization of governance to the institutions themselves. The increase in organizational autonomy is accompanied by the legal obligation to regularly account for the quality of education and research (Westerheijden et al., 2009).

The Research Evaluation System in the Netherlands

The WHW Act broadly prescribes the implementation of an instrument of continuous quality control in the higher education sector. As a response, the VSNU has developed guidelines for a periodical, disciplinary research assessment procedure encompassing all Dutch universities. The so-called VSNU protocols formalize the general aims, scope, procedures and responsibilities of all actors involved. Additionally, disciplinary protocols set up by the standing disciplinary chambers of the VSNU account for the specificities of the disciplines to be evaluated. The framework aims at quality maintenance and improvement, providing suggestions for institutional research management and accountability to the government and society at large. However, there is no link between evaluation and the allocation of basic funding to the universities.

The system of quality care is comprehensive in that all disciplines are to be evaluated every five years on a rolling schedule on research programme level. The evaluation is based on a self-assessment report and optional site visits by a review committee consisting of international, independent experts. The experts are called to review the scientific productivity, (scientific) relevance and viability of research programmes. The protocol leaves room for a discipline-specific interpretation of the assessment criteria (van der Meulen, 2007 VSNU, 1994).The predominant evaluation method according to the VSNU protocol is peer review. However, if deemed feasible by the standing disciplinary committees of VSNU bibliometrics were recommended as additional data.

After two evaluation cycles, the VSNU protocol was evaluated and modified substantially into the Standard Evaluation Protocol (SEP) in 2003. The SEP is jointly set up by VSNU, KNAW and NWO and now also includes the research institutes of KNAW and NWO. The guideline extends the evaluation cycle to six years and includes an institutional, internal mid-term review after three years. The assessment procedure applies to the level of the research institute and to research programmes. Significant changes apply to the scope of the assessment, the evaluation criteria used and the responsibility for the procedure: First, the national, disciplinary scope was abandoned as a response to criticism from the academic community (KNAW, NWO, & VSNU, 2001; Interviews with VSNU and KNAW stakeholders). Second, the evaluation criteria have been broadened to include a notion of societal relevance of research. In the latest version of the SEP 2015-2021, societal relevance even assumes the same importance within the evaluation criteria as does scientific relevance (VSNU, NWO, KNAW, 2015). Additionally, the productivity criterion was discarded in the light of increasing criticism (Dijstelbloem, Huisman, Miedema, & Mijnhardt, 2013). Third, the responsibility for the implementation of the assessment devolved from the university association to the universities themselves. The university boards decide on university specific terms of reference denoting schedule, size and scope of evaluation units as well as selection and appointment of the review committee members (van Drooge, Jong, Faber, & Westerheijden, 2013; VSNU, NWO, KNAW, 2003). This implies that research units of one discipline or sub-discipline may be evaluated individually, in cooperation with a few selected or all universities, depending on the agreement of the respective university boards (van Drooge et al., 2013). The use of bibliometric methods and data by evaluated units and review committee is voluntary as in the predecessor of the SEP.

Italy

The Research System in Italy

The Italian research system is dominated by publicly funded higher education institutions, which are under the jurisdiction of the central government (Italian Ministry of Education, Universities and Research–MIUR). Overall, there is little structural variation (there is e.g. only a small non-university research institutions sector, and the HE system is dominated by public universities). The government has far-reaching top-down regulatory competencies with regards to academic and research programmes or institutional structures (Biesenbender, 2019; Dobbins, 2016; Rebora & Turri, 2013). While university autonomy was already strengthened in the late 1980s, it was only by the end of 2010 that far-reaching reforms were passed (law 240/2010, the so-called Gelmini reform). The law combines a number of measures to enhance strategic governance in universities without limiting state interventions (autonomy vs. accountability; cf. Donina, Meoli, & Paleari, 2015). It introduced a number of measures that rely on (standardized) research information and evaluation of both individual scientists and institutions. On the one hand, it states that the results of comparative performance evaluations should determine the allocation of funding between state universities from 2014 on. On the other hand, the law outlines a two-step process for professorial appointments that leaves the initial selection of candidates to a government agency (Dobbins, 2016). For this reason, the demand for research information and its management through appropriate systems have gradually evolved over the recent years (Galimberti & Mornati, 2017).

Despite small structural horizontal differentiation between HEIs, the sustained North–South gap continuously plays a role in the ongoing considerations in the design of MIUR's public policies and programmes.

The most important source of university funding in Italy is block funding. While 80 per cent of state funding is being distributed according to the institutions' financial commitments (for personnel, teaching etc.), 20 per cent are currently being allocated based on the institutions' performance in the central evaluation procedure, which focuses on the quality of academic products or outputs.

The Research Evaluation System in Italy

The central evaluation procedure for the Italian science system is – since its second iteration – organized and implemented by the government agency ANVUR (Agenzia Nazionale di Valutazione del Sistema). The first system-wide evaluation of this kind was the VTR (Valutazione triennale della ricerca) covering the years 2001 to 2003, followed by the first and second rounds of the VQR (short for Valutazione della qualità della ricerca, hereinafter referred to as VQR1, 2004-2010, and VQR2, 2011-2014 respectively) (Rebora & Turri, 2013).

Both, the VTR and the VQR focus on evaluating the quality of academic research (or more precisely, the quality of products). While the VTR was exclusively based on peer-review ratings, the VQR leaves it to the evaluation panels to specify the method of evaluation for each of the type of outputs: bibliometric citation analysis or peer-review by external reviewers (Abramo, D'Angelo, & Di Costa, 2011).

The composition and disciplinary focus of the panels of experts is determined by the official list of Academic Disciplines for Italian Universities Research and Teaching, which was developed in 1973 and which is nowadays a widely used four-level categorisation scheme. In its current version the categorisation scheme contains 14 academic areas (highest level of aggregation), 86 macro-sectors, 191 recruitment fields and 367 academic disciplines (lowest level). There is one evaluation panel for each of the 14 disciplinary areas (two of the areas are further divided into two sub-panels). In order to be eligible as panel member, interested experts may apply to the government agency ANVUR.

Evaluation focusses on academic products or outputs by academic staff in Italian public HEIs and research institutions. The list of academic products eligible for the last evaluation rounds has been defined by ANVUR (ANVUR, 2011, ANVUR, 2015). Research institutions were called to select and report a certain number of research products for each staff member. The calls contain detailed provisions with regard to the number of products for different types of staff (in VQR 2, it is 2 to 3 research products per person for a period of four years). In VTR it was up to the university to select the requested number of academic products (regardless of their distribution over disciplines or departments), whereas VQR takes into account publications selected by the researchers themselves.

The selection process of academic products involves both academic staff and university administration with the latter ensuring that academic products with multiple authors from the same institution be reported only once. The reporting process and technological systems are fairly standardized: Reporting of academic products for

VQR is being done through an interface developed by the Italian inter-university consortium Cineca, which has made it highly advisable for universities to implement Cineca's CRIS solution IRIS that is tailored to the procedural exigencies of the VQR (Biesenbender, 2019; Galimberti & Mornati, 2017; interview with Italian HEI representative, 2017).

The reporting of academic products requires – next to the full texts – detailed meta information: external identifiers and subject codes of the publication, ORCID ID, disciplinary codes language information, abstract, information on whether the output requires peer evaluation (e.g. because it belongs to emerging, highly specialized or inter-disciplinary areas) and a "description of the importance of the research output in the international scientific context and the impact that the research output has had" (ANVUR, 2015, p. 12).

Before evaluating academic products of their areas, panel members agree on the method of evaluation by type of product: qualitative (peer-review) vs. quantitative (bibliometric). They may also further specify the classification of scientific products or outputs or limit the list of outputs to be considered for evaluation. The criteria of evaluation are specified and identical for all panels (originality, methodological rigor and attested or potential impact).

The United Kingdom

The Research System in the UK

The research system in the UK is characterized by a diverse set of private and public institutions. There are currently about 140 universities in the UK; exact enumeration remains difficult (Tight, 2011). With the exception of five fully private universities, they are at least partially publicly funded. In addition, there are more than 800 private HEIs in the UK (Hunt & Boliver, 2019). Main representative bodies undertaking advocacy and policy development work for HEIs are Universities UK (UUK) and GuildHE.

HEIs in the UK are formally independent entities operating within a legal and policy framework set by the government. Higher Education is a devolved matter, with the UK government being responsible for England. Public funding is provided by the four national Higher Education Funding Councils (HEFCs) and United Kingdom Research and Innovation (UKRI), a body established in 2018 comprising the seven UK research councils, the innovation agency Innovate UK and Research England, a council with England-only responsibilities for administering research assessment and funding. Additionally, private sources, especially student tuition fees, make up an increasingly large part of HEI's funding. The sector is highly stratified, with competitively distributed funding predominantly going to top 'research-intensive' universities (Arnold et al., 2018; Hamann, 2016).

Governance of the Higher Education sector has been shaped by numerous government and funding reforms (that can be broadly characterized as New Public Management (NPM) techniques) since the 1960s, which have tightened state regulation and external control and increased demands for public accountability, transparency and performance (Ntim, Soobaroyen, & Broad, 2017). Conditions attached to public funding have been one of the principal mechanisms for external regulation, and research assessment exercises of increasingly comprehensive scope undertaken since the 1980s.

The Research Evaluation System in the UK

The quality of research carried out in UK HEIs has since the 1980s been assessed through national evaluation exercises of increasingly comprehensive scope. The first *Research Selectivity Exercises* (RSEs) in 1986 and 1989, intended to selectively fund research and ensure efficient spending, likely constituted the first attempts by any country to systematically assess research quality and had limited implications for funding allocation (Jones & Sizer, 1990). Subsequent *Research Assessment Exercises* (RAEs) conducted by the four UK country Higher Education Funding Councils (HEFCs) informed the allocation of the overwhelming share of the funding councils' budgets (Bence & Oppenheim, 2005; Stern, 2016). From 1986 to 2008, six exercises were conducted. The RAE has since been succeeded by the *Research Excellence Framework* (REF), which broadened assessment criteria to include both descriptions of impact and research environment in its first iteration of 2014 (Arnold et al., 2018).

HEIs make submissions to discipline-based Units of Assessment (UoA) operating under main panels. The panels develop both demarcation and assessment criteria for the UoA within a common framework. The number of UoA was greatly reduced from RAE to REF, as was the number of main panels (REF, 2015; Stern, 2016). While the configuration of the UoA does not immediately follow from existing classifications, they have become more aligned with the departmental reporting structure of HESA 'cost centres' for finance, staff and student records (REF, 2015, p. 32).

From early on, the mode of research quality assessment employed in these exercises has been expert peer review informed by research information on, among others, staff, research outputs (most prominently, publications), and external research income. Only a selection of research is assessed: From RAE 1992 onwards, HEIs have been asked to select 'research-active' staff for which to submit a set number of research outputs. While HEIs themselves choose staff to submit (and their mapping to UoA), detailed eligibility criteria for both staff categories and types of outputs are set by the REF team for the whole exercise (e.g. REF, 2011). The assessment of outputs has become increasingly comprehensive: From five publications per subject area (RSE 1986) to two publications per staff (RAE 1992) to four publications/outputs per staff (RAE 1996-REF 2014) to 2.5 times the summed full-time equivalent of a unit's submitted staff (REF 2021) (REF, 2019a; Stern, 2016). Since REF 2014, sub-panels can decide on the use of supplementary citation data to inform assessment (REF, 2019b, REF, 2015; Stern, 2016).

The panels provided quality rankings for each submission on a single scale until RAE 2008, when quality profiles were introduced, with weighting of the individual components decided by the main panels (RAE, 2005). Since REF 2014, weightings have been set by the REF team, with 'Outputs' accounting for 65 per cent and 'Impact' for 20 per cent (25 per cent in REF 2021) (REF, 2019a, REF, 2011). Both the rating scales and corresponding funding thresholds have been continuously adapted for each exercise, with funding successively concentrated at higher grades (Arnold et al., 2018; de Boer et al., 2015).

FINDINGS

The following analysis focuses on the use of semantic and procedural assessment standards in the central evaluation instruments of the three countries under study. The case studies differ with regard to the focus and degree of standard specification and the rules and practices of implementation of these standards (e.g. the ways through which evaluation objects are being assigned to classes (disciplines, publication types etc.)).

These rules, practices and classifications impact in different ways the diversity and transparency of the information basis and procedures for research assessment – and hence their adequacy for the evaluation instrument. The case descriptions first identify central semantic and procedural standards in use in the three science systems and second relate them to perceived effects on the diversity and adequacy of the evaluation procedure, reporting opinions from stakeholders of the science systems and the scientific literature.

Assessment Standards in the Netherlands

Terminological Standards in the Dutch Central Assessment Exercise

Semantic standards for RI in the Netherlands originate from governmental and institutional governance. First, semantic standards with regard to subject categories originate from the classification of disciplines in the so called bi-annual Higher

Education and Research Plans (Dutch abbreviation HOOP), a governmental planning instrument introduced in 1988 (van Vught, 1997).

Second, semantic standards regarding staff and research output are related to annual reporting duties of the universities to the Ministry of Science and Education. In the mid-nineties, the university association developed a set of key reporting figures for university research (Kengetallen Universitair Onderzoek, KUOZ), comprising agreed upon and periodically revised definitions of research input and output which are laid down in an agreement called "Definitie-afspraken wetenschappelijk onderzoek" (VSNU, 2019).

These semantic standards for RI were adopted for the national evaluation protocols. The VSNU protocol and the SEP stipulate the provision of self-assessment reports in a standardized format corresponding to the guidelines of the mandatory annual scientific reports of the universities. (VSNU, 1994; 1998; VSNU, NWO, KNAW, 2003; 2009; 2015).

While the semantic standards are therefore imported into the assessment context from the general requirement to research reporting in the course of ministerial and then institutional governance of research, the subsequent evolution and change dynamics of these standards are strongly shaped by the modifications of the protocols in the light of current policy debates and evaluations of the instrument itself.

The semantic assessment standard of **staff categories** comprises staff categories differentiated into tenured and non-tenured academic ranks. Across the different versions of the evaluation protocols this standard displays hardly any change except for a decreasing differentiation into academic ranks as of the SEP and the additional consideration of support staff as of the SEP 2009-2015.

The semantic assessment standards specifies **academic publications** broadly as the descriptions of the results of scientific work in bibliographically traceable forms (VSNU, 1994, VSNU, 1998). In the first VSNU protocol, the definition comprises the publication types of PhD theses, scientific publications, professional publications, annotations and patents. The latter three types only need to be supplied if deemed necessary by the complementary disciplinary protocols (VSNU, 1994).

In the subsequent versions of the VSNU protocol and the SEP, more publication types are added and differentiated: popular publications aiming at the presentation of academic knowledge to the larger public, poster presentations, internal reports, book chapters and monographs as well as conference papers (VSNU, 1998, pp. 442–444). This change to the RI standard of publications is related to the change in the overall focus of the assessment: Reviewers are asked to contribute not only to the quality assessment but also to deliver an appraisal of the research groups and institutes mission in an effort to value context-specific aspects (VSNU, 1998, Preface). Additionally, the variety of different disciplinary and interdisciplinary publication practices is acknowledged by this differentiation of publication output.

A marked re-organization of the semantic RI standard of publications takes place in the most recent version of the SEP (2015) which distinguishes into research products for peers (refereed or non-refereed research articles, books or other research outputs such as software tools, datasets or instruments and infrastructure) and for societal target groups (reports, articles in professional journals, instruments, infrastructure, datasets, outreach activities) (VSNU, NWO, KNAW, 2015, p. 25). This opening up of publication types and inclusion of additional forms of output is due to the marked shift in focus to include societal relevance of research on an equal footing with scientific relevance.

These standard dynamics affect the level of diversity and transparency of assessment: The growing differentiation of publication output increases the diversity of academic products considered for evaluation, thereby acknowledging differing disciplinary publication practices and varying institutional missions. Procedural transparency with regard to the data classification is assured since the definitions of publication types and most recently also activities indicating societal impact are continuously updated and revised in the "Definitie afspraken" issued by VSNU, which also provide a mapping between SEP and KUOZ output types (VSNU, 2019).

Semantic assessment standards regarding **subject categories** or disciplines originate from the former governmental planning instrument HOOP. In the VSNU protocols, around 26 disciplines are listed as part of the rolling evaluation schedule without further differentiation into sub-disciplines (VSNU, 1994; 1998). This standard was met with substantial criticism for lumping together research fields into disciplines that are not strictly comparable (KNAW et al., 2001; Interviews with VSNU and KNAW stakeholders), contributing to the transition to the SEP. In the successor protocols subject categories are not oriented towards HOOP areas anymore but to SEP units (VSNU, 2019). Their scope and size is defined by the university boards who assume responsibility for the assignment of evaluation units. Some evaluations are still organized in a disciplinary manner across universities; whereas "in some disciplines virtually every university organizes an independent evaluation" (van Drooge et al., 2013, p. 7) or evaluations take place at sub-discipline or interdisciplinary level (van Drooge et al., 2013). The flexibility in the designation of the scope evaluation units affects diversity in a positive manner since it allows for a better representation of for example interdisciplinary research and broad institutional missions. However, this impedes a traceable and stable definition of evaluation units over time.

Procedural Standards in the Dutch Central Assessment Exercise

Currently, the Dutch CRIS landscape is characterized predominantly by a commercial institutional CRIS, called Pure, developed by Elsevier. Pure is used by at least 10 out of 13 Dutch universities who purchased individual subscriptions. The system harvests different types of institutional and external RI databases complemented by manual entries of publications by scholars or institutional CRIS managers. Many Dutch universities have set policies in place that base any kind of research assessment on the output registered in CRIS only (Fondermann & van der Togt, 2017).

The manual entry and classification of publication types takes place both at the "shop floor" by the researchers themselves and at the central or faculty level of the university. Universities have created positions such as dedicated RI managers, assigned responsibility for the management of RI to program coordinators or tasked the library with verifying publication entries (Fondermann & van der Togt, 2017; Kaltenbrunner & Rijcke, 2017). These positions provide a major venue for exercising powerful decisions as to what counts as research output and how to classify it. They are not exempt from power play especially when classification practices conflict around definitions, the wrong assignment of publications to publication or journal categories or the duplication of entries in the case of co-authorships (Interviews KNAW, University representatives, 2018).

The **registration and processing of RI** for the SEP is facilitated by specific modules of the **CRIS** Pure. Uniform specifications of publication types are incorporated into these modules based on the semantic standard set by VSNU. The strengthened focus of the SEP on societal relevance necessitates both new categories of RI and modifications to the semantic standard of output types. Pure attempts to standardize outputs with societal impact in the category of "activities" which encompasses for example invited lectures, seminars or memberships in advisory bodies. However, the technical template contains classifications that do not always fit with the institutional conception of the societal impact of research activities; therefore Pure doesn't provide a seamless technical translation of the semantic assessment standards of the SEP (Interview KNAW, University representative, 2018).

The protocols prescribe the **tasks of the review committees** to varying degrees of specificity.

The primary task of the review committee is to form an assessment of the evaluation units by the given criteria in the respective protocol on the basis of the documentation, i.e. the self-assessment reports provided and a site visit. The protocols refrain from prescribing any form of evaluation method to be used by the peers.

After the assessment of the material provided to the committee and the site visit, the review committee is obliged to produce an evaluation report. The degree of specifications regarding the structure and content of this report vary throughout the different versions of the protocols. Whereas in the VSNU protocols and the latest version of the SEP only the major sections are specified, such as descriptions of the evaluated units together with the verdict on their quality, and in the case of the VSNU protocols a national appraisal of the disciplines from an international view point, the procedural standards for the compilation of the evaluation report are very elaborate in the SEP 2003-2009 and 2009-2015. They include a richer description of the institutes and programmes starting with a reflection of leadership, strategy and policy and an assessment of the quality of resources, funding policies and facilities. They explicitly ask for a "quantified assessment of the quality, productivity, relevance and prospects of the research programme" (VSNU, NWO, KNAW, 2003, p. 16). The procedural evaluation standards emphasize a strong focus on productivity and output in quantitative terms. This resulted in criticism leading to the amended SEP in 2015 (KNAW, 2005). The current SEP also prescribes a distinct format for the evaluation report, however with fewer specifications regarding the structure of the report. It calls for a report evidencing a combined and balanced qualitative and quantitative assessment of research quality, relevance to society and viability (VSNU, NWO, KNAW, 2015).

The decreasing degree of standardization of the reporting of the evaluation committee corresponds to a significant expansion of the possible range and type of research products that are allowed to be submitted for the self-assessment report (VSNU, NWO, KNAW, 2015, p. 25). Here as well a substantive decrease in the degree of standardization can be observed.

The impact of procedural standards on transparency and diversity needs to be differentiated according to the institutional and formal level of the protocol regulations. On the institutional level, transparency is enhanced by the common use of a CRIS adapted to the national assessment context which also attempts to incorporate new policy directions such as the impact agenda (Interview, KNAW representative, 2018). However, variations and conflicts in local data registration practices may produce intransparencies and inconsistencies of evaluative information with regard to the commonly agreed semantic RI standards.

At the level of the protocols, overall much leeway is granted to reviewers in terms of methods used and focal points in reporting with the exception of the formerly detailed specifications in the first SEP protocols. Varying documentation requirements regarding key reporting areas affect the transparent, consistent as well as comparable display of evaluation results by allowing differing degrees of emphases of selected evaluation results. This in turn possibly enhances the acknowledgement of diversity in terms of organizational missions and research practices.

Assessment Standards in Italy

The institutional collection and management of research information in Italy takes place in a regulatory environment with potentially favourable conditions for standardization. The ministry's (MIUR) strong regulatory competencies were further enhanced in 2010, when the Gelmini reform was passed to strengthen the role of evaluation as an instrument for the science system (Donina, Meoli, & Paleari, 2015; Rebora & Turri, 2013). The long tradition and availability of standards for the classification of academic disciplines and the availability of the respective data in the ministry has facilitated their immediate use also in the context of the central assessment instrument in Italy (VTR, VQR). The definition and classification of "academic products" however constitutes a rather recent RI standard developed in the context of the assessment exercise.

Terminological Standards in the Italian Central Assessment Exercise

Next to fundamental differences in their scope, the two types of evaluation exercises (VTR vs. VQR1 and VQR2) make use of and perpetuate different existing classification schemes of the Italian science system. In this context, three evaluation-relevant terminological RI standards stick out.

First, the official four-level categorisation scheme of **Academic Disciplines** for Italian Universities Research and Teaching is nowadays a widely used classification standard (Bellotti, Kronegger, & Guadalupi, 2016; Bianchi & Carusi, 2019). Every scientist in an Italian public research institution and every academic department is being assigned one (and only one) academic discipline, and MIUR maintains up-to date lists of academic staff by discipline (lowest level) and (public) research institution (Interview with representative of the Italian public administration, 2017). In the central evaluation process (VTR and VQR) academic disciplines play a central role, because they determine the number, extent, composition and focus of the evaluation panels and the bibliometric thresholds for evaluation. There is constant controversy regarding the broad focus to be taken within some of the 14 academic areas and the heterogeneity of research and publication cultures to be covered in one panel. In addition, there is wide criticism in the academic community against the use of academic areas or disciplines as benchmarks for the products under evaluation. The issue becomes even more controversial in light of the freedom of each panel to choose its evaluation method by research product (Interviews with Italian HEI representatives, 2017; Interview with representative of the Italian public administration, 2017).

In other words, the use of the classification of academic disciplines clearly enhances the reliability of the publication and staff data (and their categorization), because they are validated against central databases with MIUR, with positive effects for the transparency of the evaluation process. Yet, there is wide criticism regarding its fit for the evaluation and hence its ability to maintain an adequate level of diversity: while expert panels are considered too broad (with 14 panels not being able to adequately consider disciplinary specificities), the assignment of publications and persons to disciplines seems to be too rigid and fundamentally determines the respective method of evaluation with negative effects for the validity of the evaluation results (Interviews with representatives of the Italian public administration, 2017).

Second, MIUR maintains detailed and up-to-date lists of university staff by institution and staff category. Similar to the classification of academic disciplines, **staff categories** constitute a terminological standard with growing relevance in the governance of the Italian science system. With regard to the central evaluation procedure they are also key for the number – and hence the characteristics and types – of the publications to be considered for central assessment. VQR 2 for instance limited the number of products eligible for evaluation for full professors or researchers in universities to two. In practice however, staff categories play a comparatively small role for the diversity and transparency of the evaluation because there is only small variance with regard to the number of academic products per category.

Third, a list of so-called **academic products or outputs** – a further terminological standard – was specified and applied in the context of setting up the VQR instrument. It contains different types of publications and patents (ANVUR, 2015; Franceschini & Maisano, 2017). While the VTR call contained a loose definition of "research products" in a footnote of the respective call including book and journal contributions, but also "projects", "designs" and "performances" (CIVR, 2004), VQR1 and even more so VQR2 presented a more tailored list of products up for consideration: In VQR2, these have been categorized as (a) academic publications comprising scientific monographs (with 11 sub-types); (b) journal contributions (with six sub-types); (c) book contributions (with eight sub-types); (d) other scientific outputs (comprising 11 sub-types ranging from compositions to psychological tests); and (e) patents (see ANVUR, 2011, ANVUR, 2015). The classification of academic products is of fundamental relevance for the evaluation instruments in both direct and indirect ways. First, it defines the object of evaluation and states what type of research output is eligible for assessment (also explicitly specifying excluded types of outputs). Second, it serves as a classification instrument for the expert panels to decide which method of evaluation to apply to the different classes of products. Moreover, expert panels are free to reduce or to further specify the list of products according to their disciplinary focus. The list of outputs has been compiled specifically for the evaluation instrument (Interview with Italian HEI representative, 2017; Interview with representative of the Italian public administration, 2017). Over the three rounds of evaluation, clarity and differentiation of the classification of academic products have grown with positive effects on the evaluation's transparency. However, the combination of a white list (included types of outputs) and a black list (excluded types of outputs) in VQR 2 might negatively impact on the diversity of the evaluation instrument by limiting the set of eligible types of outputs.

Procedural Standards in the Italian Central Assessment Exercise

Not only has the central assessment instrument entailed the perpetuation of terminological standards in the Italian science system. They have also led to considerable professionalization and **standardization of the institutional management and processing of research information**. While in 2004 for the VTR reporting, only a minority of universities was able to draw on institutional CRIS (Galimberti & Mornati, 2017; Interview with Italian HEI representative, 2017), reporting provisions for VQR2 (2014) made the use of the standard CRIS platform IRIS highly advisable. To this end, a ministerial decree tasked Cineca (an Italian inter-university consortium) with the development of the software, which by now is in use in more than 65 Italian universities (Biesenbender, 2019; Bollini, Mennielli, Mornati, & Palmer, 2016; Galimberti & Mornati, 2017; interview with Italian HEI representative, 2017). The CRIS platform offers more than just a tool for the institutional reporting of research information for the purpose of evaluation: it also serves as a standardized institutional repository of academic products (publications and patents) with different monitoring and outreach functionalities. In other words: the standardization of the institutional management and processing of research information through a CRIS solution tailored to the exigencies of the evaluation instrument, has further catalysed the establishment of a number of terminological standards (i.e. the classifications of academic disciplines and academic products) with positive effects on the institutional harmonization and transparency of institutional information management.

As for the **expert-panel based evaluation process**, the assessment guidelines are rather flexible and unspecific. Overall, the evaluation panels are given considerable leeway to adjust the evaluation procedure to their disciplinary needs: First, they may alter (further specify or reduce) the list of academic products to the considered. Second, they are entitled to decide on the method of evaluation for the single classes of products under consideration. These procedures ensure certain levels of diversity as they allow panels to consider discipline-specific types of outputs and publication cultures with negative consequences for the transparency (and reliability) of the evaluation procedure.

Assessment Standards in the UK

The fragmented nature of the Higher Education information and RI landscape and its corresponding reporting infrastructure in the UK has long been recognized (Arnold et al., 2018; Deloitte, 2013; KPMG, 2015; Mahieu, Arnold, & Kolarz, 2014; Waddington et al., 2013). In recent years, several initiatives by Jisc (a not-for-profit company providing digital services to HEIs), the Higher Education Statistics Agency

(HESA), RCUK and others have furthered the development of a national reporting landscape in the UK in order to reduce the associated burden on HEIs (Arnold et al., 2018). Stakeholder involvement is an important mode of coordination of RI standardization efforts in the UK, and participation of HEIs in these initiatives is high. While there is a strong interest in harmonization and standardization of RI collection and reporting across the sector, enthusiasm for a single national research reporting system is low, as stakeholders have already made substantial investments in RI infrastructure (Jörg, Waddington, Jones, & Trowell, 2014; Waddington et al., 2013; Waddington et al., 2014). Thus, existing initiatives focus predominantly on the interoperability of existing systems. Against this background, the development and specification of standards for research information is often confined to specific assessment instruments, such as the RAE/REF.

Terminological Standards in the UK Research Assessment Exercise

While the research assessment exercises have undergone significant change since their inception in the 1980s, a number of terminological and procedural standards have emerged that continuously shape its implementation. In addition, terminological standards of external data sources are increasingly used for data verification and audit.

First, the specification of **staff categories** and corresponding eligibility criteria for REF submission constitutes an important terminological standard that shapes both number and composition of submitted staff and, by extension, the outputs eligible for assessment. Since RAE 2008, no information about non-submitted staff is collected (RAE, 2005). While some differentiation is made between status groups, the individual's involvement in (independent) research is the main eligibility criterion (e.g. REF, 2019a; 2011) and HEIs can in principal submit the same number of outputs for all personnel fulfilling the requirements of the respective staff categories. REF 2021 will see the decoupling of staff and outputs, but output submission will continue to depend on the number of staff submitted. Within the realms of the eligibility criteria provided, staff selection remains at the discretion of the HEIs, and strategic exclusion of staff has been subject of much critical debate. In a shift from previous exercises, REF 2021 will require the return of all eligible staff with significant responsibility for research and will verify data submissions against external HESA records. Given these requirements, the decoupling of staff and outputs as well as the increasing recognition of staff circumstances, the standard ought to have a positive effect on both transparency and diversity of the exercise.

The classification of publications and other **outputs** constitutes another terminological standard applied in the exercise, providing information on the categories of output types, definitions, and collection formats. Given the high percentage of the overall quality rating determined by output assessment, the standard plays an important role in the evaluation process. In contrast to its detailed specifications, panels have been instructed to assess all types of research on their own merit, without regard for publication types, since RAE 1996 (Martin & Whitley, 2010). In addition, panels can make adjustments to the types of outputs and their eligibility for assessment. Overall, the standard therefore formally enhances transparency and diversity of publication output. However, the considerable leeway in the implementation of the standard impedes an assessment of the standard's impact on these values.

Third, the **Units of Assessment** (UoA) that submitted staff and their outputs are mapped to represent a terminological standard that is of great relevance for the (fundamentally discipline-based) assessment of research quality conducted in the exercises. Initially based on existing subject-based committees (Stern, 2016), the latter were quickly abandoned in favor of disciplinary UoA, which HEIs were invited to define themselves, embracing all subjects (Jones & Sizer, 1990). This resulted in 152 UoA for RSE 1989. Since then, the number of UoA has shrunk to 34 UoA in REF 2021. Demarcation between the UoA is not clear-cut, and panels are requested to specify definitions and anticipate legitimate topical overlap. While mapping of staff to UoA is done by the submitting HEIs, records are validated against external terminological standards: the HEI's annual staff returns to HESA.

The standard's slight fuzziness retains certain levels of flexibility for HEIs. Measures to potentially increase its transparency via the use of external standards have been met with criticism, such as the latter's fitness for evaluative purposes. The classification of eligible staff and their subsequent allocation to UoAs constitute important arenas of standardization and HEIs have been wary of the potential implications that changes to these standards could entail for the governance of the exercise.

Procedural Standards in the UK Research Assessment Exercise

As indicated above, the guidelines setting out the assessment criteria and working methods for the **evaluation process** grant the expert panels a certain leeway, albeit within the confines of the general assessment framework set by REF demanding equity, equality, and transparency (REF, 2019a). As such, they may e.g. choose to consult additional information and citation data to inform the peer review process, adapt assessment criteria in order to account for disciplinary idiosyncrasies regarding, for example, publication types and their weighting, develop guidance on the kind of evidence appropriate to include in impact case studies, and, to a lesser extent, handling of interdisciplinary research submissions (REF, 2019b). Consequently, the standard allows for a high level of diversity while negatively impacting transparency and reliability of the evaluation procedure

Since the RAE 1996, data submission has been conducted electronically, in a common format, and using custom-build, standardized software provided to the HEIs (Page, 1997). In contrast to the other two country cases described above, however, there is no standardization of the CRIS landscape in the UK. Nevertheless, experiences with the **data collection and management processes** for RAE 2008 and involvement in a bibliometrics pilot exercise for REF 2014 constituted significant drivers for the implementation and/or improvement of **institutional CRIS** in UK HEIs and the development of bibliometrics expertise, both in anticipation of REF requirements and for internal strategic purposes (REF, 2015; Technopolis, 2009). As a result, procurement of commercial CRIS, at the time deemed to approach maturity, rapidly increased (Russell, 2012). Given the fragmented nature of the research information landscape outlined above, institutional CRIS are the central source of data about research in HEIs and thus play a major role in research reporting processes, including, but not limited to, REF (e.g. McGrath & Cox, 2014). As of 2017, more than 60 HEIs have installed such systems (Burland & Grout, 2017), with providers offering dedicated REF-modules aiding submission. As such, transparency is enhanced by the requirement to use CRIS for data collection and processing. This effect is mitigated by the variety of systems used.

Summary Of Standardization Dynamics Across The Three Cases

The following table (Table 1) provides a brief summary of the characteristics of the standardization regimes within the three national evaluation systems in the Netherlands, Italy and the UK. Two characteristics are highlighted: First, the origins of procedural and semantic standards. These can be either internal to the assessment, denoting standards created for the purpose of the evaluation or external, denoting standards that originate within other policy or reporting contexts. Second, the standard's degree of formal specification as an overall trend across the development of the evaluation regimes ranging from low to high. A high degree of specification of an assessment standard however does not automatically imply a high compatibility with the design of the evaluation instrument and its purpose (e.g. the distribution of research funding). Formal specifications may be partly decoupled from actual practices.

DISCUSSION AND CONCLUSION

Standards represent a feasible way of governing processes of academic quality control because of their voluntary, yet (often) consensual and rule-guided nature.

Table 1. Characteristics of the assessment standardization regimes in the three countries

	NL	IT	UK	NL	IT	UK
	Origin of standard			Degree of specification		
Semantic						
Staff categories	external	external	internal	High →medium	Medium	High →medium
Publication types	external	internal	internal	Low →high	Low →high	High →medium
Subject categories	external	external	internal	Medium →low	High	Medium
Procedural						
Reviewer guidelines	internal	internal	internal	Medium	Medium	Medium
Use of CRIS for data collection & processing	external	internal	external	Yes	Yes	No

Notes: Procedural standards regarding reviewer guidelines denote specifications of evaluation methods or documentation. CRIS originate from within the evaluation context in case they have been introduced for the primary purpose of supporting the national evaluation scheme. The degree of specification of procedural standards regarding CRIS establishes whether any specifications exist regarding the use of CRIS for data collection and processing.

Coordination by standards in the field of research evaluation resembles the modes of coordination in scientific communities (Gläser, 2006). Standards are therefore a fundamental component of all three assessment exercises though to different degrees.

Generally, they fulfill several important functions: First, assessments standards provide a comprehensive *information basis* for all participants of the evaluation process which encompasses both procedural guidelines as well as specific content (evaluation criteria, data to be submitted, etc.). Especially procedural assessment standards *guide and prescribe activities and actions* of the involved actors (for example through guidelines for the structure of the evaluation report or the focus of assessment, such as 'productivity' or 'quality'). Second, they act as *selection* and *classification* devices. Semantic assessment standards specify the types of information submitted for evaluation.

In the following, the commonalities and differences in assessment standard functions as well as their change related to the evolution of the evaluation frameworks will be examined comparatively across all cases.

A striking observation across the countries studied is that Italy and the UK display a much tighter linkage between the classification, selection and information function of semantic assessment standards than the Netherlands where such a linkage only loosely exists. In the Italian assessment exercise, categories for subjects, staff and academic products are strongly intertwined, the same holds true for the tight and also much criticized connection between research staff and outputs in the UK. In the Dutch case, the selective capacity of the semantic standard of subject categories is weakened with the transition to the SEP where disciplinary assignment to evaluation units depends on organizational and procedural decisions of the university boards.

The empirical cases illustrate that assessment exercises with a funding mechanism (Italy and the UK) have a stronger propensity to rely on terminological standards regarding several types of RI than the system without any funding implications (the Netherlands). In this context, the empirical evidence suggests that strong top-down regulatory competences of the government or the responsible ministry (such as e.g. in Italy) favor high levels of standardization.

In all countries, semantic standards display a higher degree of specification than procedural standards, albeit to a slightly lesser extent in the Netherlands.

Regarding the interaction between semantic assessment standards and procedural standards of collecting, processing and reporting RI using CRIS, the cases of the Netherlands and the UK illustrate that the underlying definitions of RI (e.g. what is counted and registered as a 'project' or a 'publication') cannot be consistently implemented in CRIS because they are mediated and transformed by CRIS users. As opposed to this, the Italian example shows how terminological and procedural standards are harmonized by means of design standards for CRIS that focus on the national assessment as primary reporting context.

When comparing standardization dynamics with regard to CRIS and RI in evaluative reporting contexts, all countries show long traditions of reporting using CRIS or RI.

While – for pragmatic reasons – the Italian evaluation instrument draws on two established terminological standards that have been designed and established in different policy contexts and for other purposes, the evaluation instrument in the Netherlands constitutes the main context for further developing terminological standards (rather than to perpetuate existing classifications). In the UK semantic standards originate predominantly in the assessment context and are tied to the procedural standards.

The development context for standards is expected to determine its 'fit' for the specific evaluation instrument and constitutes an important criterion from the perspective of responsible research evaluation.

Lastly, the impact of semantic and procedural standardization on the transparency and diversity of the evaluation instruments is reviewed. The responsible research evaluation discourse maintains the following premise: Generally, a high level of specification of semantic and procedural standards leads to increased transparency regarding the assessed content and the procedures to be followed because a consistent verification is possible. This in turn however leads to a decreasing diversity of the information provided and of related evaluation practices.

Our findings indicate that especially semantic standards affect these values in more variegated manner: In the UK and the Netherlands, standards for subject categories are similar with regard to delegating the responsibility for the assignment of evaluation units to subjects to the institutional level. This has negative consequences for transparency but positively impacts diversity. The opposite is true for Italy, leading to substantial criticism against the use of the established classification of academic disciplines for both the composition and disciplinary focus of the expert panels and the selection as well as evaluation of academic outputs (with potentially distortive consequences for the diversity of the evaluation instrument). Standardization of academic outputs in the UK illustrates the difference between standard-setting and implementation. On the formal level semantic standards with regard to outputs enhance transparency and diversity. However, this does not imply that these standards and values are adopted in the reviewer's evaluation practice, respectively. The case of the UK is also unique in that it displays negative impacts on transparency and diversity on the standards for staff categories because of their tight coupling with output standards.

With regard to procedural standardization and their impact on the values of responsible research assessment the cases display similarities. In all countries the use of CRIS for data collection and processing enhances the transparency of the evaluative information base (at least on a formal level). As opposed to this, low procedural standardization of reviewer's evaluation repertoire and reporting enhances diversity at the cost of the transparency and visibility. The overall shift towards acknowledging and accounting for societal impact especially in the Netherlands and the UK softens semantic standards leading to a greater variety of considered research outputs at the cost of reduced transparency.

Only few examples show high levels of transparency and diversity: the Italian list of academic outputs was specifically designed to meet the requirements of the central evaluation scheme but has been implemented in a consistent and transparent way throughout the Italian science system. The continuous tradeoff between transparency and diversity is being counterbalanced in all countries by compensating a higher level of semantic standardization with lower degrees of procedural standardization.

In general, it can be noted, that assessment standards are loaded with additional values. In the UK and in Italy they are impregnated by a logic of accountability and control due to the formative nature and allocative function of the evaluation schemes (and beyond) whereas in the Netherlands the focus on organizational learning, quality enhancement and prospective development implies a counseling and advisory logic of the evaluation system.

The present study may serve as a starting point for the under researched field of assessment standards. The conceptual categorization into semantic and procedural standards offers a useful frame to foster our understanding of standardization in (responsible) research assessment. Yet, the results of the qualitative analysis based on three country cases are clearly of limited generalizability. Overall, future work would benefit from a more systematic approach (e.g. through a quantitative research design and/or a broader empirical basis). In addition, it should consider a stronger theoretical take on the issue, e.g. by providing a more fine-grained categorization and operationalization of assessment standards and by embedding them further in theoretical models of research governance. Furthermore, the concepts of "transparency" and "diversity" are worth being operationalized in a systematic way. While the exploratory case studies of this contribution qualitatively report opinions and assessments by stakeholders and representatives of the three science systems under study, further research might develop methods and procedures to qualitatively and quantitatively assess the effects of standards and other features of the evaluation instruments on the transparency and diversity of evaluation. This includes approaches to evaluate the quality of classifications (semantic standards; see Bianchi & Carusi, 2019; Coen & Smiraglia, 2019; Hancock, 2013; Sile, Guns, Vandermoere, & Engels, 2019; Smiraglia, 2019), assessments of the architecture and coherence of evaluation processes and its stages (see Fig. 1) as well as analyses regarding the "fit" of the different components and standards with regard to purpose of evaluation. Last, the relationship between degree of standardization and acceptance and perceived fairness of the evaluation instrument (by the 'objects' of evaluation, i.e. the researchers themselves) is worth further investigation.

ACKNOWLEDGMENT

This research was supported by the German Federal Ministry of Education and Research [grant number KDS2016].

REFERENCES

Abramo, G., D'Angelo, C. A., & Di Costa, F. (2011). National research assessment exercises: A comparison of peer review and bibliometrics rankings. *Scientometrics*, *89*(3), 929–941. doi:10.1007/s11192-011-0459-x

ANVUR. (2011). Valutazione della Qualità della Ricerca 2004-2010 (VQR 2004-2010): Bando di partecipazione. Retrieved from https://www.anvur.it/wp-content/uploads/2011/11/bando_vqr_def_07_11.pdf

ANVUR. (2015). Evaluation of Research Quality 2011-2014 (VQR 2011-2014): Call for participation. Retrieved from https://www.anvur.it/wp-content/uploads/2015/11/Bando%20VQR%202011-2014_secon~.pdf

Arnold, E., Simmonds, P., Farla, K., Kolarz, P., Mahieu, B., & Nielsen, K. (2018). Review of the Research Excellence Framework: evidence report. Retrieved from technopolis group UK website: https://assets.publishing.service.gov.uk/government/uploads/system/uploads/attachment_data/file/768162/research-excellence-framework-review-evidence-report.pdf

Bellotti, E., Kronegger, L., & Guadalupi, L. (2016). The evolution of research collaboration within and across disciplines in Italian Academia. *Scientometrics*, *109*(2), 783–811. doi:10.1007/s11192-016-2068-1 PubMed

Bence, V., & Oppenheim, C. (2005). The evolution of the UK's Research Assessment Exercise: Publications, performance and perceptions. *Journal of Educational Administration and History*, *37*(2), 137–155. doi:10.1080/00220620500211189

Bianchi, G., & Carusi, C. (2019). Debunking the Italian Scientific Sectors' classification system: preliminary insights. In ISSI - the International Society for Informetrics and Scientometrics (Chair), 17 International Conference on Scientometrics & Informetrics. Sapienza University of Rome.

Biesenbender, S. (2019). The governance and standardisation of research information in different science systems: A comparative analysis of Germany and Italy. *Higher Education Quarterly*, *73*(1), 116–127. doi:10.1111/hequ.12193

Biesenbender, S., & Herwig, S. (2019). Support structures to facilitate the dissemination and implementation of a national standard for research information – the German case of the Research Core Dataset. *Procedia Computer Science*, *146*, 131–141. doi:10.1016/j.procs.2019.01.088

Blind, K., & Gauch, S. (2009). Research and standardisation in nanotechnology: Evidence from Germany. *The Journal of Technology Transfer*, *34*(3), 320–342. doi:10.1007/s10961-008-9089-8

Bollini, A., Mennielli, M., Mornati, S., & Palmer, D. T. (2016). IRIS: Supporting & Managing the Research Life-cycle. Universal Journal of Educational Research, 4(4), 738–743. doi:10.13189/ujer.2016.040410

Boyatzis, R. E. (1998). *Transforming qualitative information: Thematic analysis and code development.* Atlanta, Ga.: Sage.

Brunsson, N., Rasche, A., & Seidl, D. (2012). The Dynamics of Standardization: Three Perspectives on Standards in Organization Studies. *Organization Studies, 33*(5-6), 613–632. doi:10.1177/0170840612450120

Burland, T., & Grout, C. (2017). Standards and Interoperability: How Jisc's Work Supports Reporting, Communicating and Measuring Research in the UK. *Procedia Computer Science, 106,* 276–282. doi:10.1016/j.procs.2017.03.026

Butler, L. (2007). Assessing university research: A plea for a balanced approach. *Science & Public Policy, 34*(8), 565–574. doi:10.3152/030234207X254404

Cagan, R. (2013). The San Francisco Declaration on Research Assessment. *Disease Models & Mechanisms, 6*(4), 869–870. doi:10.1242/dmm.012955 PubMed

CIVR. (2004). Valutazione triennale della ricerca (VTR): Bando di partecipazione all'esercizio 2001-2003. Retrieved from https://www.unipd.it/sites/unipd.it/files/Bando%20n.35%2016%20marzo%202004.pdf

Coen, G., & Smiraglia, R. P. (2019). Toward Better Interoperability of the NARCIS Classification. *Knowledge Organization, 46*(5), 345–353. doi:10.5771/0943-7444-2019-5-345

De Boer, H., Jongbloed, B. W., & Benneworth, P. S. (2015). *Performance-based funding and performance agreements in fourteen higher education systems. Center for Higher Education Policy Studies.* CHEPS.

de Jong, S. P. L., Smit, J., & van Drooge, L. (2015). Scientists' response to societal impact policies: A policy paradox. *Science & Public Policy, 43*(1), 102–114. doi:10.1093/scipol/scv023

De Vries, H. J. (2006). IT standards typology. In K. Jakobs (Ed.), Advanced Topics in Information Technology Standards and Standardization Research (Vol. 1, pp. 1–26). IGI Global; doi:10.4018/978-1-59140-938-0.ch001.

De Vries, H. J., Jakobs, K., Egyedi, T. M., Eto, M., Fertig, S., Kanevskaia, O., ... Mirtsch, M. (2018). Standardization: Towards an agenda for research. *International Journal of Standardization Research, 16*(1), 52–59. doi:10.4018/IJSR.2018010104

Deloitte. (2013). Redesigning the higher education data and information landscape. Strand 1 project report.

Dijstelbloem, H., Huisman, F., Miedema, F., & Mijnhardt, W. (2013). Why science does not work as it should. And what to do about it. Science in Transition Position Paper. Retrieved from http://www.scienceintransition.nl/app/uploads/2013/10/Science-in-Transition-Position-Paper-final.pdf

Dobbins, M. (2016). Convergent or divergent Europeanization? An analysis of higher education governance reforms in France and Italy. *International Review of Administrative Sciences*, *83*(1), 177–199. doi:10.1177/0020852315580498

Donina, D., Meoli, M., & Paleari, S. (2015). Higher Education Reform in Italy: Tightening Regulation Instead of Steering at a Distance. *Higher Education Policy*, *28*(2), 215–234. doi:10.1057/hep.2014.6

Egyedi, T. M., & Ortt, J. R. (2017). Towards a functional classification of standards for innovation research. In R. Hawkins, K. Blind, & R. Page (Eds.), Handbook of innovation and standards (pp. 105–132). Cheltenham, Northampton, MA: Edward Elgar Publishing; doi:10.4337/9781783470082.00013.

Fondermann, P., & van der Togt, P. L. (2017). How Wageningen University and Research Centre managed to influence researchers publishing behaviour towards more quality, impact and visibility. *Procedia Computer Science*, *106*, 204–211. doi:10.1016/j.procs.2017.03.017

Franceschini, F., & Maisano, D. (2017). Critical remarks on the Italian research assessment exercise VQR 2011–2014. *Journal of Informetrics*, *11*(2), 337–357. doi:10.1016/j.joi.2017.02.005

Friedman, B., Kahn, P. H., & Borning, A. (2008). Value sensitive design and information systems. The Handbook of Information and Computer Ethics, 69–101.

Galimberti, P., & Mornati, S. (2017). The Italian Model of Distributed Research Information Management Systems: A Case Study. *Procedia Computer Science*, *106*, 183–195. doi:10.1016/j.procs.2017.03.015

Gläser, J. (2006). *Wissenschaftliche Produktionsgemeinschaften: Die soziale Ordnung der Forschung*. Frankfurt am Main: Campus-Verl.

Gläser, J., Lange, S., Laudel, G., & Schimank, U. (2010). Informed authority? The limited use of research evaluation systems for managerial control in universities. In R. Whitley, J. Gläser, & L. Engwall (Eds.), *Reconfiguring Knowledge Production: Changing Authority Relationships in the Sciences and their Consequences for Intellectual Innovation* (pp. 149–183). Oxford, UK: Oxford University Press.

Gläser, J., & Laudel, G. (2007). The social construction of bibliometric evaluations. In R. Whitley & J. Gläser (Eds.), Sociology of the Sciences Yearbook: Vol. 26. The Changing Governance of the Sciences: The Advent of Research Evaluation Systems (pp. 101-123). Dordrecht: Springer Netherlands. doi:10.1007/978-1-4020-6746-4_5

Hamann, J. (2016). The visible hand of research performance assessment. *Higher Education*, *72*(6), 761–779. doi:10.1007/s10734-015-9974-7

Hancock, A. (2013). Best practice guidelines for Developing International Statistical Classifications. Expert Group Meeting on International Statistical Classifications.

Hansson, F. (2010). Dialogue in or with the peer review? Evaluating research organizations in order to promote organizational learning. *Science & Public Policy*, *37*(4), 239–251. doi:10.3152/030234210X496600

Hicks, D. (2012). Performance-based university research funding systems. *Research Policy*, *41*(2), 251–261. doi:10.1016/j.respol.2011.09.007

Hicks, D., Wouters, P., Waltman, L., de Rijcke, S., & Rafols, I. (2015). The Leiden Manifesto for research metrics. *Nature*, *520*(7548), 429–431. doi:10.1038/520429a PubMed

Higginbotham, B. D. (2017). *The Standardization of Standardization: The Search for Order in Complex Systems*. Fairfax, VA: George Mason University; Retrieved from http://jbox.gmu.edu/xmlui/bitstream/handle/1920/11295/Higginbotham_gmu_0883E_11559.pdf?sequence=1&isAllowed=y

Houssos, N., Jörg, B., Dvořák, J., Príncipe, P., Rodrigues, E., Manghi, P., & Elbæk, M. K. (2014). OpenAIRE Guidelines for CRIS Managers: Supporting Interoperability of Open Research Information through Established Standards. *Procedia Computer Science*, *33*, 33–38. doi:10.1016/j.procs.2014.06.006

Hunt, S., & Boliver, V. (2019). Private providers of higher education in the UK: mapping the terrain. Centre for Global Higher Education working paper series No. 47. Retrieved from https://www.researchcghe.org/perch/resources/publications/to-publishwp47.pdf

International Organization for Standardization. (2001). *International Classification for Standards*. Geneva, Switzerland: ICS.

Jakobs, K. (2006). ICT standards research-Quo Vadis. *Homo Oeconomicus*, *23*(1), 79–107.

Jones, P., & Sizer, J. (1990). The universities funding council's 1989 research selectivity exercise. *Beiträge Zur Hochschulforschung*, *4*, 309–348.

Jongbloed, B. (2018). Overview of the Dutch science system. CHEPS Working Papers 201804, University of Twente, Center for Higher Education Policy Studies (CHEPS). Retrieved from https://ideas.repec.org/p/chs/wpachs/201804.html

Jörg, B., Waddington, S., Jones, R., & Trowell, S. (2014). Harmonising Research Reporting in the UK – Experiences and Outputs from UKRISS. *Procedia Computer Science, 33,* 207–214. doi:10.1016/j.procs.2014.06.034

Kaltenbrunner, W., & de Rijcke, S. (2017). Quantifying 'output' for evaluation: Administrative knowledge politics and changing epistemic cultures in Dutch law faculties. *Science & Public Policy, 44*(2), 284–293. doi:10.1093cipolcw064

KNAW. NWO, & VSNU. (2001). Kwaliteit verplicht. Naar een nieuw stelsel van kwaliteitszorg voor het wetenschappelijk onderzoek: Rapport van de werkgroep Kwaliteitszorg, Wetenschappelijk Onderzoek en standpuntbepaling KNAW, NWO en VSNU. Amsterdam: Author.

KNAW. (2005). Judging research on its merits. An advisory report by the Council for the Humanities and the Social Sciences Council. KNAW. Retrieved from https://www.knaw.nl/en/news/publications/judging-research-on-its-merits

KPMG. (2015). The blueprint for a new HE data landscape: Final report.

Kurihara, S. (2008). Foundations and Future Prospects of Standards Studies: Multidisciplinary Approach. *International Journal of IT Standards and Standardization Research, 6*(2), 1–20. doi:10.4018/jitsr.2008070101

Lepori, B., Reale, E., & Spinello, A. O. (2018). Conceptualizing and measuring performance orientation of research funding systems. *Research Evaluation, 27*(3), 171–183. doi:10.1093/reseval/rvy007

Mahieu, B., Arnold, E., & Kolarz, P. (2014). *Measuring scientific performance for improved policy making. Science and Technology Options Assessment (STOA) Study, European Parliamentary Research Service (EPRS).* Brussels: European Union; Retrieved from https://www.europarl.europa.eu/stoa/en/document/IPOL-JOIN_ET(2014)527383

Martin, B. R., & Whitley, R. (2010). The UK Research Assessment Exercise: A Case of Regulatory Capture? In R. Whitley, J. Gläser, & L. Engwall (Eds.), Reconfiguring Knowledge Production: Changing Authority Relationships in the Sciences and their Consequences for Intellectual Innovation (pp. 51–80). Oxford, UK: Oxford University Press; doi:10.1093/acprof:oso/9780199590193.003.0002.

McGrath, A., & Cox, M. (2014). Research Excellence and Evaluation Using a CRIS: A Cross-institutional Perspective. *Procedia Computer Science, 33*, 301–308. doi:10.1016/j.procs.2014.06.048

Moed, H. F., & Halevi, G. (2015). Multidimensional assessment of scholarly research impact. *Journal of the Association for Information Science and Technology, 66*(10), 1988–2002. doi:10.1002/asi.23314

Narin, F. (1976). Evaluative bibliometrics: The use of publication and citation analysis in the evaluation of scientific activity. Report to the National Science Foundation.

Ntim, C. G., Soobaroyen, T., & Broad, M. J. (2017). Governance structures, voluntary disclosures and public accountability. *Accounting, Auditing & Accountability Journal, 30*(1), 65–118. doi:10.1108/AAAJ-10-2014-1842

Page, E. S. (1997). Data Collection for the 1996 Research Assessment Exercise: Review (No. M2/97). Retrieved from https://webarchive.nationalarchives.gov.uk /20120118212839/http://www.hefce.ac.uk/pubs/hefce/1997/m2_97.htm

Picciotto, R. (2005). The value of evaluation standards: A comparative assessment. *Journal of Multidisciplinary Evaluation, 2*(3), 30–59.

Power, M. (2015). How accounting begins: Object formation and the accretion of infrastructure. *Accounting, Organizations and Society, 47*, 43–55. doi:10.1016/j. aos.2015.10.005

RAE. (2005). Guidance on submissions (No. 03/2005). RAE.

Ràfols, I. (2019). S&T indicators in the wild: Contextualization and participation for responsible metrics. *Research Evaluation, 28*(1), 7–22. doi:10.1093/reseval/rvy030

Rebora, G., & Turri, M. (2013). The UK and Italian research assessment exercises face to face. *Research Policy, 42*(9), 1657–1666. doi:10.1016/j.respol.2013.06.009

REF. (2011). Assessment framework and guidance on submissions (No. 02.2011). Retrieved from https://webarchive.nationalarchives.gov.uk/20170302114208/http:// www.ref.ac.uk/pubs/2011-02/

REF. (2015). Research Excellence Framework 2014: Manager's report. Retrieved from https://webarchive.nationalarchives.gov.uk/20170302114114/http://www.ref. ac.uk/pubs/refmanagersreport/

REF. (2017). Consultation on the second Research Excellence Framework: Summary of responses (No. 2017/02). Retrieved from https://www.ref.ac.uk/media/1046/ ref_2017_02.pdf

REF. (2019a). Guidance on submissions (No. 2019/01). Retrieved from https://www. ref.ac.uk/media/1092/ref-2019_01-guidance-on-submissions.pdf

REF. (2019b). Panel criteria and working methods (No. 2019/02). Retrieved from https://www.ref.ac.uk/media/1084/ref-2019_02-panel-criteria-and-working-methods.pdf

Reinhart, M. (2012). *Soziologie und Epistemologie des Peer Review*. Baden-Baden: Nomos; doi:10.5771/9783845239415

Russell, R. (2012). Adoption of CERIF in Higher Education Institutions in the UK: A Landscape Study. Version 1.1.

Saldaña, J. (2013). *The coding manual for qualitative researchers* (2nd ed.). Thousand Oaks, CA: Sage.

Seawright, J., & Gerring, J. (2008). Case Selection Techniques in Case Study Research: A Menu of Qualitative and Quantitative Options. *Political Research Quarterly*, *61*(2), 294–308. doi:10.1177/1065912907313077

Sile, L., Guns, R., Vandermoere, F., & Engels, T. (2019). Comparison of classification-related differences in the distribution of journal articles across academic disciplines: the case of social sciences and humanities in Flanders and Norway (2006-2015). In ISSI - the International Society for Informetrics and Scientometrics (Chair), 17 International Conference on Scientometrics & Informetrics. Sapienza University of Rome.

Sivertsen, G. (2017). Unique, but still best practice? The Research Excellence Framework (REF) from an international perspective. Palgrave Communications, 3(1), 725. doi:10.1057/palcomms.2017.78

Smiraglia, R. P. (2019). Trajectories for Research: Fathoming the Promise of the NARCIS Classification. *Knowledge Organization*, *46*(5), 337–344. doi:10.5771/0943-7444-2019-5-337

Stern, N. (2016). Building on success and learning from experience: an independent review of the Research Excellence Framework. Retrieved from Department for Business, Energy & Industrial Strategy website: https://www.gov.uk/government/publications/research-excellence-framework-review

Technopolis. (2009). Identification and dissemination of lessons learned by institutions participating in the Research Excellence Framework (REF) bibliometrics pilot: Results of the Round Two Consultation. Retrieved from https://webarchive.nationalarchives. gov.uk/20180103220839/http://www.hefce.ac.uk/data/year/2009/Identification,and ,dissemination,of,lessons,learned,by,institutions,participating,in,the,Research,Exce llence,Framework,REF,bibliometrics,pilot,Results,of,the,Round,Two,Consultation/

Timmermans, S., & Epstein, S. (2010). A World of Standards but not a Standard World: Toward a Sociology of Standards and Standardization. *Annual Review of Sociology, 36*(1), 69–89. doi:10.1146/annurev.soc.012809.102629

Universities, U. K. (2017). Universities UK response to the UK Funding Councils consultation on the second Research Excellence Framework. Retrieved from https:// www.universitiesuk.ac.uk/policy-and-analysis/reports/Documents/2017/second-ref-consultation-response.pdf

Van de Kaa, G. (2013). Responsible innovation and standardization: A new research approach? *International Journal of IT Standards and Standardization Research, 11*(2), 61–65. doi:10.4018/jitsr.2013070105

Van der Meulen, B. (2007). Interfering governance and emerging centres of control. In P. Weingart, R. Whitley, & J. Gläser (Eds.), The Changing Governance of the Sciences (Vol. 26, pp. 191–203). Dordrecht: Springer Netherlands; doi:10.1007/978-1-4020-6746-4_9.

Van der Meulen, B., & Rip, A. (1998). Mediation in the Dutch science system. *Research Policy, 27*(8), 757–769. doi:10.1016/S0048-7333(98)00088-2

Van Drooge, L., Jong, S., Faber, M., & Westerheijden, D. F. (2013). *Twenty years of research evaluation*. The Hague, Netherlands: Academic Press.

Van Leeuwen, T. (2004). Descriptive Versus Evaluative Bibliometrics. In H. F. Moed, W. Glänzel, & U. Schmoch (Eds.), Handbook of Quantitative Science and Technology Research: The Use of Publication and Patent Statistics in Studies of S&T Systems (pp. 373–388). Dordrecht: Springer Netherlands; doi:10.1007/1-4020-2755-9_17.

Van Steen, J. (2012). *The science system in the Netherlands: An organisational overview*. Den Haag: Academic Press.

Van Vught, F. A. (1997). Combining planning and the market: An analysis of the Government strategy towards higher education in the Netherlands. *Higher Education Policy, 10*(3-4), 211–224. doi:10.1016/S0952-8733(97)00014-7

VSNU. (1994). *Quality Assessment of Research, Protocol 1994*. Utrecht: VSNU.

VSNU. NWO, & KNAW. (2003). Standard Evaluation Protocol 2003-2009 for public research organisations. Utrecht: Author.

VSNU. (2009). *NWO, KNAW 2009–2015*. Amsterdam: Standard Evaluation Protocol.

VSNU. (2015). *NWO, KNAW 2015–2021*. Amsterdam: Standard Evaluation Protocol.

VSNU. (2019). *Definitieafspraken Wetenschappelijk Onderzoek: Toelichting bij KUOZ*. Den Haag: VSNU.

Waddington, S., Joerg, B., Jones, R., McDonald, D., Gartner, R., Ritchie, M., . . . Trowell, S. (2014). UK Research Information Shared Service (UKRISS) Final Report, July 2014. Technical Report. Retrieved from JISC website: http://bura. brunel.ac.uk/handle/2438/10192

Waddington, S., Sudlow, A., Walshe, K., Scoble, R., Mitchell, L., Jones, R., & Trowell, S. (2013). Feasibility Study Into the Reporting of Research Information at a National Level Within the UK Higher Education Sector. New Review of Information Networking, 18(2), 74–105. doi:10.1080/13614576.2013.841446

Westerheijden, D. F., de Boer, H., & Enders, J. (2009). Netherlands: An 'Echternach' Procession in Different Directions: Oscillating Steps Towards Reform. In C. Paradeise, E. Reale, I. Bleiklie, & E. Ferlie (Eds.), University Governance: Western European Comparative Perspectives (pp. 103–125). Dordrecht: Springer Netherlands; doi:10.1007/978-1-4020-9515-3_5.

Whitley, R. (2007). Changing Governance of the Public Sciences. In R. Whitley & J. Gläser (Eds.), Sociology of the Sciences Yearbook: Vol. 26. The Changing Governance of the Sciences: The Advent of Research Evaluation Systems (pp. 3–27). Dordrecht: Springer Netherlands. doi:10.1007/978-1-4020-6746-4_1

Whitley, R. (2011). Changing governance and authority relations in the public sciences. *Minerva*, *49*(4), 359–385. doi:10.1007/s11024-011-9182-2

Wilsdon, J., Allen, L., Belfiore, E., Campbell, P., Curry, S., Hill, S., . . . Johnson, B. (2015). The Metric Tide: Report of the Independent Review of the Role of Metrics in Research Assessment and Management. Retrieved from https://responsiblemetrics. org/the-metric-tide/

Wurster, S., Egyedi, T. M., & Hommels, A. (2013). *The development of the public safety standard TETRA: lessons and recommendations for research managers and strategists in the security industry*. IEEE.

ADDITIONAL READING

Abramo, G., D'Angelo, C. A., & Di Costa, F. (2011). National research assessment exercises. A comparison of peer review and bibliometrics rankings. Scientometrics, 89(3), 929–941. doi:10.1007/s11192-011-0459-x doi:10.100711192-011-0459-x

Butler, L. (2007). Assessing university research. A plea for a balanced approach. Science & Public Policy, 34(8), 565–574. doi:10.3152/030234207X254404 doi:10.3152/030234207X254404

Cronin, B., & Sugimoto, C. R. (2014). Beyond bibliometrics: Harnessing multidimensional indicators of scholarly impact. MIT Press. doi:10.7551/mitpress/9445.001.0001 doi:10.7551/mitpress/9445.001.0001

Egyedi, T. M., & Ortt, J. R. (2017). Towards a functional classification of standards for innovation research. In R. Hawkins, K. Blind, & R. Page (Eds.), Handbook of innovation and standards. Edward Elgar Publishing. doi:10.4337/9781783470082.00013 doi:10.4337/9781783470082.00013

Hicks, D., Wouters, P., Waltman, L., Rijcke, S., & Rafols, I. (2015). The Leiden Manifesto for research metrics. Nature, 520(7548), 429–431. doi:10.1038/520429a PubMed doi:10.1038/520429a PMID:25903611

Ràfols, I. (2019). S&T indicators in the wild: Contextualization and participation for responsible metrics. Research Evaluation, 28(1), 7–22. doi:10.1093/reseval/rvy030 doi:10.1093/reseval/rvy030

Timmermans, S., & Epstein, S. (2010). A World of Standards but not a Standard World. Toward a Sociology of Standards and Standardization. Annual Review of Sociology, 36(1), 69–89. doi:10.1146/annurev.soc.012809.102629 doi:10.1146/annurev.soc.012809.102629

Whitley, R. (2011). Changing governance and authority relations in the public sciences. Minerva, 49(4), 359–385. doi:10.1007/s11024-011-9182-2 doi:10.100711024-011-9182-2

Whitley, R., & Gläser, J. (2007). The changing governance of the sciences. The Advent of Research Evaluation Systems (Vol. 26). Springer. doi:10.1007/978-1-4020-6746-4_1 doi:10.1007/978-1-4020-6746-4_1

Wilsdon, J., Allen, L., Belfiore, E., Campbell, P., Curry, S., Hill, S., ... Johnson, B. (2015). The Metric Tide: Report of the Independent Review of the Role of Metrics in Research Assessment and Management. London. doi:10.4135/9781473978782 doi:10.4135/9781473978782

KEY TERMS AND DEFINITIONS

Assessment Standard: Assessment standards refer to written procedural guidelines and rules regarding the planning and implementation of national or institutional evaluation processes, established by consensus by recognized stakeholders and approved by the scientific community.

Current Research Information System (CRIS): Current research information systems comprise software solutions that merge research information from different sources and databases in order to describe and report on research (activities) in institutions and their organisational units.

Governance: Describes the coordination of political, economic and public actors in order to guide and regulate action and achieve common goals. Major coordination modes are hierarchy, the market und networks.

National Research Evaluation System: A set of procedures and guidelines set up by science policy stakeholders and the scientific community to regularly assess the quality, impact and performance of publicly funded research for the purpose of accountability, funding allocation or improving research quality.

Peer Review: Assessment of the merits of research contributions by esteemed members of the scientific community ('peers'). Peer review serves as the dominant evaluation method in a variety of evaluative contexts (publications, project proposals, applications for promotion and tenure, prizes and awards, etc.)

Research Information (RI): Research information describes an institution's research activities. It comprises information on a research institution's (scientific) staff and structure, projects, third-party funding, publications, patents, etc.

Research Metrics: Research metrics refers to the measurement of research performance or impact through (quantitative) indicators. They form an integral part of research assessment methods with varying implications and inadvertent consequences for science.

Responsible Research Evaluation: Responsible research evaluation focuses on producing research metrics that adhere to certain principles, such as data accuracy, transparent data collection and analysis or making use of a diversity of indicators

Section 2
Participation in Standards Setting

Chapter 4

Individual Participation in Standards Setting:
Role, Influence, and Motivation

Jonas Lundsten
Malmö University, Sweden

Jesper Mayntz Paasch
Universty of Gävle, Sweden & Aalborg University, Denmark

ABSTRACT

Since standardization is essential and additionally has organizational effects, studying motivation for participating in the standardization processes is important. A phenomenological study of descriptions made by individual participants in project teams for geographical information at the Swedish Standards Institute, SIS, was conducted 2016-2017. The study indicated that participants were motivated, but there were different motivators depending on the participants' differing contexts. For most participants, the main personal meaningful goal was to be at the forefront of development. For participants employed by organizations with frequent interactions with stakeholders, the main personal meaningful goal was to satisfy the stakeholders' needs. This study also showed that several members felt that they do not have sufficient time for working with standardization asks due to the fact that their daily work in their organizations often has higher priority in relation to standardization work. This may slow down the development of standards and other publications due to lack of resources.

INTRODUCTION

DOI: 10.4018/978-1-7998-2181-6.ch004

This chapter explores motives for individual participation in formal standardization processes for geographic information in Sweden and is a continuation of research presented in Lundsten and Paasch (2017; 2018; 2019). Geographic information and geodata are common terms for information describing the physical world around us,for example buildings, roads, forests and features related to location, for example administrative boundaries.

Participation in a formal standardization process may require huge resources from the participants (Riillo, 2013). However, standards are not "trade secrets", but available for anyone, such as competitors, for a fee charged by the standardization body. The motives for participation do therefore not rely on the protection of ideas for the companies involved. A motive can also be to share technical and/or strategic knowledge and/or access to markets (Bild & Mangelsdorf, 2016; Riillo, 2013), thereby gaining either technical and/or economic advantages.

Geographical information has gained much interest during the last decades due to increased
use and exchange of digital data ("maps") describing physical and administrative features. Standards and related documents, such as specifications and code lists, play an important part in this.

The benefits of standardization in the field of geographic information are well known and the development of formal standards have in Sweden been in focus for several years, e.g. by public and private stakeholders participating in technical committees, TC, at the Swedish Standards Institute, SIS, for more than two decades. Examples are Lantmäteriet [the Swedish mapping, cadastral and land registration authority], Trafikverket [the National Transport Administration] which have been involved in formal standardization since the late 1980-ies, being part of a national initiative concerning a standardization programme for geographic information at the Swedish Standards Institute.

There is a long tradition for implementing international standards for geographical information and to develop national standards when international standards are not available. Examples are the International Organization for Standardization's [ISO] 19100 series of standards for geographical information, which, among other things, specify how to describe geographic information (ISO, 2014) which has been implemented as a Swedish standard (Swedish Standards Institute [SIS], 2014) and the nationally developed Swedish standards for application schemas for municipal zoning plans, SS 637040:2016 (SIS, 2016) and road and railway networks, SS 637004:2009 (SIS, 2009). Sweden has recently adopted a national strategy for advanced cooperation for open and usable geographic information via e-services (Lantmäteriet, 2016). The strategy state, among other things, that the use of standards is of major importance for achieving an effective infrastructure for, among others, data exchange, digitization of public administration, more effective social planning processes, defense and civil contingencies. Standards are in other words an important part of the nation's "invisible infrastructure", a term coined a decade ago by the Swedish government in regard to increased cooperation concerning IT standardization in the public sector (Swedish government, 2007).

Standardization plays a vital part in the national Swedish strategy for geographic information infrastructure 2016-2020 (Lantmäteriet, 2016). An example is the initiative providing governmental agencies, municipalities and other organizations easy access to data within the Swedish geodata cooperation initiative. A third example illustrating the importance of geographical information standards is the financial agreement between SIS and Lantmäteriet, the Swedish mapping, cadastral and land registration authority, allowing the free-of-charge use of a number of standards within the Swedish geographic information sector (SIS & Lantmäteriet, 2017).

Since previous studies show a clear correlation between motivation and performance (Chaudhary & Sharma, 2012), it's essential to understand motivation on individual level to contribute to standardization processes. The authors have not identified research on how individuals are motivated in standardization work in geographic information and hope this article will be a contribution to this field of study.

BACKGROUND

Geographical information has gained much interest during the last decades due to the increased use and exchange of digital maps describing geographical and administrative features. Standards and related documents, such as technical reports, play an important part in this. Examples are the technical guidelines (data specifications) specifying common data models, code lists, etc., to be used when exchanging geographic datasets in accordance with the European INSPIRE directive providing a spatial infrastructure for Europe (European Union, 2007). The benefits of standardization in the field of geographic information are well known and the development of formal standards have been in focus for several years, e.g. by private and public stakeholders participating in technical committees, TC (TK in Swedish), at the Swedish Standards Institute, SIS, for more than two decades. The authors have not identified research on how individuals are motivated in standardization work in geographic information and hope this article will be a contribution to this field of study. There is a long tradition for implementing international standards for geographical information and to develop national standards when international standards are not available. Examples are the International Organization for Standardization's [ISO] 19100 series of standards for geographical information, i.e. specifying how to describe geographic information (ISO, 2014), the Swedish standards for application schemas for municipal zoning plans, SS 637040:2016 (Swedish Standards Institute [SIS], 2016) and road and railway networks, SS 637004:2009 (SIS, 2009). Sweden has recently adopted a national strategy for advanced cooperation for open and usable geographic information via e-services (Lantmäteriet, 2016). The strategy state, among other things, that the use of standards is of major importance for achieving an effective infrastructure for, among others, data exchange, digitization of public administration, more effective social planning processes, defense and civil contingencies. Standards are in other words an important part of the nation's "invisible infrastructure", a term coined a decade ago by the Swedish government in regard to increased cooperation concerning IT standardization in the public sector (Swedish government, 2007).

Standardization in the field of geographic information is a central part in the Swedish land use and planning infrastructure and, for example, play a vital part in the national Swedish strategy for geographic information infrastructure 2016-2020 (Lantmäteriet, 2016). An example is the initiative providing governmental agencies, municipalities and other organizations easy access to data within the Swedish geodata cooperation initiative. A third example illustrating the importance of geographical information standards is the financial agreement between SIS and Lantmäteriet, the Swedish mapping, cadastral and land registration authority, allowing the free-of-charge use of a number of standards within the Swedish geographic information sector (SIS & Lantmäteriet, 2017).

MAIN FOCUS OF THE CHAPTER

The chapter presents the results of research concerning individual participants' personal motives for participating in formal standardization work at the Swedish Standards Institute, SIS, concerning the production of standards and related documents (such as national profiles and other publications) for geographic information.

PROBLEM DESCRIPTION

The Swedish Standards institute´s TC for geographic information stated in 2012 that it sometimes is difficult to recruit new participants to the technical committees (SIS, 2012). This is also an observation shared by one of the authors after having been involved in TC-work for more than a decade.

The research question investigated here is how a standardization project, intended to develop standards, technical reports and other guidelines for geographic information, is perceived as motivating by the project team members.

Method

SIS had when the Lundsten and Paasch (2017) investigation was conducted 9 technical committees, working with geographical information: TK320 (Road and railroad information), TK323 (Framework for Geographic Information), TK452 (Water systems), TK466 (Addresses), TK533 (Building information), TK538 (Forestry information), TK489 (Metadata for geographic information), TK501 (Physical planning) and TK570 (Webb cartography). The TC's were mainly working with national Swedish standardization and the ISO standards for geographic information. The individual TCs were not subject for individual research, but were treated as one entity.

Semi-structured interviews were conducted with TC members and chairmen to get the involved participants perspective on the standardization projects. An interview guide was constructed, based on Leontiev's (1978) theory on the relationship between an individual's goal and the motive of a collective activity. In the beginning of each interview, the interviewees were asked to describe the project, the goal, the stakeholders' expectations, the interviewees experiences of the process, and the performances in the project team. The following questions concerned the interviewees' view of the motives' behind the project and their employing organization. Thereafter, the interviewees were asked about their personal meaningful goals and how it was related to the project's motive. Finally, they were asked about the conditions for the project's succeeding. In order to understand how the projects were experienced by the interviewees and why they were experienced that way the Meaning Constitution Analysis, MCA (Sages & Lundsten, 2004) method was used. In a first step of the analysis each interview was divided into meaning units. Each meaning units consisted of one or a few clauses. The meaning units were then categorized into themes. The interviews were then compared in order to find differences and similarities. The interviews were categorized based on the motives behind the standardization processes. Based on the categorization the interviewees were divided into groups. For instance, in some interviews the motive could be related to "stakeholders", whereas in other interviews the motive could be related to "the employing organization. If "stakeholders" was mentioned as the central aspect for the standardization process in one group of interviews the interviewees were categorized into one group in contrast to those interviewees indicating that "the employing organization" was the central aspect. The case study was conducted by interviewing individual present and former TC members. The interviewees were randomly selected by studying their presence at committee meetings, documented in the meeting minutes where available, and through discussions with the author's colleagues involved in TK standardization work. 23 present and former members were contacted. In total, 18 present and former committee members were interviewed;

13 members active in some of the TCs (seven chairmen and six team members), two former team members having left their TCs due to reorganizations, but have been replaced with others from their respective organizations, and three former team members whose organizations have left their TCs. The 9 TCs consist today of 81 members representing 43 different public and private organizations. Several organizations are represented in more than one TC. The TC chairmen were included in the study since they are responsible for managing the committee and appointed by SIS after the recommendation from the participating organizations (Beskow, 2017), often employed by one of the organizations participating in the TC and normally much engaged in the TCs daily work. The TC team members are appointed by the participating organizations (Beskow, 2017). In the following text "member" indicate chairmen and team members unless otherwise noted. All interviews were conducted by personal meetings or by telephone/Skype, supported by open ended questions. The authors have refrained from sending out questionnaires to all TC members, which may have increased the number of interviewees, but with answers on pre-formulated questions.

Instead, the approach of in-depth interviews based in fewer open-ended questions were chosen to allow narrative interviews concerning their individual motives. The interviewees were, for example, asked about the motivation of the organization they represent and their personal motives for being involved in standardization, the support they receive from their home organization and the view of their home organization on standardization. It must be noted that this study does not include the formal motives of the participating organizations and level of support, but the motives and support as perceived and described by the interviewees. SIS facilitate the TC work by supplying a project manager and by being responsible for formal, administrative matters.

STANDARDIZATION

Previous Research on Standardization Processes

The selection of stakeholders for participating in standardization projects is essential. There are cases where stakeholders from larger organizations tend to influence the standardization in a way that makes the standards more complex (de Vries, 2006). The motives for participating in standardization work are many, for example Blind and Mangelsdorf (2016), Blind and Gauch (2009), Mangelsdorf/2009), Blind (2006), and Jacobs, Procter, and Williams (1996; 2001). However, the authors have not identified research on the influence of stakeholders on standardization of geographical information. Contributing to standardization demands managing information, implying that standardization is complex, see e.g. Hanseth, Jacucci, Grisot, and Aanestad (2006). Previous research has shown a relationship between performance in complex tasks and motivation (Amabile, 1982), implying that motivational factors need to be considered. According to self-determination theory, SDT, there are three fundamental psychological needs: Autonomy, Competence, and Relations (Ryan & Deci, 2000). The concept Autonomy refers to an individual's experience of being able to control a situation, the concept Competence refers to a process of learning new skills or knowledge, and the concept Relations refers to a feeling of involvement in a social context. In an activity in which these three needs are met a state of autonomous motivation arises. A prerequisite for the basic psychological needs to be met in a work situation is that the individual has a certain degree of freedom, the work involves a certain level of challenge and that performances lead to involvement in a social context.

Consultants may not be able to recover all their individual costs by billing their clients their total expenses (Steinfield, Wigand, Markus & Minton, 2007) and that their participation therefore competes with fee-generating work. However, this behavior may be voluntary since there may be an eventual later payoff in future business development since they may have obtained a knowledge gap in relation to non-participating competitors (Steinfield, et al., 2007, p. 182). Another individual reason for many to participate is a personal interest in the subject-matter to be standardized. This may result in the will to participate more or less on one´s private, free time, as one interviewee expressed (Steinfield, et al., 2007, p. 182). Another reason to invest private time into the project was that they became committed to the cause or to the other participants (Steinfield, et al., 2007, p. 182). Frequent and lasting interaction among experts working in a group tend to forge groups together (Isaak, 2006). However, not much research about motivation in geographical information standardization teams has been identified. However, one such publication is a report from the Swedish Standards Institute (2012).

ORGANIZATIONAL MOTIVES

Since people are dependent on collective processes (Leontiev, 1978), understanding organizational motives is essential to understand individuals' motivation. Apart from the product of the standardization per se, additionally motives can coexist (de Vries, 2006). See Table 1. That is, there can be both explicit and implicit motives. A study of 626 Swedish governmental organizations indicated that their primary motive was to get insight into the process of developing standards, identify needs for standardization, and comment on the processes. Producing standards was a secondary motive (Swedish government, 2007, pp. 354-356).

Table 1. Motives for governmental agencies to participate in standardization organization. Translated from Swedish government (2007, p. 356)

Motive to Participate in a Standardization Organization	Number of Agencies Who Answered Not Important at All / Not that Important	Number of Agencies Who Answered Quite Important / Very Important	Did Not Know
Monitor development in one's area of responsibility	6	52	4
Point at the needs for standardization in the sector	11	47	4
Influence the development by giving comments on the content and design of standards	8	50	4
Participate in the production of standards	38	20	4
Take initiative to development of sector specific standards regardless of content	28	29	5

An organizational motive is basically to satisfy a need, which could be people's material needs (Leontiev, 1978) or the need to maintain the organizational routines (cf Leontiev, 1978). Organizational activities result in processes beyond the organizations (Tobach, 1999). By that, multiple activities can be interdependent. Developers from different organizations are involved in the development of standards for geodata. Standardization processes are not directly dependent on the motives of the involved organizations. Meeting the expectations of the Swedish national strategy for geographic information infrastructure 2016-2020 (Lantmäteriet, 2016) is an example of a motive shared between multiple organizations. The motives can differ, but there are organizational routines dependent on standardization or the standardization process per se.

Organizational Routines and Standardization

The concept *organizational routines* refers to repetitive behavior (Feldman & Pentland, 2003), implying that there is a clear relationship between organizational routines and standardization. According to Nelson and Winter (1982) an organization basically consists of routines. Organizations are situated in an unpredictable environment. However, the organizational routines make the intra- and inter-organizational behaviors predictable (Nelson & Winter, 2005). There are considerable similarities between routines and biological genes (Hodgson, 2013), even though there are differences as well. The evolution of organizations proceed in the same basic steps as the evolution of biological organisms. These steps are: variation, selection, and retention (Mesoudi, Whiten, & Laland, 2006). Originally, there is a variation of routines. Routines possible to perform in differing contexts and with interdependent relationships with other routines have a higher tendency to be selected. When selected, some routines are spread to other organizations. What genes are for biological organisms, routines are for organizations. The set of routines constituting an organization are linked together because there is room for them, not necessarily because there is an intentional reason for keeping them (Stanczyk-Hugiet, 2014). Standardization implies routinization, which have organizational effects. Firstly, standardization processes generate routines and can, by that, be components in the constitution of an organization. Secondly, standardization facilitates retention of organizational routines, implying that organizations involved in standardization tend to influence their environment to a higher extent than organizations who are not. In the long run, organizations involved in standardization should have an evolutionary advantage. Thirdly, standards clarify the organizational routines. Regarding geodata, standards clarify the routines for processing of geographic information for each employee. Clarified routines facilitates perceptions of the organizational activity as personally meaningful for the employees (cf. Leontiev, 1978). That is, employees experience a relationship between the routines and their personal meaningful goals, implying that the routines make sense for them. People involved in developing standards should therefore have a higher motivation if they interact with people affected by the standards in their daily work.

The difference between organizational motives and organizational routines is that the former represents a striving towards need satisfaction and the latter represents repetitive actions coordinated between multiple individuals.

Personal Meaningful Goals and Standardization

An organizational context affects people's motivation (Deci, Connel, & Ryan, 1989; Gagné & Deci, 2005), implying that understanding motivation requires understanding the organizational structure. Leontiev's (1978) theory on the relationship between an individual's goal and the motive of a collective activity bridges the gap between the individual level and the organizational level. Satisfaction of the basic psychological needs in a task makes the goal of the task personally meaningful for the individual (cf. Gagné & Deci, 2005). When people are involved in an activity, their personal meaningful goals are related to the motive of the activity. By that, people can be motivated to follow the organizational routines. A goal is a person's imagination of a desirable state in the future, whereas a motive is the kit linking people in a collective activity. The motive forms the frame in which the individuals can fulfil their personal meaningful goals and, by that, be motivated (Leontiev, 1978). When an organization communicates the expectations on standardization, the individual relates these expectations to personal meaningful goals. The expectations can be unrelated to personal meaningful goals and thus the individual will not be motivated.

The expectations can also encourage the individual to strive for development of personal competence along with standard development. A motive originates in a real or perceived need among a group of people (Leontiev, 1978). If the motive forms the activity in a way that makes it satisfy the psychological needs, autonomy, competence, and relations (cf. Ryan & Deci, 2000) the personal meaningful goal is related to the activity itself (cf. Leontiev, 1978). In a standardization project an individual's personal meaningful goal can be to develop the personal competence by participation in the project and, by that, satisfy psychological needs. Multiple organizations, with differing motives, are involved in standardization projects. Consequently, the team members have several motives to consider in relation to their personal meaningful goal.

Multiple activities can share an object, in spite of differing motives. For instance, the motive for one activity can be to develop a product. The motive for another activity can be to distribute the product. The product is the object for both activities. The differing motives make people in the activities perceive the object from different perspectives, when the object is shared and people from separate activities interact. In these interactions people can learn from activities beyond their own (Engeström, 2001). Previous studies indicate that personal interactions enhance motivation (Bent & Freathy, 1997), which can be explained by the psychological need for relations (Gagné & Deci, 2005). Additionally, the psychological need for competence (Gagné & Deci, 2005) is satisfied by the learning process in interactions between activities. That is, interactions between activities can affect people's autonomous motivation, implying that personal meaningful goals can be achieved.

Interactions between standard developers and stakeholders in standardization projects can have a positive effect on motivation (cf. Bent & Freathy, 1997). To understand activities, their networks need to be studied along with them (Spinuzzi, 2011). Spinuzzi's (2011) theory describe relationships between multiple activities. An object, shared in a network, tend to be inconstant, making it perceived differently in different activities. In a network of activities, which takes place in standard development, a single person can be involved in multiple activities (Miettinen, 1998). Thereby, a person constitutes a link between different activities and transfer understanding of an ambiguous object. In some cases, the object is unclear. That is, people involved in such network do not have a clearly defined aim to strive for (Spinuzzi, 2014). In standardization of geodata the object should be rather clear. However, there can be implicit motives for participation in standardization (Swedish government, 2007, pp. 354- 356). Consequently, there can be several motives for the individual standard developer to take into respect, which affects the individual's motivation.

RESULTS

Motivation Among Members in Technical Committees

The interviewed chairs' main motives for participation in the standardization work was to structure geographic data. Two of the interviewed chairmen also stated that the wish to improve/facilitate interaction among the team members was an additional motive, since they experienced lack of engagement among team members as a hindrance in the work process. Time constraints in the projects are also considered as a reason for the lack of commitment among project team members. The individual members are not able to influence the workload placed on them in the organizations, but their motivation may still be relevant. With a high degree of motivation, an employee will be more inclined to prioritize the task, even if it means working extra, unpaid hours.

The team members' descriptions showed considerable differences. The members, except one, from public organizations expressed the view that their work in the technical committees were not prioritized in regard to their daily working tasks in their organizations. They were obliged to focus on the organization's core activities.

One of the team members, representing an interest organization predominantly for small sized companies, expressed that the organization was dependent on the work done in the technical committee. Many of the companies needed accessible geographic data. In order to satisfy this need, the organization engaged itself in a technical committee. The relations between the companies and the interest organization made the representative being motivated to participate in the technical committee. The project manager did not need to focus on interactions between team members; the project proceeded driven by the motivation to solve the needs of companies indirectly involved by the interest organization.

In all interviews the interviewees said that the standardization projects demanded a considerable effort from them. For some of the interviewees the standardization project was related to an unpleasant personal situation. However, the standardization projects had different motives and goals for the interviewees.

Organizational Motives and Personally Meaningful Goals

The interviewees described five different motives for participation: 1) to develop standardized structures for geographic information, 2) to take part in technical development, 3) to minimize resource waste, 4) to run the organization based on national perspectives, 5) to facilitate information transmission. Six interviewees described the object for their activity as structure of geographic information. Geographic data needs to be structured in order to enable information transfer between users. There is a need for standardization in the organizations, which made them engage in the standardization projects. As described by the interviewees, the main obstacle was committee member's engagement. Insufficient communication came as an effect of lacking engagement.

The object is structure of geographic information in the beginning of the project. . During the project the object changes. In a later state the object is the communication in the committee. In order to structure data multiple perspectives from different branches are needed. In turn, interactions in project teams were needed to synthesize the multiple perspectives. The interviewees described two aspects of clarification as a personal meaningful goal. The first aspect was clarification of their own and committee members' roles in the standardization projects. Their roles and the expectations on each committee member were unclear, which hindered the projects from proceeding effectively. The second aspect was clarification of the explicit purpose of the standardization projects.

The second group, of two interviewees, described their object as technical development. In contrast to the previously mentioned interviewees, for them the objective was not social interactions, but plans for development of the technical aspects of standardization. The interviewees described making contributions to the community benefit as a personal meaningful goal. The third group, of four interviewees, described the object as minimized resource waste. The standardization projects were not prioritized by their organizations. Therefore, the amount of time spent on standardization needed to be minimized. Still, these interviewees were involved in standardization projects and they had a value for them, namely insight into other organizations. They learned from others in the standardization projects, regardless of the lack of focus on standardization per se. The objects described by the interviewees differed and were not associated with standardization. Likewise, the personal meaningful goals differed. For two interviewees, the personal meaningful goal concerned their organization. The other two interviewees described learning from other committee members as their personal meaningful goal. A fourth group, of three interviewees, described the object as enabling the activity of their organizations. They emphasized the organization's national perspective on standardization. The main objective was establishment of guidelines for standardization of national geographic data. Two interviewees talked about technology as a tool for communication. One of the interviewees talked about the final standards as a tool for communication. That is, the interviewees emphasized different aspects of communication; technology per se vs the final standards. Facilitating the transmission of information was described as a personal meaningful goal, implying that the personal meaningful goal corresponded to the motive of the activity. The fifth group of interviewees differed from the former four groups. In the fifth group, one interviewee represented a governmental authority, one of the interviewees represented an interest organization, and one interviewee represented a profit driven company. Among these organizations, a network with frequent interactions with stakeholders was a common feature. The interviewees in group 1, 2, 3, and 4 represented a governmental authority. Possibly, representing a non-governmental organization makes commission members more prone to perceive stakeholders' needs and satisfaction as a personal meaningful goal. This is however subject for further research.

The interaction of private and public actors are often blended to combine their advantages, such as providing technical expertise from the private sector and mobilization of state power (Abbott & Snidal, 2001, p. 363). They focused in their study on international standards and international governance. The authors, however, see no reason why their conclusions should not be valid for domestic standardization.

The SIS interest organization's stakeholders were mainly small firms. The interest organization monitored these interests. In turn, the governmental authority was in frequent contact with the interest organization and additionally with similar interest organizations. The profit driven company was in frequent contact with customers communicating standardized solutions for e-services. The interviewees in the fifth group had frequent interactions with clients. In these interactions, the clients expressed their needs. That is, the interviewees considered the standardization projects being related to people's needs (see Table 2).

ANALYSIS AND DISCUSSION

The study showed that a major motive for organizations and individuals to participate in formal standardization is to contribute to the development of standards for the description and exchange of geographic information. That is, maintaining the organization's routines is a critical motive. However, there were differences depending on the relationship between the interviewees and the stakeholders. Interviewees with frequent interactions with stakeholders perceived the standardization project being a personal meaningful goal. The frequency of interactions with stakeholders was a result of their organizations' routines. One of these organizations was an interest organization and the other was a profit driven small firm, relying on frequent personal interactions with customers. This finding corresponds to the research results presented by Bent and Freathy (1997), implying that personal interactions with clients facilitate motivation.

None of the interviewees mentioned their participation in standardization work as an individual strategic personal career planning aiming at, for example, a higher/ better position in the organization or higher salary. That is, the motivator was not mainly related to an extrinsic reward. According to the interviewees they were intrinsically motivated, implying that their basic psychological needs of autonomy, competence, and relations, were met (cf. Gagné & Deci, 2005). On the contrary, for

Table 2. Representing in relation to personal meaningful goals (Lundsten & Paasch, 2017, p. 23)

Group	No. of Interviewees	Representing	Personal Meaningful Goal in Relation to Standardization
1	6	Governmental authority	To structure geographic information.
2	2	Governmental authority	Technical development through standardization
3	4	Governmental authority	Meaningful goals concerning organizations Learning from others as meaningful goal
4	3	Governmental authority	Enabling the activity of their organizations National perspective on standardization Technology as means for communication
5	3	Governmental authority Interest organization Profit driven company	Satisfaction of stakeholders' needs

15 interviewees in the first four groups, participation in standardization was related to an increased workload, knowing that one cannot make a proper contribution due to other priorities in the participant's organization. That is, standardization did not fully correspond to the organizational routines, They were not able to meet the expectations set on them in the standardization projects. For some of these interviewees a personal goal was to learn from other commission members. This implies there were contradictions between organizational routines and the personal meaningful goals. In this situation, the individual risks to feel alienated, resulting in absence of motivation (Gagné & Deci, 2005). For the interviewees in the fifth group, the relation to the organization's stakeholders, standardization was perceived as a tool for facilitating stakeholders' activities. For them standardization was both related to organizational routines and a personal meaningful goal, which increased their motivation. In these cases the standardization process was an organizational routine which was spread to their stakeholders. The reason why the standardization process was selected in the variation of routines (cf. Mesoudi, Whiten, & Laland, 2006), was that the organizations had frequent contact with stakeholders in need of standards. In this way the organization's external relations affected the selection of routines. Additionally, project team members, employed in these organizations, experienced a connection between the organizational routines on one hand and their daily work and their personal meaningful goals on the other hand.

Participation in the formal standardization process is voluntary and in line with the Swedish principles of governmental autonomy. Lantmäteriet was in 2006 appointed as responsible for facilitating increased cooperation concerning geographic information among stakeholders in Sweden by the Swedish government (Swedish government, 2006; 2009). This appointment does however not include any mandate to instruct other public agencies or other parties to participate.

The Swedish system of public agencies is based on a centuries old principle of rather independent agencies, where tasks are meant to be solved in cooperation, not by one agency mandating another agency to do specific tasks. Swedish governmental agencies therefore hold a considerable high level of autonomy and are independently managed under performance management by the government (Hall, Nilsson & Löfgren, 2011), even if the level of autonomy among agencies in general differs (Niklasson and Pierre (2012).

This autonomy is constitutionally enshrined. The responsibilities of each governmental agency are specified in their governmental instructions, for example Lantmäteriet´s instructions (Swedish government, 2009). This autonomy means that agencies can make their own decisions concerning if, and how, they want to participate in national and international standardization (Swedish government, 2007, p. 123), unless they receive specific, governmental instructions.

This principle is an organizational challenge, based on the risk that participation in standardization may not be prioritized by the organization itself by allowing their employees sufficient time to work with these issues (cf. Riillo, 2013).

One of the findings of this study is that the reason why the invested resources in standardization by some of the participating of the participating organizations are insufficient is the result of that standardization seem not prioritized in relation to their main routines (cf. Riillo, 2013). They have nevertheless invested resources to a specific, albeit not sufficient, extent. They are officially involved by the invested resources. Previous studies show that networking tend to lead organizations to aiming at their self-representation per se (Spinuzzi, 2014). In some contexts, an organization can improve its self-representation by investments of resources in a standardization project.

FUTURE RESEARCH DIRECTIONS

A larger study encompassing the majority of organizations in the investigated technical committees is being planned as either a stand-alone study of more participants from the technical committees, or as part of a comparative study of one or more technical committees within the information sector. Future research should even have a broader perspective on organizational aspects of participation. For example, how organizations prioritize and implement standards on geographic information and whether it is possible to measure the societal and economic impact of degrees of motivation.

CONCLUSION

This study focused on investigating individual motives for participation in formal standardization of geographic information, and a selection of chairmen and members of Technical Committees at the Swedish Standards Institute were interviewed.

The majority of interviewees expressed a strong personal motivation in standardization of geographic data. A minority expressed a lack of motivation for participating in standardization projects. The interviewees motivation corresponded to the interest of their organization. It is not sufficient to support the financial obligations of being part of a technical committee by paying participation fees, etc. If the individual participants' time is not allocated for the specific purpose to participate in the technical committee it may lead to lack of motivation due to the feeling of not being able to participate in an optimal way and that the work is regarded as less important than other work activities closer to daily life activities. This view has also been expressed by some of the interviewees.

Interviewees representing organizations with frequent contacts with private stakeholders described the standardization as personally meaningful for themselves. According to the analyses the individuals´ interactions with stakeholders made the purpose of standardization clear. The stakeholders' needs were related to the standardization projects.

The individual participants' daily work in their respective organizations has often higher priority in relation to standardization work. This is in contrast with the organizational motive of the participating organizations and may slow down the development of standards and other publications due to lack of resources.

ACKNOWLEDGMENT

The authors are indebted to the members of the technical committees participating in this study. This research received no specific grant from any funding agency in the public, commercial, or not-for-profit sectors.

REFERENCES

Abbott, K. W., & Snidal, D. (2001). International "standards" and international governance. *Journal of European Public Policy*, 8(3), 345–370. doi:10.1080/13501760110056013

Amabile, T. M. (1982). Social psychology of creativity: A consensual assessment technique. *Journal of Personality and Social Psychology, 43*(5), 997–1013. doi:10.1037/0022-3514.43.5.997

Bent, R., & Freathy, P. (1997). Motivating the employee in the independent retail sector. *Journal of Retailing and Consumer Services, 4*(3), 201–208. doi:10.1016/S0969-6989(96)00045-8

Beskow, C. (2017). *Regler för arbete i teknisk kommitté (SIS/TK)* [Rules for working in a Technical Committee (SIS/TK)]. Stockholm, Sweden: Swedish Standards Institute.

Blind, K. (2006). Explanatory factors for participation in formal standardisation processes: Empirical evidence at firm level. *Economics of Innovation and New Technology, 15*(2), 157–170. doi:10.1080/10438590500143970

Blind, K., & Gauch, S. (2009). Research and standardisation in nanotechnology: Evidence from Germany. *The Journal of Technology Transfer, 34*(3), 320–342. doi:10.100710961-008-9089-8

Blind, K., & Mangelsdorf, A. (2016). Motives to standardize: Empirical evidence from Germany. *Technovation, 48–49*, 13–24. doi:10.1016/j.technovation.2016.01.001

Chaudhary, N., & Sharma, B. (2012). Impact of employee motivation on performance (productivity) private organization. *International Journal of Business Trends and Technology, 2*, 29–35.

de Vries, H. J. (2006). Standards for business - How companies benefit from participation in international standards setting. In A. L. Bement, T. Standage, T. Sugano, & K. Wucherer (Eds.), *International Standardization as a strategic tool - Commended papers from the IEC Centenary Challenge 2006* (pp. 130–141). Geneva, Switzerland: IEC.

Deci, E. L., Connel, J. P., & Ryan, R. M. (1989). Self-determination in a work organization. *The Journal of Applied Psychology, 74*(4), 580–590. doi:10.1037/0021-9010.74.4.580

Engeström, Y. (2001). Expansive learning at work: Toward an activity theoretical reconceptualization. *Journal of Education and Work, 14*(1), 133–156. doi:10.1080/13639080020028747

European Union. (2007). *Directive 2007/2/EC of the European Parliament and of the Council of 14 March 2007 establishing an Infrastructure for Spatial Information in the European Community (INSPIRE)*. Brussels, Belgium: European Union.

Feldman, M. S., & Pentland, B. T. (2003). Reconceptualizing Organizational Routines as a Source of Flexibility and Change. *Administrative Science Quarterly, 28*(1), 94–118. doi:10.2307/3556620

Gagné, M., & Deci, E. L. (2005). Self determination theory and work motivation. *Journal of Organizational Behavior, 26*(4), 331–362. doi:10.1002/job.322

Hall, P., Nilsson, T., & Löfgren, K. (2011). *Bureaucratic autonomy revisited: Informal aspects of agency autonomy in Sweden*. Paper presented at the Permanent Study Group VI on Governance of Public Sector organizations, Annual Conference of EGPA, Bucharest, Romania.

Hanseth, O., Jacucci, E., Grisot, M., & Aanestad, M. (2006). Reflexive standardization: Side effects and complexity in standard making. *Management Information Systems Quarterly, 30*, 563–581. doi:10.2307/25148773

Hodgson, G. M. (2013). Understanding organizational evolution: Toward a research agenda using generalized Darwinism. *Organization Studies, 34*(7), 973–992. doi:10.1177/0170840613485855

International Organization for Standardization. (2014). *ISO 19115-1:2014 Geographic information - Metadata - Part 1 - Fundamentals*. Geneva, Switzerland: International Organization for Standardization, ISO.

Isaak, J. (2006). The role of individuals and social capital in POSIX standardization. *International Journal of IT Standards and Standardization Research, 4*(1), 1–23. doi:10.4018/jitsr.2006010101

Jakobs, K., Procter, R., & Williams, R. (1996). Users and standardization - Worlds apart? The Example of electronic mail. *StandardView, 4*(4), 183–191. doi:10.1145/243492.243495

Jakobs, K., Procter, R., & Williams, R. (2001). The making of standards: Looking inside the work groups. *IEEE Communications Magazine*, (April): 2–7.

Lantmäteriet. (2016). *The national geodata strategy 2016-2020*. Report no. 2016/7. Gävle, Sweden: Lantmäteriet.

Leontiev, A. N. (1978). *Activity, consciousness, and personality*. Englewood Cliffs, NJ: Prentice-Hall.

Lundsten, J., & Paasch, J. (2017). Motives for Participation in Formal Standardization Processes for Geographic Information - An Empirical Study in Sweden. *International Journal of Standardization Research, 15*(1), 16–28. doi:10.4018/IJSR.2017010102

Lundsten, J., & Paasch, J. M. (2018). Individual's Motivation in Standardization of Geographic Information. *Proceedings of FIG Congress 2018*.

Lundsten & Paasch, J. M. (2019, Feb.). Why do people participate in standardization of GI? *Coordinates*, 36-39.

Mangelsdorf, A. (2009). *Driving factors of service companies to participate in formal standardization processes: An empirical analysis*. doi:10.2139srn.1469512

Mesoudi, A., Whiten, A., & Laland, K. N. (2006). Towards a unified science of cultural evolution. *Behavioral and Brain Sciences*, *29*(4), 329–383. doi:10.1017/S0140525X06009083 PMID:17094820

Miettinen, R. (1998). Object Construction and Networks in Research Work: The Case of Research on Cellulose degrading Enzymes. *Social Studies of Science*, *28*(3), 423–463.

Nelson, R. R., & Winter, S. G. (1982). *An Evolutionary Theory of Economic Change*. Cambridge, UK: Belknap Press.

Niklasson, B., & Pierre, J. (2012). Does agency age matter in administrative reform?: Policy autonomy and public management in Swedish agencies. *Policy and Society*, *31*(3), 195–210. doi:10.1016/j.polsoc.2012.07.002

Riillo, C. (2013). Profiles and motivations of Standardization Players. *International Journal of IT Standards and Standardization Research*, *11*(2), 17–33. doi:10.4018/jitsr.2013070102

Ryan, R. M., & Deci, E. L. (2000). Intrinsic and extrinsic motivations: Classic definitions and new directions. *Contemporary Educational Psychology*, *25*(1), 54–67. doi:10.1006/ceps.1999.1020 PMID:10620381

Sages, R., & Lundsten, J. (2004). The ambiguous nature of psychology as science and its bearing on methods of inquiry. In M. Lahlou, & R. B. Sages (Eds.), Mèthodes et Terrains de la Psychologie Interculturelle (pp. 189- 220). Lyon, France: L'Interdisciplinaire, Limonest.

Spinuzzi, C. (2011). Losing by expanding: Coralling the runaway object. *Journal of Business and Technical Communication*, *25*(4), 449–486. doi:10.1177/1050651911411040

Spinuzzi, C. (2014). How noemployer firms stage-manage ad-hoc collaboration: An activity theory analysis. *Technical Communication Quarterly*, *23*(2), 88–114. doi:10.1080/10572252.2013.797334

Stanczyk-Hugiet, E. (2014). Routines in the process of organizational evolution. Management, 18, (2), pp. 73-87. *Technical Communication Quarterly*, *23*(2), 88–114. doi:10.1080/10572252.2013.797334

Steinfield, C., Wigand, R., Markus, M. L., & Minton, G. (2007). Promoting e-business through vertical information systems standards: Lessons from the US home mortgage industry. In S. Greenstein & V. Stango (Eds.), *Standards and Public Policy* (pp. 160–207). Cambridge, UK: Cambridge University Press.

Swedish government. (2006). Förordning (2006:1009) om ändring i förordningen (1995:1418) med instruktion för det statliga lantmäteriet [Ordinance (2006:1009) concerning changes in ordinance (1996:1418) for the governmental Lantmäteriet]. Svensk författningssamling 2006:1009. Stockholm, Sweden: Ministry of the Environment.

Swedish government. (2007). *Den osynliga infrastrukturen - om förbättrad samordning av offentlig ITstandardisering. SOU 2007:47* [The invisible infrastructure - concerning improved coordination of public ITstandardization. SOU 2007:47]. Stockholm, Sweden: Ministry of Enterprise and Innovation.

Swedish government. (2009). Förordning (2009:946) med instruktion för Lantmäteriet [Ordinance with instructions for Lantmäteriet]. Svensk författningssamling 2009:946. With later amendments. Stockholm, Sweden: Ministry of Enterprise and Innovation.

Swedish Standards Institute. (2009). *SS 637004:2009. Geografisk information - Väg- och järnvägsnät - Applikationsschema* [Geographic information - Road and railway networks - Application schema]. Stockholm, Sweden: Swedish Standards Institute.

Swedish Standards Institute. (2012). Rapport om förslag till utveckling av Stanlis metodik [Report on suggestions for development of the STANLI methology]. 2012-05-25. Stockholm, Sweden: Swedish Standards Institute, technical committee TK323.

Swedish Standards Institute. (2014). *SS-EN ISO 19115-1:2014. Geografisk information - Metadata - Del 1: Grunder (ISO 19115-1:2014)* [ISO 19115-1:2014 Geographic information -- Metadata -- Part 1: Fundamentals]. Stockholm, Sweden: Swedish Standards Institute.

Swedish Standards Institute. (2016). *SS 637040:2016. Geografisk information - Detaljplan - Applikationsschema för planbestämmelser* [Geographic information - Detail plan- Application schema for planning instructions]. Stockholm, Sweden: Swedish Standards Institute.

Swedish Standards Institute & Lantmäteriet. (2017). *Avtal nr LMV8589* [Agreement no. LMV8589]. Stockholm, Sweden: Swedish Standards Institute and Gävle, Sweden: Lantmäteriet.

Tobach, E. (1999). Activity theory and the concept of integrative levels. In Y. Engeström, R. Miettinen, & R.-L. Punamäki (Eds.), *Perspectives on activity theory* (pp. 133–146). New York, NY: Cambridge University Press. doi:10.1017/CBO9780511812774.011

ADDITIONAL READING

Lundsten, J., & Paasch, J. M. (2017). Motives for Participation in Formal Standardization Processes for Geographic Information - An Empirical Study in Sweden. *International Journal of Standardization Research*, *15*(1), 16–28. doi:10.4018/IJSR.2017010102

Lundsten, J., & Paasch, J. M. (2018). Individual's Motivation in Standardization of Geographic Information. In *Proceedings of FIG Congress 2018*. Istanbul, Turkey, May 6–11, 2018.

KEY TERMS AND DEFINITIONS

Geographic Information: Information describing geographical features, such as coastlines, buildings and boundaries. Also called geospatial information.

Motivation: Peoples' striving for satisfaction of psychological or material needs.

Organizational Routine: Behaviors that are repeatedly performed by multiple individuals.

Standardization Institute: Organization responsible for national standardization. Often (part) financed by the government.

Chapter 5
Participation in the Standards Organizations Developing the Internet of Things:
Recent Trends and Implications

Justus Alexander Baron
Northwestern University, USA

ABSTRACT

This chapter explores patterns and recent trends in meeting attendance at four standard development organizations (SDO): 3GPP, IETF, IEEE 802.11, and One M2M. Average meeting attendance has slightly increased over the last two decades. It is rare for individuals to attend meetings in different SDOs. IETF has the least attendee overlap with other SDOs and the lowest attendee affiliation concentration. Nevertheless, 3GPP attendance has become more diverse and IETF attendance more concentrated. The affiliations of attendees of 3GPP and IETF have become more similar over time while OneM2M attendance has become more distinct from other SDOs. IEEE 802.11 attendance has become significantly less diverse since 2007. Until 2014, there was a significant convergence with 3GPP. Since 2014, this trend has reversed, and attendance at IEEE 802.11 has become more similar to IETF. The author explores implications of the described evidence for differences between telecommunications and internet standardization, companies' standardization strategies, and consequences of the patent policy change at IEEE.

DOI: 10.4018/978-1-7998-2181-6.ch005

INTRODUCTION

A number of Standard Development Organizations (SDOs) currently develop the standards that will support a large range of technologies for the communication from machine to machine (M2M), collectively labeled the Internet of Things (IoT). While several detailed studies have investigated specific aspects of standardization processes in individual organizations, SDOs such as the 3rd Generation Partnership Project (3GPP), the Institute of Electrical and Electronics Engineers Standards Association (IEEE-SA), the Internet Engineering Task Force (IETF), and OneM2M increasingly interact in the development of standards (indeed, 3GPP and OneM2M are themselves the result of extensive collaboration between SDOs). For a better understanding of the standardization processes in these SDOs and the behavior and strategies of the participating individuals and organizations, it is important to analyze individuals' and firms' participation in and across various SDOs.

Participation in standardization processes has many facets, including actively developing technical contributions to standardization problems, and implementing standardized technologies in new products and services. In this chapter, I focus on one dimension of participation in standardization – attendance of SDO meetings. Meeting attendance is more systematically observable than other, more complex forms of participation. Furthermore, meeting attendance data covers large parts of the diverse group of individuals and organizations participating in standardization, such as companies competing for leadership over standardization projects, research organizations presenting new technical ideas, downstream firms eager to learn about new standards in order to develop new products and services, and individual technology or standardization enthusiasts. I collected, compiled and cleaned the publicly available attendance lists of meetings at 3GPP, IEEE 802.11, IETF, and OneM2M and created a database with 325,371 attendance records in 3,369 SDO meetings. Over the past 20 years, more than 40,000 individuals representing 6,466 different organizations participated in at least one meeting of one of these four SDOs. In this chapter, I present patterns and recent trends in the attendance data. In particular, I document changes in attendance frequencies, co-attendance patterns across SDOs, and concentration of individual attendees' affiliations.

These SDOs have very different processes, so that the nature of meetings as well as the role of meeting attendees differ substantially from one SDO to the other. Nevertheless, there are some common patterns across organizations. The overall population size, i.e. the number of individuals attending at least one SDO meeting per year, has not markedly increased at any SDO over time, and has significantly decreased at IETF from a peak in 2000. Nevertheless, individuals that are active in SDOs attended a significantly larger number of meetings in 2017 than at the beginning of the respective observation periods. Therefore, total meeting attendance and the average number of attendees per meeting steadily increased at 3GPP, and increased at IEEE 802.11 up to 2015.

At the affiliation level, participation in 3GPP, IEEE-SA, and IETF has become significantly more similar over time. At the beginning of the observation period, corporate entities entirely dominated at 3GPP, whereas non-corporate entities (such as universities, public administrations, public research institutes, and non-profit organizations) played a larger role at IEEE-SA and IETF. Nevertheless, the share of attendees with corporate affiliations (and in particular network operators) declined at 3GPP, and the share of company affiliates among attendees is no longer a significant differentiating factor among SDOs. Furthermore, IETF and IEEE-SA 802.11 have historically been characterized by a greater degree of openness to smaller entities, whereas a smaller number of larger actors dominated at 3GPP. Nevertheless, 3GPP participation has become significantly more diverse in terms of affiliations over time, whereas affiliations of IETF and especially IEEE-SA 802.11 attendees have become significantly more concentrated. The increasing similarity of these SDOs in terms of the share of non-corporate attendees and the diversity of attendees' affiliations is also reflected in a greater degree of co-participation by the same organizations in the three SDOs.

Nevertheless, there has not been a generalized convergence among SDOs over the observation period. First, over the few years since its creation, OneM2M has become significantly more distinct from other SDOs (and in particular 3GPP) in terms of both individual attendees and their affiliations. This suggests that a distinct standardization community specializing on IoT standardization and specifically focused on OneM2M has quickly emerged and grown increasingly independent of 3GPP and other incumbent SDOs. Second, at the individual level, overlap between different SDOs has always been low, and has not significantly increased over time.

A recent event that has sparked significant interest in indicators of SDO participation was the update of IEEE's patent policy in 2015. Several studies have analyzed whether there were significant changes in measures of stakeholders participation in IEEE activities in the wake of the change. In this study, I contribute to this nascent body of empirical evidence.

In the remainder of this article, I review the related literature, describe the methodology of data collection and processing, briefly discuss the institutional differences between SDOs, and present and discuss the evidence on SDO participation patterns and their implications.

RELATED LITERATURE

There is a large and quickly growing empirical literature on standard development processes in SDOs (see e.g. Baron and Spulber, 2018, for a review). Nevertheless, there are significant gaps in this literature. First, for the largest part, this literature has focused on firm participation in SDOs, and has paid less attention to the individuals participating in standard development.[1] Second, most of the empirical research on SDOs either uses highly aggregated and indirect measures of participation in standards development, or is limited to analyses of individual SDO working groups. Consequently, there is a dearth of in-depth research comparing detailed measures of participation in various significant SDOs.

There are few systematic studies of the role of individuals in standard development processes. Nevertheless, the existing evidence suggests that this role may be significant. Jakobs et al. (2001) survey senior members of working groups at IETF, the International Telecommunications Union (ITU), and the International Organization for Standardization (ISO). Only a fourth of the respondents from IETF viewed themselves as representatives of a company or a country, while the majority viewed themselves as "techie" or "user advocate". Even at ISO, about one third of the respondents identified individuals as the most powerful influencing factor. Baron et al. (2019b) study SDO processes for making decisions on rules and policies, and find that many SDOs allow or require individuals to participate in these processes in their personal capacity.

In a case study of a standardization project mostly carried out at IEEE-SA, Isaak (2006) finds that the goals of individual participants may significantly differ from those of their employers, and that individuals have significant influence over standardization outcomes that is distinct from the influence of their employers. Isaak (2006) and Dokko and Rosenkopf (2010) highlight the role of the social capital that individuals build through their participation in SDO working groups, and that individuals may use these social ties to act as boundary-spanners between different firms. In a comprehensive history of standardization since the 19th century, Yates and Murphy (2019) similarly highlight the role of individual goals and social ties between individual participants of the "standardization movement".

Some analyses of individual SDO participants specifically focus on scientists. Zi and Blind (2015) and Blind et al. (2018) survey employees of a German public research institute to investigate the motivations and implications of individual scientists' involvement in SDOs. Nevertheless, Simcoe's (2012) research on IETF suggests that the behavior of academic researchers in SDOs differs significantly from the behavior of SDO attendees with a corporate affiliation (the "beard-to suit ratio" e.g. is a significant predictor of the speed of standard development). Overall, as our own data will confirm, academics and other scientists are not a very significant demographic among SDO attendees. Baron and Spulber (2018) note that membership in the 191 SDOs in their sample very predominantly consists in companies. Few studies on SDOs distinguish between participation by firms and participation by their individual employees. A rare exception is a study on the SDO meeting attendance records of inventors listed in declared standard-essential patents (SEP) by Kang and Motohashi (2015).

The existing studies suggest that the behavior of individuals in standard development cannot be fully explained in terms of their employers' standardization strategies, and that decision-making at the individual level is an important but understudied research topic. Nevertheless, comprehensive empirical research on individuals in standards development is limited by data availability. Existing studies are based on surveys of small samples of individuals or case studies of individual working groups. Contreras (2014) provides more comprehensive empirical evidence on the demographics of IETF meeting attendees, but also this study is limited to a single SDO. This study will contribute to the nascent body of empirical evidence on the role of individuals in SDOs by presenting and describing data on individual participation in SDOs that are much more comprehensive than what has so far been available. The descriptive evidence in this chapter may open new avenues for more in-depth research on the role of individuals in SDOs.

Studies of companies' involvement in SDOs on one hand have often used coarse measures of SDO participation, such as binary indicators based on surveys or observed participation in individual SDOs or committees (Haudeville and Wolff, 2004; Blind and Thumm, 2004; Riillo, 2014; Blind and Mangelsdorf, 2016), or SDO membership counts (Baron et al., 2019a). On the other hand, a number of studies (e.g. Ranganathan and Rosenkopf, 2014; Bar and Leiponen, 2014; Ranganathan et al., 2018; Jones et al., 2018) analyze firm interactions in single SDOs or SDO committees using granular data, including ballots and individual contributions to working group discussions.

Nevertheless, standard development within an SDO working group does not take place in isolation. Several studies have documented how SDO processes are affected by member firms' collaboration in related standards consortia (Leiponen, 2008; Delcamp and Leiponen, 2014; Baron et al., 2014). There are also significant interactions between different standard development processes in different SDOs. Companies' behavior with respect to the large number of different SDOs with their different processes and rules has often been analyzed through the lens of SDO competition, or companies' 'forum shopping' for a favorable standardization venue (Lerner and Tirole, 2006; Chiao et al., 2007; Lerner et al., 2015). Nevertheless, qualitative research suggests that forum shopping is often not an option for stakeholders with respect to large and established SDOs such as 3GPP, IEEE, or IETF (Baron et al., 2019b). Qualitative case studies of SDO standardization processes (e.g. de Lacey et al., 2006) offer a more subtle take on the interactions between related SDOs.

A serious limitation to the research on interactions between SDOs is the paucity of empirical data on companies' and individuals' participation in multiple SDOs. Detailed empirical studies on SDO participation (e.g. Simcoe, 2012; Contreras, 2014; Baron and Gupta, 2018; Ranganathan et al., 2018; Jones et al., 2018) are limited to single SDOs. Consequently, little is known on patterns of co-participation, which could provide some indication on the nature of the relationship between different SDOs. Furthermore, it is difficult to compare the results of studies that use data from different SDOs, as they use different measures and metrics. This study will contribute some of the first empirical evidence on individuals' and firms' co-participation in different SDOs, and will provide comparative evidence on patterns of participation in different SDOs.

In addition to the aforementioned studies of standard development processes in SDOs, some studies have analyzed trends and changes in measures of participation in SDOs over time; in particular after changes of important SDO policies (e.g. Contreras, 2011; Stoll, 2015; Gupta and Effraimidis, 2018). SDOs frequently make changes to their rules; in particular rules on Intellectual Property Rights (IPR) (Tsai and Wright, 2015). In some instances, these changes have been viewed as very significant, such as the introduction of mandatory or potentially mandatory royalty-free licensing policies for SEPs at W3C and OASIS (Stoll, 2015; Baron et al., 2019b), or mandatory ex-ante disclosure of most restrictive licensing terms at VITA (Contreras, 2011). More recently, in 2015, IEEE-SA made several significant changes to its patent policy, including changes to the definition of "reasonable" licensing terms on which owners of SEPs commit to make licenses available to standard implementers.

The change has been widely discussed in the literature (see e.g. Sidak, 2016; Zingales and Kanevskaia; 2016). A number of empirical studies have analyzed trends and changes in measures of innovation and standardization activities related to IEEE-SA standards (Katznelson, 2016; Pohlmann, 2017; Gupta and Effraimidis, 2018). While Katznelson (2016) highlights an increase in the number of patent holders declaring not to be willing to abide by IEEE's patent policy (negative declarations) and a decline in the number of licensing commitments made under the policy, Pohlmann (2017) finds sustained rates of new standardization projects and contributions to standard development at IEEE after the change. Similarly to our study, Gupta and Effraimidis (2018) focus on the working group IEEE 802.11, which is responsible for wireless communication standards, and document a decrease in the number of new projects and an increase in the duration of standardization processes until completion. In this study, I provide evidence on several pronounced changes at IEEE 802.11 occurring after 2015, which may hint at causal effects of the patent policy change that have so far not been documented.

METHODOLOGY

To analyze patterns and trends in SDO participation at different SDOs, I created a database with meeting attendance records at IETF, 3GPP, IEEE-SA, and OneM2M. I selected these SDOs, because they all significantly contribute to the development of IoT-related standards, and all are global organizations with significant participation from private and public actors from many different countries. In addition, each of these organizations provides publicly available meeting attendance logs or records on its website. Other global SDOs that are relevant for IoT-related standards development (e.g. ITU-T and the World Wide Web Consortium, W3C) are not included because of more limited data availability. The sample of four SDOs is thus partly a convenience sample, even though the four SDOs included in the study are certainly among the most relevant SDOs in the field (as reflected in different reviews of IoT-related standardization projects and trends, e.g. Husain et al., 2014 and Palattella et al., 2016).

IETF, formed in 1986, is the standard-setting activity of the Internet Society. IETF has developed many well-known internet-related standards, in particular the different versions of the Internet Protocol (IP). IETF has no membership, and makes standards-related decisions by rough consensus. Standards development at IETF takes place in working groups that mostly operate by open mailing lists. In addition, IETF holds three annual meetings. At each IETF meeting, the active IETF working groups meet, in addition to "birds-of-feather" (BoF) meetings for the creation of new working groups. The IETF website provides attendance lists for every working group meeting, in addition to the general attendance lists of the IETF meeting.[2] For this chapter, I use information from 69 IETF general meeting attendance lists, for a total of 93,355 meeting attendance records (all numbers of attendance records are adjusted for duplicates). The meeting attendance lists provide attendee names, and varying additional information. Depending on the meeting, the list provides information on the attendee's affiliation, country, and contact information (usually e-mail, and sometimes also phone number).

3GPP was established in 1998 as a global consortium of national and regional SDOs in the field of mobile telecommunications. Today, there are seven organizational partners: Association of Radio Industries and Businesses (ARIB; Japan), Alliance for Telecommunications Industry Solutions (ATIS; USA), China Communications Standards Association (CCSA; China); European Telecommunications Standards Institute (ETSI; Europe), Telecommunications Standards Development Society

(TSDSI; India); Telecommunications Technology Association (TTA; South Korea), and Telecommunication Technology Committee (TTC; Japan). Companies and other organizations that are members of one of the organizational partners can participate in 3GPP standards development by becoming 3GPP individual members. As of October 2019, there are 686 individual 3GPP members. 3GPP makes decisions on technical specifications by consensus (requiring at least 71% of the cast votes) of the individual members, and the organizational partners publish 3GPP specifications as standards. 3GPP provides "reports" for each of its working group meetings, including meeting minutes and a spreadsheet with attendee information.[3] The spreadsheet includes the name, contact information, and affiliation ("Organization represented") of registered attendees, and indicates whether the person in fact attended, as well as the role in the meeting (e.g. chair, delegate, etc.). I compiled the information from 2,712 meetings, keeping only records of effective attendees (i.e. "attended" is "yes"; for a total of 202,451 records).

IEEE-SA is an SDO that is part of IEEE, a professional association of electrical and electronics engineers. IEEE-SA offers individual and corporate membership, and IEEE-SA working groups can develop standards as an individual or corporate project. IEEE-SA is best known for the Wireless Local Area Netwok (WLAN) standards developed in the working group 802.11.[4] IEEE-SA's working group 802.11 publishes minutes of its meetings.[5] Many albeit not all of these minutes include attendance lists in the appendix. I collected 177 meeting minutes, including 66 attendance lists with 15,595 attendance records. The data includes attendee names and affiliations.

OneM2M is the most recent organization in the dataset. Similar to 3GPP, it was founded in 2012 as a global partnership of SDOs. Its organizational partners are the same seven SDOs that form 3GPP, plus the Telecommunications Industry Association (TIA). While OneM2M specifically focuses on M2M communication technologies, its institutional setup is similar to 3GPP's. OneM2M publishes documents for each meeting of each of its working groups on a data server.[6] The documents usually include one or several documents with meeting minutes. I collected the most recent document with "meeting" in the document name. The meeting minutes often albeit not always include attendance lists in the appendix. From 877 meeting minutes, I identified 520 attendance lists with 13,970 attendance records. The data includes attendee names, affiliations, and (rarely) contact information (e-mail).

There is thus a total of 325,371 attendance records in the data. Table 1 provides an overview over the distribution of observations and meetings over the four different SDOs.

I carried out significant name cleaning and standardization efforts. First, I carried out the following automatic steps for all names: trim, standardize upper and lower case, remove middle initials, remove titles (e.g. Dr.), remove suffix (e.g. "jr." or "third"), standardize order of names (wherever first, middle and last names are

Table 1. Attendance records and meetings per SDO

Organization	Number records	Percentage	Number meetings	Earliest record	Latest record
3GPP	202,451	62.22%	2,712	1999	2019
IETF	93,355	28.69%	69	1994	2017
IEEE-SA 802.11	15,595	4.79%	66	2007	2017
OneM2M	13,970	4.29%	520	2012	2019
Total	325,371	100.00%	3,367	1994	2019

clearly identifiable, e.g. change "Doe, Jane" to "Jane Doe"), and change foreign language characters (accents, Umlaut, etc.) to their closest English equivalent (e.g. "ø" to "o", "ß" to "ss" etc.).

I then used a number of semi-manual and manual cleaning techniques to further standardize names. In particular, I manually checked all cases where different names were registered with the same phone number, fax number, or e-mail address (excluding generic phone numbers and e-mail addresses with a large number of clearly different names). I further manually checked all cases in which removal of middle names, reversal of orders between first and last name, and/or removal of hyphens would result in different names becoming identical. Furthermore, I manually checked cases in which substitution of full length first names for their common short forms would result in different names becoming identical (e.g. changing Dick to Richard or Bill to William). Finally, I manually went through the full list of names (ordered by both first and last names) to manually identify spelling varieties for the same name. In all these cases, I used additional information, and in particular affiliation and working group, to guide the assessment whether different variations of a name relate to the same individual.

These name standardization efforts result in 40,672 unique individual attendee names. In a small number of cases, I disambiguated names, in particular when there are several attendees with identical names but different affiliations listed as attending the same meeting. Nevertheless, a small proportion of the "unique" names are likely to relate to different individuals with identical names. Standardization efforts are likely to be more reliably for European language names, for which I may more easily identify abbreviations or common spelling variations. There is also more limited variation in Korean and Chinese names, resulting in a greater risk that two individuals enter the database with identical names. As these individuals tend to be affiliated with fewer and larger affiliations, affiliation information is also somewhat less helpful for disambiguation. These limitations have to be borne in mind when interpreting the results.

Next, I standardize and complete (interpolate) affiliation information. When available, I use the individual attendee's affiliation indicated in the attendance record. When this information is not available from the attendance record, I use e-mail addresses to infer the affiliation. I carried out significant manual and semi-automatic cleaning of affiliation names. These standardization efforts result in 6,466 different affiliations. Whenever possible, I standardized affiliation names to the parent entity (e.g. FutureWei to Huawei Technologies Inc., Kellogg School of Management to Northwestern University, and National Institute of Standards and Technology to U.S. Department of Commerce). I manually collected data on 239 mergers or acquisitions in the relevant high-tech sectors, so that the standardization of affiliation names at the parent level is dynamic. Consequently, the number of currently existing independent entities included in the data is somewhat lower than 6,466 (over time, Alcatel, Lucent, and Alcatel-Lucent are all included as independent affiliations in the data, in addition to the current parent entity Nokia).

I then interpolated affiliation information. If affiliation information is missing for one attendance record, but the same individual provided the same affiliation information at both an earlier and a later meeting (at the same or another SDO), I assumed that this was the individual's affiliation at the meeting for which affiliation information is missing. For the purpose of interpolation, I temporarily set a larger number of affiliations to missing, including when individuals identified standards organizations and other non-profit membership organizations as their affiliation. Many individuals have "different hats", and may provide an organization they are member of (or for which they act as chair or board member) as their affiliation, instead of their employer. If possible, I prefer to obtain the identity of the employer, which I consider the "primary" affiliation. If an individual provides the name of a standards organization or other membership organization as affiliation for a meeting, but provided another affiliation information at both an earlier and later meeting, or the company information can be inferred from the e-mail address, I change the affiliation from the standards or membership organization to this other affiliation. If I was not able to interpolate the affiliation, I set affiliation back to the standards or membership organization listed as affiliation in the original attendance records. After interpolation, I have affiliation information for 320,218 attendance records, or 96.7% of the observations (289,108 observations had affiliation information in the original data, and another 26,731 observations included e-mail addresses that could potentially be used to infer affiliations; however, as described, the affiliation from the e-mail address or interpolation sometimes overrides the affiliation information directly included in the original data).

The affiliations with the largest number of attendance records in the data are Nokia (19,886), Ericsson (18,123), Huawei (16,037), Qualcomm (8,866) and NTT (8,442). These figures however ignore substantial changes over time, as well as

Table 2. Individual attendees, affiliations, and meetings per attendee at different SDOs

Organization	Different names	Meetings per name	Different affiliations	Percentage academics
3GPP	14,459	14.00	986	0.14%
IETF	25,483	3.66	5,417	9.90%
IEEE-SA 802.11	1,986	7.85	577	3.79%
OneM2M	1,029	13.57	214	0.30%
Total	40,672	8.00	6,466	2.89%

heterogeneity across SDOs, which I will explore in greater detail. The 20 affiliations with the largest numbers of attendance records are private companies (number 21 is ETRI, a Korean governmental research institute). The 20 top affiliations together account for 151,327, or 46.5% of the attendance records in the data.

I use this information on attendees' affiliations to create categories of attendees by type of affiliation. I manually classified the largest affiliations by number of attendees. For the remainder, I used regular expression searches. I searched for expressions including 'University', 'College', 'School', 'Institute of Technology'; and common abbreviations and translations of these words, to identify academic affiliations. I identified 706 different academic affiliations (at the parent, i.e. university rather than school or laboratory level), with 3,201 different affiliated individuals and 10,173 attendance records. While non-negligible, this academic participation is small in comparison to the overall attendance data. 9,215, i.e. more than 90%, of the academic attendance records are from IETF.

I used expressions of legal form (e.g. "Inc.", "LLC", "GmbH", "S.p.A.", "AB", "Corp.", and "Pte.") to identify private companies. Among private companies, I create a special category for 46 telecommunications network operators, including (in order by number of attendees) NTT, Orange SA, Deutsche Telekom, Vodafone, and AT&T. Expressions such as "ministry", "authority", and "agency" (including their common translations) identify public authorities. I include public authorities in the category "Government", which also includes military and intergovernmental organizations. I create a special category for 41 public research institutes, which includes governmental research laboratories, as well as independent non-profit research organizations with significant government support. The largest among these organizations in terms of attendees (including, in order, the Korea-based Electronics and Telecommunications Research Institute, the Chinese Academy of Telecommunications Technology, the China Academy of Telecommunications Research, and the Taiwan-based Industrial Technology Research Institute) are all

Figure 1. Average attendance per meeting at different SDOs over time, with 95% confidence intervals

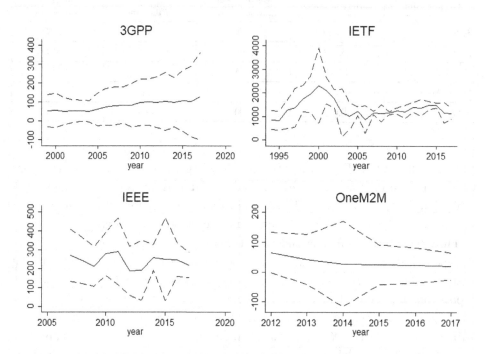

based in Asia. The largest non-Asian entity in this category is the German Fraunhofer Gesellschaft.

Overall, affiliation type is known for 296,524 attendance records, or 91.1% of the total number of records.

Table 2 presents overview information on attendees' affiliations at the different SDOs. The table illustrates the large number of different affiliations represented at IETF as compared to the other SDOs.

EMPIRICAL RESULTS

General Trends in Meeting Attendance

With 325,371 attendance records from 3,367 meetings, the average attendance per meeting in the data is 97 attendees. Given the different nature of the meetings at different SDOs, it is more informative to look at trends over time at individual SDOs.

Figure 1 displays yearly average attendance at the meetings of the four different SDOs over time, along with 95% confidence intervals.

Meeting size is highly variable also within SDOs, especially at 3GPP and OneM2M, where the data spans across meetings of all different working groups of the SDOs. Given the heterogeneity of meetings and the resulting large standard deviations, the only statistically significant time trend is a significant increase of meeting size at IETF up to 2000, followed by a significant decrease up to 2004. Average attendance has been stable at IETF since 2004. Disregarding the variance in attendance counts over different meetings, the average meeting attendance at 3GPP has continuously increased.

In Figure 2, I decompose these trends in attendance into two different contributing factors: the number of different individuals that attend at least one SDO meeting per year, and the average number of meetings each individual attendee attends per SDO and per year. IETF draws a significantly larger number of different individuals than other SDOs, but individuals attend fewer meetings per year (as there are only three meetings per year to attend, the variance among individuals is also significantly lower). At three SDOs, the average number of meetings per year and per individual

Figure 2. Trends in number of different attendees and average number of meetings per attendee and year, per SDO

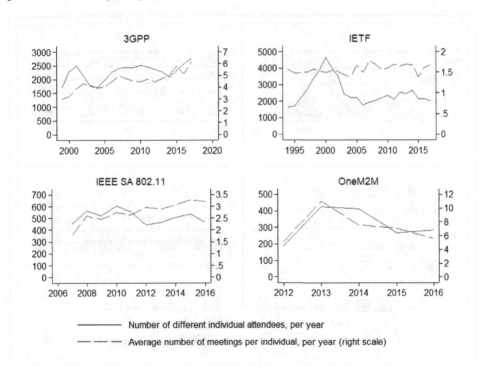

——————— Number of different individual attendees, per year

— — — — Average number of meetings per individual, per year (right scale)

has increased over time: pronouncedly at 3GPP and IEEE-SA, and more moderately at IETF. There is an apparent decline at OneM2M, but the fact that more recent meeting attendance records from OneM2M are more often missing affects such comparisons over time. At IEEE-SA, the increase in the average number of meetings per individual attendee offsets a slight decrease in the number of different individuals participating in IEEE 802.11 meetings. The divergence in these two trends is more informative than the trends themselves, as both are similarly affected by incomplete information. Incomplete information is a lesser concern for IETF and 3GPP, where attendance information is more systematically available over longer periods of time. The spike in IETF meeting attendance observed in Figure 1 can be clearly attributed to an increase in the number of different individuals participating in the meetings, whereas average attendance counts have remained stable through the spike and the subsequent drop.

There is relatively little systematic evidence on the demographics of individual SDO participants. One important variable is the type of attendees' affiliations. In Figure 3, I compare the composition of the different SDOs' attendee population by affiliation type, and its evolution over time. The composition of attendee populations at all SDOs, and particularly those that I observe over longer periods of time (3GPP

Figure 3. Trends in types of attendees' affiliations at different SDOs

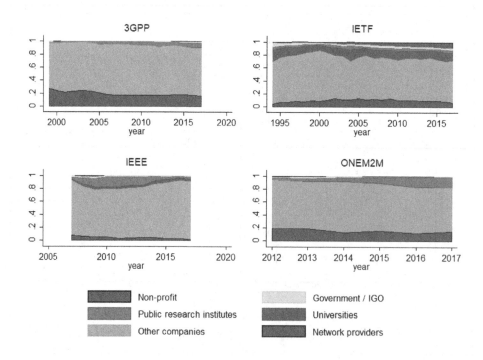

and IETF), is quiet stable. Nevertheless, there are some significant and interesting evolutions in the data.

Most attendees at all SDOs are affiliated with private companies. Nevertheless, in 3GPP and OneM2M, where the share of private companies was initially particularly large (and close to 100% at 3GPP), other affiliation types (and in particular public research institutes) have come to play an increasingly important role over time. Network operators, which have historically dominated the development of international telecommunication technology standards through bodies such as the International Telegraph and Telephone Consultative Committee (CCITT) (Russell, 2014), still play an important role, especially at 3GPP and OneM2M, even though their share in attendee affiliations in these organizations never exceeded 25% and continues to decline. Network operators however extended their participation in IETF until 2008. Over the last ten years, their share at IETF declined again, while they almost vanished from IEEE 802.11.

At IETF, the body with the most diverse set of attendees in terms of affiliation types, the share of company affiliates significantly rose during the spike in IETF meeting attendance in the late 1990s up to 2001. This came at the expense of other traditional IETF constituencies, and in particular academics and government officials. After 2001, corporate participation in IETF meetings declined more pronouncedly than participation by attendees with other types of affiliations. While universities and government did not fully recover the share that they held among IETF meeting attendees in the mid-1990s, a larger share of individuals now report affiliations with non-profit or membership organizations, and (to a lesser extent) public research institutes. Given that IETF is based on individual participation, individuals with "multiple hats" can choose more freely than at other SDOs which affiliation they report. It is thus likely that a significant number of the individuals reporting affiliations with non-profit or membership organizations also have an affiliation with another organization (which in many cases is likely to be a private company).

At IEEE-SA 802.11, participation by universities and public research institutes significantly increased between 2007 and 2013, but has strongly decreased since 2014. This trend reversal coincides with the change in the IEEE-SA patent policy, which was perceived by many observers to disadvantage entities relying on patent licensing revenue to monetize their contributions to standard development.

Patterns and Trends in SDO Co-Attendance

An important benefit of collecting similar participation data from various SDO is the possibility to study patterns of co-participation, i.e. individuals and organizations participating in multiple SDOs at once. Co-participation patterns have important implications for the degree of specialization of individuals and organizations. Larger

Table 3. Co-attendance patterns between SDOs on individual level

	3GPP	IETF	IEEE	ONEM2M	unique
3GPP		193	146	177	4,340
		4.01%	3.03%	3.67%	90.10%
IETF	193		50	51	6,152
	3.01%		0.78%	0.79%	95.86%
IEEE	146	50		16	805
	14.76%	5.01%		1.61%	80.90%
ONEM2M	177	51	16		660
	20.21%	5.82%	1.83%		75.34%
N	4,817	6,418	995	876	11,957 95.6%

co-participation for instance indicates greater mobility, suggesting that standardization efforts could more easily move from one SDO to the other. So far however, there has been no systematic evidence on the extent of such co-participation in different SDOs.

As a first step, I make a static assessment of co-participation. I set a time window in which I observe attendance in each of the four SDOs in the data, and analyze how many individuals participate in only one or multiple of the four SDOs during that time window. I set a five year time window from 2012 to 2016, inclusive. 12,512 individuals attended a meeting of at least one of the four SDOs during these five years. The results are presented in Table 3. While 7,410 or 59.2% of these individuals attended multiple meetings during this time, 11,957 or 95.6% of these individuals only attended meetings at a single SDO. 516 or 4.1% of the individuals attended meetings at two different SDOs, and only 39 (0.31%) attended meetings at three different SDOs. Even though these SDOs work on related technologies and all participate in developing the IoT, there is thus only very modest overlap between the individuals participating in the different SDOs.

Attendance at IETF is least correlated with attendance in other SDOs in the sample. 95.9% of the attendees of IETF meetings from 2012 to 2016 did not attend a single meeting at any of the other three SDOs over this same time. To some extent, this higher uniqueness is a mechanical result of the larger number of IETF attendees. Since there are many more IETF and 3GPP attendees than IEEE or ONEM2M attendees in the data, it is more likely for attendees of one of the latter organizations to also show up in the attendance records of another SDO. Nevertheless, even though IETF has a larger number of attendees than 3GPP, both IEEE and ONEM2M attendees are more likely to also attend a 3GPP meeting than an IETF meeting. Furthermore, 3GPP attendees are almost as likely to attend an IEEE-SA 802.11 or ONEM2M

Table 4. Co-attendance patterns between SDOs on affiliation parent level (angle coefficients)

SDO	3GPP	IETF	IEEE	OneM2M
3GPP		0.4826	0.5926	0.6881
IETF	0.4826		0.4105	0.4822
IEEE	0.5926	0.4105		0.6207
OneM2M	0.6881	0.4822	0.6207	

meeting as an IETF meeting, even though the overall number of attendees for these SDOs is up to seven times smaller. It is also possible to observe that OneM2M attendance is more correlated with participation in both 3GPP and IETF than is the case for IEEE. The large overlap between OneM2M and 3GPP is not surprising, as both OneM2M and 3GPP are partnerships of essentially the same organizational members. Rather, given the close institutional proximity between these SDOs, it is surprising that a large majority of attendees nevertheless specializes on only one of these organizations.

While the previous analysis assesses co-attendance on an individual level, I next analyze co-attendance of different SDOs' meetings on the affiliation level. Using the same time window as before, and removing attendance records with unknown affiliation, I count attendance counts per affiliation and SDO, and compute the angle coefficient between SDOs at the parent level.[7] The angle coefficient is a commonly used distance measure (Benner and Waldfogel, 2008). An angle coefficient of 1 would indicate that the same set of companies participate in the same proportions in two SDOs, whereas an angle coefficient of 0 indicates no overlap between affiliations participating in two different SDOs.

The results presented in Table 4 confirm the co-attendance patterns observed on an individual attendee level. To a large extent, the same firms participate in 3GPP, IEEE, and OneM2M, whereas participation in IETF is more distinct from participation in the other SDOs. The highest participation similarity rate (the highest angle coefficient) is observed between 3GPP and OneM2M.

The results discussed so far represent a static picture of co-participation in the relatively short time window from 2012 to 2016. In the following, I explore trends and shifts in these co-participation patterns over longer periods of time. I thus repeat the same analyses as before, but only take into account co-participation in different SDOs in the same year. First, I analyze co-participation at an individual level, i.e. the share of each SDO's attendees that also attended another SDO's meetings during the same year. The results are presented in Figure 4.

Figure 4. Trends in co-attendance of different SDOs, at individual level

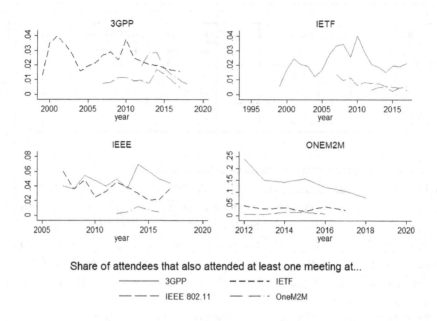

Figure 5. Trends in co-attendance of different SDOs, at the affiliation level (angle coefficients)

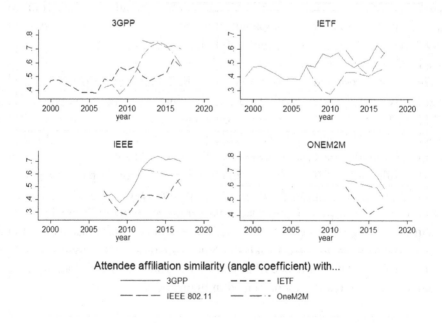

The analysis is constrained by the different observation periods for the different SDOs in the sample. The longest common observation period is between IETF and 3GPP, for which we can observe co-participation patterns from 1999 to 2018. The share of SDO attendees that attended meetings of both SDOs increased from 1999 to 2011. The increase is more pronounced as percentage of IETF attendees than as percentage of 3GPP attendees, because the population of IETF attendees shrunk significantly over this period. IETF attendees also participating in 3GPP were thus less likely to discontinue their IETF participation during this period than other IETF attendees. Since 2011, co-participation between these SDOs has declined and is now at a similar level to 1999.

While we only observe shorter periods of co-participation patterns involving other SDOs, there are some interesting trends. While the percentage of 3GPP attendees that also attended an IEEE 802.11 meeting in the same year significantly increased up to 2014, this co-participation sharply decreased in 2015 and the following years. The share of IEEE-SA attendees also attending a 3GPP meeting in the same year significantly decreased from 6.5% in 2014 to 4.5% in 2016, whereas the share of IEEE-SA attendees also attending an IETF meeting increased from 2.1 to 3.8%. There is thus some evidence for a change in the composition of the population of IEEE 802.11 attendees in the years following the IEEE patent policy update. One possible interpretation is that after the policy update, which was opposed by several patent-centric companies, attendees with 3GPP experience were more likely to discontinue their participation in IEEE 802.11 (it is also possible that attendees with a focus on IEEE discontinued participation in 3GPP).

Perhaps the most pronounced evolution in co-attendance over time is a significant decline in co-attendance between 3GPP and OneM2M. While co-attendance between these SDOs was originally widespread (in 2012, almost 25% of OneM2M attendees also attended a 3GPP meeting in the same year), this co-attendance quickly and significantly declined over time. This pattern may indicate that standard development at OneM2M becomes increasingly independent of 3GPP, even though both organizations share most of their organizational membership.

Once again, I also carry out a co-attendance analysis on the affiliation level, computing angle coefficients to measure attendance similarity across SDOs. The findings are presented in Figure 5. At an affiliation level, co-attendance between 3GPP and IETF also increased from 1999 to 2011, but did not subsequently decrease. This suggests that while individuals increasingly specialized between these SDOs, many companies continued to be active in both SDOs. Participation similarity between IETF and other SDOs has now reached a level that is comparable to the levels observed among the other SDOs.

At an affiliation level, there is an even more pronounced increase in co-participation between 3GPP and IEEE-SA from 2007 to 2014. This strong and significant increase in participation similarity leveled off after the IEEE patent policy update. Participation similarity between IEEE 802.11 and IETF in turn increased after 2015. While these descriptive findings cannot prove causal effects, they resonate with informal analyses of the nature of the debate within IEEE over the patent policy. Many of the companies that vocally opposed the 2015 changes to IEEE's patent policy had long been among the leading contributors to 3GPP standard development, where it is more common for companies to rely on royalties for SEPs as a main incentive for participating in standards development.

Overall, with the exception of OneM2M, affiliation level co-participation was at a significantly higher level in 2017 than at the beginning of the respective observation periods.

Concentration of the Affiliations of SDO Attendees

The last variable in my analysis of recent trends in SDO attendance patterns is concentration of attendees' affiliations. The mere numbers of affiliations represented in the data are testimony of the diversity of organizations involved in standard development. Nevertheless, many of these affiliations are only very marginally represented, whereas technology companies such as Huawei, Nokia, Ericsson, Qualcomm, and Samsung employ hundreds (or, in the case of Huawei, thousands) of individual attendees and are represented in meetings of every SDO working group in the data.

To compare levels of affiliation concentration among SDOs and over time, I compute the Herfindahl-Hirschman Index (HHI) of affiliations over attendance records. I thus calculate the percentage of an affiliation among the attendance records per SDO and year, and then compute the sum over the square of these percentages. An HHI of 1 indicates full concentration, i.e. all attendees were affiliated with the same affiliation, whereas an HHI close to 0 indicates that attendance is highly dispersed among different affiliations (no two attendees had the same affiliation). Similar to the angle coefficient analysis, I only take into account attendance records with known affiliation.

Overall, affiliation concentration of SDO attendees is low; and the HHI has rarely exceeded 0.05 at any SDO in the sample. This is another indicator for the healthy diversity of organizations represented in standards development. Over time, affiliation concentration has however evolved very differently at the different SDOs in our sample. 3GPP had initially relatively high levels of concentration, but has become significantly more diverse after 2003. IETF meetings on the other hand, which historically had attendees with particularly diverse affiliations, have seen a modest increase in affiliation concentration.

Figure 6. Trends in affiliation concentration at different SDOs

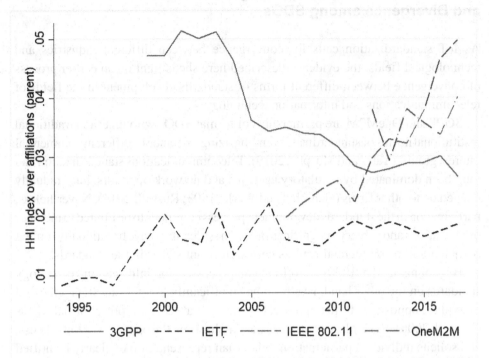

The most significant evolution in affiliation concentration has happened at IEEE 802.11. In 2007, 802.11 attendance was almost as diverse as the general attendance at IETF meetings. Nevertheless, from 2007 to 2014, the HHI increased from 0.0195 to 0.0497. Given that the IEEE data only covers a single working group, whereas the data from other SDOs spans across different working groups, the higher affiliation concentration in 802.11 is not per se surprising. Nevertheless, this difference in the nature of the data does not explain the steep trend depicted in Figure 6. Clearly, over the last years, participation in 802.11 has become increasingly driven by a smaller number of companies. This trend has significantly accelerated after 2014.

DISCUSSION

In this chapter, I presented some of the first systematic empirical evidence on individual SDO meeting attendees based on data spanning across multiple important SDOs and longer observation periods. The presented descriptive evidence sheds light on several important issues and ongoing discussions that are relevant to the future of standards development, in particular with respect to IoT technologies.

Patterns of Institutional Convergence and Divergence among SDOs

As IoT standardization calls for convergence between different industries and technological fields, the evidence described here sheds light on an earlier process of convergence between different forms of standards development in the fields of telecommunications and information technology.

3GPP and OneM2M are partnerships of formal SDOs with inherited traditional institutional norms of standardization emphasizing a balance of different commercial interest groups (Yates and Murphy, 2019). Telecommunications standardization had long been dominated by regulatory agencies and network operators, but gradually opened up to other firms (Genschel and Werle, 1993; Russell, 2014). Nevertheless, participation in the standards development process continues to be limited to member organizations and subject to significant fees. These features have traditionally limited participation to commercial entities with significant stakes in the standards.

Beginning in the 1980s, development processes for information technology standards on the other hand have become significantly less formal. IETF emerged in explicit opposition to the "political" processes at ISO and other formal SDOs (Russell, 2006). IETF places much greater emphasis on the openness of the process, and solicits individual participation rather than representation of clearly identified stakeholders (Russell, 2014). Most of the technical work takes place online, and online participation requires neither membership nor participation fees. Meeting attendance, while subject to a fee, is open to any interested individual. In its early years, most IETF participants were government officials (particularly US Department of Defense) or academics (Russell, 2006). Nevertheless, Simcoe (2012) and others have documented an increasing role of corporate participation in IETF. Waguespack and Fleming (2009) find that it is profitable for small and young entrepreneurial firms to participate in IETF meetings to gain information about recent technological developments.

IEEE-SA embodies yet another tradition of standards development, the standardization activities of engineering societies with their large and dispersed individual membership. Similar to IETF, IEEE-SA encourages individual participation. Nevertheless, IEEE-SA has opened up to company-based participation, and standards development can now take place in either individual- or organization-based mode.

The attendance patterns at the beginning of the respective observation periods still reflect these different historical origins: 3GPP and OneM2M had overwhelmingly corporate participants, and higher levels of affiliation concentration, whereas IETF and IEEE-SA 802.11 displayed a (somewhat) larger share of non-corporate attendees and a greater dispersion of attendee affiliations. Nevertheless, the trends in the attendance data document a further erosion of these differences. Non-corporate participation in 3GPP and OneM2M has significantly increased, particularly at the expense of network operators. At the same time, attendees' affiliation concentration has continuously decreased at 3GPP, while increasing slowly and continuously at IETF, and more sharply at IEEE 802.11. In all these SDOs, attendees predominantly but not exclusively represent private companies; and processes are now similarly diverse in the four SDOs in terms of represented organizations. This convergence is also reflected in the rising co-participation of the same organizations in different SDOs. To a significantly larger extent than just 10 or 15 years ago, the same organizations are represented in 3GPP, IEEE-SA 802.11, and IETF meetings.

At the same time, there is no universal tendency towards blurring the boundaries between SDOs. The stark decline in individuals' and organizations' co-participation in 3GPP and OneM2M over a short period of time is evidence of the formation of a new independent organization with its own social networks and commercial stakeholders. Furthermore, among all SDOs in the sample, participation of the same individuals in different SDOs is rare, and has not become more common over time.

Patterns of Individuals' and Organizations' Co-Participation in Different SDOs

Even though the same companies are often represented in the meetings of the four SDOs in our sample, it is rare for individuals to participate in multiple SDOs. Furthermore, as we have seen, this distinction has deepened over time, as the affiliations of attendees at IETF, IEEE-SA and 3GPP have become more similar over time, whereas attendee overlap at the individual level has not significantly increased.

To some extent, participation in different SDOs is likely to require very different technical knowledge and expertise. Nevertheless, individuals tend to specialize on single SDOs even among IEEE-SA 802.11, 3GPP, and OneM2M, which all develop wireless communication technology standards. The sharp decline in individuals' co-attendance in OneM2M and 3GPP nicely reflects this process of specialization. While both organizations draw from the same pool of organizational partners, a relatively autonomous "OneM2M community" seems to have emerged in only a few years. This specialization at individual level is consistent with existing evidence on the importance of social networks that individuals create through participation in an SDO (Isaak, 2006; Dokko and Rosenkopf, 2010). It also suggests that individuals participating in a standard development effort acquire project-specific technical expertise that is difficult to transpose to a different standards development project in a different SDO.

This specialization at individual level raises questions about the low and declining level of specialization at company level. Existing theoretical models of firms' strategies with respect to SDO participation predict that firms pick the SDO with the most attractive rules, and that powerful companies may use competition among SDOs to obtain concessions (such as overly lenient Intellectual Property Rights policies; Lerner and Tirole, 2006; Chiao et al., 2007). Furthermore, theoretical economic analysis suggests that a main benefit of standardization is to promote modularity and specialization (e.g. Spulber, 2013). Given that the four SDOs in my sample constitute different institutions with separate networks, different rules and traditions, and different individual participants, one may thus have expected increasing specialization among companies according to their preferred standardization rules or their relative technological advantage in the different standard development processes.

The significant and increasing extent of participation of the same companies in different SDOs thus suggests that there are benefits to participation in multiple SDOs that outweigh incentives for specialization. Some of these benefits may be strategic. Firms co-participating with other firms in multiple SDOs on multiple projects may form strategic relationships, which may increase the participating firms' capacity to influence different standardization outcomes (Leiponen, 2008; Ranganathan and Rosenkopf, 2014). Multiplying co-participation with the same partners in multiple projects may also reduce firms' incentives to behave opportunistically, if such opportunistic conduct negatively affects the firm's standing in other SDOs (Larouche and Schuett, 2019). The fact that the same set of companies co-participate in different SDOs thus helps to maintain SDO participants' incentives to collaborate, and reinforces trust among different participants.

In addition to these strategic factors, participation by the same firms in different SDOs may facilitate information flows between different standardization projects, and improve the coordination between different SDOs. These firms may direct their individual employees to avoid wasteful duplication of efforts, and encourage them to complement rather than compete with each other. The emerging literature on the role of individuals in standards development has shed light on the boundary-spanning role of individual working group participants, which can facilitate coordination between firms (Isaak, 2006; Dokko and Rosenkopf, 2010). At the same time, firms employing individuals that participate in different SDOs may play a boundary-spanning role between SDOs and SDO working groups, and facilitate the coordination between different standard development projects. While detailed case studies have shed light on coordination processes among individuals in SDO working groups, there is relatively little evidence on firms' internal organization of their SDO participation, which may shed light on the coordination function of firms and other benefits of firms' involvement in multiple SDOs. This seems to be an important task for future research.

IEEE-SA Patent Policy Change

The recent trends in IEEE 802.11 participation have attracted significant interest, as researchers and practitioners have searched for evidence for causal effects of the 2015 patent policy update (Pohlmann, 2017; Gupta and Effraimidis, 2018). While the descriptive findings presented in this chapter cannot provide such causal evidence, they nevertheless highlight several previously unreported significant trends and trend breaks that occurred over the recent years.

While attendance at 802.11 meetings has remained stable or increased slightly from 2007 to 2017, this attendance has become significantly less diverse in terms of individuals and affiliations. Until 2014, IEEE 802.11 was also increasingly driven by affiliations that also strongly participate in 3GPP, reaching very high levels of participation similarity. More recently, and in particular after 2014, this trend towards greater participation similarity with 3GPP has discontinued, whereas participation similarity with IETF has recovered. The trend towards greater affiliation concentration however has not reversed, but rather strongly accelerated. Finally, the share of attendees affiliated with universities or public research institutes has significantly increased from 2007 to 2014, but since 2014, these "R&D specialists" have reduced the extent of their participation.

It is possible to tentatively interpret these evolutions as possible indications for causal effects of the patent policy change. The patent policy change was seen by many observers as placing greater restrictions on the licensing and assertion of SEPs related to IEEE standards and disadvantaging companies that rely on SEP licensing for a substantial share of their revenue. The significant decline in the participation by universities and public research institutes in IEEE 802.11 at a time when they expanded their participation in the other SDOs is consistent with this concern. Universities and public research institutes are R&D specialists with little or no downstream presence in industries where the standards are implemented. Similarly, the fact that IEEE-SA 802.11 participants became less similar to 3GPP participants (albeit at a high level of similarity) and more similar to IETF participants may indicate a gradual change in the composition of IEEE-SA's attendee population. SEP licensing has traditionally played a more important role at 3GPP and in telecommunication standardization in general, as compared to IETF and other internet-oriented SDOs.

Nevertheless, these descriptive findings do not constitute causal evidence. All the studies on the effects of the IEEE-SA patent policy change are limited by the fact that the patent policy change did not occur exogenously, but through the endogenous decisions of IEEE-SA and IEEE governance bodies. There were significant changes in IEEE-SA attendance patterns prior to the policy change, and some of these pre-existing trends continued after 2014 (for instance, the significant increase in affiliation concentrations). The endogenous nature of the change and the existence of pre-existing trends challenge any causal interpretation of observed changes after 2014. For instance, the patent policy change may partly have been a reaction to some of the prior trends also highlighted in this analysis, such as the significantly increasing share of IEEE-SA attendees affiliated with R&D specialists and firms also participating in 3GPP. The presented descriptive findings can only provide tentative indications for such explanations; a more comprehensive analysis with an explicit identification strategy would be required to disentangle the different causal effects.

CONCLUSION

I have used publicly available meeting attendance records to study attendance patterns and recent trends at some of the SDOs that are poised to lead IoT standards development. Over the past few decades, some of the basic characteristics of standard development in these SDOs have been remarkably stable. In spite of the increasing importance of the standards developed by these SDOs, the population of engineers participating in their working groups has not significantly increased. In most SDOs however, the meeting workload of individual attendees has increased. Furthermore, while there is increasing overlap between the organizations represented in IEEE 802.11, IETF, and 3GPP meetings, most individual SDO attendees continue to specialize on single SDOs. Also, SDOs continue to draw participants from a remarkably large and diverse set of companies and other organizations. While some new significant players have emerged over this period, there is no generalized trend towards greater concentration of attendee affiliations.

Nevertheless, this seeming stability in the overall data masks pronounced changes occurring in individual SDOs. Some of these changes may illustrate slow processes of institutional convergence. The affiliations of IETF and 3GPP attendees, originally perhaps the most different SDOs in our sample, have become more similar over time in terms of type and diversity. In the case of OneM2M however, which arose from the same set of organizational partners as 3GPP, the data illustrates a process of quickly increasing specialization on both the level of individual attendees and their affiliations. Finally, significant changes and trend reversals in IEEE-SA 802.11 participation patterns may hint at causes and causal effects of the 2015 patent policy change.

These descriptive findings, and the underlying data, open many opportunities for in-depth quantitative research. Future research may investigate the causes behind some of the trends and changes observed in this chapter. In particular, this research may corroborate the existence of a link between the IEEE patent policy update and the observed evolutions in IEEE 802.11 attendance. Another important task for future empirical research is to investigate the consequences of the strongly increased participation by Huawei and other Chinese actors in international SDOs. This task has recently become even more important, as the US government has voiced its strong concerns about Huawei's prominent and quickly strengthening role in some of the technological areas perceived as key for the future IoT. Future research should combine data on working group meeting attendance with other detailed measures of SDO participation, such as submissions of technical documents and leadership roles in SDOs and SDO working groups.

REFERENCES

Bar, T., & Leiponen, A. (2014). Committee composition and networking in standard setting: The case of wireless telecommunications. *Journal of Economics & Management Strategy, 23*(1), 1–23. doi:10.1111/jems.12044

Baron, Contreras, Husovec, Larouche, & Thumm. (2019b). *Making the Rules: The Governance of Standard Development Organizations and their Policies on Intellectual Property Rights.* JRC Science for Policy Report, EUR 29655.

Baron, J., & Gupta, K. (2018). Unpacking 3GPP standards. *Journal of Economics & Management Strategy, 27*(3), 433–461. doi:10.1111/jems.12258

Baron, J., Li, C., & Nasirov, S. (2019a). *Why Do R&D-Intensive Firms Participate in Standards Organizations? The Role of Patents and Product-Market Position.* Working paper.

Baron, J., Meniere, Y., & Pohlmann, T. (2014). Standards, consortia, and innovation. *International Journal of Industrial Organization, 36*, 22–35. doi:10.1016/j.ijindorg.2014.05.004

Baron, J., & Spulber, D. F. (2018). Technology standards and standard setting organizations: Introduction to the Searle Center Database. *Journal of Economics & Management Strategy, 27*(3), 462–503. doi:10.1111/jems.12257

Bekkers, R., Bongard, R., & Nuvolari, A. (2011). An empirical study on the determinants of essential patent claims in compatibility standards. *Research Policy, 40*(7), 1001–1015. doi:10.1016/j.respol.2011.05.004

Benner, M., & Waldfogel, J. (2008). Close to you? Bias and precision in patent-based measures of technological proximity. *Research Policy, 37*(9), 1556–1567. doi:10.1016/j.respol.2008.05.011

Bernard, H., & Wolff, D. (2004). Enjeux & déterminants de l'implication des entreprises dans le processus de normalisation. *Revue d'Economie Industrielle, 108*(4), 21–40.

Blind, K., & Mangelsdorf, A. (2016). Motives to standardize: Empirical evidence from Germany. *Technovation, 48*, 13–24. doi:10.1016/j.technovation.2016.01.001

Blind, K., Pohlisch, J., & Zi, A. (2018). Publishing, patenting, and standardization: Motives and barriers of scientists. *Research Policy, 47*(7), 1185–1197. doi:10.1016/j.respol.2018.03.011

Blind, K., & Thumm, N. (2004). Interrelation between patenting and standardisation strategies: Empirical evidence and policy implications. *Research Policy, 33*(10), 1583–1598. doi:10.1016/j.respol.2004.08.007

Chiao, B., Lerner, J., & Tirole, J. (2007). The rules of standard-setting organizations: An empirical analysis. *The Rand Journal of Economics, 38*(4), 905–930. doi:10.1111/j.0741-6261.2007.00118.x

Contreras, J. L. (2011). *An empirical study of the effects of ex ante licensing disclosure policies on the development of voluntary technical standards.* National Institute of Standards and Technology, No. GCR (2011): 11-934.

Contreras, J. L. (2014). Divergent patterns of engagement in Internet standardization: Japan, Korea and China. *Telecommunications Policy, 38*(10), 914–932. doi:10.1016/j.telpol.2014.09.005

DeLacey, B. J. (2006). *Strategic behavior in standard-setting organizations.* Academic Press.

Delcamp, H., & Leiponen, A. (2014). Innovating standards through informal consortia: The case of wireless telecommunications. *International Journal of Industrial Organization, 36*, 36–47. doi:10.1016/j.ijindorg.2013.07.004

Dokko, G., & Rosenkopf, L. (2010). Mobility of Technical Professionals and Firm Influence in Wireless Standards Committees. *Organization Science, 21*(3), 677–695. doi:10.1287/orsc.1090.0470

Gandal, Gantman, & Genesove. (2004). *Intellectual property and standardization committee participation in the US modem industry.* Academic Press.

Genschel, P., & Werle, R. (1993). From National Hierarchies to International Standardization: Modal Changes in the Governance of Telecommunications. *Journal of Public Policy, 13*(3), 203–225. doi:10.1017/S0143814X00001045

Gupta & Effraimidis. (2018). *IEEE Patent Policy Revisions: An Empirical Examination of Impact.* Available at SSRN 3173799

Husain, Prasad, Kunz, Papageorgiou, & Song. (2014). Recent Trends in Standards Related to the Internet of Things and Machine-to-Machine Communications. *Journal of Information Communication Convergence Engineering, 12*(4), 228-236.

Isaak, J. (2006). The Role of Individuals and Social Capital in POSIX Standardization. *International Journal of IT Standards and Standardization Research, 4*(1), 1–23. doi:10.4018/jitsr.2006010101

Jakobs, K., Procter, R., & Williams, R. (2001, May). The Making of Standards: Looking Inside the Working Groups. *IEEE Communications Magazine, 39*(4), 102–107. doi:10.1109/35.917511

Kang, B., & Motohashi, K. (2015). Essential intellectual property rights and inventors' involvement in standardization. *Research Policy, 44*(2), 483–492. doi:10.1016/j.respol.2014.10.012

Katznelson, R. D. (2016). *The IEEE controversial policy on Standard Essential Patents–the empirical record since adoption.* Presentation to the Symposium on Antitrust, Standard Essential Patents, and the Fallacy of the Anticommons Tragedy.

Larouche, P., & Schuett, F. (2019). Repeated interaction in standard setting. *Journal of Economics & Management Strategy, 28*(3), 488–509. doi:10.1111/jems.12287

Leiponen, A. (2008). Competing through cooperation: The organization of standard setting in wireless telecommunications. *Management Science, 54*(11), 1904–1919. doi:10.1287/mnsc.1080.0912

Lerner, J., & Tirole, J. (2006). A model of forum shopping. *The American Economic Review, 96*(4), 1091–1113. doi:10.1257/aer.96.4.1091

Lerner, J., & Tirole, J. (2015). Standard-essential patents. *Journal of Political Economy, 123*(3), 547–586. doi:10.1086/680995

Palattella, M. R., Dohler, M., Grieco, A., Rizzo, G., Torsner, J., Engel, T., & Ladid, L. (2016). Internet of Things in the 5G Era: Enablers, Architecture, and Business Models. *IEEE Journal on Selected Areas in Communications, 34*(3), 510–527. doi:10.1109/JSAC.2016.2525418

Pohlmann, T. (2017). *Empirical study on patenting and standardization activities at IEEE.* Available at https://www.iplytics.com/wp-content/uploads/2018/01/IPlytics_2017_Patenting-and-standardization-activities-at-IEEE.pdf

Ranganathan, R., Ghosh, A., & Rosenkopf, L. (2018). Competition–cooperation interplay during multifirm technology coordination: The effect of firm heterogeneity on conflict and consensus in a technology standards organization. *Strategic Management Journal, 39*(12), 3193–3221. doi:10.1002mj.2786

Ranganathan, R., & Rosenkopf, L. (2014). Do ties really bind? The effect of knowledge and commercialization networks on opposition to standards. *Academy of Management Journal, 57*(2), 515–540. doi:10.5465/amj.2011.1064

Riillo, C. F. A. (2014). *ICT Standardization and use of ICT standards: a firm level analysis*. MPRA Paper No. 63436.

Russell, A. (2006). 'Rough Consensus and Running Code' and the Internet-OSI Standards War. *IEEE Annals of the History of Computing, 28*, 48–61. doi:10.1109/MAHC.2006.42

Russell, A. (2014). *Open Standards and the Digital Age – History, Ideology, and Networks*. Cambridge University Press. doi:10.1017/CBO9781139856553

Sidak, J. G. (2016). Testing for Bias to Suppress Royalties for Standard-Essential Patents. *Criterion J. on Innovation, 1*, 301.

Simcoe, T. (2012). Standard setting committees: Consensus governance for shared technology platforms. *The American Economic Review, 102*(1), 305–336. doi:10.1257/aer.102.1.305

Stoll, T. P. (2014). Are You Still in?–The Impact of Licensing Requirements on the Composition of Standards Setting Organizations. In *The Impact of Licensing Requirements on the Composition of Standards Setting Organizations*. Max Planck Institute for Innovation & Competition Research Paper 14-18.

Tsai, J., & Wright, J. D. (2015). Standard setting, intellectual property rights, and the role of antitrust in regulating incomplete contracts. *Antitrust Law Journal, 80*(1), 157–188.

Waguespack, D. M., & Fleming, L. (2009). Scanning the commons? Evidence on the benefits to startups participating in open standards development. *Management Science, 55*(2), 210–223. doi:10.1287/mnsc.1080.0944

Zi, A., & Blind, K. (2015). Researchers' participation in standardisation: A case study from a public research institute in Germany. *The Journal of Technology Transfer, 40*(2), 346–360. doi:10.100710961-014-9370-y

Zingales & Kanevskaia. (2016). The IEEE-SA patent policy update under the lens of EU competition law. *European Competition Journal, 12*(2-3), 195-235.

ENDNOTES

[1] A large share of the literature on firm participation in SDOs has concentrated on the relationship between firms' patenting and standardization strategies (e.g. Blind and Thumm, 2004; Gandal et al., 2004; Bekkers et al., 2011; Baron et al., 2019a).

[2] e.g. https://www.ietf.org/proceedings/86/attendee.html

[3] e.g. https://www.3gpp.org/ftp/TSG_RAN/WG1_RL1/TSGR1_92b/Report/

[4] Other IEEE-SA working groups are also relevant for IoT standardization, such as 802.15 developing standards for Wireless Personal Area Networks (WPAN) used in technologies such as Bluetooth and Zigbee.

[5] mentor.ieee.org//802.11/dcn/17/11-17-0339-01-0000-minutes-working-group-march-2017.doc

[6] http://ftp.onem2m.org/Meetings/ARC/2014%20meetings/20140626_ARC11.1/

[7] To measure similarity in attendance affiliations between SDO i and SDO j, I count attendance records $a_{i,k}$ by affiliation k and SDO. The angle coefficient is then defined as $\dfrac{\sum_k a_{i,k} a_{j,k}}{\sqrt{\sum_k a_{i,k}^2 \sum_k a_{j,k}^2}}$

Section 3

Shedding Some More Light on ISO9001

Chapter 6

Does Innovation Flourish With the Implementation of Certified Management Systems?
A Study in the European Context

Vasileios Mavroeidis
Hellenic Open University, Greece

Petros E. Maravelakis
Department of Business Administration, University of Piraeus, Greece

Katarzyna Tarnawska
European Commission, Belgium

ABSTRACT

Existing literature states that standardization and certification are not only crucial for enterprises, but they have a positive impact on productivity, international trade, innovation, and competition as well. This research employs data derived by the European Innovation Union Scoreboard and the International Standardization Organization from 2005 to 2014 to investigate the relation between innovation and certified quality management systems according to ISO 9001. Using suitable panel data analysis, the authors analyse the data gathered form a panel accounting for the different countries and different years. The main result of this study is that we are able to provide evidence to policymakers, academics, and entrepreneurs that there is a statistically significant relationship between innovation and certified quality management systems. The originality of this chapter stems from the fact that up to now, to the authors' knowledge, the impact of ISO 9001 on innovation has not been examined in the European context.

DOI: 10.4018/978-1-7998-2181-6.ch006

1. INTRODUCTION

Quality may be considered as a systemic way to express customer expectations in a changing environment. Quality Management Systems (QMS), derived by the scientific field of Quality, emphasize to organisational systems rather than to product or services specifications. ISO 9001 (International Organisation for Standardization) is one of the most popular standards addressing QMS leading to Certified Quality Management Systems. It should be noted that certification of QMS (i.e. ISO 9001) is part of the National Quality Infrastructures (NQI) which all together form the competitive advantage of an economy.

Research on the impact assessment of QMS as part of NQI is carried out on macroeconomic, sector and firm levels. Comprehensive studies of the whole NQI system are rare. Concerning methodology, scholars employ pure descriptive methods in the form of case studies based on reports and interviews. Statistical and econometric analyses are also performed on the grounds of correlation, regression and growth models.

There exist analyses on impact of standardisation on various macro microeconomic variables like business performance, also on different phases of innovation process and development. There are in particular studies investigating linkages between standardisation and intellectual property rights, especially patents (see for example Blind et al. 2018) and connection between standardisation and socioeconomic development (see for example Fura and Wang 2017). Research on relationships between certified QMS and innovation are rare. Numerous theoretical and empirical studies illustrate how certification may influence macroeconomic performance. Most of these studies focus on impact of certification on business performance and some on innovation as case study analysis (see for example Mir et al. 2016 and references therein) rather than evaluating public data provided by the databases like the Innovation Union Scoreboard and ISO databases. Moreover empirical studies focus very often on a limited number of objects (countries) and variables.

This research paper contributes to filling this gap through development of a statistical model to investigate relationship between standardisation and innovation in the area of QMS. In Sections 2 and 3, the authors present a review of existing literature in the field describing linkages between quality and innovation, standardisation and innovation and quality management systems and innovation. In Section 4, the authors give the research hypotheses and the methodology used for the analysis. The results and their discussion is given in Section 5. Finally, in Section 6 some conclusions, recommendations and limitations are given.

2. LINKAGES BETWEEN QUALITY AND INNOVATION

The Schumpeterian concepts of innovation (Sengupta 2014) assume that it is closely related to radical or incremental changes. In general, there are two approaches to innovation: one regards innovation as a process while the other one as an event, object or product. Further elaboration on these approaches entails creation of many innovation concepts that are basically related to organisational processes and technical development of certain products (for thorough reviews see Kotsemir et al. 2013). Managing innovation is one of the key strategic tasks which organisations face. Knowledge becomes a primary task requiring building innovation routines (Bessant 2003). According to Igartua et al. (2010) innovation management can be defined as the creation of preconditions to promote human creativity but also as a process to foster the application of knowledge.

The notion of total quality (TQ) comprises two areas: holistic and continuous improvement (McAdam et al. 1998). The holistic view incorporates business process re-engineering, benchmarking and total productive maintenance including business proficiency and efficiency. Continuous improvement is defined as a mechanism and a cultural definition of TQ. It is based on the following assumptions: customer satisfaction is vital, internal customers are real, all work is a process, measurement is essential, teamwork is the preferred work mode, people achieve continuous improvement, and continuous improvement cycle is sacrosanct. López-Mielgo et al. (2009) distinguish two components of TQM: hard components which are mechanistic elements of quality assurance and soft components seeking to gain the involvement of managers and employees in the quality management like training, learning and internal cooperation teamwork.

Several scholars admit that there is a close relationship between TQM and innovation. This statement can be found in the work of Prajogo and Sohal (2003) who offer the literature review on this topic arguing that TQM embodies principles that are congruent with innovation like linking learning promoted by TQM practices and innovation. Other aspects of this relationship are mentioned by Los Reyes et al. (2006) who discuss the impact of strategic quality management on innovation management and claim that at individual level, people have the ability to both be creative and pay attention to detail. Organizational innovativeness is supported by a team work based on the principles of empowerment and involvement. Organisations focused on consumer needs trigger innovative approach, development and introduction of new products on the market. Improvements require change and innovative thinking. Galia and Pekovic (2008) note that "the motivation of both performances, quality and innovation, is satisfaction of customer requirements with the need to make continuous improvements". They add that ISO certification provides a foundation for TQM. McAdam et al. (1998) who make distinction between radical and incremental innovation argue that the TQ process can reinforce incremental innovation. Zairi (1994) argues that TQM gives organisations the impetus and commitment required for establishing climates of innovations. Leavengood, et al. (2014) claim that TQM makes a basis for innovation and significantly and positively impacts quality and innovation performance. The same approach may be found in López-Mielgo et al. (2009) analysis that invoking literature review state that firms implementing soft TQM components tend to be more innovative especially in terms of incremental innovations. Also the other way round companies which are already innovative and spend on R&D tend to apply quality control practices. López-Mielgo et al. (2009) note that both the theoretical and empirical literature suggest that high innovation capabilities may reduce the costs of implementing the quality standards and ensure profitability of investments needed for controlling quality.

Other researchers see contradiction between TQM and innovation. Focus on customers may also provoke failure to explore customers' latent needs and lack of continuous improvement. Certain level of rigidity triggered by routine, standards or regulations may be detrimental to innovation due to lock-in into outdated and inefficient technologies (Prajogo and Sohal 2003). There is also question if companies are able to concentrate on both management and innovation performance or should choose between the two. López-Mielgo et al. (2009) admit that some authors argue that hard components of TQM inhibit innovation in particular a radical one since the efficiency goals and strict measures imposed on the production process prevent creativity while radical innovation requires improvisation.

3. STANDARDIZATION AND INNOVATION

Research analyses describe also the link between standardisation and innovation. Standards are important for companies concerning development of products and also research and development activities as well as marketing instruments for innovation (Blind 2013).

Standards are a part of the mechanisms of knowledge transfer, as a codified knowledge and best practice they are direct input to innovation system, may be a complementary knowledge asset or be a contributor to the creation of market demand.

A study prepared by Optimat for CEN/CENELEC (2014) stresses that "standards play a multiple and catalytic role in innovation and growth systems. Although the degree of take up varies, standards are pervasive elements in the innovation system, as initially highlighted in the literature review". Specific conclusions state that standards are important for research projects and improvement of marketability of research although they are more important for innovation itself than for more fundamental research. In innovation system standards serve as tools for measurement and terminology, specification of processes and performance and interoperability between components and systems. Standardization can be considered as providing a catalyst for various linkages within 'science, technology, innovation, and growth (STIG) systems (Optimat 2014). Standards have a particular potential concerning incremental innovation as they provide the basis to demonstrate that new products are both fit for purpose and offer advantages over existing products or, in the important case of complementarities, are compatible with them (Optimat 2014). Analysis carried out by Miotti (2009) based on interviews with managers (response sample of 1790 respondents) proves that standardisation supports dissemination of innovation and is a selection tool of products.

On the other hand standards limit variety by defining technology and norms and in this way constraining innovation (Swann 2000). Standards may have also an adverse effect on innovation through decrease of the speed of innovation activities (Butter et al. 2007). Innovations that require standards are costly to develop because standards which are not internationally recognized do not bring network externalities. It is also very risky to develop such innovations due to the fact that there is no certitude that a new technology will become a recognized standard. Although there are negative aspects of relationship between standards and innovation the net effect is positive meaning that standards have a positive impact on innovation activities (Butter et al. 2007). On the other hand, according to Blind (2013) "the various studies on the macroeconomic level, and the microeconomic ones based on company or expert surveys and on specific case studies are able to show the positive correlation or the complementarily between standards and innovation, but not necessarily the causality of standardization promoting innovation. For such complex analyses controlling for the endogenous of standardization, i.e. the approved influence of innovation, not only time series of data, but additional complementary data to construct instruments is necessary. However, this type of data is currently not available, but partly under construction".

3.1. Certified Quality Management Systems and Innovation

Innovation and certified quality management systems are often perceived as opposite because innovation is the realization of something new while certification is an on-off process of certain standardized criteria often criticised as source of bureaucracy. However, literature review on innovation has emphasized the positive role that standards leading to certified quality management systems play in the commercial success of new goods and services (Swann 2000, Blind 2004, Hesser et. al. 2007, Egyedi and Blind 2008, Mangiarotti and Riillo 2010).

To gain advantages from innovation efficient diffusion of a new technology is necessary (DIN 2000). Standards play an important role in technological diffusion, empirical evidence shows that standards have a positive influence on innovative potential (e.g. DIN 2000; Gausch et al. 2007). Moreover DIN report (2000) emphasizes that "standards were at least as important for technical innovation as patents. This makes it clear that innovation potential is not the only deciding factor in economic development, but that it must also be broadly disseminated by means of standards and technical rules". Standards fortify credibility and are a source of information for innovation activities. Standards can reduce the transaction and search costs that are caused by imperfect information. This is a role of minimum safety standards, but it can also be accomplished by quality standards and product description standards (Gausch et al. 2007). Blind (2009) enumerates other, less direct positive impacts of standards on innovation which include reduction of the time to market of inventions, research results and innovative technologies; promotion of competition which encourages innovation; strengthening of network industries (compatibility standards) which develop new technologies and promotion of trust in innovative products (minimum requirements standards). Swann (2009) lists four channels by which standards have impact on innovation: standards support division of labor which upholds some innovations; standards help to open up markets and allow new entrants; measurement standards allow proving superiority of innovative products and finally standards help to derive the greatest value from networks. Role of standards in exploitation of network effects is emphasized by Gausch et al. (2007) who notes that standards may increase direct network externalities by allowing products to work as part of a system or network and also increase indirect network externalities when they allow users to derive benefits from a system involving two or more complementary components.

ISO 9001 is an international standard leading to certification and can raise effectiveness of the operations, increase customer satisfaction and facilitate penetration in new market. Galia and Pekovic (2008) claim that "the ISO standards were created to facilitate mutual understanding of quality management system requirements in national and international trade". Moreover, ISO 9001 is voluntary; however, certification from accredited third party has the advantage to signal to the market the commitment to quality. The validity of a certificate is generally three years, but practice proves that it gets mature after two years. The benefits of ISO certification among others include: increased customer preference, better quality perception and increased competitiveness on the market and compliance with customer expectations (Galia and Pekovic 2008).

The number of ISO 9001-certified companies is significantly high when compared with the remaining management systems, thus reflecting the huge importance that ISO 9001 certification has assumed for companies worldwide. According to the ISO Survey (ISO 2013), the number of ISO 9001 issued certificates in Europe represents 48% of the worldwide number of issued certificates.

Da Costa Araujo Sampaio et al. (2014), identified clusters of countries with different ISO 9001 evolution stages, derived from the ISO 9001 per 1000 inhabitants' scores and countries' growth indices. The authors developed ISO Scoreboard across EU to categorise and rank countries based on the quality management systems evolution (growth rates). This scoreboard is an instrument to provide a comparative assessment of quality management practices over the EU states, leading to the dynamic evaluation of their 'macroquality' levels achieved, according to such a standard.

The effect of ISO 9001 on innovation is considered also through enterprise performance which is debated in literature. The effects can be classified along two main categories: internal and external business dimensions (Sampaio et al. 2009). Internal dimensions affected by ISO 9001 are related with the knowledge effect of the standard and includes organization, efficiency and quality of production process. Corbett et al. (2005) compare financial performance of ISO 9001 companies against not certified but otherwise similar firms, reporting superior performance in terms of return on asset and sales. External dimensions are mainly related with the minimum quality assurance. Terlaak and King (2006) develop a signalling effect and argue that growth performance of ISO 9001 is superior to other companies even it has no impact on operational dimensions. Moreover, ISO 9001 supports the codification of tacit knowledge and enhances the development of new knowledge (Bénézech et al. 2001, Pekovic and Galia 2009).

Only a few empirical studies have been identified to explain the complex relationship of innovation and certified management systems. Mangiarotti and Riillo (2010) have investigated empirically the impact of ISO 9001 on companies' innovation capabilities using the logit regression. They have analysed data received by Community Innovation Survey (CIS) for Luxembourg for year 2006 along to ISO 9001 certified companies and concluded that ISO 9001 certification affects positively and significantly the probability of innovation in terms of organisational and marketing effects, considering that the magnitude and significance of impact are progressively reduced when more restrictive definitions of innovation are made. It is revealed that ISO 9001 certified management systems increase technical innovation capabilities of manufacturing companies and non-technical innovation capabilities of other service sectors, but effect of ISO 9001 systems decrease with firms' size. However, this research is limited considering that only one year is considered (2006) and time maturity of certification is not considered adequate to reveal complex relationships between certification and innovation.

Pekovic and Galia (2009) claim basing on empirical survey that ISO 9001 has a positive impact on innovation while Terziovski and Guerrero- Cusumano (2009) report the opposite effect.

Delic et al. (2014) carried out in Serbia a study to determine the relationships between certified quality management systems according to ISO 9001 and organisational performance over a sample of 160 organisations. Using structural equation modelling as the methodology to examine the relationships between quality management and organisational performance the authors identified that ISO 9001 certified systems significantly affect performance considering "organisational climate maturity".

According to the findings, it is seen that time element as maturity of quality management systems should be considered when examining the relationships between organisational performance, innovation and quality management systems.

4. RESEARCH HYPOTHESES

Based on the literature review of sections 2 and 3, which revealed diverse views if there is a relation between ISO 9001 and innovation, we will examine if there is a statistically significant relationship between innovation and certified quality management systems in the European countries context. To address this issue, the following hypotheses are formulated:

Hypothesis 0 (H0): ISO 9001 certified quality management systems have no impact on innovation,
Hypothesis 1 (H1): ISO 9001 certified quality management systems have impact on innovation.

The way to measure ISO 9001 certified quality management systems and innovation is not uniquely defined. Therefore, different variables were used to assess these quantities.

The above hypotheses are considered for 34 European countries (table 1) and for the periods of (2005 – 2012) as input and (2007 – 2014) as output. These yearly data allowed authors to check for possible relationships with and without lag.

4.1. Data Description

The research utilises two databases public available to proceed to panel data analysis. The first database is obtained by International Standards Organisation (ISO) and is based on its 2013 Survey. The database contains relevant data for ISO 9001 certifications and ISO Withdrawn certifications, in 34 European countries (table 1).

The database (2013 Survey) includes only certificates accredited by national accredited bodies and members of the IAF (International Accreditation Federation). In this research, all data are considered of the database of ISO for 34 countries and

Table 1. European countries under study

Austria	France	Luxembourg	Slovenia
Belgium	Germany	Malta	Spain
Bulgaria	Greece	Netherlands	Sweden
Croatia	Hungary	Norway	Switzerland
Cyprus	Iceland	Poland	The former Yugoslav Republic of Macedonia
Czech Republic	Ireland	Portugal	Turkey
Denmark	Italy	Romania	United Kingdom
Estonia	Latvia	Serbia	
Finland	Lithuania	Slovakia	

for the period of (2005 – 2012). Input or independent variable is measured by the number of ISO 9001 certifications and withdraws, for the period of (2005 – 2012).

The second database is obtained by the European Commission (2017a), DG Growth, the European Innovation Scoreboard – previously Innovation Union Scoreboard, 2015. This database provides a comparative analysis of innovation performance in EU Member States, other European countries, and regional neighbours. It assesses relative strengths and weaknesses of national innovation systems and helps countries identify areas they need to address (European Commission, Innovation Scoreboard).

Innovation performance is measured using a composite indicator – the Summary Innovation Index (SINI) – which summarizes the performance of a range of different indicators. The Innovation Union Scoreboard distinguishes between 3 main types of indicators – Enablers, Firm activities and Outputs – and 8 innovation dimensions, capturing in total 25 indicators (table 2).

Specifically, panel data on the summary innovation index (SINI) and its components like SMEs innovating in-house, SMEs introducing product or process innovations and SMEs introducing marketing/organisational innovations. Research accounts for variation over time (different years-within variation) and across individuals (different countries–between variation).

Output or dependent variable is measured by the Summary Innovation Index, for the period of (2007 – 2014) for the same countries indicated in table 1.

In Table 3, some descriptive statistics are presented for all the variables used in this study. Specifically, it is presented the minimum (min), the 25th (Q_1), 50th (Q_2, median), 75th (Q_3) percentage point, the maximum (max), the mean and the standard deviation (Std) of the Summary Innovation Index (SINI), SMEs innovating in-house (SMEh), SMEs introducing product or process innovations as % of SMEs (SMEp),

Table 2. Summary innovation index components (source: Innovation Union Scoreboard 2015)

ENABLERS
Human resources
1.1.1 New doctorate graduates
1.1.2 Population completed tertiary education
1.1.3 Youth with upper secondary level education
Open, excellent and attractive research systems
1.2.1 International scientific co-publications
1.2.2 Scientific publications among top 10% most cited
1.2.3 Non-EU doctorate students
Finance and support
1.3.1 Public R&D expenditure
1.3.2 Venture capital
FIRM ACTIVITIES
Firm investments
2.1.1 Business R&D expenditure
2.1.2 Non-R&D innovation expenditure
Linkages & entrepreneurship
2.2.1 SMEs innovating in-house
2.2.2 Innovative SMEs collaborating with others
2.2.3 Public-private co-publications
Intellectual Assets
2.3.1 PCT patent applications
2.3.2 PCT patent applications in societal challenges
2.3.3 Community trademarks
2.3.4 Community designs
OUTPUTS
Innovators
3.1.1 SMEs introducing product or process innovations
3.1.2 SMEs introducing marketing/organisational innovations
3.1.3 Fast-growing firms in innovative industries
Economic effects
3.2.1 Employment in knowledge-intensive activities
3.2.2 Contribution of MHT product exports to trade balance
3.2.3 Knowledge-intensive services exports
3.2.4 Sales of new to market and new to firm innovations
3.2.5 Licence and patent revenues from abroad

Table 3. Descriptive statistics for the variables used in this study

	min	Q_1	Q_2	Q_3	max	mean	Std
SINI	0.16	0.33	0.45	0.61	0.82	0.47	0.17
SMEh	10.13	19.62	28.18	36.93	46.29	27.86	9.77
SMEp	5.16	25.34	32.61	40.86	57	33.05	11.24
SMEm	13.93	29.05	36.95	44.08	68.18	36.83	11.47
ISOCert	13	1528	4277	11479.5	143121	13125.54	24782.07
ISOWith	1	43.75	157	578.25	13504	686.89	1661.58

SMEs introducing marketing/organisational innovations (SMEm), ISO Certifications (ISOCert) and ISO Withdrawn certifications (ISOWith).

4.2. Methodology

In this research panel data model analysis is applied. There are three types of panel data models: the pooled model, the fixed effects model and the random effects model. The pooled model is given by the equation $y_{it} = a + x_{it}'\beta + u_{it}$. In this model it is assumed that the coefficients are constant which is the usual assumption for cross-sectional analysis. If it is further assumed that there is unobserved heterogeneity across individuals, then it is needed to consider a_i in order to account for this behaviour. If the individual-specific effects a_i are correlated with the regressors then the fixed effects model is used, otherwise the random effects model is considered.

The fixed effects model is given by the equation $y_{it} = a_i + x_{it}'\beta + u_{it}$. It is observed that under this model each individual has a different intercept term and the same slope parameters. The random effects model is described by the equation $y_{it} = x_{it}'\beta + (a_i + e_{it})$, where $\varepsilon_{it} = a_i + e_{it}$ is a composite error term. In this model, the effect a_i is included in the error term and everyone has the same slope parameters.

In order to choose between the fixed and the random effects model the Hausman test (Baltagi 2013) is applied. This test assesses whether there is a significant difference between the fixed and random effects estimators or not. If the Hausman test is insignificant the random effects model is used otherwise the fixed effects model is considered. There is also a check between the pooled and the random or fixed effects models. For the random effects versus pooled model the Lagrange multiplier test is used and in the case of the fixed effects versus pooled model a suitable F test (Sun 2014) is considered. In both cases if the test is not significant the pooled model is chosen. Furthermore, since the data refer to few years a test for serial correlation is not applied as it is not expected to identify such an effect. For more details about these methods the interested reader may refer to Baltagi (2013) or Wooldridge (2010).

In this paper and for all the research equations, all three types of models are considered. For all the computations the statistical software R (see www.r-project. org) is used and the type I error is considered 5%.

Note that the use of panel data analysis has a number of advantages compared to other possible choices. As Hsiao (2007) stated the three main advantages are that using pooled data we get more accurate inference of model parameters, we are able to model more efficiently complex data of human behaviour than single cross-section or time series data and that computation and statistical inference is simpler

Table 4. Panel model for SINI with ISO certifications

	Estimate	Std.Error	t-value	P-value
Intercept	0.4245	0.01869	22.71	0.000
ISO Certifications	0.0000027	0.0000012	2.31	0.028
$R^2 = 0.603$				

than expected. In this paper the data at hand are analysed using panel data models because we can take into consideration both the cross-sectional and the time series dimension of the data.

5. EMPIRICAL ANALYSIS AND DISCUSSION

As already stated the main question in this paper is to test if there is a statistically significant relationship between innovation and certified quality management systems (QMS). At first, the variable Summary Innovation Index (SINI) is used as the variable measuring innovation and the variable ISO Certifications as the variable measuring QMS. The first question that needs to be answered is whether there is a statistically significant relationship between the independent variable ISO Certifications and the dependent variable SINI.

The results are given in Table 4. It must be noted that in this model and all the following models the categorical variables year and country are used as control variables. Moreover, the between estimator is used in these results which means that variation across individuals is only considered (time averages are used).

From the results in Table 4 it is concluded that there is a statistically significant effect of ISO Certifications on SINI since p=0.028. The interpretation of the model is that if the average number of ISO Certifications increases by one then there is a positive effect of 0.0000027 on the SINI index. Moreover, it is R^2 =60.3% therefore this model can explain 60.3% of the total variation of the SINI index.

A point that has to be stressed is that the use of the SINI index as an innovation index stems from the fact that it is used for this purpose by the European Commission (2017a). To be more specific one can argue that there are subcategories of the SINI index that seem to have little to do with the ISO Certifications (e.g., number of graduate students). Therefore, in this study the variables used are those that seem to be strongly related to innovativeness. According to the European Commission (2017b) 99% of all the enterprises operating in the European Union in 2016 were small and medium enterprises (SMEs) and this percentage rises up to 99.8%

Table 5. Panel model for SMEs innovating in-house and the independent variables ISO certifications and ISO withdrawn certifications

	Estimate	Std.Error	t-value	P-value
Intercept	0.4785	0.02517	19.014	0.000
ISO Certifications	0.0000025	0.00000098	2.581	0.011
ISO Withdrawn	-0.0000422	0.0000160	-2.631	0.009

$R^2 = 0.712$, p=0.009 (for the model)

taking into account the non-financial business sector. Consequently, the variables SMEs innovating in-house, SMEs introducing product or process innovations and SMEs introducing marketing/organisational innovations will be used as innovation indices since these variables measure innovativeness in SMEs. Additionally, both ISO Certifications and ISO Withdrawn Certifications variables will be used as independent variables to study their effect on the three SMEs that will be used as dependent variables each.

As already stated in section 3.1. Galia and Pekovic (2008) claim that the validity of an ISO certificate is generally three years, but practice proves that it gets mature after two years. This actually means that an applied ISO 9001 system takes about two years to give innovation results measured by the Innovation Scoreboard. Therefore, under the scenario that there are two years difference a possible relationship between the dependent and the independent variables will be checked. Therefore, when the values for each of the dependent SMEs variables are given for example for year 2010 the corresponding values for variables ISO Certifications and ISO Withdrawn certifications are given for year 2008.

The results of the model having as the dependent variable SMEs innovating in-house and as the independent variables ISO Certifications and ISO Withdrawn certifications using the pooled model are given in table 5.

The model is statistically significant since p=0.009. The interpretation of the model is that if the average number of ISO Certifications increases by one then there is a positive effect of 0.0000025 on the SMEs innovating in-house provided that ISO Withdrawn remains constant. Moreover, if the average number of ISO Withdrawn certificates increases by one then there is a negative effect of -0.0000422 on the SMEs innovating in-house provided that ISO Certifications remains constant. Obviously the sign of the two independent variables is the expected one. The R^2 =71.2% therefore the model explains 71.2% of the total variation of the SMEs innovating in-house.

Table 6. Panel model for SMEs introducing product or process innovations as % of SMEs and the independent variables ISO certifications and ISO withdrawn certifications

	Estimate	Std. Error	t-value	P-value
Intercept	0.4959	0.023605	21.007	0.000
ISO Certifications	0.000001	0.00000093	1.096	0.275
ISO Withdrawn	-0.0000411	0.0000149	-2.757	0.007
$R^2 = 0.703$, p=0.024 (for the model)				

In table 6, the presented results refer to the model having as the dependent variable SMEs introducing product or process innovations as % of SMEs and as the independent variables ISO Certifications and ISO Withdrawn certifications again using the pooled model.

The model is statistically significant since p=0.024. From the results it is seen that ISO Certifications have a positive effect on the dependent variable, but this effect is not statistically significant given that ISO Withdrawn and the intercept are already included in the model. On the other hand ISO Withdrawn certificates have a negative effect and it is statistically significant. The $R^2 = 70.3\%$ therefore the model explains 70.3% of the total variation of the SMEs introducing product or process innovations as % of SMEs.

The statistical pooled model when the dependent variable is SMEs introducing marketing/organisational innovations and the independent variables are ISO Certifications and ISO Withdrawn certifications is given in Table 7.

The model is statistically significant since p=0.022. The interpretation of the model is that if the average number of ISO Certifications increases by one then there is a positive effect of 0.0000019 on the SMEs introducing marketing/organizational innovations provided that ISO Withdrawn remains constant. Moreover, if the average

Table 7. Panel model for SMEs introducing marketing/organisational innovations and the independent variables ISO certifications and ISO withdrawn certifications

	Estimate	Std. Error	t-value	P-value
Intercept	0.4837	0.02144	22.559	0.000
ISO Certifications	0.0000019	0.00000083	2.325	0.021
ISO Withdrawn	-0.0000315	0.0000134	-2.346	0.020
$R^2 = 0.733$, p=0.022 (for the model)				

number of ISO Withdrawn certificates increases by one then there is a negative effect of -0.000032 on the SMEs introducing marketing/organizational innovations provided that ISO Certifications remains constant. Since $R^2 = 73.3\%$ the model explains 73.3% of the total variation of the SMEs introducing marketing/organisational innovations.

As it can be observed in tables 4-7 the ISO Certifications have a positive effect on different aspects of innovation. It is clear that this result offers a view of the importance of ISO Certifications on the economy of a country. Consequently, political decisions supporting the quality culture is very important to improve innovation. It should be stressed that authors don't support that only ISO Certifications is important for innovation. But ISO Certifications among others are evidently a crucial factor.

At this point authors focus on the very interesting result that withdrawn certificates have a negative effect on innovation. An ISO Certificate can be withdrawn for a number of reasons like non-elimination of serious nonconformities within agreed term discovered during surveillance or breaking of information duty – in communication of changes, which essentially influence management system function etc. The results in Tables 5-7 clearly present the importance of withdrawn ISO Certifications in innovation. Therefore, it is very important for an economy to focus on ISO certification and the preservation of these certificates to have a positive impact on innovation.

6. CONCLUSION

Quality has become one of the most crucial factors influencing business performance. There is a debate if pursuing quality supports or hinders innovation. A similar discussion refers to the problem if standardization has a positive or negative impact on innovation. In both cases the opinions are divided.

Empirical analysis carried out in this paper reveals a statistically significant effect of ISO Certifications on SINI index. Moreover, there is a statistically significant relationship between ISO Certifications as well as ISO withdrawn certifications on SMEs innovating in-house, SMEs introducing product or process innovations and SMEs introducing marketing/organisational innovations. Therefore, Hypothesis 1 (H1) is confirmed as mentioned in section 4 that "ISO 9001 certified quality management systems have impact on innovation".

The results in Tables 4-7 reveal the necessity of taking into consideration the ISO certifications issued and withdrawn in the innovation policy. The results pinpoint the necessity of the European countries to give emphasis on QMS. Standardization is shown to have a positive effect on innovation therefore it is an issue that should attract government attention. Obviously, innovation should be one of the key factors in the development of an economy and the results in this paper can help to move in this direction.

However, authors highlight that more data are needed to have a clear positive decision about the impact of QMS. Data for more years or even better in a monthly scale could improve the applicability of the studied models. Another issue to be referred to is the quality of the data. The countries should emphasize on the immediate and accurate recording of the information. Otherwise, it might be experienced a non-significant relationship when one exists or the opposite.

The studied models have not included economic indicators from other aspects of the economy in the models. Moreover, other forms of management systems (e.g. ISO 14001, etc.) could be used as independent variables in the models. The aforementioned points can be checked in future research.

REFERENCES

Baltagi, B. H. (2013). *Econometric Analysis of Panel Data* (5th ed.). John Wiley and Sons.

Bénézech, D., Lambert, G., Lanoux, B., Lerch, C., & Loos-Baroin, J. (2001). Completion of knowledge codification: An illustration through the ISO 9000 standards implementation process. *Research Policy*, *30*(9), 1395–1407. doi:10.1016/S0048-7333(01)00158-5

Bessant, J. (2003). *High involvement innovation*. Chichester, UK: John Wiley and Sons.

Blind, K. (2004). *The economics of standards: theory, evidence, policy*. Edward Elgar Publishing.

Blind, K. (2009). Standardisation: A Catalyst for Innovation, Inaugural Address. Rotterdam School of Management, Erasmus Universiteit Rotterdam. Retrieved from http://repub.eur.nl/pub/17558/EIA-2009-039-LIS.pdf

Blind, K. (2013). The Impact of Standardization and Standards on Innovation. Nesta Working Paper No. 13/15. Retrieved from https://media.nesta.org.uk/documents/the_impact_of_standardization_and_standards_on_innovation.pdf

Blind, K., Pohlisch, J., & Zi, A. (2018). Publishing, patenting, and standardization: Motives and barriers of scientists. *Research Policy*, *47*(7), 1185–1197. doi:10.1016/j.respol.2018.03.011

Butter, F. A. G., Groot, S. P. T., & Lazrak, F. (2007). The Transaction Costs Perspective on Standards as a Source of Trade and Productivity Growth. Tinbergen Institute Discussion Paper, TI 2007-090/3. Retrieved from http://personal.vu.nl/f.a.g.den. butter/TIstandards07090.pdf

Corbett, C. J., Montes-Sancho, M. J., & Kirsch, D. A. (2005). The financial impact of ISO 9000 certification in the United States: An empirical analysis. *Management Science, 51*(7), 1046–1059. doi:10.1287/mnsc.1040.0358

Da Costa Araujo Sampaio, P. A., de Andrade Saraiva, P. M. T. L., & Gomes, A. C. R. (2014). ISO 9001 European Scoreboard: An instrument to measure Macroquality. *Total Quality Management, 25*(4), 309–318. doi:10.1080/14783363.2013.807683

Delic, M., Radlovacki, V., Kamberovic, B., Maksimovic, R., & Pecujlija, M. (2014). Examining relationships between quality management and organisational performance in transitional economies. *Total Quality Management, 25*(4), 367–382. doi:10.108 0/14783363.2013.799331

DIN. (2000). *Economic Benefits of Standardization: Summary of Results*. Berlin: Beuth Verlag GmbH and Deutsches Institut für Normung.

Egyedi, T. M., & Blind, K. (2008). *The Dynamics of Standards*. Cheltenham, UK: Edward Elgar.

European Commission. (2017a). DJ Growth. European Innovation Scoreboard. Retrieved from http://ec.europa.eu/growth/industry/innovation/facts-figures/ scoreboards_en

European Commission. (2017b). Annual Report on European SMEs 2016/2017. Retrieved from http://ec.europa.eu/docsroom/documents/26563/

Fura, B., & Wang, Q. (2017). The level of socioeconomic development of EU countries and the state of ISO 14001 certification. *Quality & Quantity, 51*(1), 103–119. doi:10.1007/s11135-015-0297-7 PubMed

Galia, F., & Pekovic, S. (2008). From Quality to Innovation: Evidence from Two French Employer Surveys. Proposal for the 1st DIME Scientific Conference "Knowledge in space and time: Economic and policy implications of the Knowledge-based economy" BETA, University Louis Pasteur, Strasbourg, France.

Guasch, J. L., Racine, J.-L., Sánchez, I., & Diop, M. (2007). Quality systems and standards for a competitive edge (Directions in Development). Washington, DC: World Bank Publications; doi:10.1596/978-0-8213-6894-7.

Hesser, E. J., Feilzer, A. J., & de Vries, H. J. (2007). *Standardisation in Companies and Markets*. Helmut Schmidt University Hamburg.

Hsiao, C. (2007). Panel data analysis—Advantages and challenges. *Test*, *16*(1), 1–22. doi:10.1007/s11749-007-0046-x

Igartua, J. I., Garrigós, J. A., & Hervas-Oliver, J. L. (2010). How innovation management techniques support an open innovation strategy. *Research Technology Management*, *53*(3), 41–52. doi:10.1080/08956308.2010.11657630

ISO. (2013). ISO Survey of Management System Standard Certifications. ISO 9001. Quality Management System. International Organisation for Standardization. Retrieved from www.iso.org

Kotsemir, M., Abroskin, A., & Meissner, D. (2013). Innovation concepts and typology – an evolutionary discussion. HSE Working papers with number WP BRP 05/STI/2013.

Leavengood, S., Anderson, T. R., & Daim, T. U. (2014). Exploring linkage of quality management to innovation. *Total Quality Management*, *25*(10), 1126–1140. doi:10.1080/14783363.2012.738492

López-Mielgo, N., Montes-Peón, J., & Vázquez-Ordá, C. J. (2009). Are quality and innovation management conflicting activities? *Technovation*, *29*(8), 537–545. doi:10.1016/j.technovation.2009.02.005

Los Reyes, E., Vega, J., & Martínez, A. (2006). ISO 9000 in SMEs. The mediating role of quality systems in the innovation performance. CINet.

Mangiarotti, G., & Riillo, A. F. (2010). ISO 9000 Certification and Innovation: an Empirical Analysis for Luxembourg. Economie et Statistiques working paper du STATEC, No 46.

McAdam, R., Armstrong, G., & Kelly, B. (1998). Investigation of the relationship between total quality and innovation: A research study involving small organisations. *European Journal of Innovation Management*, *1*(3), 139–147. doi:10.1108/14601069810230216

Miotti, H. (2009). *The Economic Impact of Standardization*. Technological Change, Standards Growth in France. AFNOR.

Mir, M., Casadesus, M., & Petnji, L. H. (2016). The impact of standardized innovation management systems on innovation capability and business performance: An empirical study. *Journal of Engineering and Technology Management*, *41*, 26–44. doi:10.1016/j.jengtecman.2016.06.002

Optimat. (2014). Research Study on the Benefits of Linking Innovation and Standardization. Final Report, CEN/CENELEC. Retrieved from https://www.cencenelec.eu/research/news/publications/Publications/BRIDGIT-standinno-study.pdf

Pekovic, S., & Galia, F. (2009). From quality to innovation: Evidence from two French Employer Surveys. *Technovation, 29,* 829–842.

Prajogo, D. I., & Sohal, A. S. (2003). The relationship between TQM practices, quality performance, and innovation performance: An empirical examination. *International Journal of Quality & Reliability Management, 20*(8), 901–918. doi:10.1108/02656710310493625

Sampaio, P., Saraiva, P., & Rodrigues, A. G. (2009). ISO 9001 certification research: Questions, answers and approaches. *International Journal of Quality & Reliability Management, 26*(1), 38–58. doi:10.1108/02656710910924161

Sengupta, J. (2014). Schumpeterian Innovation. In Theory of Innovation. Cham: Springer; doi:10.1007/978-3-319-02183-6_3.

Sun, Y. (2014). Fixed-smoothing Asymptotics and Asymptotic F and t Tests in the Presence of Strong Autocorrelation. In *Essays in Honor of Peter C. B. Phillips.* Emerald Group Publishing Limited; doi:10.1108/S0731-905320140000033002

Swann, G. M. P. (2000). *The economics of standardization. Final report for Standards and Technical Regulations Directorate.* Department of Trade and Industry.

Swann, G. M. P. (2009). The Economics of Metrology and Measurement. Retrieved from http://webarchive.nationalarchives.gov.uk/+/http://www.nmo.bis.gov.uk/fileuploads/NMS/Prof_Swann_report_Econ_Measurement_Revisited_Oct_09.pdf

Terlaak, A., & King, A. (2006). The effect of certification with the ISO 9000 Quality Management Standard: A signalling approach. *Journal of Economic Behavior & Organization, 60*(4), 579–602. doi:10.1016/j.jebo.2004.09.012

Terziovski, M., & Guerrero-Cusumano, J.-L. (2009). ISO 9000 Quality Systems Certification and Its Impact on Innovation Performance. Academy of Management Annual Meeting Proceedings.

Wooldridge, J. M. (2010). *Econometric Analysis of Cross Section and Panel Data* (2nd ed.). Cambridge, MA: MIT Press.

Zairi, M. (1994). Innovation or innovativeness? Results of benchmarking study. *Total Quality Management, 5*(3), 27–44. doi:10.1080/09544129400000023

Chapter 7

Managing the Standardization Knowledge Codification Paradox:
Creative Experience and Expansive Learning

Hiam Serhan
AgroParisTech, France

Doudja Saïdi-Kabeche
iD https://orcid.org/0000-0002-7235-3708
AgroParisTech, France

ABSTRACT

In a connected society and organizations working with digitized business models, standards will have more important roles than ever in shaping activity systems content, structure, and governance. While the standardization conformity/innovation duality has received great attention in literature, little research has been done on the role of managers in managing the tensions of knowledge codification required during ISO 9001 standard implementation. By utilizing Danone's Networking Attitude experience as a case study, the authors address this gap by exploring how managerial skills and practices were used to overcome the cognitive and emotional tensions related to internal knowledge codification, transfer, and use. The main contribution is to elucidate the role of managers in resolving these paradoxes and creating innovation capabilities. Further, they demonstrate the mutually beneficial relationship between knowledge codification and innovation if knowledge management is approached more as an evolving pragmatic knowing than a technical means that may create rigidity and resistance.

DOI: 10.4018/978-1-7998-2181-6.ch007

INTRODUCTION

In a connected society and organizations working with digitized business models and knowledge management processes, technical and management systems standards will have more important roles than ever in shaping innovation strategies and activity systems content, structure and governance. In organizations the challenge of managing standardization - i.e. implanting and maintaining a standardized system to continuously improve strategic process (Asif & DeVries, 2015) - relates to the management of tensions and paradoxes that emerge in activity systems during the implementation of standards. The paradoxes and tensions occur when the routines of an established system collide with the standard's new requirements, and where the actors' know-how is challenged with external new knowledge.

Managing an organization's paradox that oscillate between stability and innovation has become a central concern for business improvement and routines' evolution (Smith et al., 2017; Engeström, 2015; Lewis & Smith, 2014). Management system standards are considered key instruments to manage business ambidextrous orientations as they are conceived to achieve simultaneously standardization through the codification and exploitation of good practices (GP), and innovation through the exploration of new knowledge and innovation opportunities (Hamdoun et al., 2018; Brunsson & Jacobsson, 2005; Lambert & Loos-Baroin, 2004). In practice, the implementation of standards' requirements is a knowledge management process (Serhan, 2018; Asif & De Vries, 2015; Saulais & Ermine, 2012; De Vries & Van Delden, 2006; Jashapara, 2004). These include acquiring new knowledge, learning and applying it for process improvement, identifying and codifying internal operational good practices, and diffusing and sharing the new procedures throughout the organization to promote organizational learning. These practices create cognitive and emotional tensions in organizations and between employees. These tensions can lead to an implementation failure, or, can be used as opportunities to create new organizational capabilities that create and maintain stability and creativity (Smith et al., 2017; Engeström, 2015; Takeuchi & Osono, 2008). The success of a manager in charge of implementing improvement tools in activity systems and leadership to enable strategic paradoxes (Smith et al., 2011) can depend upon their style and dynamic managerial capabilities (Helfat & Martin, 2015).

Researchers have long studied and responded to the dual role of exploitation/ exploration related to the standardization effort in organizations (Ahmad, 2017; Evangelos et al., 2013; Lambert & Ouedraogo, 2009; Lambert & Loos Baroin, 2004). However, there is no research exploring the combined benefits of these paradoxical strategies and the role of managers in confronting and managing the tensions of the knowledge codification paradox inherent in the ISO 9001 standard requirement to simultaneously achieve stability and long-term sustainability (Smith et al., 2011).

In this chapter, through a case study - Danone's Networking Attitude experience - we fill this gap in the literature by focusing on the managers' role and practices used to manage the cognitive and emotional tensions related to internal knowledge codification, transfer, and use in Danone's community. We use Engeström's cultural-historical activity system as a theoretical model to explain how Danone's knowledge managers overcome these tensions by focusing not only on the knowledge to identify and codify, but also, and mainly, on knowing the established system as a cultural activity, mediated with established tools, and contested by individuals who have routines and values and work according to a certain division of labor. We chose Danone's experience because it illustrates the role of managers in implementing standards as a knowledge management process to simultaneously achieve stability and innovation, and in managing the tensions that emerge among practitioners during the standardization process.

The main contribution of this chapter is to elucidate the role of managers in resolving these paradoxes. We demonstrate the value of paradoxes as a locus for addressing organizational tensions and unleash creativity and innovation capabilities that can emerge during the implementation of quality management practices (Donate & Sanchez de Pablo, 2015; Xie et al., 2016). Further, we demonstrate that there is a mutually beneficial relationship between knowledge codification and organizational learning and innovation, when the knowledge management process is approached more from a social practice perspective with the goal of creating flexibility, rather than as a technical fix that fosters stability and rigidity (Brown & Duguid, 2001).

This chapter is structured as follows. The first section presents the paradoxes and tensions that emerge in evolving organizations. It also highlights the paradoxes that arise when introducing the ISO 9001 quality management standard with respect to standardization and innovation. The second section explains how the activity system model can be used as tool to manage paradoxes and tensions and expand organizational knowledge and learning. The third section develops the case study, Danone's Networking Attitude experience, which was introduced with goal of codifying, diffusing and using corporate internal and external knowledge. This is followed by the discussion and conclusions.

Because knowledge assets enhance today's organisations to achieve better results than their competitors, managing knowledge creation and sharing has become an important source of competitive advantage for firms. Innovation has been taken as a main solution for the difficulties that companies faced in the highly competitive environment. But the existence alone does not help the organisation without properly utilised it. Therefore, this proposal is important to activate knowledge sharing activity in order to transfer and share tacit knowledge in the organisation. This paper uses design science research method to integrate knowledge management and innovation management in order to practice knowledge sharing, knowledge capital and knowledge value. The basic objective is to recommend a strategic management framework as a conceptual model for organisations performance.

THE ORGANIZATIONS' PARADOXES: STABILITY AND CREATIVITY

In a turbulent environment, organizations can evolve through solving paradoxes (Handy, 1994; 1995) and overcoming their underlying tensions. To understand these changes, organizations seek to manage the various tensions that emerge in their ecosystems and in the work place. Often, these organizations must be both local and global or maintain their current expertise and yet develop new knowledge to create new value. Employees must be capable of acting autonomously, while also working in different teams. Managers must be "Masters of Paradox" (Hampden-Turner, 1994) by both monitoring and delegating; decentralising, while remaining integrated; and satisfy existing mass consumers, while discovering new niche markets. They must introduce new technology that allows workers to control their own destiny; and yet find ways to increase variety and quality, while operating under unrelenting cost pressure. They have, in short, to find a way to reconcile what appear to be opposites, instead of choosing between them (Jay, 2013; Smith & Tushman, 2005; Tushman & O'Reilly, 1996).

Managers must discover new tangible and intangible resources and exploit existing good practices and specialized skills. To manage the paradoxes of a perpetually changing environment, the managerial challenge is to identify the organization's core competences that must be continuously improved and leveraged (Saulais & Ermine, 2012).

New management tools and ideas can then be adopted and integrated to support change programs. Among the diversity of improvement management tools, this paper focuses upon ISO 9001 standard for quality management systems (QMS). This generic standard aims to manage quality management systems and can be considered as a management innovation (Ansari et al., 2010; Birkinshaw et al., 2008; Hamel, 2006; Serhan, 2017), i.e. "a new management practice, process or structure that significantly alters the managers' way of thinking (Hamel, 2006), how the managerial work is performed, and is intended to further the business performance goals to innovate with internal and external knowledge sourcing and knowledge management practices (Hamel, 2006; Birkinshaw et al., 2005).

MANAGEMENT PARADOXES OF THE ISO 9001 STANDARD: CONFORMITY AND INNOVATION

ISO 9001 generic standard is based upon a number of quality management principles including a customer focus, the motivation and involvement of the top management, a process approach, and continual improvement of key processes, customers and other stakeholder relations, organizational knowledge management and risk management (ISO, 2015).

The management challenge for ISO 9001 is to maintain and continuously improve key processes and products through using Deming's Plan, Do, Check, Act improvement process. Planning consists of identifying the internal good practices to standardize and dysfunctions to establish and improve the appropriate quality management instruments and improvement goals.

In quality management, this improvement cycle is a knowledge management process (Asif & De Vries, 2015; De Vries & Van Delden, 2006; Jashapara, 2004; Serhan, 2017). It consists of introducing, identifying, selecting, codifying employees' good practices, and replicating them throughout the organization. These processes create tensions within organisations and conflicts between employees due to the paradox of knowledge codification processes. In practice, knowledge codification, which is meant to make visible and give access to the organisation's relevant knowledge and skills, is often resisted by employees (Lambert & Loos-Baroin, 2004). Employees often perceive the act of writing what they do and how they do it, as an act that dispossesses them of their 'know-how' (by making their skills public) and jeopardises their positions. These tensions could provoke the failure of the implementation process or help organizations discovering their employees' relevant know-how. The success or failure in implementing quality management systems depends on the quality manager's management style or capability for implementing organizational change and resolving its underlying paradoxes and tensions.

ISO 9001 Standard: A Management Tool for Conformity and Innovation

The ISO 9001 standard is the most studied management systems standard in quality management literature. It is based on a set of principles to set a quality management system (QMS). Some have suggested that a standardization effort is a tool to achieve conformity, but conversely it hampers innovation (Benner & Tushman, 2003), others find that it can initiate exploration and innovation when it is employed in an ambidextrous way (Asif & De Vries, 2015). They argue that it is possible to include and align the exploitation of good practices to satisfy customers' needs, and the exploration of opportunities that can be leveraged by quality management to create new values and product/service innovation. In line with Asif and De Vries, we argue throughout this paper, that organizational, managerial, individual, product/service innovations related to the ambidextrous structure and orientation of ISO 9001 standard's requirements, depend on the organisation's quality goals, the degree of commitment of top and middle management, and the managerial philosophy in place to manage the paradoxes and tensions that will arise during the implementation process.

We consider and study ISO 9001 standard as a management tool structured and functions with three interdependent elements: The first element is the role of conformation of practices to the pre-established rules (role of standardization).The second element is to investigate internal knowledge and competences. The third element is to explore the relevant external knowledge and relationships that can leverage organization's core competence with new values (role of innovation). These three elements structure the following:

1) The *technical substratum or artifact* that contains the rules or requirements to be implemented. Each of these rules is made of encoded expert scientific and technical knowledge (Brunsson et al., 2012; Brunsson & Jacobsson, 2005).

2) The implementation of these requirements is influenced by the managerial style or *the management philosophy* that deploys, interprets, and implements them with the appropriate quality management methods, tools and techniques (Asif & De Vries, 2015). The management style may be enabling or coercive to employee learning (Adler & Borys, 1996). Managers can be participative or directive (Likert, 2012). When the manager or someone responsible for quality adopts a participative style, employees are asked to write down the procedures or operational routines, i.e., what they do in their daily practices, how they do it, and in which sequence. With a directive style, some quality management functions are delegated to a qualified supervisor, which may be an external consultant. They will define and write the new procedures to be integrated in operations, without involving the employees. Without their involvement, the employees, who play a crucial role in the appropriation of new quality rules (Benezech et al., 2001), will feel dispossessed from their know-how and may resist the change program. This resistance can lead to the failure of the standardization effort (Serhan, 2017; Lambert & Loos-Baroin, 2004).

The third component of ISO 9001 is a simplified view of the knowledge and relations that compose an organization. This is because the standards were conceived through a progressive distillation of their developers' expertise so that they were generic and applicable to a wide variety of organizations (Brunsson et al., 2012).

These generic characteristics have a pragmatic ambiguity that enlarges the interpretive variability and ensures their adaptability to various contexts and goals (Ansari et al., 2010; 2014; Giroux, 2006).

Managerial style can play a critical role in individual and organizational learning, and in managing this pragmatic ambiguity. It helps overcome the cognitive and emotional tensions that emerge during the standardization process, in particular, those driven by the knowledge management and knowledge codification processes.

ISO 9001 Requirements Implementation: Organizational Knowledge Expansion and Learning

Standardization praxis is a poorly understood discipline, and most of the academic studies are of little assistance to practitioners (Cargill, 2011). One way to understand the ISO 9001 standard is as a set of "ostensible routines" (Feldman & Pentland, 2003) that can frame and manage the "performative routines" or operational actions in organizations. These performative routines adapt the standard's generic requirements to the organizational context such as mission, vision, values, and culture, and thus, mitigate the possibility that implementation might fail (Cargill, 2011). To better understand the reasons of failures, the implementation of these ostensible routines should not be examined from the focus of whether the standard or its specification were implemented, but rather from the viewpoint of whether the practitioners involved in the new rules appropriation, learned, achieved their goals, and helped further the organizational goals.

The standard appropriation means devising new rules appropriate to the specific use in the organization and creating a specific value for the system (organization, product, process, relationship, etc.) meant to be improved by quality principles (Grimand, 2006). Through this process, the standard is reinvented by its users, and the users' practices are transformed by the new knowledge introduced into the existing system (Grimand, 2006; Hatchuel, 2005). This transformation can be understood through the expansive individual and organizational learning process proposed by Engeström (2001; 2015). The expansive learning process occurs as a dynamic fit between the adopter's practices and the organizational goals. The individual learning is operational and incremental. It is achieved through a "learning the code" process (Lambert & Loos-Baroin, 2004). The organizational learning is conceptual and is achieved through a "learning by the code" process. In this process, skilled managers learn from the contradictions how to change the goals or objects of their activities and put into practice new instruments that help overcome the contradictions and tensions caused by the newly adopted change program (Engeström, 2001). If "learning the code" could be achieved by the application of a new procedure, it can induce the expansion of the organisation's knowledge, strategic goals and relationships.

Tensions Related to Quality Management Systems

The introduction of ISO 9001 standard's requirements is also the introduction of new operational rules. This induces three paradoxes (Lewis, 2000) that are manifested through three tensions or conflicts at both individual and organizational levels: First, the "interpretative tension" related to the contradiction between the standard's demand for both conformity and exploration (organizing paradox). Second, the "confrontation tension" between the standard's abstract rules and the existing routines (learning paradox). Third, the tensions related to the knowledge codification process, namely the learning and belonging paradoxes (Table 1). The learning paradox refers to the opposition between the simultaneous desire to achieve stability and seek sensing and seizing the opportunities that can reconfigure the organization's products and services with new values. The paradox of belonging signifies complex relationships between the self and other, highlighting the problematic nature of individuality, group boundaries, and globalization (Lewis, 2000). In the belonging paradox, employees try to find the best way to integrate into a group while preserving their own skills and know-how. In organizations, all of these paradoxes appear as emotional and cognitive tensions. They create anxiety that prevents the employees and the company from learning how to expand their knowledge and competences.

In this paper, we focus particularly on the knowledge codification paradox that emerges during the implementation of "writing of procedures and identification of GP" requirement. This knowledge management process aims at identifying, selecting, codifying and diffusing the good practices throughout the organization

Table 1. Paradoxes, tensions and their impact during the implementation of ISO 9001 requirements

Tension	Source of Tension	Paradox	Organizational Impact
Interpretative tension	Contradiction between the role of conformity and exploration	Organizing paradox	Management seeks to involve its employees in the process of change, even if they are resistant and lose confidence
Confrontation tension	Contextualization of the standard's abstract rules within the operational routines	Learning paradox	Opposition between compliance procedures and exploration practices
Tensions of knowledge codification	Opposition between stability and innovation needs	Learning and belonging and paradoxes	Managers seek organizational learning and employees fear losing their know-how. Emergence of emotional and cognitive tensions.

for replication. These processes enhance the organizational learning by gathering specialized - but fragmented - knowledge from individuals and subsidiaries (Kim, 1993; Grant, 1996).

This knowledge management process can be achieved through two complementary approaches: The process and the practice approach (Leidner et al., 2006). Within the 'process approach', the organizational knowledge is more or less reduced to a codifiable object (Cook & Brown, 1999) and KM practices focus on managing explicit knowledge stock, i.e. knowledge that can be articulated and written. The "writing of procedures" requirement is a codification process that creates new information but is partially representative of the activity, as only verbalised knowledge can be codified (Foray, 2000). The KM within the "process approach" allows ISO 9001 standard to only fulfil the role of compliance to codified good practices (GP). This produces "first-order or dead routines" (Collis, 1994) as they induce incremental improvements and provoke rigidity and inertia that hinder the functions of exploration and innovation. Moreover, the cognitive distance between the creator of the GP and the actor applying them can lead to a negative transfer experience, i.e., a misunderstanding of the sense and value of GP (Heimeriks et al., 2012).

In organizations, other individual and organizational knowledge is more difficult to codify. The abilities to do ("doing know-how"), understand ("understanding know-how"), and combine ("combinatory know-how"), represent expertise specific to the individual, and remain attached to a particular mode of organization and deployment (Hatchuel & Weil, 1999). Such 'tacit knowing' (Polanyi, 1958) can only be handled and assessed in a "practice approach" that helps managing these personal abilities by involving the GP's users in socialization practices to share their experiences and know-how and create new value (De Vries & Van Delden, 2006; Nonaka et al., 2008).

To counterbalance the blind spots of codified tools, organizations concentrate upon a practice approach to manage the tacit knowledge and knowing at both the individual and organizational levels (Brown & Duguid, 2001). At the individual level, by describing their functions and daily procedures, employees can make visible their competences and their knowledge gaps. This knowledge audit (De Vries & Van Delden, 2006) can facilitate acceptance of the change program and the integration of the new rules into operations. This permits the evolution of their practices and skills (Cochoy et al., 1998). On the organizational level, the identification of the various specialized but fragmented individuals' knowledge can be understood as an explorative knowledge management practice. It allows the organization to discover the relevant knowledge and competences it holds and to develop the "higher-order routines" that permit sensing and seizing the opportunities that can reconfigure the organization's product and services' values (Teece, 2007).

Two higher-order routine practices that have been identified are risk management and tacit knowledge transfer (Heimeriks et al., 2012). Risk management practices aim to facilitate the integration of codified GP in practices to ensure operational improvements. For example, the presence of a quality manager during the implementation of a new rule reduces the risk of its misunderstanding and negative transfer, i.e., deviation from its proper use. The tacit knowledge transfer practices are based on extensive personal contact, including training by integration experts that are experienced corporate executives or external consultants or sessions between different business unit managers involved in the standardization program. These practices elevate the understanding of acquisition/integration of GPs from the "what" (declarative knowledge) and the "how" (procedural knowledge) to the "why" (causal knowledge) (Cohen & Bacdayan, 1994). Thus, they narrow the knowledge gap between those who create the codified tools and those who are applying them (Heimeriks et al., 2012). These practices can be mainly developed through experiences that involve managers and employees who collectively question the blind spots of codification processes and the sense, value, and orientations of their activities. In QMS, the introduction of knowledge codification process as a creative experience requires participative managers who are competent in understanding paradoxes, tensions and find the best ways to manage them.

The literature of paradox management distinguishes three ways of dealing with paradoxes: 1) Acceptance, 2) Transcendence and 3) Confrontation (Schneider, 1990). Acceptance occurs as a group of individuals work together to manage a paradox. The global performance of their activity system is achieved under the supervision by leaders. Transcendence refers to the ability to think paradoxically in order to develop a more complicated repertoire of understandings and behaviours that better reflect the organization's intricacies. Confrontation refers to a process by which the tensions are discussed to socially construct a more accommodating understanding or practice. By identifying and discussing their underlying logic, actors might subject their ways of thinking to critique, thereby raising their chances of escaping paralysis. This allows the construction of a new working framework that overcomes the contradictory individual rationales and emotional tensions to reach a cognitive equilibrium (Lewis, 2000). The management challenge and role is to know how to focus on cognitive conflicts and avoid emotional ones, by valuing the intersection of diverse employees' knowledge and skills and reducing the power imbalance between managers and employees (Lewis, 2000; Josserand & Perret, 2003). The confrontation process can become an opportunity for fostering ideas and new solutions likely to bring about cognitive 'jumps' within the organisation (Josserand & Perret, 2003). The use of humour is a 'low risk' means of confrontation in the management of paradoxes (Hatch & Ehrlich 1993). In certain circumstances, it reduces emotional tensions (individual goals) and highlights the cognitive tensions (organizational goals).

While the literature explains the nature and origins of some organizational paradoxes, it is as yet unclear how organizations can manage them in practice and what are the outcomes of their emerging tensions. The management of paradoxes entails exploring rather than suppressing tensions and its analysis requires more than a definition of the paradox's characteristics. This management requires a tool or a framework to help exploring it and better understanding the reasons and outcomes of the contradictions that emerge in the transforming system (Cameron & Quinn, 1988). To facilitate the exploration of the Danone case study, we use Engeström's model of activity system and expansive learning (Engeström, 2001; 2015) as an interpretative framework for understanding the learning, disturbances, failures and innovations that emerged during Danone's experience introducing the knowledge codification process in its activity system.

MANAGING PARADOXES BY ACTIVITY SYSTEM AND EXPANSIVE LEARNING THEORY

Engeström's model of activity system theory and expansive learning (2001) builds on and completes the activity theory initiated by Vygotsky (1934) and Leont'ev (1981). The activity system model (Engeström, 2001; 2015) aims to reveal the learning, tensions, and expansion of knowledge of any practitioner (subject) who interacts with his/her internal collaborators and external stakeholders (community) to implement cultural artifacts with respect to some rules, in order to reach an objective (object, goal or outcome) (Figure 2). Objects are concerns, generators and foci of attention, motivation, effort and meaning. They are moving targets to continuously improve (expansive learning) by moving from an initial concept or unclear state, situationally-given "raw material" (object of concept 1) to a collectively meaningful object constructed by the activity system (object of concept 2), and then to a potentially shared or jointly-constructed object (object of concept 3) constructed by the community's actors (Figure 3).

In activity systems, contradictions appear when the goals of an individual and his/her community differs, or when a new rule collides with an old one. The contradictions generate disturbances and conflicts. However, these can be the triggers for the evolution of established routines, and also an opportunity to create new concepts through collective interpretation.

The relevance of Engeström's concept of cultural-historical activity theory to study the standardization effort is twofold: First, this model refers to groups of individuals acting within a community using various tools according to a particular division of labour with a set of beliefs to achieve a common object. In our case the ISO 9001 standard is a socio-technical artifact. To introduce the standard means that it must be contextualized in an already existing system. This entails reconciling the standard being introduced with context in the focal organization implementing the

Figure 1. Engeström's activity system model (2001)

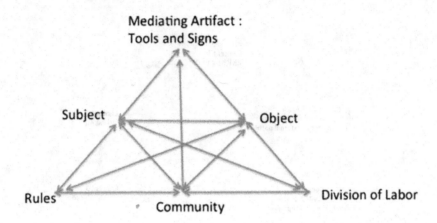

standard. The Engeström model is a powerful tool for understanding the process by which managerial standards are introduced and normalized, and the complexities of "socially distributed activity systems" in which incoherencies, paradoxes and tensions are inevitable in a change. This model allows showing how managers can use these paradoxes and conflicts as a driving force for change, and a tool to drive the constant effort to create new meanings and values in activities.

Figure 2. Expansive learning cycle (Engeström, 2001)

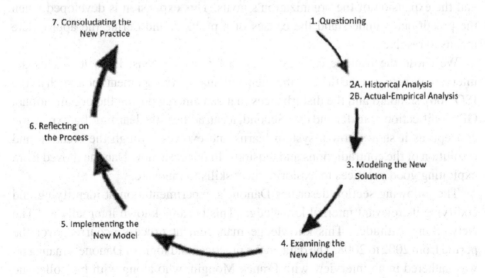

Figure 3. The expansive learning cycle applied to the networking attitude experienced at Danone

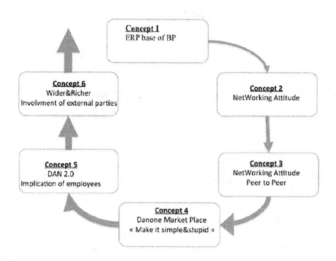

The socially constructed new meaning creates new knowledge (expansive learning) in a cyclical process that consists of several phases of learning (see Figure 2). Through this cycle, successive concepts are elaborated and presented as a new solution to a disturbance in the system (Figure 3 for the case of Danone). Expansion refers to the generation of new knowledge and practices from the organization's conflicts and the expansion of the organization's goals. This expansion is developed when the practitioners understand the causes of a problem and define the appropriate means to resolve it.

We chose the Danone case as a model for two reasons. First, it reveals the interactions between the three components of quality management tools such as the ISO 9001 standard and the disturbances that can emerge during the organizational GPs codification, transfer and use. Second, it can address the learning-by-expansion concept, as it shows how a system learns and evolves through the creation and resolution of the contradictions and tensions. In our case, how Danone moved from exploiting good practices to exploring new skills to innovate.

The following section describes Danone's experimentation at identifying and codifying its relevant internal knowledge. This became known internally as "The Networking Attitude." This knowledge management process occurred over the period from 2002 to 2008. The data on the practices and logic of Danone's managers was gathered in an interview with Franck Mougin, who along with his colleague

Mr. Benedikt Benenati, developed the concept. We also drew upon articles they published in "Les amis de l'Ecole de Paris, *Danone se raconte des histoires, une version latine du knowledge management*" and "Danone tells stories, a Latin version of knowledge management" (Mougin & Benenati, 2005; Edmondson et al., 2008).

THE DANONE CASE STUDY

The Context of Danone

Danone defines itself as a 'glocal' multinational, and as such experiences the paradox of "integration-decentralisation," a difficulty that many multinational firms face. This forces Danone to look beyond current market demands to anticipate future competition. For Franck Riboud (Chairman & Chief Executive Officer of Danone Groupe), Danone's threats are partially determined by its limits. It is smaller than some of its direct competitors (Nestlé and Unilever), and therefore, cannot compete directly with them in mass production. As a result, it aims to become and remain faster by introducing new distinctive products, services and values. This innovation strategy is one of using "continuous innovation" (Verona & Ravasi, 2003) or innovations in rapid succession (Deschamps & Nayak, 1997).

To achieve the goal of more rapid innovation, Danone invests in the management of its knowledge and skills, scattered among its factories, subsidiaries and individuals throughout the world. To maintain its place among the world market leaders, it aims to merge this specialized but scattered knowledge into a repertoire of "common knowledge". Danone aims to use this 'knowledge reservoir' (Becker & Lazaric, 2003) to build the organizational capabilities that facilitate maintaining its competitive advantage by developing rare or difficult-to-imitate innovations. Such innovations should be distinctive, as they are grounded on internal routines and considered as knowledge-based innovations (Saulais & Ermine, 2012).

The international context of Danone's activities' systems constitutes the implementation starting point of ISO 9001 standard of quality management and later of ISO 22005 for food security and traceability. These standards provide companies and their stakeholders a common language to continuously improve their processes and products (Berget, 2008). Danone's fundamental objective is to promote organizational learning to stimulate creativity and innovation across all its units. From this perspective, the codification of GPs among all its subsidiaries is vital but difficult to achieve for two reasons: First, knowledge codification and the development of GPs require the participation of the largest possible number of practitioners. Second, to achieve a successful knowledge transfer, appropriate dissemination tools and integration practices are required. To encourage all of its employees to collaborate in this process, Danone invented the basics to facilitate the participation it wanted. To reinforce the feeling of belonging of its practitioners to the company and the image and culture of the group, Danone created a common language, an identity for its collaborators and a system to share its knowledge. Danone's employees became 'Danoners'. They worked in a 'Danone Community' within a 'Danone Way' organised around 'storytelling' or stories of good practices developed in its units. These stories were meant to be exchanged within the group.

Danone's Approach to Knowledge Management and the Knowledge Codification Paradox

Applying an Activity System Model

In Danone, the aim to manage the paradox of 'maintaining autonomy' while 'integrating entities' on an organizational and cultural level, led two directors of the group, Franck Mougin (General Director of Human Resources) and Benedikt Benenati (Director of Organizational Development and Knowledge-Networking) to imagine a new method to manage Danone's knowledge, The NetWorking Attitude (NWA). NWA was made up of 'good networking practices'. We detail below the successive stages of development of this initiative, by first specifying the primary system requirements, the objective to be achieved through the implementation of the tool (concept 1), and the disturbances or conflicts that emerged while putting the concept into practice. These disturbances led to the creation of a new Concept 2, and then another Concept 3, Concept 4, and further in a cycle of learning and practice evolution. The sentences in italic are verbatim translation from our interview with Franck Mougin, one of the developers of the tool and from the two articles that the protagonists wrote.

The first step of this "nice story" stems from a strategic paradox in the group's management system - the integration/decentralization of its activities.

To continuously and rapidly improve quality management practices, the transformation of behaviours in the activity system from controlled participation to autonomy was needed.

System Requirements: The continuous improvement of quality management by avoiding a pyramid approach to solving problems: *"When a front-line manager encounters a problem, he turns to his boss, who in turn consults his own boss, and so on, until the point where the heads of different entities discuss the manager's problem in a transversal manner. The problem moves from one unit to another searching a solution, then climb back up the hierarchical pyramid for application before going down to another unit."*

Object to achieve: Permit the exchange of GPs between different units without a pyramidal consultation.

Concept 1: Implementation of a Tool (Entreprise Resource Planning) to Manage the Codified Knowledge of Business Units

This tool aimed to provide a system to set up files, manage data and facilitate the transfer of managers' good practices through networking. This concept allowed the incorporation of 144 GPs into the system.

Contradiction (a): *"This virtual system did not work, the actors did not engage in exchange, and the database was not used. Scaling complicates the problem, takes up time and leads to online loss," "This tool was countercultural, simply because at Danone we are not process driven," "Being controlled by headquarters has always been a challenge for Danone."*

Another key reason of this tension is related to the knowledge gap or cognitive distance between the creators and implementers of the codified GP. Implementers lack time to search for the appropriate solution and have limited understanding of the cause-and-effect relationships that underpin acquisition/ integration process.

To alleviate this problem, adopters need practices that facilitate their understanding of the causal effects between the procedures applied and the results obtained. An improvement of the concept was needed. Another tool had to be found that was composed of less "technical material" and was more socialization-oriented as it had to manage knowledge.

Concept 2: The Networking Attitude, NWA

Object 2: Allow direct discussions about GP in managers' meetings to speed up the transfer of knowledge to different functions, units and countries.

Contradiction (b): Bosses were reluctant to let their teams engage in direct discussion.

    Contradiction (c): Danone employed 90,000 people; therefore, direct contact to find solutions and resolve problems was impossible.

This contradiction in Concept 2 had to be improved by focusing the object of codifying knowledge only for front- line managers.

Concept 3: Networking Attitude 'Peer-to-Peer'

Object 3: *"A front-line manager must consult his colleague rather than his boss." This means reaching the 8,400 front-line managers"*.

In practice, this concept means that managers will be opposed to their skills and know-how, thus a double bind emerged: contradictions (d) and (e). In each contradiction, the manager is confronted to two conflicting choices.

Contradiction (d): The manager's anxiety about becoming redundant and losing skills: *"If a collaborator applies an efficient practice that he/she has developed, he/she risks losing control of it and to be not useful anymore. This practice also calls back the syndrome of "not invented here."*

Contradiction (e): Fear of being judged incompetent by superiors: *"Adopting someone else's solution means that I do not know how to resolve the problem myself. The fear is shared equally by bosses; if managers find solutions by consulting their colleagues, then managers are of no further use."*

The fear of showing "unresolved problems and the need for help" in the activity system of each manager led to the development of a new innovative experience.

Concept 4: "Make it Simple and Stupid" Danone MarketPlace of Best Practices (DMP)

Object 4: The goal of this concept is to implement direct, improvised and fast exchanges of good practices between experts to forge a "community of communities of practices" (Brown & Duguid, 2001). This fits perfectly the goal of organizational learning set by Danone at the beginning of its knowledge management program.

The developers of the DMP justify their choice: *"When instructions are too sophisticated, people will not understand them, and it is therefore necessary to be intelligent to give simple instructions"*. Simplicity is complicated, and therein lies the mangers' skills and dynamic managerial capabilities

The *Danone Marketplace* can be understood as an organised bazaar. It looks like the classic idea of any market with supply and demand), but one in which GPs not products are exchanged . The actors of this market are front-line managers from different units and subunits (R&D, food security, stock management, etc.) from the three core group businesses (dairy products, water and biscuits). These managers appear unexpectedly for a short time in a meeting or a conference in an informal manner (disguised) to propose good practices for "sale." *"The disguise does away with hierarchical ranks and overcomes inhibitions, thus reduces emotional and cognitive tensions related to GP exchange."* Each DMP was conceived around a different theme (Provincial-style market, Hungarian market, Star Wars, the American West, etc.). The GP creators, prepare the presentation of their "offer" that must not exceed ten minutes. At the presentation, "givers" distribute to potential "takers" or future implementers, a little book of GPs, in which the codified good practices are written as nice stories that can be told in 30 seconds. In each page of this booklet is displayed a GP summing up the problem, the solution, the tangible advantages, and the practical details of putting it into practice. After a brief and informal discussion between the two parties (creators and implementers of GP), if a taker buys a GP, he receives a check to symbolise the act of payment (the transaction) and the promise of its implementation in their unit. The giver keeps the check to help him following the traces of the GP in Danone's community and eventually recount beautiful stories.

In this concept, the GP reference document, according to the theory of activity system of Engeström, operates as a mediating-tool between the subject, object and the community. In this informal way of improving work practices, learning is not considered as distant from work problems as it is in the first stages of the concept. The discussion between actors on the market represents a tacit knowledge transfer practice (Heimeriks et al., 2012). Such discussions are risk management practices for quality management systems. They reduce the GP's negative deviation from the sense it was given where it was created. Moreover, in this market between the givers and takers, there is a facilitator, whose role is *"to make sure that the selection of a GP to resolve a certain problem is correctly done."*

By providing ample opportunity for in-depth discussion of specific issues that a given manager, or a team is facing, the tacit knowledge transfer practice goes beyond what codified tools can offer. They elevate understanding of acquisition - integration from the "what" and the "how" to the "why" (causal knowledge) (Cohen & Bacdayan, 1994), thus narrowing the gap between those who create and those who will apply the creations. The DMP was proposed to facilitate sharing and improve performance of units: *"We should sell the idea by explaining things in a simple way, almost simplistic." "When the 'taker' has met the 'giver' and an exchange has taken place, beneficial results obtained by the articulation of know-how of both actors, could be seen in terms of time saved and errors avoided; this becomes a 'nice story' to tell."*

But a new tension occurred when some top managers decided that the DMP concept should be expanded (virtually) from managers to employees, while others remained reluctant and believed that the contribution of non-managers to total performance does not merit including them in networking activities and would consume time to make it happen and with uncertain benefits. For Mougin, involving all Danone employees (90,000 persons) in this experience was vital for both employees and the group: *"This is about empowerment and appraisal."* Mougin had tested this belief himself with a marketplace for assistants that worked well, with some assistants claiming that it was the first time anyone had asked their opinion.

The organizational learning from this knowledge management program led to the emergence of a new concept that widened the object "peer-to-peer NWA" to all employees. It was termed the "Who's Who" concept. Launched in 2007, this concept was an internal directory on the Danone intranet that had a box entitled "Networking Attitude". Any practitioner who wanted to take part in sharing his GP could check saying "I'm happy to share". The idea is that if an employee has a problem, he can with a few search words find someone who can help him. This concept was rapidly judged as inappropriate or entrapped by its own mode of functioning, since it is based on keywords for seeking a competent person. For example, *"if you typed in the word "diversity", then you would see all the people that listed this as a competence in their profile."* This intranet directory was not useful and failed (Edmondson et al., 2008). The failure opened up another discussion to address some new questions about the relevance of making this space/tool available for all employees and how this should be done to enhance not only learning at the organizational level, but also innovation .

Previously, innovation had not been introduced as a goal to achieve through the GP exchange program. Thus, another concept emerged to bridge workplace practices, learning and innovation in the whole Danone community.

Concept 5: Dan 2.0, Managing Knowledge for Competitive Advantage
Object 5: the object of this concept was to involve more employees in the GPs exchanging experience.

Dan 2.0 was a new program of organizational change. It required a strong commitment from the top management to support the 'democratic principles' of this participative philosophy of management, which was "user-centric" (Rolland, 2012). Nicolas Rolland, the creator of Dan 2.0 concept argued that with this approach, each employee should be considered as potentially possessing knowledge that could be a source of a competitive advantage. This new concept aimed to modify the object of knowledge management from sharing codified knowledge to creating new knowledge on which Danone could rely on to innovate. The first problem of this system lay in language. Danone operates in 140 countries and the language barrier may reduce the value of the GP and can also demotivate certain employees. A second disadvantage was related to the time factor. Employees have to dedicate a certain amount of time to codify their knowledge in a simple form, clear and accessible.

But the developers pointed out a key problem in the project: knowledge till now is only shared in the form of a good practice. GPs are zero-order routines that allow implementers to efficiently apply lessons learned from the Danone's prior experience and similar problems. And despite the critical role in reducing the cognitive distance and the risk of misapplication of GP, tacit knowledge transfer practices are in DMP, only optimizers of selection. They do not capture and align the full story of knowledge management of Danone with its strategic goal and mission: managing knowledge to create new products faster than its competitors. *"If we just keep sharing practices we are not going to survive, because the good practices of today are not going to be the good practices of tomorrow."*

To be richer, the tool had to go wider and open the knowledge management processes to creativity and innovation. Therefore, an innovation challenge to GP exchange was declared.

Concept 6: Peripheral Expansion of the Object, "Wider and Richer"
Object 6: The new object of the innovation challenge was to build external bridges to partners, suppliers, customers and consumers.

Danone had tested marketplaces with suppliers that competed to introduce the best solution for Danone on a strategic business issues that Danone had communicated to them in advance. The supplier with the best solution won a contract .

Danone also invited consumers to discuss products in development. Sharing GPs with retailers such as Wal-Mart and Carrefour was an option for Danone, as it lacked direct contact with consumers. Collaboration with the mass retailers could help find ways to ensure on-shelf availability. When there is a shortage on the shelf, Danone is penalized by the retailer for the loss of sales. It also gives the employees access to information about products and feedback into the innovation process based on consumers' requirements and needs. By giving consumers the opportunity to express their needs and insights, Danone could react more quickly than its competitors: *"Nestlé has 10 times as many resources as we do, but we still manage to create new solutions and processes"* (HRD at Danone Waters France) (Edmondson et al., 2008).

This analysis of the Danone NWA illustrates how a management tool can gradually be transformed into an established activity system (culture, daily routines, way of thinking of people), and, at the same time, how it transforms the actors' identity and knowledge during its diffusion. This transformation can be related to the successive learning stages that occurred gradually in the system and facilitated the adoption of the management innovation. The divisibility of the tool's principles (applied at first in a small-scale trial), and the simplification of its complexity (inventing methods like marketplaces with disguised participants) were innovative methods to facilitate the appropriation of the tool's requirements (Ansari, 2010). The NWA made GPs accessible to 5,000 of the 9,000 managers worldwide. Between 2004 and 2007, employees exchanged 640 GPs.

Danone has published the innovations that were obtained through the GPs exchange at Lu France. It shows that between 2003 and 2006, the problems of food security and the time to resolve them has decreased by 25% (Edmondson et al., 2008).

This experience shows also that the social interaction in this system constitutes a prerequisite to 'internalize' new knowledge for implementors and to 'externalize' know-how of the GPs creators. This cycle of knowledge conversion enabled Danone to introduce innovations at the workplace, behavioural, and development levels. These include the introduction of:

- Taillefine: In a "little book" in Brazil, a story entitled "If time is not on your side" describes how the Brazilian marketing team helped the French marketing team introduce a 0% fat dessert, the 'Taillefine', through an exchange of good practices;
- Essensis: This yoghurt that 'nourishes skin from the inside' was achieved through a centralised effort with three local ideas. This concept was then decentralised by calling for a collaborative project between several teams in several countries. As a result, *"the cross-functional team managed to get the product to the market in seven months."*

This innovation is related to the pooling of separate functions, talents and codified GPs. It embodies the principle of 'cross-functional teams', highlighted by Juran (1998) as the practice that makes possible the intersection of standardization and innovation.

DISCUSSION AND CONCLUSION

The activity system model used to analyse the knowledge codification paradox explains the tensions, learning mechanisms, and innovation that emerged during the implementation of new tools and rules into Danone's established systems. The praxis was the meeting point of the new rules and the operational routines, and it revealed the limits of the tool. During the deployment and diffusion process of the new rules, the three elements that compose generic management tools were contextualized with Danone's context and mission. First, new procedures adapted to Danone's performance improvement strategies to be codified and diffused. Second, the management philosophy to implement quality management tools changed. It evolved from a linear and rigid management style based on a "codify, apply, check" process approach, to a practice approach based on the practitioners' socialization and tacit-knowledge exchange to promote creativity and innovation. Third, the knowledge management processes helped codify Danone's internal and external relevant knowledge, and identify the key relationships composing the company's community that can affect or be affected by its actions, objectives and policies. The reconstitution of Danone's activity system and quality management strategy was facilitated by Danone's managers' efforts and competences that helped overcoming the emotional and cognitive tensions related to the knowledge codification processes by considering conflicts as constructive elements for learning, i.e., as neither good nor bad, but as the appearance of difference, difference in opinions, interests (Follett, 1925). These managers were critical in getting the technical tool to be accepted in the organization. This allowed learning and knowledge expansion for both individuals and the organization.

The expansion of the object from individual learning, to collective (front-line managers) and then to the organizational level (all employees) was followed by the introduction of another activity system that extended beyond the Danone's boundaries. This system integrated Danone's suppliers, customers, consumers and retailers. This expansion revealed new contradictions and ignited another cycle of learning. In fact, exposing organizational knowledge to the concerned external parties confronted Danone with another paradox. Not involving external parties meant depriving the company of useful knowledge for innovation, but, by doing so, it could result in a leak of the company's expertise to its competitors (Szulanski, 1996). There were two "paradoxical" concepts at the heart of the NWA:

1)   Autonomy Under Control

Even in the marketplace where GPs are exchanged and tacit knowledge was transferred, there was always a manager named a "transaction facilitator" who checked the coherence between the "buyer's" need and the "seller's" solution. The facilitator's role consisted of managing the risk of a negative transfer experience. He ensured that the right solution was sold to the right person and in an adequate format. This risk management practice triggered the variation stage of ad hoc problem solving, and the tacit knowledge transfer practices between managers were optimized at the selection stage. If knowledge transfer is a crucial practice to contribute to organizational learning, knowledge assimilation by those receiving it indicates knowledge transfer success (Hamdoun et al., 2019). As such, this practice represents a complementary mechanism through which higher-order routines manifest themselves through a deliberate effort to develop effective organizational learning capabilities.

2)   Standardization as the Crucible of Innovation

To drive the process of developing new GPs, Danone encouraged all its employees to participate in the standardization process with the goal of developing innovative concepts and products. But for this participation to be possible, and for innovation to be generated, a GP must be standardized so that it can be diffused and combined with others GPs.

The analysis of Danone's experience, shows that the product innovations developed through the NWA were exploitative knowledge-based innovations (Chanal & Mothe, 2005). They were the outcome of diverse specialized and codified knowledge combination. These new products allowed Danone to continuously introduce new innovative and targeted products. Examples of this are the "Taillefine" and "Essensis" yoghurts, that were targeted services. Essensis was for beauty and Taillefine was for health.

Danone's experience also shows that practitioners are not neutral observers of the change process, and neither is the management tool when it comes to learning and transformation. They interact and mutually reinforce the goals of each other. We have shown that knowledge expansion was not due to standards' requirements, but an outgrowth of the response to their limits and rigidity when put into practice. It also was an outcome of the management philosophy and style adopted for managing people and tools, standardization and innovation. Perceived as a management innovation, the knowledge codification paradox changed the way through which work is performed, and transformed practitioners, top managers and employees, into resources that can be used by the entire organization (Burns and Stalker, 1961).

Engeström's activity system model provided an important tool to describe how the knowledge expansion process contributes to standardization and knowledge codification. The model showed that to achieve learning, knowledge expansion and innovation through standardization, separating individual from collective and social forms of learning from the technical requirements should be avoided. By focusing on knowing as a situated, pragmatic, socio-cultural activity rather than a static form of knowledge, Danone's managers facilitated the adoption and the appropriation of the standard requirements at different levels of the organization.

Role of Managers' Philosophy and Skills to Manage Tensions and Change

Although the NWA experiment at Danone was not initiated within the framework of implementing ISO 9001, it illustrates the tensions and learning that emerged due to the knowledge codification requirements and the strategies for managing the paradoxes and contradictions related to QMS adoption. Humour was an important tactic that the developers of NWA used to assist in the uneasy, embarrassed, or chronically anxious quest for knowledge about what the individual should be doing, or what is expected of him, and similar apprehensiveness about what others are doing (Burns & Stalker, 1961). It facilitated the identification of tensions that could hinder practitioners from sharing their GPs and assisted in overcoming anxiety linked to a loss of skills, the fear of being judged incompetent, and conflicts regarding belonging. It allowed groups to exchange knowledge and capabilities that they valued with other actors that they did not know.

In implementing standardization and quality management systems top management and middle managers play a crucial role. For example, after Mr. Mougin left Danone in 2008, the MarketPlace program ended, as did the social and practice processes built up by the GP exchange. Only the Dan 2.0 remained as a social network to exchange GP of the group.

To conclude, this research found that strategy practices are embedded in broad organizational capabilities and technologies. We contribute to better understanding ISO 9001 requirements' implementation and the benefits a company can achieve through the management of its contradictions for both exploitation of good practices and exploration of opportunities that can leverage corporate core competence in the name of quality.

Finally, our conclusions can be generalised to understanding the codification and diffusion of good practices in an activity system and to management systems, in general. These can be applied to any process of implementing management standards, not just the ISO standard. Indeed, the process of implementing standards is one in which contradictions and paradoxes arise. For success, it is necessary to go beyond what codified tools generate and create a process that requires thinking of the organization as a system for developing creativity and innovation.

Our case study shows how Danone dealt with the contradiction and tensions in the standardization process and our granular exploration about how ISO management system standards and knowledge management processes were introduced and diffused provides insight that managers can use and upon which other researchers can build.

In the future, organizations will be ever more enmeshed in webs of relationships. Knowing that their partners have developed predictable processes that can generate reproducible outcomes is ever more necessary. Standards will be vital for ensuring intra- and inter-firm communication and process and product reproducibility particularly in firms with multinational operations.

The increasingly rapid introduction of innovations are continuously transforming the identity and functions of organizations and products. Organizations must develop innovations that address the global socio-economic and environmental challenges and standards are necessary to be judged as a reliable partner. Moreover, standards are necessary to successfully manage globally distributed business operations and eco-design new products and services.

ACKNOWLEDGMENT

The authors gratefully acknowledge the editor and the reviewers for their thoughtful and helpful comments.

REFERENCES

Adler, P. S., & Borys, B. (1996). Two types of bureaucracy: Enabling and Coercive. *Administrative Science Quarterly*, *41*(1), 61–89. doi:10.2307/2393986

Ahmad, W. (2017). ISO 9001 ISO 9001 Transition and its Impact on the Organizational Performance: Evidence from Service Industries of Pakistan. *International Journal of Research in Business Studies and Management*, *4*(3), 39–54. doi:10.22259/ijrbsm.0403004

Ansari, S. M., Fiss, P. C., & Zajac, E. J. (2010). Made to fit: How practices vary as they diffuse. *Academy of Management Review*, *35*(1), 67–92. doi:10.5465/AMR.2010.45577876

Ansari, S. M., Reinecke, J., & Spaan, A. (2014). How are Practices Made to Vary? Managing Practice Adaptation in a Multinational Corporation. *Organization Studies*, *35*(9), 1313–1341. doi:10.1177/0170840614539310

Asif, M., & De Vries, H. (2015). Creating ambidexterity through quality management. *Total Quality Management & Business Excellence*, *26*(11-12), 1226–1241. doi:10.1080/14783363.2014.926609

Asif, M., De Vries, H., & Ahmad, N. (2013). Knowledge creation through quality management. *Total Quality Management & Business Excellence*, *24*(5–6), 664–677. doi:10.1080/14783363.2013.791097

Becker, M., & Lazaric, N. (2003). The influence of knowledge in the replication of routines. *Economia Aplicada*, *LVI*(3), 65–94.

Benezech, D., Lambert, G., Lanoux, B., Lerch, Ch., & Loos-Baroin, J. (2001). Completion of knowledge codification: An illustration through the ISO 9000 standards implementation process. *Research Policy*, *30*(9), 1395–1407. doi:10.1016/S0048-7333(01)00158-5

Benner, M. J., & Tushman, M. L. (2003). Exploitation, exploration, and process management: The productivity dilemma revised. *Academy of Management Review*, *28*(2), 238–256. doi:10.5465/amr.2003.9416096

Berget, D. (2008). *Danone, géant mondial de l'alimentation, un des premiers adeptes de l'ISO 22000. ISO Management systems.* Mai-Juin.

Birkinshaw, J., Mol, M., & Hamel, G. (2005). *Management Innovation.* Advanced Institute of Management, Research Paper No. 021.doi:10.2139srn.1306981

Birkinshaw, J., & Mol, M. J. (2008). Management innovation. *Academy of Management Review, 33*(4), 825–845. doi:10.5465/amr.2008.34421969

Brown, J. S., & Duguid, P. (2001). Knowledge and organization: A social Practice perspective. *Organization Science, 12*(2), 198–213. doi:10.1287/orsc.12.2.198.10116

Brunsson, N., & Jacobson, B. (2005). *A world of standards.* Oxford University Press.

Brunsson, N., Rasche, A., & Seid, D. (2012). The Dynamics of Standardization: Three Perspectives on Standards in Organization Studies. *Organization Studies, 33*(5-6), 613–632. doi:10.1177/0170840612450120

Burns, T., & Stalker, G. M. (1961). *The management of innovation.* London: Tavistock.

Cargill, C. F. (2011). Why standardization efforts fail? *The Journal of Electronic Publishing: JEP,* 14.

Chanal, V. & Mothe, C. (2005). Concilier innovations d'exploitation et d'exploration – Le cas du secteur automobile, *Revue française de gestion, 154,* 173-191.

Cochoy, F., Garel, J. P., & De Terssac, G. (1998). Comment l'écrit travaille l'organisation: Le cas des normes ISO 9000. *Revue Francaise de Sociologie, 39*(4), 673–699. doi:10.2307/3323006

Cohen, M. D., & Bacdayan, P. (1994). Organizational Routines Are Stored as Procedural Memory: Evidence from a Laboratory Study. *Organization Science, 5*(4), 554–568. doi:10.1287/orsc.5.4.554

Collis, D. J. (1994). How valuable are organizational capabilities? *Strategic Management Journal, 1*(S1), 143–152. doi:10.1002mj.4250150910

Cook, S., & Brown, J. S. (1999). Bridging epistemologies: The generative dance between organizational knowledge and organizational knowing. *Organization Science, 10*(4), 381–400. doi:54 doi:10.1287/orsc.10.4.381

Deschamps, J. P., & Nayak, P. R. (1997). *Les maîtres de l'innovation totale, traduit de Product juggernauts.* Paris: Éditions d'Organisation.

DeVries, H. J. & Van Delden, M. (2006). *How to integrate standardization in knowledge management.* ISO Focus.

Donate, M. J., & Sanchez de Pablo, J. D. (2015). The role of knowledge-oriented leadership in knowledge management practices and innovation. *Journal of Business Research, 68*(2), 360–370. doi:10.1016/j.jbusres.2014.06.022

Edmondson, A. C., Moingeon, B., Dessain, V., & Jensen, A. D. (2008, Apr.). Global Knowledge Management at Danone. *Harvard Business School Review.*

Engeström, Y. (2001). Expansive learning at work: Toward an activity theoretical reconceptualization. *Journal of Education and Work, 14*(1), 133–156. doi:10.1080/13639080020028747

Engeström, Y. (2015). *Learning by expanding, an activity theoretical approach to developmental research* (2nd ed.). Cambridge University Press.

Evangelos, L. P., Pantouvakis, A., & Kafetzopoulos, D. P. (2013). The impact of ISO 9001 effectiveness on the performance of service companies. *Managing Service Quality: An International Journal, 23*(2), 149–164. doi:10.1108/09604521311303426

Feldman, M. S., & Pentland, B. T. (2003). Reconceptualizing organizational routines as a source of flexibility and change. *Administrative Science Quarterly, 48*(1), 94–118. doi:10.2307/3556620

Follett, M. P. (1925). Constructive conflict. In P. Graham (Ed.), Mary parker Follett: Prophet of management. Boston: Harvard Business School Press.

Foray, D. (2000). *L'économie de la connaissance*. Paris: La Découverte.

Giroux, H. (2006). It was such a handy term: Management fashions and pragmatic ambiguity. *Journal of Management Studies, 43*(6), 1227–1260. doi:10.1111/j.1467-6486.2006.00623.x

Grant, R. M. (1996). Towards a knowledge-based view of the firm. *Strategic Management Journal, 17*, 109–122.

Grimand, A. (2006). *L'appropriation des outils de gestion, vers de nouvelles perspectives théoriques?* Publications de l'Université de Saint-Etienne.

Hamdoun, M., Jabbour, Ch. J. Ch., & Ben Othman, H. (2018). Knowledge transfer and organizational innovation: Impacts of quality and environmental management. *Journal of Cleaner Production, 193*, 759–770. doi:10.1016/j.jclepro.2018.05.031

Hamel, G. (2006). The why, what and how of management innovation. *Harvard Business Review, 84*(2), 72–84. PMID:16485806

Hampden-Turner, Ch. (1994). *Corporate Culture*. London: Hutchinson.

Handy, C. (1994). *The age of paradox*. Cambridge, MA: Harvard Business School Press.

Handy, C. (1995). *The empty raincoat: Making sense of the future*. Random House Business.

Hatch, M. J., & Ehrlich, S. B. (1993). Spontaneous humor as an indicator of paradox and ambiguity in organizations. *Organization Studies*, *14*(4), 505–526. doi:10.1177/017084069301400403

Hatchuel, A. (2005). *Entre connaissances et organisation: l'activité collective, Pour une épistémologie de l'action, l'expérience des sciences de gestion*. La découverte.

Hatchuel, A., & Weil, B. (1999). *L'expert et le système*. Paris: Economica.

Heimeriks, K. H., Koen, H., Schijven, M., & Gates, S. (2012). Manifestations of higher-order routines: The under-lying mechanisms of deliberate learning in the context of post-acquisition integration. *Academy of Management Journal*, *55*(3), 703–726. doi:10.5465/amj.2009.0572

Helfat, C. E., & Martin, J. A. (2015). Dynamic managerial capabilities: Review and assessment of managerial impact on strategic change. *Journal of Management*, *41*(5), 1281–1312. doi:10.1177/0149206314561301

Jashapara, A. (2004). *Knowledge Management, an integrated approach*. Prentice Hall, Financial Times.

Jay, J. (2013). Navigating paradox as a mechanism of change and innovation in hybrid organizations. *Academy of Management Journal*, *56*(1), 137–159. doi:10.5465/amj.2010.0772

Josserand, E., & Perret, V. (2003). Pratiques organisationnelles du paradoxe. Le paradoxe: penser et gérer autrement les organisations, 165-187.

Juran, J. (1998). *Juran's Quality handbook* (5th ed.). McGraw Hill.

Kim, D. H. (1993). The Link between Individual and Organizational Learning. *Sloan Management Review*, *35*(1), 37–50.

Lambert, G., & Loos-Baroin, J. (2004). Certification ISO 9000 et création de connaissances opérationnelles et conceptuelles: Une étude de cas. *Finance Contrôle Stratégie*, *7*(1), 53–79.

Lambert, G. & Ouedraogo, N. (2009). Rôles des normes de management de la qualité sur l'apprentissage organisationnel selon les raisons de leur mise en œuvre. *Congrès annuel de l'Administrative Sciences Association of Canada*.

Leidner, D. E., Alavi, M., & Kayworth, T. (2006). The role of culture in knowledge management: A case study of two global firms. *International Journal of e-Collaboration*, 2(1), 17–40. doi:10.4018/jec.2006010102

Leont'ev, A. (1981). *Problems of the Development of the Mind*. Moscow: Progress Publishers.

Lewis, M. W. (2000). Exploring Paradox: Toward a More Comprehensive Guide. *Academy of Management Review*, 25(4), 760–776. doi:10.5465/amr.2000.3707712

Lewis, M. W., & Smith, W. K. (2014). Paradox as a Metatheoretical Perspective. *The Journal of Applied Behavioral Science*, 50(2), 127–149. doi:10.1177/0021886314522322

Lickert, R. (2012). Management systems and styles. In *Jean Michel Plane, Théorie et Management des Organisations, Management, Ressources Humaines*. Dunod.

Moisdon, J. C. (1997). *Du mode d'existence des outils de gestion: les instruments de gestion à l'épreuve de l'organisation*. Seli Arslan.

Mougin, F. & Benenati, B. (2005). Danone se raconte des histoires, une version latine du knowledge management. *Séminaire des affaires organisé grâce aux parrains de l'école de Paris*.

Nonaka I., Toyama R., & Hirata., T. (2008). *Managing flow: A process theory of the knowledge-based firm*. doi:10.1057/9780230583702

Polanyi, M. (1958). Personal knowledge, towards a post critical philosophy. Chicago Press.

Riboud, F. (2013). *Danone Rapport économique et social*. Academic Press.

Rolland, N. (2012). *L'entreprise 2.0 en France en 2012: Mythe et Réalité*. Etude réalisée par l'Institut de l'Entreprise 2.0 de Grenoble Ecole de Management.

Saulais, P., & Ermine, J.-L. (2012). Innovation fondée sur les connaissances: Une expérimentation sur l'innovation technique incrémentale. In GeCSO Gestion des Connaissances dans la Société et les Organisations. Montréal, Canada: Mai.

Schneider, K. J. (1990). *The paradoxical self: Toward an understanding of our contradictory nature*. New York: Insight Books, Plenum.

Serhan, H. (2017). *Pratiques d'appropriation et dynamique des connaissances de la norme ISO 9001: outil de conformation et creuset d'innovation* (Thèse de doctorat). AgroParisTech, Université Paris-Saclay, Paris, France.

Serhan, H. (2018). Creating conformity, facilitating innovation: A practice-based study of implementing ISO 9001 standard. In Congrès RRI – VIII Forum de l'innovation, Les nouveaux modes de l'organisation. IUT Nîmes – Université Montpellier 1.

Smith, W. K., Lewis, M. W., Jarzabkowski, P., & Langley, A. (2017). *The oxford handbook of organizational paradox*. OUP. doi:10.1093/oxfordhb/9780198754428.001.0001

Smith, W. K., Lewis, M. W., & Tushman, M. L. (2011). Organizational sustainability: Organization design and senior leadership to enable strategic paradox. In K. Cameron, & G. Spreitzer (Eds.), The Oxford handbook of positive organizational scholarship (pp. 798-810). New York, NY: Oxford University Press.

Smith, W. K., & Tushman, M. L. (2005). Managing strategic contradictions: A top management model for managing innovation streams. *Organization Science*, *16*(5), 522–536. doi:10.1287/orsc.1050.0134

Szulanski, G. (1996). Exploring internal stickiness: Impediments to the transfer of best practice within the firm. *Strategic Management Journal*, *17*(S2), 27–43. doi:10.1002mj.4250171105

Takeuchi, H., & Osono, E. (2008). The contradictions that drive Toyota's success. *Harvard Business Review*, *86*(6), 96. PMID:18411967

Teece, D. J. (2007). Explicating dynamic capabilities: Nature and microfoundations of sustainable enterprise performance. *Strategic Management Journal*, *28*(13), 1319–1350. doi:10.1002mj.640

Tushman, M. L., & O'Reilly, C. A. I. III. (1996). Ambidextrous organizations: Managing evolutionary and revolutionary change. *California Management Review*, *38*(4), 8–30. doi:10.2307/41165852

Verona, G., & Ravasi, D. (2003). Unbundling dynamic capabilities: An exploratory study of continuous product innovation. *Industrial and Corporate Change*, *12*(3), 577–606. doi:10.1093/icc/12.3.577

Vygotski, L. (1934). Pensée et langage. la dispute.

Xie, Z., Hall, J., McCarthy, I. P., Skitmore, M., & Schen, L. (2016). Standardization efforts: The relationship between knowledge dimensions, search processes and innovation outcomes. *Technovation*, *48*(4), 69–78. doi:10.1016/j.technovation.2015.12.002

Section 4
Legal and Regulatory Aspects

Chapter 8
Standardisation, Data Interoperability, and GDPR

Harshvardhan Jitendra Pandit
 https://orcid.org/0000-0002-5068-3714
Trinity College Dublin, Ireland

Christophe Debruyne
 https://orcid.org/0000-0003-4734-3847
Trinity College Dublin, Ireland

Declan O'Sullivan
Trinity College Dublin, Ireland

Dave Lewis
 https://orcid.org/0000-0002-3503-4644
Trinity College Dublin, Ireland

ABSTRACT

The General Data Protection Regulation (GDPR) has changed the ecosystem of services involving personal data and information. It emphasises several obligations and rights, amongst which the Right to Data Portability requires providing a copy of the given personal data in a commonly used, structured, and machine-readable format – for interoperability. The GDPR thus explicitly motivates the use and adoption of data interoperability concerning information. This chapter explores the entities and their interactions in the context of the GDPR to provide an information model for the development of interoperable services. The model categorises information and exchanges and explores existing standards and efforts towards use for interoperable interactions. The chapter concludes with an argument for the use and adoption of structured metadata to enable more expressive services through semantic interoperability.

DOI: 10.4018/978-1-7998-2181-6.ch008

INTRODUCTION

Standards emerge when operations have consequences and an agreement is essential for co-operation between stakeholders. In today's world, interoperability is essential for the smooth running of businesses and services that are increasingly dealing with data through the medium of the Internet. With the advent of the Internet as a marketplace with global outreach, the progression of online services has increasingly indulged in personalisation and targeted advertisements. To counter unchecked pervasiveness and instill the responsible use of personal data, privacy laws are enacted and updated to keep pace with ever-evolving technology. The latest of these is the European Council's General Data Protection Regulation ('Regulation (EU) 2016/679...', 2016), which was adopted on 14th April 2016 and entered into force on 25th May 2018. It is the topic of global interest due to the potential of significantly high fines on the order of 20 million euros or 4% of an organisation's global turnover – whichever is higher. Now past its first year, GDPR still continues to be a topic of development and innovation due to its extent of requirements and lack of technological solutions and guidance to address compliance (Good, Rubinstein, & Maslin, 2019).

The GDPR provides the data subject (an individual whose personal data is being processed) with several rights that form an obligation for organisations in order to be compliant. These rights require the provision of information concerning processing in a transparent manner (A12-14) regarding how their personal data is or will be collected, processed, stored, and used along with the specific purposes (A15). The Right to Data Portability (A20) enables the data subject to request a copy of personal data provided to the Data Controller (organisation determining the purposes of processing), or to request it be directly moved, copied, or transferred to another Data Controller. This data is required to be provided in a commonly used, machine-readable, and interoperable format. Thus, the GDPR explicitly mentions and uses interoperability as a means to ensure a common understanding of data between different Data Controllers, through which it provides the data subject with the freedom to reuse their personal data.

Along with regulating how personal data is used and shared through various processes, the GDPR also provides guidelines, requirements, and obligations on how information is shared or communicated between various entities. For example, when a Data Controller shares data with a Data Processor (organisation performing processing for a Data Controller), the Data Processor is required to carry out its processing limited to the explicit instructions provided by the Controller. These instructions are required to be maintained by the Processor for verifying compliance and ensuring accountability, as well as to clarify the legal responsibilities of each party. Within this arrangement, the Data Processor cannot determine the purpose of the processing, but the Data Processor can share the data with another Data

Processor (a Sub-Data Processor) to carry out the processing on its behalf. In such a case, the Data Processor will share the instructions with the Sub-Data Processor, who will, upon completion, notify the Data Processor. The Data Processor will, in turn, notify the Data Controller –thereby establishing a chain where information flows between entities and establishes points of interaction.

While there is no legal requirement for maintaining and using data in a structured and interoperable form, doing so has several benefits for the post-GDPR ecosystem. For Data Subjects and Data Controllers, (semantic) interoperability provides consistency in terms of the understandability of personal data across organisations. For Data Controllers and Data Processors, interoperability enables seamless operations through common mechanisms that also act towards maintaining and demonstrating legal compliance. For Regulatory and Supervisory Authorities, interoperability provides a uniform entry point when conducting investigations into processing operations, and specifically in the case where information flows involve multiple organisations.

In this chapter, we explore these issues of standardisation and data interoperability shaped by the requirements of GDPR and its compliance.

ENTITIES AND INFORMATION IN GDPR

Entities Defined by the GDPR

Entities in the context of GDPR are defined and categorised through their roles and responsibilities towards the information required to fulfill the requirements and obligations of compliance. The categorisation of entities also enables identification of relationships through provision and exchange of information between them. Through this, a model emerges representing the commonality and interoperability of information, which is useful to identify and discuss the suitability and applicability of standards for representation, as well as avenues for future work in the standardisation domain.

The model, the entities, and their interactions are visualised in Figure 1. At a broad and abstract level, entities can be categorised into Data Subject (DS), Data Controller (DC), Data Processor (DP), and Supervisory Authority (SA). A Data Subject is an identifiable natural person whose personal data is being processed, and are the user or recipient of a system or service. A Data Controller is an entity that determines the purposes and means for processing of personal data under their control. A Data Processor is an entity that processes personal data on behalf of a Data Controller based on explicitly provided instructions. A sub-processor is a processor acting under another processor. A Sub-Data Processor is bound by the same rules as a Data Processor in terms of limiting processing as per provided

Figure 1. Model of entities and their interactions based on the GDPR (Pandit, Debruyne, et al., 2018)

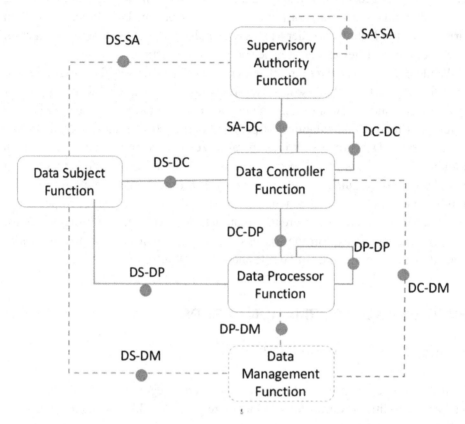

instructions. The Supervisory Authority or Data Protection Authority or Regulatory Authority is a governmental institution responsible for monitoring the application of data protection laws.

In addition to these, Data Management (DM) is a virtual entity responsible for the handling and management of information on behalf of a Data Controller or Processor. In this context, "Virtual" refers to the DM not being a separate entity in the legal sense of the term, but being distinct from a DC or DP in terms of functionality and control by virtue of abstraction or automation. An example of a Data Management entity is the use of automated software for interaction with users in an online service, where the Data Subject interacts only with the automated DM for exercising of rights. The DM can be an external interface provided by a third party or a Data Processor contracted by the Controller to act on its behalf. The DM is of interest as the same set of services can be deployed by different Controllers or Processors, thereby providing commonality in terms of functionality and information flows. GDPR can also be interpreted to define more entities such as an Agent or a Representative acting on behalf of another entity such as the Data Subject or Data Controller, Data Protection Officers, organisations that issue certifications, and courts and other authorities involved in the compliance process.

Interactions Between Entities

An *interaction* is defined as the exchange of information between two entities irrespective of their type. An interaction between two entities, even of the same type, can be considered as an interoperability point if it involves the communication of some information or structured data between them. Understanding the requirements of this interaction in terms of associated information and context of exchange provides the basis for exploring opportunities towards standardisation of information practices. In the case of GDPR compliance, the law itself motivates adopting standard practices in terms of interactions between entities – such as in the case of Right to Data portability, which is an interaction between a Data Controller and Data Processor.

Considering all possible combinations of interactions between entities provides a total of six points of interaction without considering the direction of interaction. Also, by including interactions between the same entity types, we have 9 points of interactions, excluding those between Data Subjects as it has no legal basis. For simplicity, we exclude the Data Management functionality as it is a virtual entity and has no mention or role in the GDPR. Similarly, we also exclude the size (large, medium, small, or individual) and nature (commercial, governmental, or not-for-profit) of the entity under the assumption that it has no bearing on the requirements of interoperability within the point of interaction. For specific domains and business sectors, such as health or finance, additional information is exchanged based on specific requirements, which requires a more in-depth review of the domain and its applicable laws. In the case of governmental institutions and organisations that are in a position where information communication needs to be made available for dissemination to the public, the interaction requires such data to be in an 'open' and 'consistent' format, where *open* is defined as being transparent and interoperable towards other entities, and *consistent* is defined as not having temporal changes. Where the interaction is concerned with provision of commercial services, the exchange of information is more concerned with consistency, structure, and correctness.

The interactions between a Data Subject and a Data Controller (other than those governed by the Right to Data Portability), or between a Data Controller and a Data Processor, only require that the provider provides the consumer with the required information in a format that can be understood and used. This provided data is not inherently intended to be made available to anyone else (such as a third-party in this case) and therefore has no requirements in terms of standards as long as the involved entities agree upon the method for sharing of data. Contrast this with the case where a public body such as the Supervisory Authority is involved. Communication from Data Controllers or Data Processors with a Supervisory Authority would have to take into consideration the sensitivity of the private information being shared and therefore would require secure forms of communications that also require security in information itself, such as through encryption or establishment of secure channels. Any warning or ruling by the Supervisory Authority, whether public or private, is also similarly governed by requirements regarding its sensitivity. While currently the SA publishes details of cases (where publicly available) along with decisions through a website, the importance of this information provides incentive to represent it in a more structured format in the future. This representation can adopt existing metadata-rich formats that are used to publish legal documents such as court proceedings and legislations.

Interactions Between Data Subjects And Data Controllers

The interaction between Data Subjects and Data Controllers is one of the critical points of interaction addressed by the GDPR. The interoperability between these entities involves the Data Subject providing personal data to Data Controller, which will be in whatever form the Data Controller accepts (by design). However, the Data Subject also provides consent to the Data Controller (which from a legal point of view is specified as the Data Controller collecting consent from Data Subject), which needs to follow specific guidelines stipulated by the GDPR regarding compliance which affects the way consent is collected and stored. Though this does not restrict how the Data Controller obtains consent from the Data Subject, the onus is on the Data Controller to ensure the obtained consent satisfies obligations stipulated by the GDPR for demonstrating the validity of such consent. Therefore, it would be prudent for the Data Controller to obtain or convert consent into a form that makes this process of GDPR compliance more manageable. Storing information about obtained consent bings in requirements towards how this information is structured regarding its representation, storage, and querying and how it can assist in the demonstration of the required compliance.

The interaction of a Data Controller towards Data Subjects also includes the provision of certain information as mandated under the GDPR such as that provided under the Right to Access. Data Controllers also have to provide this information regarding exercising of rights such as the Right to Data Portability through which a Data Subject can request the Data Controller to provide a copy of their personal data. GDPR also defines the conditions regarding the provision of this data such as its structure or format. Additionally, GDPR also provides Data Subjects the right to have their personal data transferred from one Data Controller to another upon request. The exercising of this right requires both controllers to have some form of interoperability mechanism for mutually understanding the concerned data. This extends to the entity generating it as well as accepting or consuming this data. Such requirements shape the information flow and, therefore, the interoperability of information, and have a role to play in the functioning of the entity and also towards legal compliance. For practical reasons, it is impossible for all entities to have an interoperability agreement or arrangement with each other. Therefore, the provision of such information must be made through open standards and formats that are also commonly used. GDPR provides the same argument for data provided under the Right to Data Portability.

Interactions Between Data Controllers And Data Processors

For interactions between Data Controllers and Data Processors, or Data Controllers and Data Controllers, or Data Processors and Data Processors, these already have some ongoing and existing information exchanges outside of GDPR that involve interoperability as part of an organisation's operational practices. Common examples include business arrangements or outsourcing of operations for cost and profit reasons. While such activities are considered a common industry practice, GDPR explicitly mentions the categories of information shared in the operation of such services between these entities. An example of this is the explicit list of instructions provided by the Data Controller to a Data Processor for processing activities over the personal data it provides. The legal acknowledgment of such information-sharing makes its documentation important from the point of compliance. This provides an opportunity for exploring whether a structured and commonly used format can provide advantages to existing practices regarding the sharing of such information.

An approach suggesting an entirely new or different interoperability model would be difficult to uptake due to the diversity and variance of existing infrastructures as well as the cost of changing and adopting them. Therefore, the cost of adopting new practices provides inertia towards keeping existing methods of operation. It is possible to construct a practical interoperability model based on the existing practices with a view towards extending them in an achievable and consistent manner for entities involved. However, this is difficult to achieve in reality due to the earlier mentioned inertia and the cost of change. Since legal compliance is a necessity and GDPR requires operational changes for its obligations, this can be exploited in the adoption of the interoperability model. An approach concerning only that information which is necessary for legal compliance can be proposed as a solution that augments existing services rather than replaces them. Under this, interactions and exchanges between entities through new activities as well as changes to existing ones are defined by the requirements provided by GDPR compliance.

Interactions With Supervisory Authorities

Interoperability as part of GDPR compliance is primarily outlined by the interactions of the Supervisory Authorities with the Data Controllers and Data Processors. Compliance information refers to the data required to demonstrate and determine the organisation's compliance, which legally is acceptable to be in any suitable form as long as it contains the required information. For organisations, the process of maintaining, sharing, and demonstrating compliance using this information becomes a challenge as other entities become involved. For example, under the GDPR, the Data Controller also is concerned with the compliance of the Data Processor as they are provided with the right to carry out reasonable audits for ensuring the Data Processor is acting in accordance with its instructions. Legally, the Data Controller is not responsible for the compliance of the Data Processor. However, since it provides an explicit list of instructions for activities over its personal data, there is a specific and defined relationship between the compliance of two entities. This motivates towards looking at alternate approaches that can help with the compliance aspect of where information and activities are shared across different entities.

One such example is where information is linked to specific activities associated with the processing of information, which is relevant for compliance. A structured approach that provides an efficient and effective way of storing, managing, and querying of this information presents a technologically structured way to use this information in the demonstration of compliance. In addition, when there are multiple entities involved in the compliance process, the sharing of structured contextual information related to compliance can assist both entities in the demonstration of their compliance. Such requirements also shape the information exchanged between entities and are a part of the interoperability model.

Categorising Information in Interactions

Each interaction point has requirements from multiple GDPR articles that affect the information and activities associated with governing the interoperability between entities. These can be summarised into four categories: Requirements, Processes, Data/Information, and Data Formats. A more detailed exploration of this associates clauses of the GDPR with information and categories and also presents them in a comprehensive tabular format (Pandit, Debruyne, et al., 2018).

The category of 'Requirements' reflects a requirement for interoperability that entities are expected to follow or fulfill for compliance. GDPR only states but does not stipulate how this requirement should be fulfilled. The category of 'Processes' by contrast, concerns an activity or action as presented in the clause of GDPR, and which leads to processes for the usage, sharing, publication, or exchange of information. For example, Article 16 of the GDPR concerns the Right of Rectification that enables Data Subjects to have their data rectified by the Controller upon request. In this case, the clause specifies the process of rectification, and the requirement for its provision – without specifying how the right should be provisioned.

Where the information consists of some structure or categorisation, it is associated with the 'Data' category. Where additional information about category or type of data is specified, this is associated with the 'Data Format' category. An example of this is Article 12, which concerns the provision of information about rights in a concise, transparent, intelligible, and easily accessible format. In this case, the clause refers to a process for provision of specific information with criteria for it being valid and compliant.

These requirements do not have a direct bearing on the processing of personal data, but they are useful towards discussions involving requirements gathering, including communication between entities, where standards can be compared or evaluated based on compliance with a requirement or the implementation of a process. For example, Article 30 requires controllers to maintain logs or records of processing activities. While this can refer to abstract information associated with processing activities, it can also be used to formulate records of activities into structured information useful towards demonstration and verification of compliance.

The information associated with information flows can be categorised based on its context and intended usage into five categories - Provenance, Agreements, Consent, Certification, and Compliance. These categories reflect information associated with compliance and organisational processes rather than the personal data that is being processed. The information categories broadly shape and classify the interaction points between entities and refer to the information exchanged. The classification provides a way to refer to the specific type or category of information along with its context without explicitly dealing with specific use-cases or examples of its usage. This abstraction is beneficial towards exploring broad standards towards its representations, such as those for representing provenance or agreements.

The dependence between these categories and their association with interactions between entities suggests an argument for creating create more efficient representations that can enable automation. This can be achieved by integrating the different types of information into a single cohesive model that operatives at a higher and more abstract level by representing the state of interactions within a system and highlights points of interoperability internally within an organisation.

This presents the possibility of utilising forms of interoperability between the various information categories such that they are capable of referencing each other as required. Such a cohesive set of information forms the basis of the interoperability model, which allows information to be structured systematically for the purposes of storage, querying, and sharing with others. An example can be seen in the case of acquisition of consent, where the consent is represented as an agreement that references the specific processes that will use the data using provenance information while the given consent itself is also recorded as an event using the same or similar provenance mechanisms. This explicit linking of inherently related information allows better representation of information and leads to semantic systems that are capable of intelligent operations. In this case, at a later date, it is possible to identify the given consent for a specific user from provenance logs and to view the process it was obtained against. This itself can further be used to determine if an updated consent is required under the terms of the GDPR upon introducing a change in the process such as an addition of a feature.

Provenance

The provenance information category refers to information about entities and activities involved in producing some data or artefact, which can be used to form assessments about its quality, reliability or trustworthiness. This information is related to the compliance for activities that involve some data that needs to be linked or resolved to the activities that create, use, share, or store it. An example of this is that of consent together with the activities associated with it that obtain, update, or invalidate the consent. For demonstrating compliance, it is essential to show that these activities follow the obligations required for compliance, which requires the presence and maintenance of logs that record the functioning of these activities. These logs can be modelled as a form of provenance in which case they form the life cycle of consent tracking its creation (obtaining), use within different activities, how it is stored, and finally its deletion (invalidation) (Pandit & Lewis, 2017). Compliance then becomes a matter of verifying such provenance logs to see whether the activities recorded the correct and compliant behaviour (Bonatti, Kirrane, Polleres, & Wenning, 2017).

Another example is for checking whether one's consent was validly given, which requires that the consent should be freely given, be explicit towards specified processes, and must be unambiguous. Since detecting these conditions for validity of consent is not possible without manual oversight, the artefacts and processes involved in the obtaining of provenance can be useful in capturing the state of things as present when obtaining the consent from the Data Subject. Depending on the manner of representing provenance, the life cycle of consent can then be traced with sufficient granularity and abstraction to link it with activities that depend on it, thereby making it possible to also determine whether the consent was used as intended by the terms of the GDPR (Pandit, Debruyne, O'Sullivan, & Lewis, 2019).

As provenance information potentially encompasses all artefacts and processes requiring compliance, it can be argued that having interoperability with relation to sharing and evaluating provenance information would greatly benefit the compliance operations for both the organisation as well as the authorities. Additionally, as compliance itself involves several activities and the creation of artefacts such as compliance reports, this information can also be defined using a common (i.e., shared) provenance model for reuse and dissemination. Such forms of interoperability can be used in any interactions where provenance information needs to be shared or evaluated, such as is also the case with controllers and processors where there is a need to define activities that need to take place or to maintain a joint or collaborative record of activities undertaken that involve both entities. This is especially useful when information needs to be shared that involves life cycles of artefacts such as consent, and personal data need to be tracked or charted across activities. Provenance defined in such manner has led to approaches in the existing corpora of work to create a privacy impact assessment template (Reuben et al., 2016) and a compliance assessment framework (Kirrane et al., 2018).

We mainly identify the use of life cycles for representing the processes and artefacts, whether internal or external to the organisation, as forms of documentation. This provenance information forms the basis of other information categories as it involves documenting the use of consent and personal data, formation of data-sharing agreements, and recording compliance audits and provision of produced reports. This information is also required to be shared with other entities such as where processors are required to outline their processes to the controllers, and authorities may request to review processes for compliance. The use of provenance also allows recording the occurrence of events such as archival and deletion of consent and personal data which can be vital in the demonstration of compliance.

Data Sharing Agreements

The next category of information we consider is that involving agreements between entities such as that between a Data Controller and a Data Processor, or a Data Controller and another Data Controller, or a Data Processor and another Data Processor. The agreements between these entities have to be in a specific form based on the consideration that they can change depending on factors such as a change in consent or rights being exercised over the personal data provided under the agreement. Therefore, exploring the use of smart agreements (Steyskal & Kirrane, 2015) that can work in an automated manner to a certain extent would benefit systems where a large part of the system can operate on a similar level of automation to ensure compliance. For example, if a Data Controller receives an instruction from a data subject to update their consent for certain activities which are handled by a Data Processor, the Data Controller must update or enforce (depending on the legal term in use to describe the use-case) their agreement to get the Data Processor to also reflect this change in consent over the personal data and activities that they have/ had received from the Data Controller. Without some form of automation, such requests would need to be sent and received manually or require manual action, significantly increasing the work and time required to handle them. With automation involved in the process, the Data Controller's system (such as a Data Management interface) can automatically take care of the request by updating the agreement in place for handling the particular consent and personal data with the Data Processor, and can also await a receipt or acknowledgement from the Data Processor for the successful completion of the request. Such agreements that can be iterated, stored, and queried using systems are of benefit to the involved entities as well as other entities that might wish to introspect the agreements such as Certification Bodies and Regulatory Authorities. An example of this is data-sharing agreements that can be explicitly designed to be interoperable based on requirements of the GDPR (Hadziselimovic, Fatema, Pandit, & Lewis, 2017).

Consent

Consent in the context of the GDPR refers to assent or agreement by the data subject about their personal data for the proposed processing activities associated with one or more entities. Given consent refers specifically to the form of consent given by the data subject in relation to their personal data and the proposed usage by activities. Consent can be considered to be an agreement between the Data Subject and the Data Controller (or another entity), and can, therefore, benefit from the same approach as described for implementing data-sharing agreements. This can provide consistency in the application of technology as well as encourage adoption of uniform standards and interoperability in dealing with similar use-cases.

GDPR specifies specific requirements that guide the acquisition and demonstration of consent for it to be evaluated as valid (Mittal & Sharma, 2017). These include the stipulation that consent must be freely given, must be informed, specific, and voluntary. Of these, only the specificity of consent can be gauged from a given consent in a form such as an agreement. Given consent contains the terms which have been accepted by the user, which can be used to gauge the specificity of the agreement, and therefore decide on whether the consent itself was specific or broad under the GDPR. For other stipulations related to valid consent, it is essential to refer to the process and artefacts used to acquire the consent to understand the conditions under which the consent agreement was provided to the data subject and how it was accepted or given or agreed.

For example, in cases where the consent is acquired through a web-form, the entire web-page may need to be preserved to demonstrate that the consent acquisition process complied with the conditions under the GDPR. Therefore, while the given consent may be represented in any form, it also has to be linked to the processes responsible for acquiring the consent. Additionally, any revision of consent data such as when updating or revoking consent also needs to be stored in a way that can be linked to the processes involved in the change as well as linked to the original consent. This is important as a matter of compliance as GDPR enforcement may require demonstration that a change in consent was carried out correctly, which is only possible through introspection of what the original and changed versions of the consent are. This also introduces the dependency-like relation between data processes and consent where consent should be inherently linked to the processes that depend on it. For example, if the process of using personal data to send emails is dependent on the consent obtained from the user at the time of registration, then it is vital to show that the two are linked together, i.e. the emails are only sent based on the given consent. Such a system must also be able to demonstrate that updated consent has immediate effect on the processes that depend on consent.

These requirements show the inherent dependency of consent and personal data along with the processes involved, which presents a strong argument for representing them together using the same method of provenance. Such a method of capturing the various stages of consent and personal data as life cycles involving processes and artefacts would enable documentation representing the model of the system as a whole. The individual records or logs of activities can then be instantiated based on the model to capture user or event-specific information.

Compliance

Overseeing compliance is an ongoing and continuous process and is specified within the GDPR as an activity to be undertaken by an organisation at certain times. While the interpretation of the law by entities in terms of compliance may vary from use-case to use-case, it is clear that a responsible entity should ensure that all its activities are compliant at all stages of operation. This can be achieved by having proper practices and processes regarding evaluation of compliance from the design stage at the earliest. Such processes ensure that a new service or change in an existing service is compliant before they begin the operation. Several people might be involved in the design and operation of the system, but the responsibility of ensuring the compliance falls on the management or the/a Data Protection Officer (DPO) if appointed (Article 29 Data Protection Working Party, 2016a). In any case, such checks of compliance are integral to audits, done by the organisation itself or by a third-party hired by the organisation, for ensuring the activities meet the required compliance towards legal obligations, and are overseen by the Data Protection Officer (Korff & Georges, 2019). A record of such activities and its outcome is, therefore, an essential outcome of such audits or compliance processes and forms part of the compliance information maintained by the organisation. Such information would prove to be helpful for supervisory authorities who might wish to inspect the activities of an organisation and determine responsibility in cases where multiple entities are involved.

The information associated with compliance-related activities can be represented as provenance information though the processes and artefacts involved in this case are different from those related to the consent and personal data life cycles. To a certain extent, depending on the structuring of compliance activities, it is possible to consider the compliance-related activities as part of a compliance life cycle where the outputs of activities such as reports can be mapped along a timeline using provenance methods similar to those previously outlined. There might be additional requirements for ensuring the security and integrity of such records, though this probably would not have any bearing on the depiction of the information itself. Instead, any concerns related to the data being tampered or accessed without proper authorisation can be mitigated through proper storage and handling of this information. This also allows the provenance representation required for compliance life cycles to be consistent in its purported use-case with those related to provenance of consent and personal data life cycles.

Certifications

GDPR has provisions for seals and certifications that can help organisations with a measure of compliance as well as good practices. These have a maximum validity of three years and have certain conditions or criteria for the creation and issuing of seals and certifications pertaining to GDPR compliance. The seal or certification does not reduce or impact the responsibility of the controller or processor for compliance with the GDPR but acts as a method of displaying or providing information regarding compliance. The exact nature of such seals and certifications and their role concerning compliance-demonstration to the authorities is still under consideration (European Data Protection Board (EPDB), 2019).

An existing example of such a mechanism is European Privacy Seal ('EuroPriSe', 2019), which carries out an audit of an organisation before providing a seal that is accompanied by a public report published on its website describing the process. The document describes the processes and their compliance with respect to GDPR obligations. While the document itself may be sufficient to demonstrate certain facts regarding the organisation's processes, the fact that it is not published in a format that can be reused by the organisation restricts its usage. The organisation who was the subject of the report has only the option to refer to the report through a legal form of citation.

There are several areas of interest where the information included in the report can be structured for representation in a manner that makes it easy to store, access, query, and, most importantly, share with other entities. For example, if a particular process is responsible for sharing personal data between a controller and a processor, where the processor's processes for handling the said data have been audited through a report, then this information may prove to be sufficient for an agreement between the two entities. However, any such audit and its accompanying report having a validity of a maximum three years require the controller and processor to investigate their respective agreements at the end of this report. Agreements hence need to consider this process as a requirement that hinders the automatic resolution of agreements between the two parties. One way to mitigate this is to keep this requirement out of the automation, in which case the agreements would continue to operate even when the report validity has lapsed. Another case is where processes change, and the processor must renew its certification. If it can demonstrate the changes in its processes, the reports can be linked to the version or iteration of process it evaluated, thereby also providing a way for agreements to view and use this information. Even without use in automated agreements, structuring such information provides motivation for its use within organisation for compliance-related tasks by cross-linking or cross-referencing the information in documentation that can be continuously updated.

Existing Standards

When identifying new areas of information representation and standardisation, it is important to acknowledge the importance of reuse and commence by identifying (established) prior work, such as existing standards, and their relevance to the interactions and interoperability discussed previously. At the same time, taking an overview of work carried out within industry, as well as organisations and bodies involved in creating and overseeing standards, and academia allows an outlook into efforts towards standardisation effort. This section provides a summary of existing standards and efforts as applicable for GDPR with a specific focus on their being open for fostering better community participation and adoption.

International Organisation for Standardisation (ISO)

ISO is an international independent non-governmental body composed of representatives from its members' national standards organizations. As such, it represents a global standard-setting body and is widely utilised by the industry and community. While ISO standards are not free (a fee is required to access a standard), their use represents a global agreement, and such is lucrative for large organisations which operate in multiple jurisdictions.

The ISO/IEC 27000 (Disterer, 2013) series concerns Information Security Management Systems and is mostly relevant for the documentation of technical and organisational measures referred to by Article 32 of the GDPR. ISO/IEC 27001 (Lopes, Guarda, & Oliveira, 2019) is a standard for information security management systems and defines information security risks with appropriate measures and controls. It outlines specific requirements and controls to ensure appropriate controls are in place to manage risks to the processing operations, which in the context of GDPR includes personal data.

ISO/IEC 27018 (de Hert, Papakonstantinou, & Kamara, 2016) is a standard concerning 'Personally Identifiable Information (PII) on Public Clouds', which makes it applicable to any processing utilising the cloud. It builds on the abstract control mechanisms defined in ISO/IEC 27002 to specify security issues related to personally identifiable information stored in the cloud. It specifies privacy principles such as consent and choice, purpose legitimacy and specification, rights to access and delete data, information disclosure, and transparency. As such, it addresses several of the requirements for GDPR compliance (Tzolov, 2018), and is intended to be a valuable tool in the compliance certification process. The latest iteration, ISO/IEC 27018:2019, clarifies that it specifies additional controls and guidance for processing which is to be certified with ISO/IEC 27001, rather than a standard on its own. ISO/IEC 27018 corresponds to the ongoing efforts by regulatory bodies to establish uniform collection of standards for processing undergoing in the cloud.

While ISO standards enable agreement over the presence of information and conformance to standard business practices, how this information should be communicated to entities in an interoperable format is not addressed. For example, if a Controller wishes to engage a Processor to carry out some processing and requests information on the technical measures it utilises, the Processor can specify being certified against ISO/IEC 27002 (and 27018) to provide assurance against a standardised set of practices. This can be through a document or a spreadsheet or a list of measures undertaken – that outlines the necessary information in conformance with the ISO standard and is provided by the Processor to the Controller as documentation of its technical measures. While this is sufficient to fulfill legal obligations and business practices, the information can be better represented in an interoperable format to integrate into systems for compliance.

World Wide Web Consortium (W3C)

The World Wide Web Consortium, abbreviated as W3C, is the standards body responsible for information exchange on the Web, which itself is based on the standards and protocols of the Internet. Due to the ever-increasing usage of the Web as a medium for providing services and information, it is important to consider standards that can be readily integrated into mediums such as web pages and web services that form the backbone of interoperability for many organisations, both commercial as well as public institutions. An example of this is email, which is ubiquitous with the Web and illustrates how standards can foster better interoperability. W3C terms its standards as 'Recommendation' to signify its agreement over time by community and members, which reflects its recommended usage rather than adoption as a requirement.

For representing information, W3C has several standards regarding data formats such as XML, CSV, and JSON. These formats provide specifications for the encoding of information into interoperable data streams. The Resource Description Framework ('RDF 1.1 Primer', 2014), or RDF, is a family of specifications that were initially defined as a metadata model but has since been used to model information as web resources. RDF supports several data serialisation formats, including XML and JSON (through JSON-LD), making its usage and adoption easier for information interoperability. RDF allows expression of facts as triples consisting of the subject-predicate-object pattern. This allows the expression of knowledge as a directed graph using a collection of RDF statements, which enables sharing data representations in a consistent manner.

The Web Ontology Language ('OWL 2', 2012), or OWL, is a family of languages for knowledge representations and modelling ontologies using formal semantics built upon RDF. The use of OWL to build schemas (or ontologies) allows the expression and inference of knowledge as well as the use of semantic reasoning. This has attracted interest in the academic as well as industrial community, and there are several public ontologies, with notable examples found in the library and bio-science domains. For querying information declared using RDF, there are mechanisms such as SPARQL ('SPARQL 1.1 Query Language', n.d.) and XQuery ('XQuery', 2017) that operate on standardised forms of data (RDF and XML respectively). Approaches for validating the structure of information defined using RDF include the Shapes Constraint Language (Knublauch & Kontokostas, 2017), which is a W3C Recommendation. To take advantage of the interoperability offered by commonly used formats such as CSV and JSON, there is ongoing work in creating a standard combining these approaches with RDF. Notable examples for this include CSV on the Web (Tennison, 2016) and JSON-LD ('JSON-LD', 2014). As their names imply, the former uses CSV and the latter JSON. The reuse and combination of standards provide interoperability as well as commonality towards the underlying technology utilised to create, store, and query information represented by these standards. This demonstrates the advantage of combining existing standards towards additional functionality and semantics while ensuring their backward compatibility for technical adoption.

In terms of GDPR, and the information categorised discussed earlier, W3C standards enable the representation of information based on standards that enable machine-readable metadata using RDF, querying using SPARQL and validation using SHACL. In addition, OWL can be used to formulate logic into the metadata to express the interdependencies and relationships inherent in the data. This is especially relevant with the recent interest and trend towards utilising knowledge-graphs where capturing semantics and relationships in the data is of essence. In such a system, GDPR compliance is based on utilising the system to identify the essential information and associate its adherence and validation towards specific clauses for compliance. This has made possible by interpreting the text and concepts of the GDPR itself as machine-readable metadata using RDF in order to link or associate information with its specific clauses (European Union, Publications Office, & ELI Task Force, 2015; Pandit, Fatema, O'Sullivan, & Lewis, 2018)

The Provenance Data Model (Lebo et al., 2013), or PROV, is a W3C Recommendation that provides definitions for interchange of provenance information, which consists of entities and relations between them such as "generated by", "derived from", and "attributed to". PROV was designed to be generic and domain-independent and needs to be extended to address the requirements to represent workflow templates and executions. There are existing approaches in academia that utilise PROV for representing provenance information related to GDPR. Examples include representing the state of a system as a template (Pandit & Lewis, 2017) and representing and maintaining processing logs (Kirrane et al., 2018).

The Open Digital Rights Language (Iannella & Villata, 2018), abbreviated as ODRL, is a W3C Recommendation for policy expression language that provides a flexible and interoperable information model, vocabulary, and encoding mechanisms for representing statements about the usage of content and services. The ODRL Information Model describes the underlying concepts, entities, and relationships that form the foundational basis for the semantics of the ODRL policies. Policies are used to represent permitted and prohibited actions over a certain asset, as well as the obligations required to be met by stakeholders. Policies may furthermore be limited by constraints (e.g., temporal or spatial constraints), and duties (e.g. payments) may be imposed on permissions. ODRL can be utilised for representing agreements, which can include both data sharing agreements as required for Data Controllers and Data Processors, as well as for interpreting GDPR requirements as a policy for compliance checking (Vos, Kirrane, Padget, & Satoh, 2019).

ISA²

The Interoperability solutions for public administrations, businesses, and citizens, or ISA², is a programme that develops and provides digital solutions that enable public administrations, businesses and citizens in Europe to benefit from interoperable cross-border and cross-sector public services. The programme was adopted in November 2015 by the European Parliament and the Council of European Union. ISA² is the follow-up programme to ISA, and aims to ensure interoperability activities are well-coordinated at EU level through a structured plan consisting of a revision to the European Interoperability Framework (EIF) and the European Interoperability Strategy (EIS), along with the development of the European Interoperability Reference Architecture (EIRA) and European Interoperability Cartography (EIC) solutions.

The effort has produced a set of 'Core Vocabularies', maintained by the Semantic Interoperability Community (ALEKSANDROVA, 2016), or SEMIC. Those vocabularies provide a simplified, reusable and extensible data model for capturing fundamental characteristics of an entity in a context-neutral fashion. Existing core vocabularies include ways to define attributes for people, public organisations, registered organisations, locations, public services, the criterion and evidence required to be fulfilled by private entities to perform public services, and a public event vocabulary. SEMIC has also developed the DCAT Application Profile (DCAT-AP), based on the DCAT specification, for describing public sector datasets in Europe to enable the exchange of descriptions of datasets among data portals. GeoDCAT-AP is an extension of DCAT-AP for describing geospatial datasets, dataset series, and services, while StatDCAT-AP aims to deliver specifications and tools that enhance interoperability between descriptions of statistical data sets within the statistical domain and between statistical data and open data portals. The Asset Description Metadata Schema (ADMS) is a vocabulary to describe and document reusable interoperability solutions, such as data models and specifications, reference datasets, and open-source software. The objective of ADMS is to facilitate the discoverability of reusable interoperability solutions to reduce the development costs of cross-border and cross-sector e-Government systems.

Emerging Efforts

Along with efforts towards establishing standards and requirements, the analysis of existing work is also important to identify the potential for reuse and essential drawbacks for adoption. To this end, there have been several critical studies that provide an overview of legal ontologies to date (Leone, Di Caro, & Villata, 2019; Rodrigues, Freitas, Barreiros, Azevedo, & de Almeida Filho, 2019) that present the state of legal ontologies and their usage in the community. At the same time, there are efforts to automate the association of legal requirements with applicable standards – specifically those regarding GDPR and ISO (Bartolini, Giurgiu, Lenzini, & Robaldo, 2017). This provides an important step in the automation of legal compliance by enabling machine-readable and queryable information regarding applicable standards for a specific legal clause. Furthermore, existing work also addresses the requirements of metadata (Wenning & Kirrane, 2018) and standardisation of legal notation associated with compliance (Governatori, Hashmi, Lam, Villata, & Palmirani, 2016).

Data Privacy Vocabulary

The Data Privacy Vocabulary (Pandit & Polleres, 2019) is a work-in-progress effort by the W3C Data Privacy Vocabularies and Controls community group to provide a standardised vocabulary to represent instances of legally compliant personal data handling. It provides a modular vocabulary consisting of concepts for defining personal data categories, purposes of processing, categories of processing, technical and organisational measures, legal bases, recipients, and consent. The vocabulary is defined using RDF and OWL for encapsulating logic and relationships between concepts, which also enables extending it in a compatible manner to define domain-specific use-cases. For example, the vocabulary can be extended for the finance domain by defining the required additional concepts using the W3C standardised mechanisms. Such extensions will remain compatible with the original concepts in the vocabulary while providing domain-specific extensions in the form of a concept hierarchy or ontology. The vocabulary fills an important gap in terms of providing unambiguous definitions that enable interoperability of semantics within the privacy domain.

Consent Receipt

Consent Receipt (Lizar & Turner, 2017) is a standard developed by the Kantara Initiative for representing the consent given by an individual concerning the processing of their personal data. The standard defines the creation of receipts based on equating the giving of consent to a transaction, similar to how a receipt is generated at the end of purchase and payment. The specification requires the receipt to be in human-readable and machine-readable formats for expressing information using predefined categories for personal data collection, purposes, use, and disclosure. In its current state the consent receipt does not address the requirements specified by the GDPR. However, the receipt itself is based on the ISO/IEC 29100 privacy framework and is being discussed for further development in the context of ISO/IEC 29184 regarding online privacy notices and consent.

Data Transfer Project

The Data Transfer Project is an on-going effort to create an open-source platform to facilitate the Right to Data Portability between online services across the Web. Contributors include technology giants such as Apple, Facebook, Google, Microsoft, and Twitter. The code for the platform is currently hosted on Github. The technical approach concerns extracting different information through the available APIs of a service and translating the data to the target platform through the use of intermediate codes or services. The project represents the first step towards an industry-led effort to address the Right to Data Portability and interoperability of information on the Web. At the same time, even though the project was started on July 2018, over a year ago, it has no visible deliverables to date in August 2019.

THE FUTURE: AN ARGUMENT FOR SEMANTIC INTEROPERABILITY

SEMIC (and EIF) define Semantic Interoperability as the preservation of meaning in the exchange of electronic information (ALEKSANDROVA, 2016). In the context of information exchange, the sender and receiver should understand and interpret information in the same way. Semantic interoperability is achieved through establishment of shared agreements on the meaning and context of information exchanged. These agreements are usually formalized in an artefact called an ontology, vocabulary, or schema. Systems that have semantic interoperability can exchange information in a more flexible manner due to the nature of interpretation being based on a shared agreement for the provision of context. Such context can be represented as metadata describing the system and providing information regarding both the content and the context.

Concerning the Right to Data Portability, GDPR only stipulates that the provided data be intended towards enabling interoperability. The Article 29 Working Party in its guidelines (Article 29 Data Protection Working Party, 2016b) observes that where there are no commonly used formats used within a particular domain or context, Data Controllers should provide personal data in commonly used formats such as CSV, JSON, and XML, along with useful metadata at the best possible level of granularity. This metadata should be used to accurately describe the meaning of the exchanged information to make the function and reuse of data possible. The guidelines further call for cooperation between industry stakeholders to adopt a common set of interoperable standards and formats to deliver the requirements of the Right to Data Portability. Therefore, there needs to be an initiative to go beyond the requirements of providing the data in interoperable formats such as CSV and XML and to work towards the establishment and adoption of semantic metadata.

One possible solution is to utilise existing data formats and extending them to support additional contextual metadata. Examples of this are the CSV on the Web, which augments the CSV data format, and JSON-LD, which encodes RDF in JSON format. Adopting such data formats is easier for existing systems that already support their native formats (CSV and JSON respectively) and can provide the necessary mechanisms for representation of data semantics.

The creation of appropriate metadata to describe information should follow the general guidelines from established methods such as the Semiotic Information Theory (Stamper, 1996), which considers the information content of signs and expressions. In this case, the information content represented by the data would replace signs and expressions in the theory. The structuring of information according to this theory can be represented through Stamper's Semiotic Ladder (Stamper, 1996), which is a framework provided by semiotics to discuss and prescribe practical and theoretical methods for the design and use of information systems. This requires agreement between various stakeholders on the creation and adoption of schemas, ontologies, and vocabularies for their respective domains.

The adoption of such semantic metadata would enable better interoperability between systems in terms of requesting data from different providers under an open and shared semantic base. An example of this is requesting a user's profile information from different providers, where a profile contains personal information such as name and email as well as information such as address and references to other social media accounts. This information can be of relevance to generic services such as contact books as well as for specialised services such as other social media services. By using a common vocabulary to define these pieces of information, a single query can retrieve the information from multiple services, as well as provide it in a manner such that it can be identified by generic as well as specialised services.

A prevalent example of semantic interoperability can be observed on the Web through schema.org ('Schema.org', n.d.), which is a collaborative community effort towards creating and maintaining schemas for use on web pages. Its primary use is to act as a shared vocabulary for metadata on websites that will assist search engines understand the content on the website. A similar effort needs to be undertaken to define interoperable metadata for content being provided as part of the Right to Data Portability, and by extension, other aspects of the GDPR.

CONCLUSION

This chapter presented an exploration of data interoperability based on entities and obligations driven by the General Data Protection Regulation (GDPR). The discussion of other interactions between entities and the categorisation of information flows at such interactions presents sufficient motivation for further work towards identifying commonality and working towards standardisation of information and services based on the requirements of legal compliance with the GDPR and other legislations.

The chapter also provided an overview of existing standards and efforts towards standardisation of information and their relevance with the ecosystem brought about by the GDPR. The promise of automating compliance and its related services and systems provides an argument to also drive efforts for the other information categories identified within the chapter. At the same time, incorporating semantics into information enriches the existing information exchange and enables the creation and utilisation of services with greater flexibility and functionality. For example, a Data Controller can be utilised semantic representations of their system to create interoperable information for documentation of compliance, drafting of privacy policies, and agreements with processors – based on the commonality of information involved and the necessity to exchange this information with other entities. There are existing efforts that are working towards such semantic interoperability and are driven by the various stakeholders including academia and industry. While GDPR itself is a highly contextual domain for services and approaches, it also presents a promising avenue for further standardisation efforts driven by economic and legal incentives.

ACKNOWLEDGMENT

This research is supported by the ADAPT Centre for Digital Media Technology, which is funded by Science Foundation Ireland (SFI) through SFI Research Centres Programme and is co-funded under the European Regional Development Fund (ERDF) through Grant 13/RC/2106.

REFERENCES

Aleksandrova, Z. (2016, November 25). *Core Vocabularies*. Retrieved 23 July 2019, from ISA²—European Commission website: https://ec.europa.eu/isa2/solutions/core-vocabularies_en

Article 29 Data Protection Working Party. (2016a). *Guidelines on Data Protection Officers ('DPOs')* (No. 16/EN, WP-243).

Article 29 Data Protection Working Party. (2016b). *Guidelines on the right to data portability* (No. 16/EN, WP242).

Bartolini, C., Giurgiu, A., Lenzini, G., & Robaldo, L. (2017). Towards Legal Compliance by Correlating Standards and Laws with a Semi-automated Methodology. In T. Bosse & B. Bredeweg (Eds.), *BNAIC 2016: Artificial Intelligence* (Vol. 765, pp. 47–62). doi:10.1007/978-3-319-67468-1_4

Bonatti, P., Kirrane, S., Polleres, A., & Wenning, R. (2017). Transparent Personal Data Processing: The Road Ahead. *Computer Safety, Reliability, and Security*, 337–349.

de Hert, P., Papakonstantinou, V., & Kamara, I. (2016). The cloud computing standard ISO/IEC 27018 through the lens of the EU legislation on data protection. *Computer Law & Security Review*, *32*(1), 16–30. doi:10.1016/j.clsr.2015.12.005

De Hert, P., Papakonstantinou, V., Malgieri, G., Beslay, L., & Sanchez, I. (2018). The right to data portability in the GDPR: Towards user-centric interoperability of digital services. *Computer Law & Security Review*, *34*(2), 193–203. doi:10.1016/j.clsr.2017.10.003

Disterer, G. (2013). ISO/IEC 27000, 27001 and 27002 for Information Security Management. *Journal of Information Security*, *04*(02), 92–100. doi:10.4236/jis.2013.42011

European Data Protection Board (EPDB). (2019). *Guidelines 4/2018 on the accreditation of certification bodies under Article 43 of the General Data Protection Regulation (2016/679)*. Author.

European Union, Publications Office & ELI Task Force. (2015). *ELI: A technical implementation guide*. Luxembourg: Publications Office.

EuroPriSe. (2019). Retrieved 11 August 2019, from European Privacy Seal (EuroPriSe) website: https://www.european-privacy-seal.eu/EPS-en/Home

Good, N., Rubinstein, I., & Maslin, J. (2019). *'When the Dust Doesn't Settle' – GDPR Compliance One Year In*. Retrieved from https://www.ssrn.com/abstract=3378874

Governatori, G., Hashmi, M., Lam, H.-P., Villata, S., & Palmirani, M. (2016). Semantic Business Process Regulatory Compliance Checking Using LegalRuleML. In E. Blomqvist, P. Ciancarini, F. Poggi, & F. Vitali (Eds.), *Knowledge Engineering and Knowledge Management* (pp. 746–761). Springer International Publishing. doi:10.1007/978-3-319-49004-5_48

Hadziselimovic, E., Fatema, K., Pandit, H. J., & Lewis, D. (2017). Linked Data Contracts to Support Data Protection and Data Ethics in the Sharing of Scientific Data. *Proceedings of the First Workshop on Enabling Open Semantic Science (SemSci)*, 55–62. Retrieved from http://ceur-ws.org/Vol-1931/paper-08.pdf

Iannella, R., & Villata, S. (2018, February 15). *ODRL Information Model 2.2*. Retrieved 19 September 2018, from ODRL Information Model 2.2 website: https://www.w3.org/TR/odrl-model/

ISO/IEC 2382-1:1993. (1993). Retrieved from http://www.iso.org/cms/render/live/en/sites/isoorg/contents/data/standard/00/72/7229.html

JSON-LD. (2014, January 16). Retrieved 11 August 2019, from JSON-LD 1.0 A JSON-based Serialization for Linked Data website: https://www.w3.org/TR/json-ld/

Kirrane, S., Fernández, J. D., Dullaert, W., Milosevic, U., Polleres, A., Bonatti, P., … Raschke, P. (2018). A Scalable Consent, Transparency and Compliance Architecture. *Proceedings of the Posters and Demos Track of the Extended Semantic Web Conference (ESWC 2018)*.

Knublauch, H., & Kontokostas, D. (2017, July). *Shapes Constraint Language (SHACL)*. Retrieved 19 September 2018, from Shapes Constraint Language (SHACL) website: https://www.w3.org/TR/shacl/

Korff, D., & Georges, M. (2019, July 30). *The Data Protection Officer Handbook*. Retrieved from https://ssrn.com/abstract=3428957

Lebo, T., Sahoo, S., McGuinness, D., Belhajjame, K., Cheney, J., Corsar, D., … Zhao, J. (2013). *PROV-O: The PROV Ontology*. Academic Press.

Leone, V., Di Caro, L., & Villata, S. (2019). Taking stock of legal ontologies: A feature-based comparative analysis. *Artificial Intelligence and Law*.

Lizar, M., & Turner, D. (2017). *Consent Receipt Specification v1.1.0*. Retrieved from Kantara Initiative website: https://docs.kantarainitiative.org/cis/consent-receipt-specification-v1-1-0.pdf

Lopes, I. M., Guarda, T., & Oliveira, P. (2019). How ISO 27001 can help achieve GDPR compliance. *2019 14th Iberian Conference on Information Systems and Technologies (CISTI)*, 1–6.

Mittal, S., & Sharma, P. P. (2017). The Role of Consent in Legitimising the Processing of Personal Data Under the Current EU Data Protection Framework. *Asian Journal of Computer Science And Information Technology*, 7, 76–78.

OWL 2. (2012, December 11). *Retrieved 11 August 2019, from OWL 2 Web Ontology Language Document Overview* (2nd ed.). Retrieved from https://www.w3.org/TR/owl2-overview/

Pandit, H. J., Debruyne, C., O'Sullivan, D., & Lewis, D. (2018). An Exploration of Data Interoperability for GDPR. *International Journal of Standardization Research, 16*(1), 1–21. doi:10.4018/IJSR.2018010101

Pandit, H. J., Debruyne, C., O'Sullivan, D., & Lewis, D. (2019). GConsent—A Consent Ontology Based on the GDPR. In K. Hammar (Ed.), *The Semantic Web*. doi:10.1007/978-3-030-21348-0_18

Pandit, H. J., Fatema, K., O'Sullivan, D., & Lewis, D. (2018). GDPRtEXT - GDPR as a Linked Data Resource. *The Semantic Web - European Semantic Web Conference*, 481–495.

Pandit, H. J., & Lewis, D. (2017). Modelling Provenance for GDPR Compliance using Linked Open Data Vocabularies. *Proceedings of the 5th Workshop on Society, Privacy and the Semantic Web - Policy and Technology (PrivOn2017) (PrivOn)*. Retrieved from http://ceur-ws.org/Vol-1951/PrivOn2017_paper_6.pdf

Pandit, H. J., & Polleres, A. (2019, July 26). *DPV*. Retrieved 11 August 2019, from Data Privacy Vocabulary v0.1 website: https://www.w3.org/ns/dpv

RDF 1.1 Primer. (2014, June 24). Retrieved 11 August 2019, from RDF 1.1 Primer website: https://www.w3.org/TR/rdf11-primer/

Regulation (EU) 2016/679 of the European Parliament and of the Council of 27 April 2016 on the protection of natural persons with regard to the processing of personal data and on the free movement of such data, and repealing Directive 95/46/EC (General Data Protection Regulation). (2016). *Official Journal of the European Union, L119*, 1–88.

Reuben, J., Martucci, L. A., Fischer-Hübner, S., Packer, H. S., Hedbom, H., & Moreau, L. (2016). Privacy Impact Assessment Template for Provenance. *Availability, Reliability and Security (ARES), 2016 11th International Conference On*, 653–660.

Rodrigues, C. M. de O., Freitas, F. L. G. de, Barreiros, E. F. S., Azevedo, R. R. de, & de Almeida Filho, A. T. (2019). Legal ontologies over time: A systematic mapping study. *Expert Systems with Applications, 130*, 12–30.

Schema.org. (n.d.). Retrieved 23 July 2019, from https://schema.org/

SPARQL 1.1 Query Language. (n.d.). Retrieved 30 April 2019, from SPARQL 1.1 Query Language website: https://www.w3.org/TR/sparql11-query/

Stamper, R. (1996). Organisational semiotics. In *Information systems: An emerging discipline?* McGraw-Hill.

Steyskal, S., & Kirrane, S. (2015). If you can't enforce it, contract it: Enforceability in Policy-Driven (Linked) Data Markets. *SEMANTiCS (Posters & Demos)*, 63–66. Retrieved from https://pdfs.semanticscholar.org/f2c3/cac9b4af913f32dbd5034ed9aa1751a8a337.pdf

Tennison, J. (2016, February 25). *CSV on the Web*. Retrieved 11 August 2019, from CSV on the Web: A Primer website: https://www.w3.org/TR/tabular-data-primer/

Tzolov, T. (2018). One Model For Implementation GDPR Based On ISO Standards. *2018 International Conference on Information Technologies (InfoTech)*, 1–3.

Vos, M. D., Kirrane, S., Padget, J., & Satoh, K. (2019). ODRL policy modelling and compliance checking. *3rd International Joint Conference on Rules and Reasoning (RuleML+RR 2019)*, 16.

Wenning, R., & Kirrane, S. (2018). Compliance Using Metadata. In T. Hoppe, B. Humm, & A. Reibold (Eds.), *Semantic Applications: Methodology* (pp. 31–45). Technology, Corporate Use. doi:10.1007/978-3-662-55433-3_3

Wong, J., & Henderson, T. (2018). How Portable is Portable?: Exercising the GDPR's Right to Data Portability. *Proceedings of the 2018 ACM International Joint Conference and 2018 International Symposium on Pervasive and Ubiquitous Computing and Wearable Computers*, 911–920.

XQuery. (2017, March). Retrieved 11 August 2019, from XQuery 3.1: An XML Query Language website: https://www.w3.org/TR/xquery-31/

Chapter 9
E–Commerce in the EU:
The Role of Common Standards and Regulations

Marta Orviska
Faculty of Economics, Matej Bel University in Banska Bystrica, Slovakia

Jan Hunady
Faculty of Economics, Matej Bel University in Banska Bystrica, Slovakia

ABSTRACT

E-commerce has several advantages for customers and improves firm productivity. The research aims to examine factors determining the usage of e-commerce within the EU with the focus on problems related to standards. This includes especially a lack of interoperability and labelling problems. Firstly, the authors found rising popularity of online purchases in recent years. Despite the increase, Visegrad countries are still lagging behind the EU average. A similar increase is also evident in e-commerce engagement as well as in turnover from e-commerce. Furthermore, they also estimated logit regressions to find factors affecting the probability of firm engagement in e-commerce. Interoperability problems, when selling online, are more frequently reported by wholesale firms as well as those in the information and communication sector. The majority of firms in our sample stated that common rules of e-commerce within the EU could be beneficial. This is particularly important for those reporting problems with interoperability and different labelling.

DOI: 10.4018/978-1-7998-2181-6.ch009

INTRODUCTION

The Internet represents a very important means of achieving greater competitiveness of individual businesses as well as for the economy as a whole. Adoption of e-commerce by enterprises became popular during the recent decade and its importance will grow further in the future. Companies seek to exploit their potential and extend their capability via the Web by using it for selling or buying. For many of them, e-commerce could be an effective tool for reducing operational costs and enhancing their target market. Furthermore, we can say that online business could significantly facilitate cross border trade within the EU and globally. It is evident that more and more customers get used to shopping abroad online without actually going anywhere. On the other hand, there are of course some potential problems that could represent a barrier to online trade between countries. The lack of standards or differences in local standards could be considered one of these barriers.

Our research aim is to identify the problems associated with online international trade which are related to standards. The paper is focused exclusively on standards and legislation in the EU context. The literature has suggested and evaluated many important reasons for e-commerce intensity, adoption and diffusion, including physical vs. digital products, delivery cost and infrastructure, position in a supply chain, number and size of partners and suppliers, and cultural distance (Jennex et al., 2004; Lawrence and Tar, 2010). In our research we focus on the impact of standards related issues on e-commerce. According to the available data from Eurobarometer we narrow our focus specifically on interoperability problems and problems with different labelling. These two issues could represent significant barriers for international online trade within the EU, and both are related to the existence of common standards. Furthermore, certain common standards for product labelling in the EU could reduce the costs of product adoption for another market. Based on empirical data, we examine the incidence of selected problems in EU countries and identify the characteristic of those firms which are most exposed to each of the problems. We particularly focus our attention on problems with interoperability and problems with different labelling. We analyse both business-to-business (B2B) and business-to-customer (B2C) types of e-commerce. Furthermore, we also want to find out whether common rules for e-commerce would be beneficial for online business in the EU, although we must acknowledge that standardization and rules are not always the same concept and one does not imply the other (Blind et al., 2017). In the next section we review the literature regarding this topic. Next we describe our methodology and the dataset used in the analysis and summarize and discuss the most important results. The final conclusions and potential policy implications are made at the end. This research builds on our previous publications and represents an extended and updated version of a previously published paper (Orviska and Hunady, 2017).

LITERATURE REVIEW

E-commerce contains all types of electronic transactions, which could be either on the buy-side or the sell-side (Chaffery, 2007). E-commerce has attracted substantial interest from economists because it has been predicted to be a new driver of economic growth especially for developing countries (Zaied, 2012) and it has the potential to improve efficiency and productivity (Lawrence and Tar, 2010). E-commerce has become one of the preferred ways of shopping due to its easiness and convenience and it has the potential to enhance organizational performance to gain sustainable competitive advantage (Kasemsap, 2018). According to Kurnia et al. (2015) e-commerce can foster the growth of small and medium-sized enterprises (SMEs) in developed as well as developing countries.

However, there are still several obstacles to e-commerce adoption and growth. Although developing countries tend to have more significant problems in this area, in developed countries there are also several problems still to be solved in order to further increase e-commerce activities. With respect to country-specific problems, the lack of an adequate infrastructure, technical barriers and lack of government ICT strategies are often mentioned as significant barriers in the adoption and growth of e-commerce (Lawrence and Tar, 2010; Zaied, 2012). There are also other technical issues limiting e-commerce usage, such as Internet security (Abbad et al., 2011; Halaweh; 2011; Zaid, 2012) and payments security concerns (Halaweh, 2011; Godwin, 2001). Internet access and online payment systems costs are also not negligible. This could be one of the reasons why studies often report that SMEs lag behind large companies in the adoption of e-commerce (Chitura et al., 2015; Stockdale and Standing, 2006).

As reported by Gomez-Herrera et al. (2014), a 1% increase in the use of efficient cross-border payment systems could lead to a 7% growth in cross-border e-commerce. The authors also argue that online business gives a comparative advantage to English-language exporting countries. Furthermore, Solaymani et al. (2012) stated that a lower level of Internet service costs motivates firms to adopt e-commerce. Finally, the risk related to online trade appears to higher than for ordinary purchases. Psychological risk, performance risk and privacy risk in particular could play the most important roles (Ruiz-Mafé et al. 2009).

Several authors also emphasise the importance of the legal and regulatory environment for the adoption of e-commerce in the country (Almousa, 2013; Zaied, 2012). Legislation and regulation together with the development of technical standards such as utilities in business transaction are seen as one of the major factors affecting the diffusion of e-commerce (Andresen et al., 2004). Thus appropriate rules or regulations for e-commerce seem to be beneficial. On the other hand, significantly different rules in different countries could pose a significant problem for e-commerce activities.

Furthermore, the lack of interoperability can pose another significant barrier to international e-commerce and here the role of standards can be crucial. According to Song et al. (2019) interoperability is often classified as followed:

1. Semantic interoperability - semantic differences in data;
2. Technical interoperability - the compatibility of information and communication technologies;
3. Organizational interoperability - compatibility of business processes and people.

Based on Song et al. (2019) standardisation represents an effective tool to solve at least the problem of semantic interoperability (Henning, 2018) as well as technical interoperability (Schweinsberg and Wegner, 2017, Verma et al., 2016).

Fensel et al. (2001) argue that successful B2B e-commerce has to deal with several challenges and most of them are related to the lack of standards or the appearance and inconsistency of newly arising pseudostandards. Hence, interoperability standards in particular could play an essential role in supporting online international trade as well as the usability of traded products. On the one hand, technology standards are enablers of e-commerce itself. Particularly standardised API and transactions are important for increasing its usability (Albrecht et al., 2003). On the other hand, standards could also improve the interoperability of products, which could be beneficial especially for B2B e-commerce, but could also improve selling to the final customer. With respect to this, MacGregor and Vrazalic (2009) stated that the interoperability of applications from different vendors enabled by e-commerce standards allows the creation of more customisable and advanced systems.

The development of standards could also substantially improve firms' collaboration and the further development of joint systems, which could both lead to more B2B e-commerce (Bjørn-Andersen and Andersen, 2009). According to Kawa (2017) cross-border e-commerce requires interoperability between different systems as well as standardisation of processes. These can be especially important for shipments where labels of the loaded units have to be standardised. Furthermore, standards for labelling and product descriptions in standardised formats could help identify products matching the buyers' preferences, which could be reflected in more demand for B2C e-commerce.

According to Wang and Xu (2015), despite integration efforts, software integration and product data exchange are still challenging issues. The Internet has significantly improved opportunities for worldwide online collaboration. However, the data consistency and comparability are the key issues limiting benefits arising from such collaborative activities. Hence, data synchronization is the key to solving problems with product information sharing and improving benefits of e-collaboration (Nakatani et. al., 2006). E-business standards are crucial for electronic transactions between organizations. These standards are often developed by consortiums and later adopted by other market participants. Authors found that benefits from e-commerce standards increase faster for standard developers than for passive adopters. In some cases, such passive adopters do not even exist (Zhao, et al., 2014).

Standardization of electronic product catalogs (e-catalogs) is considered as one of the key elements of e-commerce standardization. This is true for both B2B and B2C e-commerce (Schmitz and Leukel, 2005). Most standards in this area are developed by industry consortia, but many of them address country-specific needs and their global usage is therefore limited. E-commerce standards can be distinguished based on their different levels. On the lowest level the standardization of data types is necessary. This is further followed by standardization of data elements at vocabulary level and standardization of documents at higher levels. Standardization of processes and frameworks are even more complex issue.

Data exchange standards also play an increasingly important role in reducing problems associated with Industrial Internet of Things (Kulvatunyou et al., 2019). Selected pioneer standards adopted in order to maintain data interoperability and business-to-business information exchange are shown in Table 1. With respect to web services, Web services technology in cooperation with semantic Web may be a solution to improve functional interoperability, technical interoperability, semantic interoperability (Nacer and Aissani, 2014).

Overview of standards used for maintaining data exchange interoperability is shown in Table 2. Semantic interoperability between different systems is the heart of modern IT operations. XML format takes an important role in the data exchange between interoperable systems due to its flexibility and richness in data representation (Abdalla, 2003). According to Decker et al. (2000) both XML and RDF are standards for establishing semantic interoperability on the Web, but XML addresses only document structure. Authors also argue that XML is ineffective as a tool for semantic interoperability in the long run. However, XML has become the most popular in encoding structured data for information exchange during previous years. The layering technology in XML allows it to be used independently from standardized representation and interoperate different Information Systems in exchanging valuable information. Nevertheless, these distributed information systems are always structured in multiple data formats and with different semantic meaning (Lee et al., 2010).

Table 1. Selected standard used to maintain data interoperability

Standard	Adoption	Purpose	Developer
ANSI ASC X12)	1970s	Business-to-business information exchange. Electronic Data Interchange standard (EDI).	American National Standards Institute (ANSI)
Open Network Computing Remote Procedure Cell (ONC-RPC)	1980s	Cross-platform data object interoperability. Interface definition language.	Sun Microsystems
Common Object Request Broker Architecture (CORBA)	1991	Cross-platform interoperability (different OS, programing languages and hardware) (rather difficult to use and computationally expensive)	Object Management Group
Initial Graphic Exchange Specification (IGES)	1980s	Data semantics and data exchange among computer-aided design (CAD) systems	American National Standards Institute's (ANSI)
ISO 10303 - Standard for Exchange of Product data (STEP)	1994	Based on IGES. Computer-interpretable representation and exchange of product manufacturing information.	ISO
UN/EDIFACT	1987	The United Nations rules for Electronic Data Interchange for Administration, Commerce and Transport. Standardisation of the data structure and meaning for information exchange.	United Nations - ISO

Source: Authors based on Kulvatunyou et al. (2019)

Table 2. Overview of data exchange standards and formats

Data exchange standard:	Forms of Specifications:	Exchange format:
EDI	Textual document	Text files
STEP	EPRESS language EXPRESS SysML (EXPRESS,OWL, XML, Schema etc.)	EXPRESS-XML OWL/RDF JSON-LD Protobuf, etc.
OAGIS	DTD, XML Schema CCS RDB (XML Schema, JSON schema, OWL etc.	XML JSON OWL/RDF JSON-LD Protobuf, etc.
ISO 15926	XML Schema, OWL	XML, OWL/RDF JSON-LD
MTConnect	XML Schema	XML
OPC UA	XML Schema	Binary XML
IOF	OWL	OWL/RDF, JSON-LD, etc.

Source: Authors based on Kulvatunyou et al. (2019)

Furthermore, in recent years, two other standards that facilitate information exchange between entities have been engaged in a battle for dominance. The more common Electronic Data Interchange (EDIFACT) is being challenged by the newcomer, eXtensible Business Reporting Language (XBRL) (van de Kaa et al., 2018).

Standardization aims to eliminate trade barriers and the globalization of trade only increases the need for international standardisation (de Vries, 2013). The potential effect of standards on international trade in general has been examined by several studies. Swann et al. (1996) analysed U.K. trade performance, and found that international standards can provide a trade advantage and standards could also promote interindustry trade. The results of Blind and Jungmittag (2006) also suggest a positive effect of international standards on international trade. Similarly, Portugal-Perez et al. (2010) find that the harmonization of standards for electronic products into international standards at the EU level has a significantly positive effect on trade. However, Moenius (2004) argues that in spite of certain trade benefits of bilaterally shared standards, the differences in country-specific standards could on average not be considered as a barrier to trade. On the other hand, some standards, such as quality and safety standards could hinder e-commerce growth by effectively creating a non-tariff barrier to exports (Martinez and Poole, 2004).

E-COMMERCE REGULATION IN THE EU

As previously mentioned, different rules for e-commerce in member states as well as a lack of standards within the common market could pose a barrier for more intense development of e-commerce within the EU. The regulatory framework for e-commerce has been discussed in the EU since the Bangemann report to the European Commission (Bangemann, 1994) which suggested developing a common regulatory approach. The first important EU directive on E-commerce was Directive 2000/31/EC introduced in 2000. It set a regulatory framework for the establishment of e-commerce providers and their exemption from liability. This directive is the oldest but arguably the most important one and therefore it is sometimes referred as the Mother Directive or Framework directive for e-commerce (Lodder and Murray, 2017).

Copyright and related rights and intellectual property right enforcement in the information society have been addressed in two other directives (Directives 2004/48/EC and Directive 2006/1123/EC). Furthermore, the explanation of the EU initiatives addressing e-money and payment services are summarised in the Directive 2009/110/EC on e-money and Directive 2015/2366/EU on payment services. With respect to online payments, regulation for electronic identification and electronic signature is necessary as well. These two issues have been addressed in Regulation No. 910/2014 on Electronic Identification and Trust services.

With respect to data protection and privacy issues the EU has introduced The General Data Protection Regulation (GDPR) 2016/679. It aims to strengthen privacy rights in the digital age, and introduce a common single law in the EU common market (European Commission, 2019).

The issue of e-commerce adoption, diffusion and support has been recently discussed with respect to the Digital Single Market initiative (European Commission, 2015a). This strategy is focused on the implementation of common e-commerce rules in the EU and it has the potential to reduce the level of uncertainty and reduce the costs related to online international trade. Moreover, published communication on the Mid-Term Review on the implementation of the Digital Single Market strategy (European Commission, 2017) focuses attention on interoperability problems. The European Commission (2017) stated that in the digital economy, interoperability means ensuring effective communication between digital components like devices, networks or data repositories as well as better connections along the supply chain. Standardisation has an essential role to play in increasing interoperability of new technologies and increased effort is needed to ensure that standardisation keeps pace with changes in technologies (European Commission, 2017). The Commission also plans to launch an integrated standardisation plan to identify and define key priorities for standardisation with a focus on domains that are deemed to be critical to the Digital Single Market, including essential sectoral interoperability (European Commission, 2017).

DATA AND METHODOLOGY

The main aim of our research is to identify potential problems facing firms when selling or buying online within the EU, with the focus on the issues that are related to standards and setting common rules. In order to achieve this we use secondary data collected at firm level. For the comparison of countries we decided to use aggregated data retrieved from the Eurostat database.

In the case of regression analysis we use micro-level data from the flash Eurobarometer survey 413 (European Commission, 2015b). It was conducted by TNS Political and Social at the request of the European Commission, (Directorate-General for Communication Networks, Content and Technology) and co-ordinated by the European Commission (Directorate-General for Communication). The survey was conducted between 19th January and 6th February 2015. The survey used CATI (Computer Assisted Telephone Interview) with representatives of firms. The sample consists of 8705 respondent firms from 28 EU member states. Efforts were

Figure 1. Individuals using the Internet for ordering goods or services (%)
Source: Data retrieved from Eurostat database

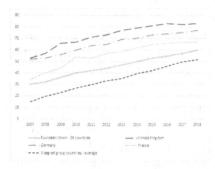

taken to ensure a representative sample. A stratified sampling approach was used, with companies selected in proportion to the population of the company size band and then randomly selecting records within the company size band[1].

Respondent firms were from the sectors of manufacturing, wholesale and retail trade, repair of motor vehicles and motorcycles, accommodation and food service activities, and information and communication (NACE codes C, G, I, J). Our sample includes mostly small and medium sized firms. Approximately 56% of firms have less than 10 employees and another 25% of them have 10 to 49 employees. The majority of respondent firms (approximately 85% of them) were established before 1 January 2009, thus they can be considered as well-established companies in their markets. More than 45% of firms included in the sample are selling their goods and services online and more than 82% are buying online. The firms that are actually selling online got on average 24.6% of their sales from e-commerce.

In this part we briefly examine the development and current state of e-commerce in the EU using selected indicators. These data have been retrieved from the Eurostat database. Firstly, we examine the development at the demand side. Figure 1 shows the share of individuals using the Internet for ordering goods or services in selected countries. We compare the share in Germany, France and UK as well as the average of EU28 countries and average of Visegrad countries (Czechia, Hungary, Poland, Slovakia). This share is the highest in the UK followed by Germany and France. The average share of individuals ordering online in Visegrad countries is lower than EU average. However, this difference is slightly decreasing over time. The general trend is evident – the share of individuals using online orders is significantly increasing over the time.

Hence, ordering goods or services on the Internet has become very popular in recent years. This trend is confirmed by the substantial increase from 30% to 60% for the EU average. Next, we focus our attention on the entrepreneur's side. We

Figure 2. Enterprises having received orders online (at least 1%) - % of enterprises
Source: Data retrieved from Eurostat database

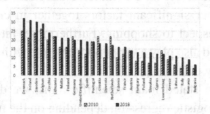

compare the share of enterprises which received orders online among EU countries. Figure 2 illustrate the differences among EU member states as well as observed change from year 2010 to 2018. Denmark, Ireland and Sweden are countries with the highest share of firms receiving at least 1% of orders online. This share has increased significantly during the last 8 years in all three leading countries as well as in the majority of EU countries. However, the percentage of enterprises receiving online orders has slightly decreased in Germany, Luxembourg, Netherlands and Croatia. This decrease can be the consequence of specific national situation, changes in regulation or an unreasonably high share of online enterprises in 2010. Overall a low share of enterprises using online orders is evident in Bulgaria, Romania and Italy.

The indicator capturing the percentage of enterprises that have received orders online shows the popularity and acceptance of internet orders, but does not accurately represent the importance of e-commerce for business sector in the country. This can be to some extent estimated by another indicator capturing the share of turnover from e-commerce. The comparison among selected EU countries is shown in Figure 3.

The highest share of turnover is arising from e-commerce in Ireland, Belgium and Czechia. These countries also experienced significant growth in this indicator during recent years. However, this trend is also evident in almost every country in our sample. There are only three EU member states where the turnover from e-commerce is slightly lower in 2018 compared to 2010 – Germany, Latvia and Lithuania.

Figure 3. Share of enterprises' turnover from e-commerce (%)
Source: Data retrieved from Eurostat database

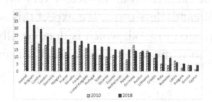

There are still several differences in regulation of e-commerce among countries, which could have some effect on e-commerce adoption. Economic development and wealth can be other significant factors together in cultural differences and national habits with respect to shopping. Furthermore, internet connectivity and ICT infrastructure could also play a very important role with respect to e-commerce adoption and frequency of its usage.

With respect to the stated main scientific aims, we decided to use logistic regression or ordered logistic regression depending on the nature of the dependent variable. This methodology helps us better determine the key characteristics of firms which are engaged in e-commerce. Moreover, we are also able to determine the key factors which impact on the problems that firms face when selling or buying online abroad. All the dependent and independent variables used in the regression analysis are summarized and described in Table 3.

We focused our analysis especially on the problems which are in some way related to standards, led by interoperability problems. This issue is clearly associated with the technical standards. Secondly, we also examine the reported problems with different labelling, which could be partially or even fully solved by applying common labelling standards. Based on the results, we can determine the key problem areas and the characteristics of the firms which are mostly affected by such problems.

RESULTS

In the analysis, we firstly focus our attention on the typical characteristics of companies involved in selling or buying online. Hence, we applied logistic regression in order to identify the associations between firms' characteristics and their engagement in international online trade. The results of the regressions are summarized in the Table 4.

These results suggest that the company size measured by the number of employees appears to have a nonlinear inverse U-shape relationship to the probability of selling online. The fact that the firm is a part of a larger international group seems to be positively related to online selling, but negatively related to online buying. This makes sense as such firms may well buy within the group. Manufacturing firms are less likely to sell online, according to our results. On the other hand, firms which are selling services are more likely to sell or buy online. The accommodation sector is an exception, because firms in this sector very often sell online, but they are buying online significantly less often. We expect this is because the majority of their purchasing is related to food, which is done locally.. Furthermore, firms which are selling more to firms rather than to final consumers also tend to buy more often online.

Table 3. Description of variables used in the analysis

Variable	Description and coding
Selling online	Does your company sell online and/or use EDI-type transactions (Electronic Data Interchange, e.g.: XML)? (Selling by email is not considered online selling). Coding: Yes=1; No = 0.
Buying online	Does your company purchase online and/or use EDI-type transactions (Electronic Data Interchange, e.g.: XML)? (Purchasing by email is not considered online purchasing.) Coding: Yes=1; No=0
Problems when selling or buying online:	*For each of the following difficulties that may present when selling/buying online or trying to sell/buy online to other EU countries, can you tell me if it has been a major problem, a minor problem or not a problem at all:*
Interoperability problems	*1. For reasons of interoperability, you cannot provide/buy your products and/or services abroad.* Coding: A major problem=3; A minor problem=2; Not a problem =1
Labelling problems	*2. Our product labelling has to be adapted* Coding: A major problem=3; A minor problem=2; Not a problem =1
Number of employees	How many employees (full-time equivalent) does your company currently have? (Exact number)
Turnover	What was your company's total turnover in 2014? (Exact number)
International group	Is your company part of an international group? Coding: Yes=1; No = 0
Independent company	Is your company independent? Coding: Yes=1; No=0;
New company	When was your company established? Coding: After 1. January 2014 = 1; later =0
Established company	When was your company established? Coding: Before 1. January 2009 = 1; earlier =0
Sell to firms	Does your company sell to other firms? Yes =1; No = 0
Sell services	Does your company sell services? Yes=1; No=0
Manufacturing sector	SECTOR OF ACTIVITY (NACE) of the company: Coding: C-Manufacturing= 1, Other=0
Accommodation sector	SECTOR OF ACTIVITY (NACE) of the company: Coding: I - Accommodation and food service activities =1; Other =0
Wholesale sector	SECTOR OF ACTIVITY (NACE) of the company: Coding: G – Wholesale and retail trade, repair of motor vehicles = 1; Other =0
Information and communication sector	SECTOR OF ACTIVITY (NACE) of the company: Coding: J - Information and communication = 1; Other =0

Source: Based on the data from European Commission (2015)

We also examine the average responses to the question regarding the problems with online buying or selling abroad. All problems mentioned in the questionnaire survey are sorted according to their importance as reported by the respondent firms. Only those firms which are currently selling online, used to sell online or

Table 4. The results of logistic regression with the selling/buying online as dependent variables

	(1) Selling online (dy/dx)	(2) Selling online (dy/dx)	(3) Buying online (dy/dx)	(4) Buying online (dy/dx)
Number of employees	0.00028*** (4.49)		-0.00002*** (-3.07)	
Number of employees^2	-1.38*10^{-8} *** (-4.15)			
Log(Turnover)		0.0027* (1.73)		0.0017 (1.50)
International group	0.0710*** (3.54)		-0.0585*** (-4.04)	
Independent company		-0.1016*** (-6.82)		0.0682 (6.19)
New company	-0.024 (-0.46)		0.0249 (0.66)	
Established company		0.0179 (1.16)		-0.0236** (-2.14)
Sell to firms		0.0123 (0.76)	0.0346*** (2.94)	0.0341*** (2.90)
Sell services	0.0665*** (5.87)	0.0659*** (5.71)	0.0294*** (3.51)	0.0284*** (3.39)
Manufacturing sector	-0.1054*** (-8.01)	-0.0990*** (-7.53)	0.0128 (1.29)	0.0114 (1.15)
Accommodation sector	0.0932*** (5.56)	0.0968*** (5.70)	-0.1011*** (-7.79)	-0.0966*** (-7.51)
Log pseudolikelihood	-5727.6	-5712.06	-3902.4	-3868.95
Wald X^2	428.49	434.84	332.75	347.39
Number of observations	8688	8640	8688	8640

Note: based on the data from European Commission (2015). Regressions done by logit and ordered logit with standard errors corrected for heteroscedasticity. Variables are all defined in an appendix. (.) denotes z statistics, */**/*** mean significance at the 10%/5%/1% levels of significance. Countries fixed effects are included in all regressions.

try to sell online have been asked for their response. The reported importance of these problems is shown in Figure 4 (the top eight problems) and Figure 5 (the bottom eight problems). Delivery cost appears to be the most important problem, followed by the cost of guarantees and returns and problems with the cross-border resolution of complaints. We cannot attribute any of the top eight problems directly to standardisation, although standardisation could still have some effect. Establishing common rules, frameworks, and payment systems would undoubtedly help cross-

Figure 4. Problems facing firms when selling online abroad (8 most important problems)
Source: Own calculations based on the data from European Commission (2015)

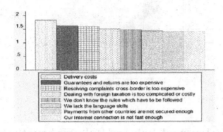

border complaint resolution, foreign taxation, lack of clarity about rules, and payment security. Problems directly related to standardization such as problems with interoperability and different labelling appear in the group of less severe problems (see Figure 5).

Turning to the issues related to buying online, fewer options are applicable compared to online selling (see Figure 6). We can see that delivery costs and the potential problems with solving complaints are once again in the top positions. Although the problems with labelling and interoperability seem to be in this case less important, the differences between the last six options are relatively small.

There are also rather significant differences in the importance of selected problems between the EU countries. We found that companies from Portugal, Greece, Italy and Bulgaria seem to have the most significant problems with interoperability when selling or buying online. It seems that adoption of interoperability standards complementary with other EU countries could be especially effective in these countries. On the other hand, significantly fewer problems with interoperability are reported by firms operating in Estonia, Slovenia, Denmark, Sweden and Finland. These countries may be able to offer best practice learnings in this aspect.

Figure 5. Problems facing firms when selling online abroad (8 less important problems)
Source: Own calculations based on the data from European Commission (2015)

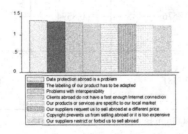

Figure 6. Problems facing by firms when buying online from abroad
Source: Own calculations based on the data from European Commission (2015)

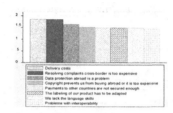

Similarly, firms from Portugal, Italy and Bulgaria have the most serious problems with the labelling and its adjustment to target markets. These are mostly the same countries as reported in the previous case. The same is true for those countries with significantly fewer problems with labelling (Estonia, Finland and Slovenia). Thus, it seems that problems of interoperability and differences in labelling could be partially correlated. In order to test the assumed correlation between these problems, we further calculated the Pearson correlation coefficients between the country averages for each of two selected problems. The results (see Table 5) suggest that there is a

Table 5. The results of Pearson correlation coefficients between the countries averages of selected problems

	Average problems with interoperability when buying online	Average problems with labelling when buying online	Average problems with interoperability when selling online	Average problems with labelling when selling online
Average problems with interoperability when buying online	1.00			
Average problems with labelling when buying online	0.9182	1.00		
Average problems with interoperability when selling online	0.8576	0.8594	1.00	
Average problems with labelling when selling online	0.7381	0.7763	0.6618	1.00

Source: Authors based on the data from European Commission (2015)

relatively strong positive correlation between the problems with interoperability and labelling regarding selling and buying. Thus, it could imply that the firms operating in the country with different standards could have problems with interoperability and labelling when selling abroad online as well as when buying online from abroad.

The relation between firms' characteristics and selected problems when selling or buying online abroad was further examined using ordered logistic regression. The results are summarized in Table 6 and Table 7. Interoperability problems could represent a potential barrier to online selling in the wholesale sector and the information and communication sector. On the other hand, manufacturing firms mostly reported more problems with labels when selling online and less of these problems when buying online. The same is also true for the firms from the wholesale sector. The sizes of the company as well as the age of the company appear to be unrelated to selected problems when selling online. However, larger companies tend to have more problems with interoperability and labelling when buying online. The results also suggest that participation of the firm in an international group could be negatively correlated with interoperability problems when selling online. Furthermore, as shown in Table 7, firms which are selling their products more to firms rather

Table 6. The results of ordered logistic regression for selected problems when selling online as dependent variables

	(1) Interoperability problems (coef.)	(2) Labelling problems (coef.)
Number of employees	-9.93×10^{-6} (-0.14)	0.00004 (0.78)
International group	-0.2899* (-1.65)	0.0564 (0.39)
Established company	0.2110 (1.54)	0.1652 (1.26)
Wholesale sector	0.4777*** (3.13)	0.8129*** (4.89)
Manufacturing sector	0.3207* (1.89)	0.5284*** (5.78)
Information and communication sector	0.5009*** (2.87)	0.2782 (1.44)
Log pseudolikelihood	-1734.09	-1851.58
Wald X^2	113.71	99.01
Observations	2396	2384

Note: based on the data from European Commission (2015). Regressions done by logit and ordered logit with standard errors corrected for heteroscedasticity. Variables are all defined in an appendix. (.) denotes z-statistics, */**/*** mean significance at the 10%/5%/1% levels of significance. Countries fixed effects are included in all regressions.

than consumers tend to have slightly fewer problems with labelling when buying online. This reflects differences in market places. Firms' sales to consumers relate to final product sales and buying online will likely be for intermediary products. Firms selling to other firms are more likely to be related to intermediate products and their purchases may be simpler, relating more to raw materials, where labelling is less of an issue.

Based on the previous results we can say that standards could play an important role in supporting online business, although they are not the only source of problems. At least the adoption of common rules in the EU could be potentially helpful. Hence, we finally focus our attention on this issue. Respondent firms were asked "whether and to what extent could the same, or standardised, rules for EU e-commerce help them to start online sales or increase their current online sales". As we have written before, the European Commission currently tries to adopt common rules for e-commerce by the Digital Single Market Strategy. It might appear self-evident that trade rules in the EU help companies engage in trade within the EU, but the responses to this question allow us to judge how important an issue this is. The proportion of responses is summarized in Figure 7. We can see that more than 60%

Table 7. The results of ordered logistic regression for selected problems when buying online as dependent variables

	(1) Interoperability problems (coef.)	(2) Labelling problems (coef.)
Number of employees	0.00017** (2.29)	0.0018** (2.42)
International group	-0.1231 (-0.99)	0.0097 (0.09)
New company	0.0604 (0.21)	0.2487 (1.02)
Sell to firms	0.0073 (0.07)	0.1790* (-1.81)
Manufacturing sector	-0.0599 (-0.76)	-0.2392*** (-3.16)
Information and communication sector	-0.1558* (-1.77)	-0.7326*** (-8.36)
Log pseudolikelihood	-3615.64	-3928.9
Wald X^2	280.69	393.61
Observations	4474	4565

Note: based on the data from European Commission (2015). Regressions done by logit and ordered logit with standard errors corrected for heteroscedasticity. Variables are all defined in an appendix. (.) denotes z-statistics, */**/*** mean significance at the 10%/5%/1% levels of significance. Countries fixed effects are included in all regressions.

Figure 7. The distribution of responses to the question whether the same rules of e-commerce in the EU would be beneficial for them
Source: Own calculations based on the data from European Commission (2015)

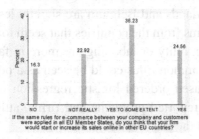

of firms reported that common rules would be beneficial for their online business and that almost a quarter of firms gave it unqualified support.

Table 8. The results of regression analysis with the attitudes towards common rules for e-commerce in the EU as the dependent variable

	(1) Common rules would be beneficial (coef.)	(2) Common rules would be beneficial (coef.)	(3) Common rules would be beneficial (coef.)
Interoperability problems	0.4458*** (5.08)		
Labelling problems			0.3842*** (4.35)
Number of employees	-0.0001* (-1.80)	-0.001* (-1.91)	-0.0001** (-1.58)
International group	0.0129 (0.07)	-0.0141 (-0.08)	0.0339 (0.19)
New company	0.2053 (0.68)	0.1052 (0.37)	0.0747 (0.26)
Wholesale sector	0.3991*** (3.16)	0.3924*** (3.06)	0.3190*** (2.54)
Manufacturing sector	0.0798 (0.56)	0.1374 (0.95)	0.0363 (0.26)
Log pseudolikelihood	-1625.85	-1583.91	-1661.76
Wald X^2	110.10	133.57	103.72
Observations	1290	1262	1310

Note: based on the data from European Commission (2015). Regressions done by logit and ordered logit with standard errors corrected for heteroscedasticity. Variables are all defined in an appendix. (.) denotes z statistics, */**/*** mean significance at the 10%/5%/1% levels of significance. Countries fixed effects are included in all regressions.

There are also some cross-country differences in the attitudes towards the common, or standardised, rules for e-commerce. Firms from Bulgaria, Poland and Romania have the most positive view on common rules, while the firms from the Czech Republic, Netherlands and Belgium are slightly less optimistic. We would like to point out that firms from the countries that seem to have the most intensive problems with interoperability or labelling are more in favour of common rules. Thus, it is likely that common rules could be seen as a possible solution of these problems. We further used ordered logistic regression in order to examine the potential link between reported problems and firms' attitudes towards common rules for e-commerce in the EU (see Table 8).

According to the results there is a strong positive link between the problems with interoperability and positive attitudes towards common rules. The same is true also for problems with labelling. Thus those firms that reported one or more of the mentioned problems tend to have a more positive view on common rules for e-commerce in the EU. Moreover, the firms from the wholesale sector appear to be also significantly more in favour of these standardised rules. The problems with interoperability and labelling can be to some extent solved by standardisation. Especially semantic and technical interoperability can be improved by common standards. This could particularly lead to higher involvement of enterprises in international e-commerce within the EU market.

CONCLUSION

Building on the previous research such as for example (Kasemsap, 2018), Kurnia et al. (2015), and Zaied (2012) it can be concluded that e-commerce activities are considered as one of the driving forces of the economy and they also have the potential to improve efficiency and productivity of companies. The share of individuals using the Internet for ordering goods or services is rising across the EU. Although Visegrad group countries are lagging behind the EU average they have made significant progress over the last few years. Furthermore, the proportion of firms that are engaged e-commerce seems to vary based on the country specific factors as well as the characteristics of the firm. Based on our results we can conclude that firms in Denmark, Ireland, Belgium, Sweden and Czechia are the most active in e-commerce activities. More than 25% of enterprises' turnover has come from e-commerce in Ireland, Belgium and Czechia. On the other hand, countries such as Cyprus, Greece, Bulgaria, Romania and Latvia are significantly lagging behind other EU member's states e-commerce engagement and e-commerce turnover. In general we can say that the differences between EU countries are still very high. However, the share of e-commerce business activities is rising significantly in the majority of EU countries during recent years. The only significant exception is Germany where we observed a decline in both the share of enterprises engaged in e-commerce as well as their relative turnover from e-commerce.

We further examine the factors affecting engagement in e-commerce at the firms' level. Based on our results, the firms in an international group as well as those selling services are more often selling online. Firms in the sector of accommodation and food services are especially successful in adopting online selling. On the other hand, manufacturing firms are less prone to sell their products online.

With respect to the negative effects on distance related trade cost, e-commerce also has the potential to enhance the actual use of the EU single market. However, there are still several problems that have to be solved in order to take advantage of its full potential. According to our results, delivery costs and costs related to guarantees are currently the most pressing problems. We can expect that the reduction of these costs within the EU could potentially lead to an increase in cross border online trade in the Single European Market. Although these problems are not directly related to standards, it is likely that standardisation could also play some role in the process of cost reduction. However, there are also several other potential obstacles of international online trade which are more directly linked with standards. One of them is the problem with interoperability. This sort of problem appears to be particularly evident in countries such as Greece, Portugal, Italy and Bulgaria. It is also more common for firms from the wholesale sector and information and communication sector. Furthermore, our results to some extent suggest that firms in an international group could have slightly less problems with interoperability when selling online. Another problem, partly related to standards is different labelling and costs related to this issue. Especially manufacturing firms often reported this problem when selling online. However, this is less of a problem for them when they are buying online. Labelling costs could be potentially reduced by the introduction of international standards or by strengthening the harmonization of products labelling within the EU.

We have also shown that most of the firms believe that common, or standardised, rules for e-commerce within the EU could lead to significant benefits for them when selling or buying online. Interestingly, especially the firms that reported problems with interoperability or labelling are more convinced that common e-commerce rules could be particularly helpful. This could represent a relatively strong supportive voice for the current Commission agenda on the Digital Single Market (European Commission, 2015a, European Commission, 2017).

ACKNOWLEDGMENT

This research was supported by the Slovak Research and Development Agency (APVV) APVV-15-0322.

REFERENCES

Abbad, M., Abbad, R., & Saleh, M. (2011). Limitations of e-commerce in developing countries: Jordan case. *Education, Business and Society, 4*(4), 280–291. doi:10.1108/17537981111190060

Abdalla, K. F. (2003, April). A model for semantic interoperability using XML. In *IEEE Systems and Information Engineering Design Symposium* (pp. 107-111). IEEE. 10.1109/SIEDS.2003.158012

Albrecht, C. C., Dean, D. L., & Hansen, J. V. (2005). Marketplace and technology standards for B2B e-commerce: Progress, challenges, and the state of the art. *Information & Management, 42*(6), 865–875. doi:10.1016/j.im.2004.09.003

Almousa, M. (2013). Barriers to E-Commerce Adoption: Consumers' Perspectives from a Developing Country. *iBusiness, 5*(2), 65-71.

Andersen, K. V., Beck, R., Wigand, R. T., Bjørn-Andersen, N., & Brousseau, E. (2004). European e-commerce policies in the pioneering days, the gold rush and the post-hype era. *Information Polity, 9*(3-4), 217–232.

Bakos, Y. (2001). The emerging landscape for retail e-commerce. *The Journal of Economic Perspectives, 15*(1), 69–80. doi:10.1257/jep.15.1.69

Bangemann, M. (1994). *Recommendations to the European Council: Europe and the global information society*. Brussels: European Commission.

Bjørn-Andersen, N., & Andersen, K. V. (2009). *Diffusion and Impacts of the Internet and e-Commerce* (No. 2003-11).

Blind, K., & Jungmittag, A. (2005). Trade and the Impact of Innovations and Standards: The Case of Germany and the UK. *Applied Economics, 37*(12), 1385–1398. doi:10.1080/13504850500143294

Blind, K., Peterson, S., & Riillo, C. A. F. (2017). The Impact of Standards and Regulation on Innovation in Uncertain Markets. *Research Policy, 46*(1), 249–264. doi:10.1016/j.respol.2016.11.003

De Vries, H. J. (2013). *Standardization: A business approach to the role of national standardization organizations*. Springer Science & Business Media.

European Commission. (2015a). *Communication from the Commission to the European Parliament, the Council, the European Economic and Social Committee and the Committee of the Regions: Digital Single Market Strategy for Europe.* Brussels: European Commission. Available at: http://eur-lex.europa.eu/legal-content/EN/TXT/?uri=celex:52015DC0192

European Commission. (2015b). *Flash Eurobarometer 413 (Companies Engaged in Online Activities).* TNS Political & Social [producer]. GESIS Data Archive, Cologne. ZA6284 Data file Version 1.0.0, doi:10.4232/1.12353

European Commission. (2017). *Communication from the Commission to the European Parliament, the Council, the European Economic and Social Committee and the Committee of the Regions on the Mid-Term Review on the implementation of the Digital Single Market Strategy - A Connected Digital Single Market for All.* COM(2017). Brussels: European Commission. Available at: http://eur-lex.europa.eu/legal-content/EN/TXT/?uri=COM:2017:228:FIN

European Commission. (2019). *Data protection in the European Union. The General Data Protection Regulation (GDPR).* Brussels: European Commission. Available at: https://ec.europa.eu/info/law/law-topic/data-protection/data-protection-eu_en

Fensel, D., Ding, Y., Omelayenko, B., Schulten, E., Botquin, G., Brown, M., & Flett, A. (2001). Product data integration in B2B e-commerce. *IEEE Intelligent Systems, 16*(4), 54–59. doi:10.1109/5254.941358

Godwin, U. J. (2001). Privacy and security concerns as major barriers for e-commerce: A survey study. *Information Management & Computer Security, 9*(4), 165–174. doi:10.1108/EUM0000000005808

Halaweh, M. (2011). Adoption of E-commerce: Understanding of Security Challenge. *The Electronic Journal on Information Systems in Developing Countries, 47.*

Henning, F. (2018). A theoretical framework on the determinants of organisational adoption of interoperability standards in Government Information Networks. *Government Information Quarterly, 35*(4), S61–S67.

Chaffey, D. (2007). *E-business and E-commerce Management: Strategy, Implementation and Practice.* Pearson Education.

Chitura, T., Mupemhi, S., Dube, T., & Bolongkikit, J. (2015). Barriers to electronic commerce adoption in small and medium enterprises: A critical literature review. *Journal of Internet Banking and Commerce*.

Decker, S., Melnik, S., Van Harmelen, F., Fensel, D., Klein, M., Broekstra, J., ... Horrocks, I. (2000). The semantic web: The roles of XML and RDF. *IEEE Internet Computing, 4*(5), 63–73. doi:10.1109/4236.877487

Jennex, M. E., Amoroso, D., & Adelakun, O. (2004). E-commerce infrastructure success factors for small companies in developing economies. *Electronic Commerce Research, 4*(3), 263–286. doi:10.1023/B:ELEC.0000027983.36409.d4

Kasemsap, K. (2018). *The importance of electronic commerce in modern business. In Encyclopedia of Information Science and Technology* (4th ed.; pp. 2791–2801). IGI Global.

Kawa, A. (2017). Supply chains of cross-border e-commerce. In Advanced Topics in Intelligent Information and Database Systems (pp. 173-183). Springer. doi:10.1007/978-3-319-56660-3_16

Kulvatunyou Oh, H., Ivezic, N., & Nieman, S. T. (2019). Standards-based semantic integration of manufacturing information: Past, present, and future. *Journal of Manufacturing Systems, 52*, 184–197. doi:10.1016/j.jmsy.2019.07.003

Kurnia, S., Choudrie, J., Mahbubur, R. M., & Alzougool, B. (2015). E-commerce technology adoption: A Malaysian grocery SME retail sector study. *Journal of Business Research, 68*(9), 1906–1918. doi:10.1016/j.jbusres.2014.12.010

Lawrence, J. E., & Tar, U. A. (2010). Barriers to e-commerce in developing countries. *Information, Society and Justice Journal, 3*(1), 23-35.

Lee, C. Y., Ibrahim, H., Othman, M., & Yaakob, R. (2010, July). Resolving semantic interoperability challenges in XML schema matching. In *International Conference on Networked Digital Technologie*s (pp. 151-162). Springer. 10.1007/978-3-642-14292-5_17

Lodder, A. R., & Murray, A. D. (2017). *EU regulation of E-commerce: A commentary.* Edward Elgar Publishing. doi:10.4337/9781785369346

MacGregor, R. C., & Vrazalic, L. (2009). E-commerce adoption barriers in small businesses and the differential effects of gender. *Journal of Electronic Commerce in Organizations, 4*(2), 1–24. doi:10.4018/jeco.2006040101

Martinez, M. G., & Poole, N. (2004). The development of private fresh produce safety standards: Implications for developing Mediterranean exporting countries. *Food Policy, 29*(3), 229–255. doi:10.1016/j.foodpol.2004.04.002

Moenius, J. (2004). *Information Versus Product Adaptation: The Role of Standards in Trade (February 2004).* Available at SSRN: https://ssrn.com/abstract=608022

Nacer, H., & Aissani, D. (2014). Semantic web services: Standards, applications, challenges and solutions. *Journal of Network and Computer Applications, 44,* 134–151. doi:10.1016/j.jnca.2014.04.015

Nakatani, K., Chuang, T. T., & Zhou, D. (2006). Data synchronization technology: Standards, business values and implications. *Communications of the Association for Information Systems, 17*(1), 44.

Orviska, M., & Hunady, J. (2017). Selected Barriers to Online International Trade Within the EU: Could Standards and Common Rules Help? *International Journal of Standardization Research, 15*(2), 76–93. doi:10.4018/IJSR.2017070105

Portugal-Perez, A., Reyes, J. D., & Wilson, J. S. (2010). Beyond the information technology agreement: Harmonisation of standards and trade in electronics. *World Economy, 33*(12), 1870–1897. doi:10.1111/j.1467-9701.2010.01300.x

Ruiz-Mafé, C., Sanz-Blas, S., & Aldás-Manzano, J. (2009). Drivers and barriers to online airline ticket purchasing. *Journal of Air Transport Management, 15*(6), 294–298. doi:10.1016/j.jairtraman.2009.02.001

Schmitz, V., & Leukel, J. (2005). Findings and Recommendations from a Pan-European Research Project: Comparative Analysis of E-Catalog Standards. *International Journal of IT Standards and Standardization Research, 3*(2), 51–65. doi:10.4018/jitsr.2005070105

Schweinsberg, K., & Wegner, L. (2017). Advantages of complex SQL types in storing XML documents. *Future Generation Computer Systems, 68,* 500–507. doi:10.1016/j.future.2016.02.013

Solaymani, S., Sohaili, K., & Yazdinejad, E. A. (2012). Adoption and use of e-commerce in SMEs. *Electronic Commerce Research, 12*(3), 249–263. doi:10.100710660-012-9096-6

Song, Z., Sun, Y., Wan, J., Huang, L., & Zhu, J. (2019). Smart e-commerce systems: Current status and research challenges. *Electronic Markets, 29*(2), 221–238. doi:10.100712525-017-0272-3

Stockdale, R., & Standing, C. (2006). A classification model to support SME e-commerce adoption initiatives. *Journal of Small Business and Enterprise Development, 13*(3), 381–394. doi:10.1108/14626000610680262

Swann, P., Temple, P., & Shurmer, M. (1996). Standards and trade performance: The UK experience. *Economic Journal (London), 106*(438), 1297–1313. doi:10.2307/2235522

van de Kaa, G., Janssen, M., & Rezaei, J. (2018). Standards battles for business-to-government data exchange: Identifying success factors for standard dominance using the Best Worst Method. *Technological Forecasting and Social Change, 137*, 182–189. doi:10.1016/j.techfore.2018.07.041

Verma, P. K., Verma, R., Prakash, A., Tripathi, R., & Naik, K. (2016). A novel hybrid medium access control protocol for inter-M2M communications. *Journal of Network and Computer Applications, 75*, 77–88. doi:10.1016/j.jnca.2016.08.011

Wang, X. V., & Xu, X. W. (2015). A collaborative product data exchange environment based on STEP. *International Journal of Computer Integrated Manufacturing, 28*(1), 75–86. doi:10.1080/0951192X.2013.785028

Zaied, A. N. H. (2012). Barriers to e-commerce adoption in Egyptian SMEs. International. *Journal of Information Engineering and Electronic Business, 4*(3), 9. doi:10.5815/ijieeb.2012.03.02

Zhao, K., Xia, M., & Shaw, M. (2007). An Integrated Model of Consortium-Based E-Business Standardization: Collaborative Development and Adoption with Network Externalities. *Journal of Management Information Systems, 23*(4), 247–271. doi:10.2753/MIS0742-1222230411

ENDNOTE

[1] Further details on the sampling procedure can be found at http://ec.europa.eu/commfrontoffice/publicopinion/flash/fl_413_en.pdf

Section 5
The Practitioners' Corner

Chapter 10
Fostering the Participation of Companies in Standardization:
A Soft Law Instrument to Reduce Risks – The Concept of Student Standardization Societies

Christophe Sene
CEN/TC-276, France

ABSTRACT

Standardization is one source of informal rules that regulate the public realm: standards are not legally-binding, but, as soft law instruments, they influence the governance, ethics, and conduct of companies. Standardization brings unique benefits to companies in term of knowledge, credibility, and risk reduction by bringing accountability and predictability. To foster active participation of companies in standardization, higher and continuous education in standardization is essential to build mutual understanding between companies and the standardization world since decision making in the former is a relatively quick top-down hierarchical process while in the latter time-consuming consensus-building is the norm. The concept of Student Standardization Societies (SSS) is introduced as the best way to promote standardization in the long term, and advice is given for the practical implementation of SSS and their relationship with Official Standardization Organizations.

DOI: 10.4018/978-1-7998-2181-6.ch010

INTRODUCTION

Standardization is a unique way of collaboration that humanity has invented a long time ago notably for commerce. In Roman time, "wine amphoras" held a standard volume of about 39 litres but there was a large variety of amphora of different standardized volumes and heights from 1.5 to 0.3 metres high. Since this dawn age, standardization has been conceptualized, formalized and refined to end up with current modern standardization systems.

It is interesting to note that nowadays **all nation states are involved in standardization** and are equipped with national Official Standardization Organizations (OSOs) covering nearly all domains from trade, techniques, quality to management and sustainability to name a few. This fact is a powerful proof that standardization fills an essential need of our current world. If not, logic has it that OSOs will exist only in some countries and dealing only with specific topics. However, independently of the cultural background, the political structure, the legal system and the economic organization, all countries have the capability to write and adopt official standards. Without standardization a gap is unfilled particularly in the economic field; therefore, economic actors should invest time to understand standardization, its benefits and its constraints: ignoring a universal tool such as standardization is never a good idea. No need to state that a lot of standards are addressing topics directly related to the economic field but also related topics such as sustainability and safety. Thus, an increasing and significant number of standards addresses societal, environmental and sustainable issues and impacts directly or indirectly companies, especially the ones having sustainability objectives and adopting triple bottom-line reporting.

It may be inferred that standardization is a tool which plays a role in the competitiveness of individual companies, economic sectors and supply chains.

The admixture of formal and informal law is a common feature of any legal order and standardisation is clear a soft law instrument. They, the interplay of soft and hard law makes standards an efficient mechanism that influences the governance and conducts of companies and governments even if they are not *stricto sensu* legally-binding and enforceable. The place of standardization in the legal system will be discussed.

All these call for an active participation of companies in standardization. What are the roadblocks to increase company participation in standardization?

The advantages associated with standardization such as in risk reduction, capability building, intelligence and better control of its environment in the long term will be discussed. This chapter per the author will show how companies can get involved in standardization and how they can benefit from such involvement.

The involvement of younger generations could be an efficient way to increase the penetration of standardization in companies and for that purpose the concept of Student Standardization Societies (SSS) will be presented.

STANDARDIZATION AS A SOFT LAW INSTRUMENT

For the layman, legislation appears as a well-defined set of texts which have been adopted by official bodies (e.g. the parliament) and must be abided by in order to be compliant with the law. In practice, legislation can be considered as a protean set of texts with a high diversity of origin, different level of requirements and enforcement. Scholars make the distinction between hard law and soft law.

The term soft law is an ambiguous term that has been coined to define a wide range of documents and instruments having some normative pretentions and which are not necessarily adopted by institutions that have the right to adopt legislation. Soft law can be adopted by a wide variety of actors: official standards that are adopted by Official Standardization Organizations fall within that definition of soft law.

Standards, Technical reports, Technical Specifications published by OSO carry some weight that bring them close to legal norm however they are not directly binding. **Binding-ness** is an essential feature of a law: this is where the key distinction between hard and soft law comes. Thus, standards in that sense are not law as such - not hard law - but can be considered as soft law. Standardization is only potentially binding. Standards materialise a form of "moral" or "political" commitment for the potential users: a standard is more than just a publication produced by a one-sided stakeholder. It comes with a form of "diverse expertise" be scientific, economic, moral or political: thus, a standard on a specific sustainability issue such as deforestation or water pollution gives rise to a non-legally binding push to use it since the genesis of standard is representative of experts in the fields and a consensus between a large community of stakeholders. Ideally, a standard is a way of sharing expertise and savoir-faire and is deemed to represent the best-in-class methodology or best practice developed by experts -even if one should never forget that the drafters of the standards are representing their own interests and defending their positions-.

A company can ignore a given norm however it is much more difficult to act in opposition: solid arguments would need to be provided to defend taking a position against a norm. It is possible but it needs be explained as it could be challenged by customers or competent authorities. Defining bio-based surfactants in a different way than the EN-17035 norm and measuring the biomass content differently than EN-16640 or ASTM-D6866-16 might be arduous to explain. **Standardization creates a** *positive* **normativity**: going against a standard induces mistrust, suspicion and sometimes a clear disapproval. Thus, as it is easier and less risky to implement standards or at least to be in line with, **standardization is clearly a mechanism that creates normativity in the long term** and therefore should be considered as part of soft law. It is worth noting that since standards are ready-to-use documents it is much easier and less time consuming to use them instead of inventing alternatives with the risks to be challenged: the majority of actors is expected to implement a norm, a virtuous circle is established by the earlier adopters and if they are sufficiently numerous the standard is becoming a market expectation or a market benchmark. In that sense standardization obeys one of the features of soft law: it is creating a **customary rule** in this case not enforceable by a public authority but by peer pressure. For example, a norm on sustainability (e.g. ISO 16128 on the natural and organic nature of cosmetic ingredients) is bringing forward knowledge, expertise and expresses an agreement between a wide variety of stakeholders: this is powerful in term of shaping practice and governance. This standard can be used to measure the "sustainability index" of a company and be used by investors in their ranking. Standardization produces soft-law instruments which can themselves be used in other soft-law instruments: thus, standardization plays a role in the multi-facet area of soft law.

Standards clearly exert a great bearing on the behaviour of a variety of economic, social and political actors. They are instruments of governance for companies and influence their conducts. Some standards can simply not be ignored: the ISO 9000 family epitomises such statement. ISO 9001 and its sector-specific versions (e.g. ISO-13485 on medicals devices or ISO/TS 29001 in petroleum, petrochemical and natural gas industries), which address various aspect of quality management, have established a certain vision of quality and are a must to do business. These standards are often legally binding via the means of commercial contracts between suppliers and customers: typically, the supplier has the contractual obligations to follow specific standard and/or be certified accordingly.

One can turn to standards to demonstrate compliance with the mandatory legal requirements. Standards can be mentioned in the legislation or they can be used as **benchmark**. For example, the European on detergents which govern the placing on the EU market of detergents directly refers to EN ISO standards and OECD guidelines (OECD 301 standards on biodegradability) to comply with the mandatory provision concerning the biodegradation of the chemical ingredients. The industrial Emission Directive 2010/75/EU which is the main EU instrument regulating pollutant emissions from industrial installations requests that best available techniques are used in the manufacturing of chemicals. Technical standards can be used to show compliance with this legal provision.

Nowadays, industrial and service companies are not only exposed to legislation - national, regional and international - which are legally binding on them, but they also must take into consideration a wide range of voluntary initiatives and schemes inter alias on sustainability and environmental issues. This voluntary framework sometimes refers to official standards. For example, the ISO 16128 on the naturality of cosmetic ingredients and the EN-17035 on bio-based surfactants are good candidates to be used in ecolabels.

Standardization produce soft law documents and instruments such as official norms and certification. As part of soft law, standardization contributes indirectly to the legal ecosystem of companies (by contractual agreement between companies or because of the legislation to be abided by) and influences the governance and conduct of companies and the legislators.

Thus, standardization plays a vital part in shaping the market directly and indirectly: (i) directly by establishing a set of references for products, applications, processes and methods and (ii) indirectly by being referred to in legislation.

STANDARDIZATION FROM THE POINT OF VIEW OF AN ECONOMIC ACTOR

What most professionals know about standardization is what they learn by themselves or by encountering standards in their professional life. Most graduate have no clue about what are standards and who issues them. Training in standardization falls between the cracks of legal, technical and business training since standardization is considered by lawyers as outside the legal field, by business representative as too slow and cumbersome, and by technical people as too procedural or outside pure technical activities. These perceptions need to be taken into account to improve access to standardization.

Standardization: A Consensus-Building Exercise

The time scale of standardization and business are inherently not the same. Normalization bodies like CEN or ISO are aware of this hurdle and have been working on speeding up and streamlining standardization processes. However, standardization is based on consensus-building and involvement of a large number of stakeholders. Consensus is a difficult exercise and time is an essential element of it: consensus cannot be forced or speed up and the construction of a common acceptable position is a time-consuming task. It takes time to build consensus, to bring diverging position closer to such proximity that the common position is acceptable for all stakeholders.

It is worth highlighting that the broader the diversity of the stakeholders the more complicated and the more time consuming the consensus building is. Consequently, the difficulty in consensus building increases logically from national level to regional or European level and then to international level. The convenors of normalization committee need to offer stakeholders space and time to share their points of view and to have the different positions understood by all stakeholders. From that point, the road to a common position which is acceptable to the all involved stakeholders are paved with difficulties including not only economic and technical but also of linguistic, cultural, behavioural nature. It is established that stakeholders in normalization come from highly diverse background: this is the value of standardization to bring together attendees from a large spectrum of organizations from private companies, non-governmental organizations, public institutes, authorities, academic institutions, trade unions or consumer associations. The high diversity of the stakeholders is a guarantee of representativeness and acceptability of the normative documents but represent a challenge that the standardization processes are designed to handle.

Cultural mapping shows that different cultures or countries have different ways to negotiate and tackle divergences. The construction of trust is necessary to negotiate successfully towards a common position and some countries achieve to trust based on the relationship while other countries build trust by the proof of tasks. A regional or international standardization committee will have to consider both task-based and relationship-based trust building before the cohesion of the committee can move to negotiating and deciding on consensus. Some cultures foster consensual deciding mechanisms while others expect top-down decisions: the former is obviously more comfortable and more time-efficient in a standardization committee than the latter. Similarly, leadership could be egalitarian or hierarchical. As disagreement is an inherent part of a committee work the attitude towards disagreement should be carefully considered by the chair of the committee: some culture may accept confrontational disagreement as part of the negotiation while others will avoid direct confrontation and will pass their disagreement through more subtle form of communication. Finally, in term of persuasion, principles or generalities should come first whereas in other cultures applications, examples and specificities should be the basis of persuasion. In short, reaching a consensus is by nature much more complex and time-consuming as each stakeholder has a different expectation in term of soft skills or soft behaviour such as in leading, deciding, disagreeing, trusting and persuading.

In companies, decisions in business are sometimes built on consensus, but in practice most of the time the process for business decisions are top down backed by a hierarchical organizational structure. Stakeholders around the negotiation table know very well their hierarchical position within the company: sharing of data and point of view take place but the decision is not the result of a vote. The decision is taken by the top of the company. Furthermore, even when a business decision is built on consensus, the process is inherently easier as the diversity of stakeholders is much narrower: individuals from the same professional communities, the same sector or same group of companies (e.g. multinational companies) share the same codes and values of their professions or sectorial environments they are evolving in. Graduates and post-graduates often benefit from similar education (e.g. chemists, business professionals, IT experts...): education is a formatting process and young graduates in business are tragically uniformly similar. Diversity does not seem to be the road for success in higher business and economic education.

In summary, consensus-building is by nature at the heat of normalization whereas in companies top-down decisions are the norm.

Dealing with Different Dynamics in Decision Making

The decision process in companies are radically different from the one in standardization. The difference in timeline and the apparent administrative burdensome of standardization are inhibiting the participation in the standardization of stakeholders from the industrial and service companies.

Generating standards suffer from one of its strong point: consensus and stakeholder participation. Both have an impact on the timeline. Drafting and adopting a standard is a relatively long process and require a medium-term approach by stakeholders: this may be conflicting with the need for a quick solution and the short-term approach of stakeholders. Individuals may be discouraged by the time required from initiation to final publication of a given standard: often more than two years are necessary, and this does not include the initial decision to use standardization as a solution for a given issue. It is not unusual to have five years before the identification of the issue and the final publication of the standard.

The dynamics in the business and standardization are radically different and the misunderstanding between the professionals working in private companies and in standardization is not self-evident. Thus, the situation could be summarized with the following statement of a business now involved in standardization: "in standardization one does not necessarily consult widely before deciding, which is possible because of our vertical structure and one is proud of our agility to react and decide quickly while in standardization the horizontal structure induces wide consultation and consensus building, the decision are slower to come. However, in business management keep changing its decision regularly for positive or negative reasons and it is not unusual to go in one direction one year and in the opposite direction the following year. In standardization a decision taken – for example a norm adopted- cannot be overturned the following day. Somehow, the agility of business decision is mirrored with instability while in standardization the apparent administrative burdensome of the decision process is mirrored by general approval, in-depth analysis and stability". This may be a caricatural statement like any generalisation but there is certainly some truth in this statement which comes to explain the frustration that business expresses toward standardization and maybe the frustration that standardization professional may feel towards the instability of business.

If one wants to increase the participation of professionals from private sectors in standardization, it is important to be aware of the **different dynamics in the decision process** in both worlds. Focusing the education on standardization only on the technical elements of the standardization process such as for example the organizational structure of a Technical Committee, the standardization processes, the key milestones or the rule on the writing of norms is not sufficient: it is key to explain why the standardization process is designed in such a way. Knowledge and acceptance of such rationales is a condition to any constructive and stimulating participation in standardization: otherwise frustration build on both sides as professionals from companies try and overcome the standardisation procedures sometimes unconsciously and standardization professionals work hard to bring them back into the official processes.

In a nutshell, standardization and private companies evolve in different spheres and both need to try and adapt to each other. Official Standardization Organizations have updated and **streamlined the standardization processes** in the past and it is important that this approach continues so that the standardization world become more business-friendly. However, it is also important that business understands the need and value for such specificities and make the most to adapt and help OSO to reform. It is worth mentioning that standardization and company business are shaped to fulfil their mission in society and there is a limit to the reform of standardisation procedures. They will remain distinct worlds with hopefully a larger overlapping area, but this is limited by the fair requests from other stakeholders: standardization need to respond to all the stakeholders and need to be friendly for all of them without providing an advantage to a specific one. Therefore, it should be emphasized the overall organization of standardization and its induced processes and timeline are themselves the fruit of a consensus between stakeholders: this is a critical consideration.

In order to promote the involvement of company professionals, academic education is an important element. Before moving into technicalities relating to standardization, it is important that education cover (i) the mission of standardization, (ii) why standardization is designed in such a way, (iii) the challenge of cultural diversity, and (iv) the fact that standardization process itself is a result of a consensus to be friendly to all stakeholders and not to a specific one like industrial or service companies. A training on (a) the organizational structure of a Technical Committee, (b) the standardization processes, (c) the key milestones and (d) the rule on the writing of norms is incomplete and should come second in the training. The training on the first part ((i) to (iv)) should promote the understanding and acceptance of the second part of the training ((a) to (d)).

The mindset in the World of standardization is different from than the one on private companies and the associated values which are praised are different. A successful participant to standardization must understand these fundamental changes and be able to change its behaviours accordingly. Is adaptability not one of the best of any quality?

Competition versus Collaboration

Humans collaborate and compete with themselves. In the economic sphere, companies collaborate in many fields and according to dynamic evolving architectures (e.g. nowadays web-based companies compete with street-based companies). Thus, companies having the same activities and who are competing on the markets for their products and service also collaborates because they share common interests and challenges. Collaboration also takes place along the supply chain: customers team up with their suppliers; and economic actors of the same value chain collaborate actively to defend their interest against other value chains or against regulatory pressure. Economic activities are a mix between collaborative and competitive behaviours: a very complex set of dynamic relationship rules by common and diverging interests are forging the alliance or opposition between economic actors. It can be said that standardization is a tool for collaboration. Thus, since a collaboration between some economic actors may represent a threat for other economic actors, standardization could represent a combination of opportunities and threats depending on the interest of a given economic actor. The discussion can be broadened to non-economic actors such as environmental and societal non-governmental organizations, trade unions, or consumer organizations. Basically, the affinity and opposition existing in the economic world is mirrored in standardization where actors sharing common interests meet stakeholders with diverging interests. However, the consensus-building principles of standardization push standardization towards the collaborative side of our human society. Standardization can be considered as a mechanism to bring together in a common forum diverging interests. As the participation to standardization is voluntary, stakeholders with diverging interests can decide to stay outside the standardization forum; however, by doing so, their interests and values are not considered. Needless to say, the non-participation to a standardization forum should be carefully assessed: there are risks associated for staying outside the forum. The risks could be limited to specific confined issues in the short term or exposed the non-participant to strategic risks in the long term.

What is at stake should be properly evaluated by professionals accustomed with standardization. Multicriteria analysis including technical, financial on the short and long term should thoroughly assessed. This mean that stakeholders should equipped itself with the knowledge on standardization either internally by developing their own experts or to use the service of external consultants in standardization.

However, often the **non-participation of stakeholders** to a technical committee is not based on a comprehensive in-depth risk assessment and critical analysis but happen because of lack of knowledge of standardization and what is at stake. Standardization may appear as an inefficient time-consuming process for which the outcome is not immediate. The timeline is certainly longer than what business dynamics would like, and standardization need a commitment for several months or years. However, standardization should be considered like any investment: financial cost, human resource, opportunities and threats should be analysed *inter alias* by a SWOT analysis for short-term and long-term. Participation of a given company to standardization should also depend on the participation of other stakeholders especially with diverging interests: basically, if one does not participate to a standardization exercise, one has no voice. Being present with converging and diverging interests enable to better understand the subject, build network, avoid missing some points and could be a way to develop stronger internal experts. Standardization often lead to better expertise skills of attendees. For company the value for its employees should be considered in term of motivation and skills: trainings and conferences are expensive and time-consuming, and, in that perspective, standardization can be a cost-efficient alternative. For company, participation to standardization fora lead to capability building in term of technical and soft skills. It is also a mechanism that should be included in company intelligence: what are your "friends" and "foes" of the market place doing and thinking? This could enable to anticipate any new development.

One should be aware that "*Stakeholder participation calls for stakeholder participation*": depending on your point of view this is a virtuous or a vicious circle. Basically, the more stakeholders in a standardization committee the more incentive to participate. A populous standardization committee is a synonym of high stakes and diverging views and probably also richness of the discussion. Therefore, it is worth attending actively to defend and promote one's position and get acquainted with the high-level context. Who are the other stakeholders, what positions do they defend, who is in our side and opposite side, what are the arguments? Because of competition law, it is tricky for companies to interact directly with their competitors and to a certain level with supply chain actors. Standardization provides such formal fora where in-depth discussions can take place on a regular basis (while still complying with competition and anti-trust law) and consensus-building often need to come with convincing elements. This could bring new light of the issue and market.

Often the difficulty is to "**prime the standardization pump**", to create a committee and attract sufficient stakeholders in order to have "interesting" discussion and obey standardization rules for example in term of number of voting and active countries (quorum). For existing standardization committee, the difficulty is to keep the momentum. Excitement on a new issue could attract active stakeholders that disappear with time as the normalization process lags. Standardization committee are also responsible for a set of published norms, technical specifications (TS) and technical reports (TR) and the business plan. These "normalisation assets" need to be updated to keep with technical or regulatory progress. For example, the classification of 1,4 dioxane has been reviewed and is now considered as a CMR and PBT substance: the analytical methods which use 1,4 dioxane need to be reviewed to substitute 1,4 dioxane with a safer solvent. This represents a significant piece of work or revalidation and round robin testing. Health and environmental considerations are important factors in analytical testing: the well-established analytical norms developed many years ago did need to be updated. It is important to note that the set of norms belonging to a committee need to be take care of to follow HSE, environmental and sustainability: this maintenance work may not be an exciting piece of work except if the committee manager creates an atmosphere of expertise sharing. Then peer-to-peer discussion lead to valuable time for the attendees as well as for the quality of the normative documents which are reviewed. ISO/TC-91 and CEN/TC-276 are the ISO and European committees on surfactants. Surfactants are a class of chemicals with specific properties. The Technical Committee is made of several working groups dealing with analytical tests, microbiology and on physico-chemical methods: the norms are commonly used in routine quality control (QC) by companies and part of the quality specifications of the commercial products. However, some tests were developed many decades ago and sometimes as far as in the 1970's: they need to be modernized and adapted to the latest analytical equipment and new HSE standards. In 2015, ISO 17280:2015 Surface active agents — Determination of 1,4-dioxane residues in surfactants obtained from epoxyethane by gas chromatography was issued to tackle the issue of 1,4 dioxane and provide companies with a reliable method with can be used to guarantee compliant ingredient for cosmetic products. This is a good example of a highly-technical method which can be used to respond to a quality and regulatory issue for a consumer (cosmetic) products: this ISO norm brings with us credibility. "From a high-tech lab to the consumer to credibility and compliance" would be a good summary in this case.

How to set up a standardization forum? A company may not participate to a standardization forum because a suitable forum does not exist. National Standardization Organization can assist a given company in such a case: either to identify a suitable Technical Committee or Working Group or to create a new one if the topic is unaddressed. Again, a proactive action by the company or stakeholder is crucial: passivity does not pay. Trade associations can be a useful resource in the field of standardization.

The Role of Trade Associations in Standardization

Trade associations are place where collaboration between competitors occur. The role of trade association is to identify and monitor the issues, explain the problem and advocate for a solution for the whole sector or subsector. For example, the European Chemical Industry Council (Cefic, ww.cefic.org) defines its policy as "to maintain and develop a prosperous chemical industry in Europe by promoting the best possible economic, social and environmental conditions to bring benefits to society with a commitment to the continuous improvement of all its activities including the safety, health and environmental performance." The scope of trade association is large and can logically encompasses lot of issues dealt by standardization. However, trade associations focus mainly on legislation and governmental policies; and tend to overlook standardization; partly because of a lack of knowledge about standardisation. The activities of a trade association is steered by the permanent staff of trade associations and by their active members: generally speaking, both groups of people lack education and knowledge about standardisation. However, all is not lost as consensus-building and collaboration rather than competition are part of the DNA of trade associations: they are uniquely positioned to participate, contribute and benefit from standardization. It is a matter of education and getting involved but the mechanism for such involvement exist in all trade associations. It is key to stress that unlike other fora with the authorities, their voices in standardization count as much as other stakeholders including official representatives: this is a truly horizontal forum. When formal vote comes in a standardization committee, industry and business stakeholders can cast their vote. This is very different from other fora, working groups, task forces (…) between industry and the Authorities where the final decision is righteously taken by the executive and/or legislative and/ or judicial powers.

To sum up, trade associations have an indisputable role to play in standardization: they could play a facilitative role to bring industrial and service at the standardization table. Small and medium enterprises are particularly in need of support, but even large companies could be encouraged to take part in standardization. To ease the access, mutualize the effort, and learn from peer, trade association **shadow standardization task force** can be set up. The concept of a shadow group is (i) to decrease the barriers to entry into standardization, (ii) to prepare a common position and (iii) to feed Technical or Strategic Committees with normative proposals or themes having a role of think tank. The first objective (i) consists in helping junior members or new companies to familiarize themselves with standardization. The second objective (ii) is to consult very widely -more widely than the members of the standardization committee- and to hold preliminary discussion maybe with a deeper data sharing than what would be advisable in term of confidentiality in the technical expert and to be able to have quicker decision amongst members already technically acquainted with the issue. For example, in order to prepare our European Norm on bio-surfactants, a shadow group was created with the surfactants companies and main users to discuss the meaning of bio-based. To the layman, this bio-based concept is akin to naturality, renewability, biodegradability, non-toxic, sustainability and even organic: a discussion within the shadow group between experts already familiar with all these concepts enable to save a lot of time and focus on the real difficulty on the issue. The Task Force can be used to propose a solution at each stage of the discussion in the standardization committee. The third objective (iii) is to analyse the gap in the set of norms and to brainstorm about future need. For example, the shadow Task Force on bio-based surfactants has brainstormed and have identified sustainability and naturality as valuable follow-up of the norm and technical report on bio-based surfactants and new topics of standardization for CEN/TC-276 or ISO/TC-91.

Companies have departments of Regulatory Affairs, Legal Affairs and External Affairs: why not creating positions of *Standardization Affairs* (a term coined by the author). It is a transversal position working all departments including Research & Department, marketing and regulatory affairs. Standardization is neither a traditional legal instrument (hard law) or a label and companies should not take for granted that standardization are taken care of if they are not attributed to a specific department or function.

Considering all these elements, it is key to realize that for an economic actor and any stakeholders the participation in standardization should be carefully evaluated. The decision is not necessarily black and white (participation and non-participation): a stakeholder can decide to be an observer, an active member or even a leader (project manager, convenor, president of Technical Committee or strategic committee). The decision should be reviewed on a regular basis and the level of participation adjusted according to the current analysis (opportunities, threats, risks) in view of the internal and external environment of the stakeholder.

STANDARDIZATION AS A MECHANISM OF RISK MANAGEMENT

Risks and uncertainties are the two sides of the same coin: the former increases with the latter. Normativity is a source of stability; and as a soft instrument, standardization is an informal source of normativity. Therefore, by creating normativity, standardization induces stability and predictability and fosters a reduction in risks. Relying on standards for its operations enables a company to externalize risks: standards make a firm base for a company: official standards can be considered as non-bias, widely accepted and best-in-class methodology, formally approved by an external board. A challenge on a standard is not directly challenging the company but the normalization committee who has adopted the standard: thus, the liability of the company is therefore tremendously reduced if it can prove that it has implement the standard in good faith. The requirements on the company is to implement thoroughly the suitable standards.

In that perspective, companies should know which standards are applicable to their internal and external activities in order to make a conscious choice on the standards to follow and the ones to ignore. This assessment should be done systematically and on a regular basis for all departments of a company: standardization occurs in all fields and no function should therefore escape from this analysis. As it is a strategic decision the board of directors should steer the assessment and make the final decisions. Obviously, this assessment needs expertise and is time-consuming; but it is beneficial since learning occurs during the evaluation process (it is a form of intelligence), risk-reduction measures are cost-efficient in the long term and is time-efficient since it enables the company to use the best from standardization (no reinvent the wheel).

Risks on quality, safety, security, digital media, finance, R&D, sustainability, eco-conception, manufacturing, engineering, customers relationship, external stakeholder's communication to name a few can be mitigated by using efficiently, cleverly and consciously the appropriate norms.

Standardization should therefore be regarded by companies as a risk-reduction tool in the long haul: this is extremely valuable for the company itself and its stakeholders especially in a civilization that advocate for zero risks (something unachievable). Pressures on quality, innovation, profits while considering sustainability and environmental issues can be eased by using standards to decrease the associated risks.

Besides, the risk reduction can be enhanced further by being more than a recipient of standards and becoming an active stakeholder in the standardization process. Actively shaping standards magnifies the benefits of standards for a company. This however comes with a price tag: standardization is a relatively slow process and involvement in standardization needs an investment over several years. Gaining influence in standardization needs time and efforts: the understanding of the overall situation and the position of each stakeholders, the evaluation of what is at stake, the development of arguments, the expertise building in standardization and finally the design of an advocacy strategy come with strong and long-term commitment. However, participating to the standardization process enables companies to have a voice in the process and advocates for its interests: the end-result is standards which are friendlier to the participating companies. The risk-reduction benefits are still therefore but because of the participation of the company in the normalization process the standards will be suitable for the company and easier to implement. The problems that companies encountered with standardization is that they do not find the appropriate standards for their needs and its implementation is difficult because they did not have a voice (the implementation requires a lot of changes and efforts). The easier is to ignore the norm missing the risk-reduction benefits, to invent their own process and to implement the standards when forced by the market or a legislation.

In summary, standardization represents an effective risk-reduction mechanism for recipient companies of standards which is topped by additional benefits in term of suitability and lower barriers to entry for companies active in the standardization process.

HIGHER EDUCATION AND CONTINUOUS EDUCATION IN STANDARDIZATION

Standards are both well-perceived and mis-understood by the public and professionals: one could even say that they are well-perceived despite being mis-understood. Professionals are referring to norms as part of their work: they are considered as useful references or providing a solution to an issue. The public is confronted with norm in their daily life especially during their act of purchasing and the acceptance level is high: polls show that the general public is trusting standards. Strangely, neither the public nor professionals understand what standards really are and how they are generated. The mandatory level of standards also remains vague for most professionals. The only community that has a good grasp of standardization is the people who have been directly involved in the standardization process.

Industrialized countries still rely on informal education and training for standardization leaving to official standardization bodies, trade associations or continuing education. Taking into account that the global market place created by globalization required creation and reconciliation of national standards on a global scale, it can be considered as an oddity not to equipped senior management with a good understanding of standardization.

The main reason for the ignorance about standards is that they are not part of the curriculum in secondary or university education. Study in law, technical and scientific education, business or humanities do not include any course on standardization: this means that what a graduate knows about standards are what in the best case they learn themselves (autodidacts, or on-the-job learning) and in most cases the perception they have about standards.

For lawyers, standards are not considered as legal instruments as such even if they are referred to in some pieces of legislation. In Europe, the so-called "new approach to technical harmonization and standards" as laid down in Council Resolution of 7 May 1985 introduces the concept of **harmonised standards** (hEN) in all areas except car, food and cosmetics and grants market compliance to products manufactured in conformity with hEN. This new approach makes a direct link between EU legislation (directives based on Article 100 of the Rome treaty) and standards: this clear links is an incentive for lawyers, and more specifically EU lawyers to study standardization. For most company employees, standards are considered as tools outside their responsibility on which they have no control: they encounter them in contracts or as management tools in quality, safety, sustainability or technical areas. In the technical sphere, many standards are available. Technicians, scientists, R&D professionals use them as references in their daily professional life for machinery, materials and methods: standards are the texts which are written as references in technical documentation or at the bottom of the page. They are considered as bringing value but cast in stone and coming from institutes or "expert committees".

Thus, standards are often considered as ready-to-use documents that are available without questioning how and who generate them. The fact that standards are generated through an open process where many stakeholders can participate is clearly not understood. Standardization is often considered as an activity performed by committees of experts in "dark rooms": serious work, boring maybe and difficult to join. The reality is far from this image.

Including training on standardization in **higher education curriculum** seems a critical step to make the best use of standardization and to demystify the subject. Standardization is a universal and flexible tool which can be applied to any field to format knowledge into a concise, clear, practical and useful form – at least this is the objective. There is no limit to the fields of application of standardization: it can bring value *inter alias* in technical to non-technical fields, in product specification, in novel technology, in management, in organizational structure, in quality, in environmental management and in sustainability. For example, recently standardization work on the human phenome was proposed at ISO level even if the subject is broad, emerging and interdisciplinary as stated by AFNOR: "phenomics is a multidisciplinary science related to NBIC (nanotechnology, biotechnology, computer science and cognitive science) and represents the next promising step for the study of diseases and mechanisms of life". Thus, standardization is a tool that can be used in all fields - **well-established and emerging** - and all postgraduate should be aware of its use and potential and how to take part in the standardization process: a level above awareness is deemed beneficial for all students. **Students** who have built their basic skills during their undergraduate studies are the most suitable to benefit from academic training on standards: it is advisable to target an intermediate level for undergraduates and an advanced level for postgraduates. As standardization is a tool of globalisation, lack of proficiency in standardization will be more detrimental to young professionals and companies in the future than it has been in the past. Therefore, a critical view should be taken for the introduction of standardization courses in higher education since missing to understand the growing importance of standards in an ever-more globalized world would be damaging to companies: immobilism is not a safe option.

This chapter per the author recommends taking an interdisciplinary approach for academic course. Standardization is typically a transversal topic and education modules on standardization could be designed accordingly for graduates or postgraduates of different faculties mixing students from different educational cursus. Developing standardization education modules which can be used in different educational cursus would be an efficient approach and would justify the introduction of a new course.

Becoming active in standardization not only brings value for the individual and its organization but to the broader community as this is a way to establish best practice, acknowledge a set of knowledge and bring a consensual solution to a given issue. Professionals with a fair level of seniority may be the ones who have an opportunity to participate to the development of standards and who will be benefiting the most from a continuous education on standardisation. This means that official standardization bodies and trade associations need to provide standard education to standard practitioners and standardization committee members. Even if a certain level of seniority and/or experience is helpful to participate to standardization committee as experts, it does not mean that younger professionals should not been exposed to basic training on standardization. Courses providing a basic knowledge on what standards are and where they originate from would be valuable to promote standardization and to make the best use from current standards. Business executives, chief technologists, R&D directors, senior engineers and senior lawyers would benefit from a more advanced training on standardization focusing on the overarching strategy values and leveraging effects.

STUDENT STANDARDIZATION SOCIETIES (SSS)

The Concept of Student Standardization Societies

For newcomers, standardization is often seen as a strenuous abstract topic full of administrative procedures. It makes sense to learn about it by practicing. The concept of **Student Standardization Societies (SSS) mimicking Official Standardization Bodies** is an efficient and convivial way to learn by doing, by role-playing, by practicing in a safe environment where mistakes have no impact and where different strategies and roles can be tested.

The type of standardization needs to be selected: Sectorial, National, Regional or International models can be used to practice standardization. The "Sectorial" model represents standardization between stakeholders of a specific sector such as cosmetics (e.g. bio-based soaps) or electric bicycles. It could be easier to start with national standardization (e.g. AFNOR for university based in France) as a model before moving to regional standardization (e.g. CEN, CENELEC or ETSI) or international standardization (e.g. ISO or IEC).

To establish an SSS, the first step is to create an **organisational structure** with a clear organigram, hierarchy and rules, operating procedures and voting rights: several technical committees dealing with specific topics need to be brought into existence and populate with active student members. Students can easily use the project they are already working on as part of their academic courses as topic for the technical committees and for their standardization exercise. Postgraduate projects (e.g. Master II level) would be nicely enriched by considering drafting a norm and eventually furthering the idea by creating a standardization working group on the topic of interest. Thus, for example, a business thesis on "novel modes of mobility", a technical thesis on "natural organic cosmetics", an LLM dissertation on "pre-market approval schemes in EU Food Law" or an engineering project on "novel eco-friendly batteries" could be improved by considering standardization. Be practical: an SSS can be initiated with only one technical committee made on one Working Group. For each committee, a president, general secretary/committee manager and project leaders need to be appointed. Working Groups (WGs) are created on different topics corresponding to items of interest to students. The important point is that the SSS are not separate from the other courses or topics that students are working on. In order to optimize the interest for SSS and the value for students, the SSS should deals with the student real concerns in the same way that standardization is dealing with real topics of concern for the stakeholders. Therefore, the SSS need to be open on the student real interests probably from ideas and subjects raised in other courses of their curriculum or their research work. Obviously, the processes in SSS would need to be adapted to the student life and its timeline: the creation of standards will need to be shortened so that students can see the benefits of their efforts before completing their studies. These adaptations do not change the concept and the value of Student Standardization Societies since one of their objectives is to induce students and academics to consider standardisation as an **additional step** in their thought process to complete academic or R&D projects.

A multi-disciplinary approach should be applied to SSS like in official standardization bodies. An approach by silo should be utterly avoided as it does not represent the reality of standardization where stakeholders of mixed background meet. Thus, SSS should not be aligned with a specific department or school: the value of an SSS would be enhanced as students from different studies joined in; for example, from the faculty of sciences and the faculty of law. Ideally students from technical fields, studies in law, economics, sciences and engineering would make SSS committees. Thus, a university made of different faculties should have one and only one Student Standardization Society where for example students in physics will interact with students in law and MBA students. The operation and procedures of an SSS will therefore be closer to what happen in real life in Official Standardization Organizations: professionals involved in standardization often praise the breadth of the interactions and the ability to mix with people with different professional backgrounds. Generally, one lives most of our professional lives in silo: agora where professionals from different backgrounds meet are rare and standardization committees are ones of these rare agora. Thus, a well-established SSS should enable to bring extra values to its student members: the opportunity for a student to interact, to confront and defend ideas and points of view with fellow students who have a totally-different academic background is unique. SSS would expand the consensus-building and negotiation skills of student members which would be an asset not only in standardization.

SSS as its name implied should be run and staffed by students but as it is beneficial for the student academic skills it would be fair for SSS to receive **encouragements and support from the university**. The support could take the form of logistics support (access to meeting rooms), ability to advertise the concept to fellow students and the incentive for students to include SSS activities in their research work or final year project. Student Standardization Societies and courses on standardization work hand in hand: the latter provides the former with the background and theory on standardization and would enable student to transfer the skill learnt in SSS in his/her future job. the former provides the latter with a sufficient number of registrants – needless to say that academic courses on standardization often fail due to the lack of registered student. SSS is deemed to be the easiest way to start with standardization - even the initial setting up of the SSS can be time-consuming - and therefore SSS is worth encouraging from an academic and holistic economic point of view.

For students to be involved in SSS an academic training on standardization would be beneficial even if learning from their fellow students already involved in SSS would occur: "learning by observing proficient students". It is fair to say that SSS would be composed of students from different academic years with novice members and experienced students. To become members of the SSS, students would be expected to take a course on standardization delivered by the university or by their fellow students. An academic course is preferable, but it is recommended that the SSS be created first and as the membership of SSS grows and reach a significant number of students establishing a course would become easier as a fair number of students would be interested in following such an academic course. Indeed, in many universities or higher education institutions, the creation of a new course is a difficult and time-consuming process and courses are discontinued because of insufficient registration: justification on the need, potential number of students are subject to the approval of the university board.

As time passes, Student Standardizations Societies will become well established and well populated, the membership to the SSS or at least the appointment in position of responsibility such as general secretary/committee manager, committee president or working group convenor shall be subject on passing honourably the academic module on standardization.

In short, SSS could be an efficient way to introduce and establish standardization as a key topic for postgraduate students in

Internationalisation of Student Standardization Societies

As aforementioned, it is advisable to have one and only one student standardization society per academic institution where students from different schools join forces. Widening the concept, the SSS of a given academic institution should collaborate with one of a different academic institution in the same way as a National Standardisation Organization from one country collaborates with one of another country. Similarly, each SSS would have to find a common ground with their counterparts of different academic institutions in order to cooperate: establishing a memorandum of understanding, **setting up common procedures, agreeing on mutual recognitions and create joints committees**. Progressively, the SSS of academic institutions will coalesce to form a national student standardization society (NSSS). Broadening the concept even further, it is not difficult to conceive a time where cooperation between NSSS would be valuable and form regional SSS: typically it is easy to conceive a European student standardization societies (ESSS or ES3) mirroring CEN, CENELEC or ETSI: the ES3 will federate National Student Standardization Societies of the European zone be created to mirror CEN or CENELEC. Finally, widening further the same principle, an International Student Standardization Society (ISSS or IS3) to mirror ISO or IEC. Intellectually speaking, establishing such network of SSS first nationally and then regionally and internationally is conceivable. The roadblock is to understand the value and importance of standardization: currently there is no impetus since the importance of standardization in a globalized world is undervalued.

Official Standardization Organizations would benefit from the creation of Student Standardization Societies as it creates a momentum towards standardization by boosting the awareness of standardization, decreasing the barriers of entry and producing graduates and postgraduates who are proficient in standardization. Trade associations would also gain from supporting SSS to boost the image of their professions. Finally, involvement in SSS standardization would endow students with additional hard and soft competences. Because of the mixing of student academic background in SSS, a more subtle benefit would be to prepare students for real working environment which are forcing employees to work with colleagues from different educational backgrounds (e.g. jurists, scientists, linguists, modern literature, accountants...). This is a win-win situation for students and their universities: successful students make successful universities (and vice-versa).

From Concept to Implementation

If one agrees that Student Standardization Society is a valuable concept, one should evaluate the processes and roadblocks to put them into practice. Getting the ball rolling is likely to be the most challenging step: due to the lack of general knowledge in standardization, raising interest of students and higher education institutes is a critical first step. Advertising the intrinsic values of standardization but also what student members could get out from a Student standardization Society. Enticing the interests of purists and novices requires a cleverly-developed advertisement strategy; and advertisement should come even before any awareness programme. This advertisement should get the support of the higher education institution. As SSS will be populated on a voluntary basis and at the beginning as an extra curriculum activity, it makes sense to involve in the advertisement campaign student organisations (student's union, student's council, student senate, students' association, guild of students ...) who are present in many universities, colleges and high schools. One should not be too ambitious at the beginning and it is perfectly fine if a SSS starts with only one working group dealing with one standardization project: priming the standardization pump is the bottleneck in the whole process of establishing SSS.

When the SSS is created it is important that the SSS do not die at the end of the academic year: the role of the first student members will be to advertise the SSS and build a critical mass of student members. The SSS cannot escape from proselytising its activity especially at its creation and during its infancy.

When the ball has started to roll, a virtuous circle is created with mature students attracting fresher students in the SSS: the natural lost of student at the end of each year will be compensated by the membership of younger students.

Administrative Aspects: Not a Big Deal!

The administrative burden of creating a SSS is twofold: (i) the legal and (ii) the logistic aspects.

Like any organization, the SSS needs to have a legal structure and one must decide what form of legal entity to establish for legal and tax considerations. The legal structure depends on the country: in most countries the law proposes some type of legal associations like the associations "loi 1901" in France or unincorporated associations in the USA. Unincorporated associations are not legal entities except in some States where legislatures have recognized the separate existence of association by statute. In any case, the SSS should be compliant with the local legislation. SSS are associations of persons who meet together for a common goal such as promotion of standardization, education of students, creating student standard. The by-laws of the SSS need to be drafted according to the mission of the SSS and in full compliance with the law. The by-law shall describe the membership rule, internal structure, internal rules, the role of the different position (e.g. of the WG convenors), voting rules, all internal processes (e.g. creation of working group): as described earlier the by-laws should mimic the ones of national Official Standardization Organization (OSO) (e.g. ANSI in the USA, ABNT in Brazil, BIS in India, IRAM in Argentina, NEN in the Netherlands, NESO in New Zealand, SABS in South Africa, SAC in China, SASO in Saudi Arabia or SII in Israel). The most difficult will be to draft the first SSS by-laws: this template could then be used and reused by other SSS of the same country and customized for SSS located in a different country. Support from academics or OSOs would be welcome.

The logistic aspects include the premises of the SSS where the standardization meetings and internal meetings (e.g. general assembly, meetings of the officers of the SSS) can take place. Access to such premise should be facilitated by the university. The virtual organization of the SSS can easily be done at a very low cost using modern IT technology: archiving the key documents (by-laws, membership list, organigrams, internal procedures...) on the digital cloud provides transparency and continuity. The activities of each Technical Committee and its Working Groups can be supported by social network and cloud computing: thus, discussion and standardization meetings can take place by web meetings; and voting or document sharing can be accomplished via social media.

It is clear that modern IT tools make possible (i) the creation of a relatively complex structure like a SSS with several Technical Committees, themselves made of several working Groups as well as (ii) the collaboration with another SSS. In the virtual world, **distance** is not a critical factor and partnership between distant SSS is perfectly possible at no or very limited cost. Modern digital tools nicely support the collaboration between SSS of different higher education institutions or between national SSS located far apart. A **network of SSS** can be established very quickly using the collaborative digital tools. The key points that need to be adequately managed are archiving, continuity, the structuration of the organisation, transparency (e.g. within a working group) as well as confidentiality (e.g. fire wall between different SSS) and flexibility of the digital structures. It should easy to add a new Technical Committee or a new standardization project. Social networks are designed for teamwork and fits very well with the required characteristics in term of open discussion, sharing point of view and consensus building that standardization work absolutely required.

After decisions have been taking in the real world such as the creation of a new technical committee, the proposal of new standard, putting dormant a working group or establishing a cooperation with another SSS, its practical implementation is only one click away: with modern digital and social tools it is quick and cheap, and for the younger generations it is also effortless and natural.

Relationship between Student Standardization Societies and Official Standardization Organisations

Official Standardization Organizations should view the Student Standardization Societies as a **pool of** trained standardization professionals. They will be proficient users of norms and be capable to participate actively to official standardization work. Furthermore, it could be asserted that students involved in SSS would naturally be **young ambassadors** for standardization in their future jobs.

Like any academic work starting with literature review, students initiating a standardization work should search not only for the current applicable published norms but also for the OSO normative work which are in progress. These normative assets will be his/her basis for any improvement. Therefore, the SSS work is immediately and irreversibly connected with OSO standardization package (norms, technical reports, technical specifications). The SSS work should not start from scratch but consider what already exists "on the market" and propose an upgrade. For example, a standard on an analytical methodology could be upgraded in light of cutting-edge equipment or by the substitution by a safer greener analytical solvent. Taking into account sustainability or environmental issues is a way to improve old standards that were drafted when these issues were reserved to a small circle of experts: nowadays sustainability, environmental and societal considerations should be considered for all standardization documents irrespectively of the field. Therefore, the work performed by SSS is complementing the work done in OSOs: the student work on standards can contribute to the enhancement of the normative assets by upgrading current standards and adding new ones. The fact that the standardization work is carried out in a well-defined environment similar to the one of Official Standardization Organizations makes the SSS work particularly useful. Thus, SSS could feed OSO with standard proposals and recommendations: the student standard drafts could be considered for official normalization.

The communication should also go from OSO to SSS: in fact, a dialogue should be established and in the longer term one could even envisage a form of collaboration between Student Standardization Society and Official Standardization Organizations such as CEN, CENELEC or ISO. This would be a win-win situation. In summary, the SSS would contribute to the dynamism of standardization helping to identify emerging trends (e.g. social or environmental) and needs on ground-breaking sciences and technologies (e.g. phenomics, IT) and bringing the gap between the academic world and the standardization sphere. The Student Standardization Societies would become the voice of the youth in standardization.

GLOBALIZATION AND STANDARDIZATION

Globalisation and standardization go hand in hand. Because of the nature of standardization, standardization is more salutary in a large diverse community: in such an environment, the benefits of standardization come to light since it helps the community to adopt the same language and agree upon on definition, description, technical specifications and methodology. The **construction of regional and global markets** calls for regional and global standards and standards are a major item on trade agenda globally. Globalisation and bilateral free trade agreement depend on the success in reducing barriers: non-tariff barriers based on standards and technical regulations are gaining in relative importance since tariff barriers are decreasing. **For good or for bad**, standards can be a way to protect national markets, but standards are also essential instruments to open markets via free trade agreements. Standards are neutral tools in term of globalisation: this is the use which is made of them that be judged. This statement is true only if all stakeholders actively participate in the genesis of the standards. In a way, the tension around fairness in globalisation and free trade agreements can be highjacked by inadequate participation of stakeholders in standardization. This is the reason why nowadays standardization is a critical instrument in international economic relation. Global trade has opened opportunity for standards: they can be used to fix cross-border issues in term of transportation, communication, health and safety, environmental issues, sustainability, technical compatibility.

In short, standards can be considered as a **form of language: they are unique "objects" that can facilitate international trade and international relationship.** Needless to say, standards go beyond the economic sphere and should not be limited to trade and economic relationship. In summary, some might say that a strategic well-thought approach to standardisation should contribute to the economic, environmental and societal performances of companies and by domino effect performances of entire economic sectors, regions and countries. Thus, considering these strategic issues, it is no surprise that industrialised nations and more recently emerging countries are the most active in standardisation.

CONCLUSION

Standardization and business fulfil different missions in society and their respective organization and decision-making processes have been designed accordingly; they are radically different -one built one consensus and the other on a hierarchical top-down process- but they need to interact for their mutual benefits. Standardization adds value to business and; vice-versa business and company professionals bring invaluable technical and non-technical benefits making standards practical and efficient. Standardization is based on a horizontal organisation, open system (i.e. open to all stakeholders) and consensus-based decision whereas as company decisions are based on a vertical hierarchical organization, close system and top-down decision. Bridging the gap is not intuitive and proactive actions are required.

Risk reduction is a prevalent and essential objective of companies to which standards can contribute positively. The current zero-risk approach of consumers, investors, public authorities and society in general makes this risk-reduction benefit extremely valuable.

Standardization has the hallmarks of soft law: it is not legally-binding but is shaping governance and conduct of companies and have varying degrees of legal force. Standards as soft law instruments can be an inspiration for hard law. Shaping standards by being active in standardization is an advantage in the long term for companies.

Providing awareness training to senior professionals as well as introducing standardization courses in higher education would be beneficial. The author submits that Student Standardization Societies is a valuable concept for promoting massively standardization among future graduates and postgraduates. The increasing involvement of companies in standardization is beneficial to the overall society since it represents a forum where stakeholders of different nature meet to share their view and through a well-established even-cumbersome procedure: the outcomes are consensual positions in a form of written documents. Since the standardization process is not self-evident, education of company staff or students remains necessary.

Standardization is dynamic system: it is a human process that has evolved for many decades to respond to real needs; and keeps evolving. The author would like to stress that standardization is not a "magic solution": practitioners will need to make efforts to learn; the results are not always ideal -for all players- but there is some magic delight when a very diverse group of stakeholders end up with a consensus. The author hopes that this will give you the endeavour to overcome the initial difficulties to enjoy this feeling: every magician has worked hard to enjoy a magic ending.

ACKNOWLEDGMENT

Horacio Hormazabal (AFNOR, CEN/TC-276) and Mojdeh R. Tabari (ISIRI, ISO/TC-91) are acknowledged for helping me navigate in the world of standardization and for fascinating discussions.

ADDITIONAL READING

Craig, P., & De Burca, G. (2011). *EU Law: Text, Cases and Materials*. Oxford, UK: Oxford University Press. doi:10.1093/he/9780199576999.001.0001

Dupuy, M.-P., & Vinuales, J. E. (2018). *International Environmental Law*. Cambridge, UK: Cambridge University Press. doi:10.1017/9781108399821

Klabbers, J. (2018). *International Law*. Cambridge, UK: Cambridge University Press.

Sands, P., & Peel, J. (2008). *Principles of International Environmental Law*. Oxford, UK: Oxford University Press.

KEY TERMS AND DEFINITIONS

Bio-Based Surfactants: Surfactants which are made from at least of 5% biomass. Minority bio-based surfactants contain from 5 to 49% biomass and majority bio-based surfactants from 50% to 95%). Wholly bio-based surfactants must contain more than 95% of biomass.

Biomass: Biomass corresponds to raw materials that originate from plants (e.g., palm oil) and animals (e.g., tallow). It excludes minerals (e.g., iron, silica) and fossil raw materials (e.g., mineral oil).

Hard Law: By opposition to soft law, hard law refers to legislation that are adopted by the formal legislative process such EU Regulations in Europe or Acts of Parliament in the UK. Hard law is legally binding and enforceable by the public authorities. Hard law is in layman language simply "law".

Soft Law: By opposition to hard law, the term 'soft law refers instruments that are non-legally binding and enforceable only to some degree. Unlike hard law, they are not adopted by a formal legislative process. Examples of soft law included decisions of G7 summits, action plan of world environmental conference or uniliteral act of a state, or gentlemen agreement between states. Soft law is usually associated with international law but can be use also in domestic law. International standards are deemed to be soft law instruments. There is an on-going debate on whether "soft law" is really law.

Student Standardization Societies (SSS): They are associations or bodies whose mission is to educate higher-education students on normalization by practicing and role-playing. Their membership is open to graduates and post-graduates. They are organized in the same way as official standardization organizations. SSS are designed to issue "student" standards.

Surfactants: Surfactants are chemicals which have surface-active properties, and which consist of a hydrophilic moiety and a hydrophobic moiety. They have unique properties due to their molecular structure. Millions of tons of surfactants are manufactured per year in the world and are used (1) in consumer products such as detergents, cosmetics and paints and (2) in industrial applications in oil-field and agrobusiness.

Chapter 11
Technology Transfer to Least Developed Countries Through Global Standards

Hans Teichmann
Independent Researcher, Switzerland

ABSTRACT

For the economic growth in least developed countries (LDCs), the transfer of technical and scientific know-how is an uncontested necessity. Poverty and underdevelopment in LDCs are interrelated features. Technology transfers may fail, however, unless varied constraints are taken into account. The focus of this study is on obstacles to an efficient technology transfer to LDCs, and on the major role which global, bilingual standards can play in this process. The global standards setting organizations International Organization for Standardization (ISO) and International Electrotechnical Commission (IEC) have recognized the need for a general, comprehensive, and effective support of the LDCs' bodies for national quality infrastructure (NQI). Standardization is not only a vital socio-economic function in itself, but standards represent part of much wider, essential infrastructures. Three stakeholder groups are particularly concerned: the users of the global standards in LDCs, the global standards setting organizations, and the individual National Quality Infrastructure bodies.

INTRODUCTION

At present a process of increasing awareness towards the needs of *underdeveloped countries* can be observed (IEC, 2019,a). Their population has often a low standard

DOI: 10.4018/978-1-7998-2181-6.ch011

of living, due to low incomes and abundant poverty. It is crucial to understand if world poverty is a *cause* or a *consequence* of lacking development. Indeed if it is a cause, it needs to be directly tackled and, if it is a consequence, the *real causes of the underdevelopment* need to be identified in order to help the poorest countries to develop, and to limit the recurring, uncontrollable migration waves.

It has already been argued that in the process of ongoing globalization usually the industrialized countries are the winners, and LDCs tend to be the losers (Ziegler, 2013). It has also been stated that in our time the term "Third World Country" seems outdated, irrelevant or inaccurate. According to the United Nations Department of Economic and Social Affairs (UN DESA), « LDCs » are Developing Countries (DCs) which exhibit the lowest indicators of socio-economic development and with the lowest Human Development Index ratings. This concept of LDCs originated in the late 1960s, and a country is now classified as such if it meets three criteria (which was the case for 47 countries in 2018).

A poverty-adjustable criterion based on the Gross National Income (GNI) per capita averaged over three years. As of 2018 a country must have a GNI per capita of less than US$ 1,025 to be included on the list, and over US$ 1,230 to graduate from it.

A human resource weakness (based on indicators of nutrition, health, education and adult literacy).

An economic vulnerability (based on instability of agricultural production, instability of exports of goods and services, economic importance of non-traditional activities, merchandise export concentration, handicap of economic smallness, and the percentage of its population displaced by natural disasters).

According to the United Nations Conference on Trade and Development (UNCTAD), the geographical distribution of the above-mentioned 47 LDCs is the following (UNCTAD, 2018):

Africa 33 countries
Asia 9 countries
Pacific region 4 countries
South America and Caribbean 1 country

Regional and global standards are developed in an international setting where the *English language* dominates, but many of the participating member countries do not have that language as their official language. It is a fact that the person who must use a foreign language to communicate can easily feel himself to be in an inferior position in relation to those who can express themselves in their mother tongue, and he can have difficulties in *completely understanding* a given issue. In the context of the 33 African countries concerned, the availability of a *French version* of the global standards is undoubtedly an important asset.

BASIC ASPECTS OF TECHNOLOGY TRANSFER

Technology transfer has been defined as « Process of transferring (disseminating) technology from the person or organization that holds it to another person or organization. It occurs along various axes: among universities, from universities to businesses (and vice versa), from large businesses to smaller ones (and vice versa), from governments to businesses (and vice versa), across geopolitical borders, both formally and informally, and both openly and surreptitiously » (Grosse, 1996). This transfer often occurs by concerted effort to share skills, knowledge, technologies, methods of manufacturing, samples of manufacturing, and facilities among governments or universities and other institutions to ensure that scientific and technological developments are accessible to a wider range of users who can then further develop and exploit the technology concerned into new products, processes, applications, materials and services. Technology transfer is closely related to *knowledge transfer. Horizontal technology transfer* is the movement from one area to another, and *vertical transfe*r occurs when technologies are moved from applied research centers to research and development departments.

Present-day research on technology transfer, combined with occasional high-profile failures, has drawn attention to the *transfer process itself.* Whilst technology transfer can involve the dissemination of *highly complex technology* from capital-intensive origins to low-capital recipients (and thereby involve aspects of dependency and fragility of systems), it can also involve *appropriate technology,* which is not necessarily high-tech or expensive, but better disseminated, yielding robustness and more independence of systems.

The actual political/economic situation can give cause to fear that, without a serious and continuous effort, the industrialized countries and a number of the economically weak LDCs may drift gradually even further apart. The focus of the present study is on the technology transfer to LDCs *by means of global ISO and IEC standards.*

In the technology transfer to LDCs through global standards, three major groups of stakeholders with different interests and motivations are involved: The standards users in the LDCs (such as local industries, trade, agriculture and national administrations) ; the Global Standards Setting Organizations, in particular ISO and IEC (with their head offices, Technical Committees (TCs), technical experts and National Committees (NCs)) ; and the NQI bodies in the LDCs (if they already exist).

OBSTACLES TO THE TECHNOLOGY TRANSFER TOWARDS LEAST DEVELOPED COUNTRIES

The difficulty for less developed countries is to find a way to reach the developed stage many other countries are at. Without a minimum of wealth, no money can be used to support the development. And if there is no financial support, there is no way to support the social areas. For example, where teachers cannot be trained, consequently education will be very insufficient and subsequently the work force will not be educated enough to boost the economy.

Technology transfer to LDCs failed sometimes in the past, a major reason being that the relevant methods and techniques had been developed in, and for the needs of, the *industrialized countries*. The applied methods were therefore geared to their own conditions. Also, in LDCs there is little or no established technical infrastructure for measurement, standards and conformity assessment. Experience has shown that the technology transfer to LDCs will not be successful unless a number of specific constraints are recognized as such, and correspondingly taken into consideration. These obstacles may be either of general nature, or related especially to the case of LDCs.

Four Common Groups of Obstacles to Technology Transfer

Dependence on Foreign Technical Assistance

This dependence is not only a burden on the country's financial resources, but unfortunately the activities of foreign consultants and suppliers were in the past not always adequately coordinated, respectively not adapted to the prevailing local conditions. For instance, the original power supply systems on different Indonesian islands had been designed by foreign consulting engineers using their own countries' techniques.

Lacking Compatibility of Equipment from Different Suppliers

Compatibility is a complex issue, related to the structure of technical systems and the interfaces between individual subsystems. In order to avoid the incompatibility of equipment, the *prospective users themselves* should specify relevant parameters as much as possible, rather than have them specified by foreign, remote and perhaps not sufficiently informed consultants or suppliers. An example well known by international travelers is today's chaotic incompatibility of plugs and socket-outlets also in the industrialized countries (Teichmann, 2016).

Need for a Socio-Economic Balance

In a *given region of the world,* the development of neighboring countries should preferably be balanced. As regards a *given country,* a balanced development of its different regions and of varied economic interests should be achieved. This will be the case only if development programs are *properly coordinated.* This aspect concerns mainly problems of the country's industrial infrastructure and the avoidance of rural exodus, usually caused by regional underdevelopment.

Language Barriers

English or French are by no means the only major world languages (Vistawide, 2019). Some figures (in millions of *first language speakers*) are: Mandarin Chinese (873), Hindi (370), Spanish (350), English (340), Arabic (260) and French (67). When factoring in second- and third-language speakers, however, *English* is the most widely used language in the world. It is therefore not self-evident that standards users in general will have sufficient language skills in English (or another official language) to be able to interpret global standards fully and correctly. The problem of language barriers is obviously of general nature and not limited to the standards users in LDCs.

Five Additional Groups of Obstacles Concerning in Particular LDCs

Need for Cooperation at the Regional, Respectively National Level

On the *national level,* there is an obvious need for efficient coordination among the relevant institutions for metrology and materials testing (if they already exist). This issue has been considered for the case of small Pacific nations (Walsh, 2011). On the *regional level,* solidarity between individual countries should lead to an increased exchange of experience and information. It is obvious that *very small countries* (industrialized or developing) and *relatively small* Developing Countries will depend to a high extent on *regional cooperation.* For instance, there are numerous small *East Pacific and Caribbean island countries,* which cannot possibly develop and support their own national technical infrastructure.

Obstacles Related to Local/Environmental Conditions

Local conditions call frequently for adjustments of foreign technology and operating methods. Examples are the sometimes indispensable need for tropicalization, the need for adaptation to local maintenance practice, and to the limited availability of spare parts and repair facilities. Industrialized countries are mostly located in temperate climatic zones and therefore less concerned by these problems.

Limited Financial Resources

Most countries with a less favored economy suffer from *financial constraints*. In addition, *natural adveristies* such as unfavorable local climatic and geographical conditions make investments in many cases difficult and expensive. In many LDCs, such constraints and underdevelopment are therefore interrelated.

Limited Human Resources

The skilled workforce in LDCs is scarce and also frequently in search for a better life and a better future abroad. It is therefore difficult to recruit qualified technical staff in their home countries. For the average technician or engineer, there is a problem of keeping abreast of a continuous technical development. A gap may also exist between the employee's training and the sophisticated equipment he has to run and to maintain. There may also be communication gaps between equipment manufacturers and the users in LDCs. Further potential problem areas are the common lack of reorientation courses and the gap between technicians/engineers and bureaucrats. The so-called brain drain tends to aggravate the situation because essentially *capable people* are involved.

Need for Renewable Energy Sources

No country can successfully develop without addressing the critical issue of growing energy demand and an adequate supply. Satisfactory solutions to the environmental problems faced today require action with long-term potential for sustainable development. In this respect, *renewable energy sources* (essentially biomass, hydropower, geothermal, wind and solar power) appear to be promising solutions, particularly in LDCs. However, the cost for the required biomass gasifiers, hydroelectric plants, wind turbine generating systems or photovoltaic energy systems is generally high and needs therefore to be kept to acceptable levels.

Effectiveness Of Global Standards In The Technology Transfer To Least Developed Countries

In the last two decades, the number of LDCs cooperating with ISO and IEC has significantly increased. These countries should make every effort to *promote standardization* in order to secure engagement and support from the stakeholders. An effective participation of their NQI bodies in international standardization is of fundamental importance. Global standards can be effective at varied levels.

Allaying the Dependence on Foreign Technical Assistance

In principle, several ways of gaining access to modern technology exist: For instance the acquisition of patents and licenses, the purchase of turnkey factories, utilization of technical books and magazines, application of other countries' national standards, or regional respectively global standards. In comparison with other technical literature, the *ISO or IEC International Standards* have major advantages:

They are classified in a logical manner, which enables the user to identify the standards which are required for the subject under consideration.
They are the result of an international consensus within competent, specialized TCs.
They are based on methods which reflect the experience acquired in numerous participating countries.
While in the past essentially countries with *highly developed economies* were involved, at present also DCs and LDCs are encouraged to defend their specific interests.
Global standards specify safety requirements without raising them to an unreasonable level.
They define the *characteristics which must be attained* in order to make the product or service in question competitive (rather than specific design features).

The global ISO or IEC International Standards can therefore be an efficient means for *gaining access to modern technology* and allaying - at least to some degree - the dependence on foreign technical assistance.

Ensuring the Compatibility of Equipment from Different Suppliers

If complex equipment is manufactured on the basis of *diverging national or regional standards,* major problems will arise: The interchangeability of individual parts of equipment is compromised; changing suppliers may be costly; it may even be impossible to use equipment from certain countries for turnkey projects. Therefore, *global standards* (rather than national or regional standards) should be preferred not only in the industrialized countries, but also in DCs/LDCs.

Contributions to a Socio-Economic Balance

Global standards can contribute in several ways to an adequate socio-economic balance:

They can support innovation and promote the adoption of new technologies in a
   number of ways, codify and spread the state-of-the-art in different areas, and
   help bridging the gap between research and end products or services.

Where products or processes were supplied by various providers and must interact
   with one another, only generally accepted standards can *provide interoperability.*
   Standards can therefore form the basis for the introduction of new technologies
   and other innovations.

Standards have also an important role to play in supporting the *competitiveness* of
   local and regional businesses in the global market: They can help to improve
   the quality of the products and services provided, and thus open the access to
   foreign businesses and markets.

Finally, global standards can contribute to *economic growth and job creation* by
   strengthening local companies.

Coping with Language Barriers

The Global Standards Setting Organizations are aware of the difficulties faced by
many standards users in general, and of the particular situation of users with a mother
tongue other than an official language. The following measures are noteworthy:

ISs (International Standards) are published - in addition to the main working language
   English - in French and sometimes in further languages.

Many ISO/IEC standards start with a « Terms and definitions » section.

IEC has prepared « Electropedia: The World's Online Electrotechnical Vocabulary
   » (IEC, 2019,f). This comprehensive online terminology database on «
   electrotechnology » contains currently more than 22.000 terminological entries
   in English and French by subject area, with equivalent terms in Arabic, Chinese,
   German, Portuguese, Russian, Spanish, etc.

Promotion of National, Respectively Regional/International Cooperation

Promotion of Cooperation at the National Level

In principle, *any economy* needs a national technical infrastructure for measurement, standards and conformity assessment. In DCs/LDCs such an institution may consist of the following elements (Walsh, 2007):

1) A *legal/government framework* covering a basic consumer protection law dealing with the requirements that goods and services shall be able to deliver, and a fair trading or competition law
2) *Metrology* which may be devided into three subfields: scientific or fundamental metrology (concerning the establishment of measurement units, unit systems, the development of new measurement methods, etc.); applied or industrial metrology (which concerns the application of measurement science to manufacturing and other processes, ensuring the suitability of measurement instruments, etc.); and legal metrology (which concerns regulatory requirements for the protection of health, public safety, the environment, etc.)
3) *Accreditation* covering the two areas laboratory accreditation of testing facilities and accreditation of management systems certification, personnel certification and product certification
4) As regards *standards development*, LDCs as well as very small other countries will in practice have to adopt one of the following options: utilization of the existing standards of more developed countries, or of Regional/Global standards.
5) *Conformity assessment*, which is defined as "demonstration that specified requirements related to a product, process, system, person or body are fulfilled". In other words, conformity testing refers to a variety of processes whereby goods and/or services are determined to meet voluntary or mandatory standards or specifications.

Regional/Interntional Cooperation

The general need for regional cooperation is now widely recognized. For example, all major international technical-scientific organizations concerned (including, but not limited to, ISO, IEC, the International Bureau of Weights and Measures (BIPM) and the International Organization for Legal Metrology (OIML)) participate in the "Network on Metrology, Accreditation and Standardization in Developing Countries" (DCMAS ; IEC, 2019,a). It should be noted that the necessary cooperation at the national and regional/international levels will function adequately only if it is supported by a *recognized system of standards.*

Consideration of Specific Local/Environmental Conditions

Numerous standards prepared by ISO's or IEC's specialized *product committees* include the consideration of environmental issues such as ambient temperatures, maintenance testing or electromagnetic compatibility. A *systematic approach* to such issues is taken by several *horizontal TCs.* For example, standards developed by the following committees are *frequently referenced* in product standards:

1) IEC/TC 77, Electromagnetic compatibility
2) IEC/TC 104, Environmental conditions, classification and methods of test
3) IEC/TC 111, Environmental standardization for electrical and electronic products and systems

Currently all essential categories of environmental conditions, including extremes putting a strain on many LDCs, are adequately covered. Admittedly, global standards cannot resolve *practical difficulties* like the lack of spare parts or the absence of accessible repair facilities. But specialized horizontal committees prepare the necessary standards and guidelines *for referencing* in product standards. Such inputs contribute, for example, to improved maintenance practice or an equipment/system design considering specific local/environmental conditions.

Allaying Obstacles Linked to Limited Financial Resources

While the utilization of global standards cannot directly remove financial constraints, it can still help to *reduce expenditures.* However, the savings which can be achieved (in general and by no means limited to the present case of LDCs) are difficult to quantify. The more important items are the following:

1) The *reduction of variety* aims obviously at reducing a product's unit cost. In this context, the utilization of national or international standards enables larger production series and thereby the achievement of major cost reductions.
2) Similarly, the technical inputs provided by standards on materials, environmental conditions, test methods, etc. contribute to *reduced design costs.*
3) Global standards reflect the experience gained in numerous industrialized and certain developing countries ; they can thus contribute to *longer equipment life* (for instance, by specifying rational maintenance methods), and to *increased*

safety of operation (for instance, by specifying performance requirements rather than merely design features).

4)   Furthermore, standardization permits to *reduce the stock of spare parts.*

5)   Last but not least, global standards provide the opportunity to *purchase equipment* on a worldwide, competitive market.

Allaying Obstacles Linked to Limited Human Resources

The technology transfer to LDCs is frequently hindered by difficulties related to the limited availability of human resources. Although global standards are not meant to be *textbooks,* they can nevertheless be useful for training purposes. Their contents provide in fact a solid technical underpinning. In this way, ISO and IEC standards represent a globally recognized, *comprehensive survey of technical recommendations* for all sectors of technology, as well as related fields.

Contributions in the Field of Renewable Energy Sources

Four specialized TCs have been contributing with particular success to the rational development of renewable energy sources (ISO, 2018; IEC, 2019,b).

1)   ISO/TC 238: Solid biofuels, prepares standards for the following purposes: Simplify the communication between fuel suppliers and consumers; assure that products and processes are compatible; provide the market with tools to determine the economic value of delivered fuels; and produce a common way to control and regulate safety demands.

2)   IEC/TC 4: Hydraulic turbines, has prepared comprehensive guidelines for the specification, testing and operation of hydraulic rotating machinery.

3)   EC/TC 82: Solar photovoltaic energy systems, is responsible for systems of photovoltaic conversion of solar energy into electrical energy, and for all the elements in the entire photovoltaic system.

4)   IEC/TC 88: Wind turbines, deals with design requirements, engineering integrity, measurement techniques and test procedures.

ESTABLISHMENT OF NATIONAL QUALITY INFRASTRUCTURES IN LEAST DEVELOPED COUNTRIES

National Quality Infrastructures in LDCs

The NQI is a country's institutional framework that establlshes and implements the practice of standardization, conformity assessment services, metrology and accreditation. It includes public and private institutions and the regulatory framework in which they operate. Unfortunately, most LDCs suffer from a *weak NQI*, which tends to be a major impediment to their integration into regional and global markets, limiting the opportunities offered by trade and hindering the ability to improve public welfare in vital areas such as health, safety and environmental protection.

Through their members, the global standards setting organizations ISO and IEC bring together international experts to share their knowledge and develop voluntary, consensus-based and market-relevant ISs that support innovations and provide solutions to global challenges. The most important resource of these organizations is their member organizations and network of experts, both at the human and organizational levels.

In the past, most LDCs did not have the nessary infrastructure for any appreciable participation in international standardization. Without an adequate NQI, they always had to struggle with a wide range of problems. At present, the LDCs' increased and effective participation in international standardization is therefore all the more important. The countries' exsting NQIs (if this is the case) usually require specific assistance to *fully exploit the value of ISs* in support of their development. Another important aspect is the *participation of LDCs* in international standardization: It is in fact essential to ensure the *global relevance* of the ISs, and contribute to the access of these countries to *world markets, technical progress and sustainable development.*

ISO Action Plan for Developing Countries 2016 - 2020

The "ISO Action Plan for developing countries 2016 - 2020", which complements the "ISO Strategy 2026 - 2020", describes the overall framework of technical assistance that ISO expects to deliver over this five-year period. The plan is intended to contribute to the economic development, social progress and protection of the environment in Developing Countries (ISO, 2018,b). It comprises five main areas of improvement, with specific focus on the *standardization pillar:*

1) Standardization shall be given a *recognized, effective role* in support of public policies: In many DCs (and even more so in most LDCs) policy makers lack detailed understanding of the role of standards.

2) The national standards bodies' *strategic capabilities* shall be strengthened: This item concerns notably the ability to identify and contribute to national priorities, secure the financial sustainability of the organization and demonstrate the value of standards to different stakeholder groups.

3) The national standards bodies' capacity shall be strengthened at the *operational and technical levels:* This item concerns the improvement of the NQI bodies' capacity to perform their mission effectively and efficiently.

4) The *involvement of developing country members* in international standardization shall be increased: Increased participation in areas of national priority is a significant enabler for a country's integration in the global market and for the development and implementation of measures of public utility.

5) *Coordination and synergies* with other organizations and among projects shall be implemented: Coordination between the different players engaged in development projects is important in order to avoid duplication of efforts and obtain multiplying effects.

IEC's "Affiliate Country Programme" as Starting Point for a National Standards Body

In many cases, DCs/LDCs do not have the necessary resources for *Full membership* or *Associate status* in IEC. The organization has met this challenge by setting up its "Affiliate Country Programme" (IEC, 2016), which enables DCs/LDCs to even take an *active part* in standards development *without becoming IEC members* (either Full IEC members or Associate members). This measure encourages LDCs to adopt IEC ISs, and make full use of *IEC's* existing 100% electronic working environment.

The IEC offers its Affiliate Countries up to 200 free ISs for adoption as national standards or for use in their regulations. In order to encourage the use of *IEC standards* rather than national/regional standards, the free ISs are intended to start a library for satisfying local needs (IEC, 2019,c). In addition, there is a possibility for *active participation* in international standardization activities : Each Affiliate Country has the opportunity to nominate five experts who are granted a username and a password, and have electronic access to documents of a maximum of ten pre-selected committees. These experts may also comment and/or submit questions on working documents. Finally, the Affiliate Countries are offered the opportunity for familiarization with the « IEC Conformity Assessment System ». The necessary training can be arranged, and the appropriate conformity assessment guidelines for DCs/LDCs are available. That way, LDCs can participate - at least to a modest degree - in international standardization activities. It should be noted in this context that for the accession to the *World Trade Organization (WTO),* a full range of standards and conformance infrastructure services is required.

Currently 87 countries are participating in the « IEC Affiliate Country Programme ». Their *geographical distribution* is the following (IEC, 2019,d ; UNCTAD 2018):

Africa 41 Countries (including 31 out of 33 the African LDCs)
Asia 18 Countries (including seven out of the nine Asian LDCs)
Europe None
Pacific region Two countries (yet none of the four Pacific Region's LDCs is included)
South America and Caribbean 26 Countries (including the only South American/ Caribbean LDC)

The *issue of multilingualism* in global standardization should not be overlooked: In the total of 39 LCDs participating in the « IEC Affiliate Country Programme » (UNCTAD 2018), numerous official languages are used.

Africa: Out of the 31 participating countries, there are nine LDCs with official language English, 15 with official language French, and seven with a different official language (among others Arabic or Portuguese ; in Africa, *French* is important also as second language).
Asia: Out of the seven participating countries, there are no LDCs with official language English or French, but all seven countries have their official language (among others Burmese or Khmer ; in Asia, *English* is important as second language).
South America and Caribbean: One participating country, with the official language French.

It should be noted that since 2009, the IEC offers in addition an « Affiliate Plus Status » (IEC, 2019,e) to those countries which have fulfilled the following two conditions:

Have declared the adoption of at least 50 IEC ISs
Have established their own National electrotechnical committee.

Since the establishment of this option, *19 Affiliate Countries* have been granted this « Affiliate Plus Status ».

CONCLUSION

General Conclusions

Underdevelopment is the lack of development in the quality of life of the population which includes economic, social, technological and political progress. The issue of poverty is both related to the causes and the consequences of underdevelopment. In other words, poverty and underdevelopment are *interrelated features*.

The transfer of technical and scientific know-how from the industrialized countries to LDCs is an uncontested necessity. It is closely related to knowledge transfer, and among other measures *ISs* can be an efficient means for the dissemination of technical knowledge. In this context, the availability of French versions of the standards and working documents is a major asset, particularly with respect to those LDCs where French is the official language or the most important second language.

Most countries with a less favored economy suffer from *financial constraints*. Increased participation in international standardization in areas of national priority is a significant enabler for an LDC's integration in the global market and the implementation of measures of public utility. In addition, international standardization is an important and effective instrument to establish and promote good practices and safety/environmental measures.

The technology transfer to DCs/LDCs through global standards occurs from the responsible International Standards Setting Organizations to the DCs'/LDCs' national institutions in an open, formal and sponsored way. Three major stakeholder groups are considered in this study: The standards users in the LDCs, the responsible Global Standards Setting Organizations, and the NQI bodies in the LDCs.

Standards Users in Least Developed Countries

Very small countries cannot possibly develop and support their own national technical infrastructure. In this situation, *global standards* can be an efficient means of providing access to modern technology and allaying, at least to some degree, the dependence on foreign technical assistance.

The population of LDCs has often a low standard of living, due to low incomes and abundant poverty. Many of these countries have in addition to cope with unfavorable local/environmental problems, such as extreme climatic conditions, the lack of spare parts or the absence of repair facilities. The standards users in these countries are mainly local industries, trade, agriculture and the national administration. Their main concern is the accessibility to markets, interoperability and the development of skills.

Global standards, which are available also in languages other than English, should be preferred to other options. They contribute to economic growth and job creation by strengthening the competitiveness of local companies. They can allay the dependence on foreign technical assistance, will ensure the compatibility of equipment from different suppliers/countries, contribute to a country's/region's socio-economic balance, facilitate the cooperation at the national/regional levels, account for environmental conditions, allay obstacles linked to limited financial/ human resources and foster the use of renewable energies.

Role of the Global Standards Setting Organization

The relevant Global Standards Setting Organizations are ISO and IEC. They bring together international experts - in the past only from industrialized countries - to share their knowledge and develop voluntary, consensus-based, English/French and market-relevant ISs to support innovations and provide solutions to global challenges. It is of great importance that in the context of technology transfer ISO and IEC do not act as competitors, but rather as complementary partners. Their main concerns are risk, interoperability, innovation and sustainability.

Both ISO and IEC have recognized the suitability of global standards for technology transfer. They have therefore developed target-oriented, ambitious plans as follows:

« ISO Action Plan for developing countries »

ISO is interested to contribute to the economic development, social progress and protection of the environment in DCs/LDCs.

IEC's « Affiliate Country Programme »

In general DCs/LDCs do not have the necessary resources for « Full membership » or « Associate membership » in IEC. The organization's « Affiliate Country programme » enables them to take anyway an active part in standards development - *without* becoming IEC members.

Mission of the National Quality Infrastructure Bodies in Least Developed Countries

NQI bodies should be both effective and efficient in the following fields: Contributing to the development of national industry and a strong export market, Fostering consumer protection and the establishment/strengthening of quality ensurance measures, and Providing support of environmental protection.

Relatively small LDCs as well as very small DCs/LDCs will depend inevitably to a high extent on *regional cooperation*. Solidarity between the individual countries should lead to an increased exchange of experience and information.

The slowly increasing participation of DCs/LDCs in international standardization is essential to ensure the *global relevance* of the ISs and contribute to technical progress and sustainable development. The main concern of the NQI bodies is costs, innovation, sustainability and available skills.

POTENTIAL FUTURE WORK

Certain aspects of the notorious migration waves from the Least Developed/ Underdeveloped Countries to the Industrialized Countries should be studied more in detail. One question is if this phenomenon is *directly rela*ted to a country's degree of underdevelopment. In other words, will a country's graduation from UN DESA's « LDC status » to « DC status » indeed *reduce* undesirable migratory movements, or might this graduation even *increase* uncontrollable migration?

REFERENCES

Grosse, R. (1996). International Technology Transfer in Services. *Journal of International Business Studies, 27.* doi:10.1057/palgrave.jibs.8490153

IEC. (2016). *Guide to the IEC Affiliate Country Programme.* Geneva: IEC.

IEC. (2019a). International Partners - DCMAS Network. Geneva: IEC.

IEC. (2019b). Renewable Energies. Geneva: IEC.

IEC. (2019c). IEC Affiliates – IEC Programme for developing countries. Geneva: IEC.

IEC. (2019d). List of IEC Affiliate Country Programme Participants. Geneva: IEC.

IEC. (2019e). Affiliate Country Programme – Affiliate Plus Status. Geneva: IEC.

IEC. (2019f). Electropedia: The World Online Electrotechnical Vocabulary. Geneva: IEC.

ISO. (2015). *ISO Strategy 2016-2020.* Geneva: ISO.

ISO. (2018a). ISO/TC 238, Solid Biofuels. Geneva: ISO.

ISO. (2018b). ISO Action Plan for developing countries 2016-2020. Geneva: ISO.

ISO/IEC. (2016). *ISO/IEC Directives, Part 1*. Geneva: ISO/IEC.

Teichmann, H. (2016). Plugs and Socket-Outlets: Pet Peeve of International Travelers and Standardizers Alike. *EURAS Proceedings 2016*.

UN. (2018). *Criteria For Identification Of LDCs*. New York: United Nations Department of Economic and Social Affairs.

UNCTAD. (2018). *What are the Least Developed Countries*. Geneva: UNCTAD.

Vistawide. (2019). *World Languages and Cultures*. Retrieved from www.vistawide.com/languages/top_30_ anguages

Walsh, P. (2007). Models for Standardization Bodies in Small and Developing Countries. *EURAS Proceedings 2007*.

Walsh, P. (2011). Governance and Structure of National Standards Bodies in Developing Countries as They Transition to Developed Status. *EURAS Proceedings 2011*.

Ziegler, J. (2013). *Betting on Famine: Why the World still Goes Hungry*. The New Press.

Compilation of References

Abbad, M., Abbad, R., & Saleh, M. (2011). Limitations of e-commerce in developing countries: Jordan case. *Education, Business and Society*, *4*(4), 280–291. doi:10.1108/17537981111190060

Abbott, K. W., & Snidal, D. (2001). International "standards" and international governance. *Journal of European Public Policy*, *8*(3), 345–370. doi:10.1080/13501760110056013

Abdalla, K. F. (2003, April). A model for semantic interoperability using XML. In *IEEE Systems and Information Engineering Design Symposium* (pp. 107-111). IEEE. 10.1109/SIEDS.2003.158012

Abramo, G., D'Angelo, C. A., & Di Costa, F. (2011). National research assessment exercises: A comparison of peer review and bibliometrics rankings. *Scientometrics*, *89*(3), 929–941. doi:10.1007/s11192-011-0459-x

Adler, P. S., & Borys, B. (1996). Two types of bureaucracy: Enabling and Coercive. *Administrative Science Quarterly*, *41*(1), 61–89. doi:10.2307/2393986

Ahmad, W. (2017). ISO 9001 ISO 9001 Transition and its Impact on the Organizational Performance: Evidence from Service Industries of Pakistan. *International Journal of Research in Business Studies and Management*, *4*(3), 39–54. doi:10.22259/ijrbsm.0403004

Akerman, M. (2003). What Does 'Natural Capital' Do? The Role of Metaphor in Economic Understanding of the Environment. *Environmental Values*, *12*(4), 431–448. doi:10.3197/096327103129341397

Albrecht, C. C., Dean, D. L., & Hansen, J. V. (2005). Marketplace and technology standards for B2B e-commerce: Progress, challenges, and the state of the art. *Information & Management*, *42*(6), 865–875. doi:10.1016/j.im.2004.09.003

Aleksandrova, Z. (2016, November 25). *Core Vocabularies*. Retrieved 23 July 2019, from ISA²—European Commission website: https://ec.europa.eu/isa2/solutions/core-vocabularies_en

Allam, Z., & Newman, P. (2018). Redefining the smart city: Culture, metabolism and governance. *Smart Cities*, *1*(1), 4–25. doi:10.3390martcities1010002

Almousa, M. (2013). Barriers to E-Commerce Adoption: Consumers' Perspectives from a Developing Country. *iBusiness*, *5*(2), 65-71.

Amabile, T. M. (1982). Social psychology of creativity: A consensual assessment technique. *Journal of Personality and Social Psychology, 43*(5), 997–1013. doi:10.1037/0022-3514.43.5.997

Ammar, M., Russello, G., & Crispo, B. (2018). Internet of Things: A survey on the security of IoT frameworks. *Journal of Information Security and Applications, 38*, 8–27. doi:10.1016/j.jisa.2017.11.002

Andersen, K. V., Beck, R., Wigand, R. T., Bjørn-Andersen, N., & Brousseau, E. (2004). European e-commerce policies in the pioneering days, the gold rush and the post-hype era. *Information Polity, 9*(3-4), 217–232.

Andonova, L. B. (2017). *Governance entrepreneurs: International organizations and the rise of global public-private partnerships*. Cambridge, UK: Cambridge University Press. doi:10.1017/9781316694015

Ansari, S. M., Fiss, P. C., & Zajac, E. J. (2010). Made to fit: How practices vary as they diffuse. *Academy of Management Review, 35*(1), 67–92. doi:10.5465/AMR.2010.45577876

Ansari, S. M., Reinecke, J., & Spaan, A. (2014). How are Practices Made to Vary? Managing Practice Adaptation in a Multinational Corporation. *Organization Studies, 35*(9), 1313–1341. doi:10.1177/0170840614539310

ANVUR. (2011). Valutazione della Qualità della Ricerca 2004-2010 (VQR 2004-2010): Bando di partecipazione. Retrieved from https://www.anvur.it/wp-content/uploads/2011/11/bando_vqr_def_07_11.pdf

ANVUR. (2015). Evaluation of Research Quality 2011-2014 (VQR 2011-2014): Call for participation. Retrieved from https://www.anvur.it/wp-content/uploads/2015/11/Bando%20VQR%202011-2014_secon~.pdf

Arnold, E., Simmonds, P., Farla, K., Kolarz, P., Mahieu, B., & Nielsen, K. (2018). Review of the Research Excellence Framework: evidence report. Retrieved from technopolis group UK website: https://assets.publishing.service.gov.uk/government/uploads/system/uploads/attachment_data/file/768162/research-excellence-framework-review-evidence-report.pdf

Article 29 Data Protection Working Party. (2016a). *Guidelines on Data Protection Officers ('DPOs')* (No. 16/EN, WP-243).

Article 29 Data Protection Working Party. (2016b). *Guidelines on the right to data portability* (No. 16/EN, WP242).

Asif, M., & De Vries, H. (2015). Creating ambidexterity through quality management. *Total Quality Management & Business Excellence, 26*(11-12), 1226–1241. doi:10.1080/14783363.2014.926609

Asif, M., De Vries, H., & Ahmad, N. (2013). Knowledge creation through quality management. *Total Quality Management & Business Excellence, 24*(5–6), 664–677. doi:10.1080/14783363.2013.791097

Bair, J., & Palpacuer, F. (2015). CSR beyond the corporation: Contested governance in global value chains. *Global Networks*, *15*(1), S1–S19. doi:10.1111/glob.12085

Bakos, Y. (2001). The emerging landscape for retail e-commerce. *The Journal of Economic Perspectives*, *15*(1), 69–80. doi:10.1257/jep.15.1.69

Baltagi, B. H. (2013). *Econometric Analysis of Panel Data* (5th ed.). John Wiley and Sons.

Bangemann, M. (1994). *Recommendations to the European Council: Europe and the global information society*. Brussels: European Commission.

Barker, R. (2019). Corporate natural capital accounting. *Oxford Review of Economic Policy*, *35*(1), 68–87. doi:10.1093/oxrep/gry031

Baron, Contreras, Husovec, Larouche, & Thumm. (2019b). *Making the Rules: The Governance of Standard Development Organizations and their Policies on Intellectual Property Rights*. JRC Science for Policy Report, EUR 29655.

Baron, J., Li, C., & Nasirov, S. (2019a). *Why Do R&D-Intensive Firms Participate in Standards Organizations? The Role of Patents and Product-Market Position*. Working paper.

Baron, J., & Gupta, K. (2018). Unpacking 3GPP standards. *Journal of Economics & Management Strategy*, *27*(3), 433–461. doi:10.1111/jems.12258

Baron, J., Meniere, Y., & Pohlmann, T. (2014). Standards, consortia, and innovation. *International Journal of Industrial Organization*, *36*, 22–35. doi:10.1016/j.ijindorg.2014.05.004

Baron, J., & Spulber, D. F. (2018). Technology standards and standard setting organizations: Introduction to the Searle Center Database. *Journal of Economics & Management Strategy*, *27*(3), 462–503. doi:10.1111/jems.12257

Bar, T., & Leiponen, A. (2014). Committee composition and networking in standard setting: The case of wireless telecommunications. *Journal of Economics & Management Strategy*, *23*(1), 1–23. doi:10.1111/jems.12044

Bartleson, K. (2013). *10 Standards Organizations That Affect You (Whether You Know It Or Not)*. Retrieved from https://www.electronicdesign.com/communications/10-standards-organizations-affect-you-whether-you-know-it-or-not

Bartolini, C., Giurgiu, A., Lenzini, G., & Robaldo, L. (2017). Towards Legal Compliance by Correlating Standards and Laws with a Semi-automated Methodology. In T. Bosse & B. Bredeweg (Eds.), *BNAIC 2016: Artificial Intelligence* (Vol. 765, pp. 47–62). doi:10.1007/978-3-319-67468-1_4

Bebbington, J., & Thomson, I. (2007). Social and Environmental Accounting, Auditing, and Reporting: A Potential Source of Organisational Risk Governance? *Environment and Planning. C, Government & Policy*, *25*(1), 38–55. doi:10.1068/c0616j

Becker, M., & Lazaric, N. (2003). The influence of knowledge in the replication of routines. *Economia Aplicada, LVI*(3), 65–94.

Beck, U. (1992). *Risk Society: Towards a New Modernity*. London: SAGE.

Bekkers, R., Bongard, R., & Nuvolari, A. (2011). An empirical study on the determinants of essential patent claims in compatibility standards. *Research Policy, 40*(7), 1001–1015. doi:10.1016/j.respol.2011.05.004

Bellotti, E., Kronegger, L., & Guadalupi, L. (2016). The evolution of research collaboration within and across disciplines in Italian Academia. *Scientometrics, 109*(2), 783–811. doi:10.1007/s11192-016-2068-1 PubMed

Bence, V., & Oppenheim, C. (2005). The evolution of the UK's Research Assessment Exercise: Publications, performance and perceptions. *Journal of Educational Administration and History, 37*(2), 137–155. doi:10.1080/00220620500211189

Bénézech, D., Lambert, G., Lanoux, B., Lerch, C., & Loos-Baroin, J. (2001). Completion of knowledge codification: An illustration through the ISO 9000 standards implementation process. *Research Policy, 30*(9), 1395–1407. doi:10.1016/S0048-7333(01)00158-5

Benner, M. J., & Tushman, M. L. (2003). Exploitation, exploration, and process management: The productivity dilemma revised. *Academy of Management Review, 28*(2), 238–256. doi:10.5465/amr.2003.9416096

Benner, M., & Waldfogel, J. (2008). Close to you? Bias and precision in patent-based measures of technological proximity. *Research Policy, 37*(9), 1556–1567. doi:10.1016/j.respol.2008.05.011

Bent, R., & Freathy, P. (1997). Motivating the employee in the independent retail sector. *Journal of Retailing and Consumer Services, 4*(3), 201–208. doi:10.1016/S0969-6989(96)00045-8

Berget, D. (2008). *Danone, géant mondial de l'alimentation, un des premiers adeptes de l'ISO 22000. ISO Management systems*. Mai-Juin.

Bernard, H., & Wolff, D. (2004). Enjeux & déterminants de l'implication des entreprises dans le processus de normalisation. *Revue d'Economie Industrielle, 108*(4), 21–40.

Bernstein, S. (2002). Liberal Environmentalism and Global Environmental Governance. *Global Environmental Politics, 2*(3), 1–16. doi:10.1162/152638002320310509

Beskow, C. (2017). *Regler för arbete i teknisk kommitté (SIS/TK)* [Rules for working in a Technical Committee (SIS/TK)]. Stockholm, Sweden: Swedish Standards Institute.

Bessant, J. (2003). *High involvement innovation*. Chichester, UK: John Wiley and Sons.

Bevilacqua, M., Ciarapica, F. E., & Giacchetta, G. (2008). Value Stream Mapping in Project Management: A Case Study. *Project Management Journal, 39*(3), 110–124. doi:10.1002/pmj.20069

Bianchi, G., & Carusi, C. (2019). Debunking the Italian Scientific Sectors' classification system: preliminary insights. In ISSI - the International Society for Informetrics and Scientometrics (Chair), 17 International Conference on Scientometrics & Informetrics. Sapienza University of Rome.

Biesenbender, S. (2019). The governance and standardisation of research information in different science systems: A comparative analysis of Germany and Italy. *Higher Education Quarterly*, *73*(1), 116–127. doi:10.1111/hequ.12193

Biesenbender, S., & Herwig, S. (2019). Support structures to facilitate the dissemination and implementation of a national standard for research information – the German case of the Research Core Dataset. *Procedia Computer Science*, *146*, 131–141. doi:10.1016/j.procs.2019.01.088

Birkinshaw, J., Mol, M., & Hamel, G. (2005). *Management Innovation.* Advanced Institute of Management, Research Paper No. 021.doi:10.2139srn.1306981

Birkinshaw, J., & Mol, M. J. (2008). Management innovation. *Academy of Management Review*, *33*(4), 825–845. doi:10.5465/amr.2008.34421969

Bjørn-Andersen, N., & Andersen, K. V. (2009). *Diffusion and Impacts of the Internet and e-Commerce* (No. 2003-11).

Blind, K. (2009). Standardisation: A Catalyst for Innovation, Inaugural Address. Rotterdam School of Management, Erasmus Universiteit Rotterdam. Retrieved from http://repub.eur.nl/pub/17558/EIA-2009-039-LIS.pdf

Blind, K. (2013). The Impact of Standardization and Standards on Innovation. Nesta Working Paper No. 13/15. Retrieved from https://media.nesta.org.uk/documents/the_impact_of_standardization_and_standards_on_innovation.pdf

Blind, K. (2004). *The economics of standards: theory, evidence, policy.* Edward Elgar Publishing.

Blind, K. (2006). Explanatory factors for participation in formal standardisation processes: Empirical evidence at firm level. *Economics of Innovation and New Technology*, *15*(2), 157–170. doi:10.1080/10438590500143970

Blind, K., & Gauch, S. (2009). Research and standardisation in nanotechnology: Evidence from Germany. *The Journal of Technology Transfer*, *34*(3), 320–342. doi:10.1007/s10961-008-9089-8

Blind, K., & Jungmittag, A. (2005). Trade and the Impact of Innovations and Standards: The Case of Germany and the UK. *Applied Economics*, *37*(12), 1385–1398. doi:10.1080/13504850500143294

Blind, K., & Mangelsdorf, A. (2016). Motives to standardize: Empirical evidence from Germany. *Technovation*, *48–49*, 13–24. doi:10.1016/j.technovation.2016.01.001

Blind, K., Peterson, S., & Riillo, C. A. F. (2017). The Impact of Standards and Regulation on Innovation in Uncertain Markets. *Research Policy*, *46*(1), 249–264. doi:10.1016/j.respol.2016.11.003

Blind, K., Pohlisch, J., & Zi, A. (2018). Publishing, patenting and standardization: Motives and barriers of scientists. *Research Policy*, *4*(7), 1185–1197. doi:10.1016/j.respol.2018.03.011

Blind, K., Pohlisch, J., & Zi, A. (2018). Publishing, patenting, and standardization: Motives and barriers of scientists. *Research Policy*, *47*(7), 1185–1197. doi:10.1016/j.respol.2018.03.011

Blind, K., & Thumm, N. (2004). Interrelation between patenting and standardisation strategies: Empirical evidence and policy implications. *Research Policy*, *33*(10), 1583–1598. doi:10.1016/j.respol.2004.08.007

Boisvert, V., Méral, P., & Froger, G. (2013). Market-Based Instruments for Ecosystem Services: Institutional Innovation or Renovation? *Society & Natural Resources*, *26*(10), 1122–1136. doi:10.1080/08941920.2013.820815

Bollini, A., Mennielli, M., Mornati, S., & Palmer, D. T. (2016). IRIS: Supporting & Managing the Research Life-cycle. *Universal Journal of Educational Research*, *4*(4), 738–743. doi:10.13189/ujer.2016.040410

Bonatti, P., Kirrane, S., Polleres, A., & Wenning, R. (2017). Transparent Personal Data Processing: The Road Ahead. *Computer Safety, Reliability, and Security*, 337–349.

Boyatzis, R. E. (1998). *Transforming qualitative information: Thematic analysis and code development*. Atlanta, Ga.: Sage.

Boyd, J., & Banzhaf, S. (2007). What are ecosystem services? The need for standardized environmental accounting units. *Ecological Economics*, *63*(2–3), 616–626. doi:10.1016/j.ecolecon.2007.01.002

Bracking, S. (2015). Performativity in the Green Economy: How far does climate finance create a fictive economy? *Third World Quarterly*, *36*(12), 2337–2357. doi:10.1080/01436597.2015.1086263

Brink, L., Folmer, E., & Jakobs, K. (2019). Coping with Multi-Disciplinarity in Standardisation. In *Proc. 24th EURAS Annual Standardisation Conference – Standards for a Bio-Based Economy* (pp. 453-466). Mainz Publishers.

Brown, A., Amundson, J., & Badurdeen, F. (2014). Sustainable value stream mapping (Sus-VSM) in different manufacturing system configurations: Application case studies. *Journal of Cleaner Production*, *85*, 164–179. doi:10.1016/j.jclepro.2014.05.101

Brown, J. S., & Duguid, P. (2001). Knowledge and organization: A social Practice perspective. *Organization Science*, *12*(2), 198–213. doi:10.1287/orsc.12.2.198.10116

Brunsson, N., & Jacobson, B. (2005). *A world of standards*. Oxford University Press.

Brunsson, N., Rasche, A., & Seidl, D. (2012). The Dynamics of Standardization: Three Perspectives on Standards in Organization Studies. *Organization Studies*, *33*(5-6), 613–632. doi:10.1177/0170840612450120

Burland, T., & Grout, C. (2017). Standards and Interoperability: How Jisc's Work Supports Reporting, Communicating and Measuring Research in the UK. *Procedia Computer Science, 106*, 276–282. doi:10.1016/j.procs.2017.03.026

Burns, T., & Stalker, G. M. (1961). *The management of innovation.* London: Tavistock.

Busch, L. (2011). *Standards: Recipes for Reality.* Cambridge, MA: The MIT Press. doi:10.7551/mitpress/8962.001.0001

Butler, L. (2007). Assessing university research: A plea for a balanced approach. *Science & Public Policy, 34*(8), 565–574. doi:10.3152/030234207X254404

Butter, F. A. G., Groot, S. P. T., & Lazrak, F. (2007). The Transaction Costs Perspective on Standards as a Source of Trade and Productivity Growth. Tinbergen Institute Discussion Paper, TI 2007-090/3. Retrieved from http://personal.vu.nl/f.a.g.den.butter/TIstandards07090.pdf

Cagan, R. (2013). The San Francisco Declaration on Research Assessment. *Disease Models & Mechanisms, 6*(4), 869–870. doi:10.1242/dmm.012955 PubMed

Cargill, C. F. (2011). Why Standardization Efforts Fail. *The Journal of Electronic Publishing: JEP, 14*(1). doi:10.3998/3336451.0014.103

Cargill, C. F. (2011). Why standardization efforts fail? *The Journal of Electronic Publishing: JEP, 14*.

Castree, N. (2010). Neoliberalism and the biophysical environment: A synthesis and evaluation of the research. *Environment and Society: Advances in Research, 1*(1), 5–45. doi:10.3167/ares.2010.010102

Chaffey, D. (2007). *E-business and E-commerce Management: Strategy, Implementation and Practice.* Pearson Education.

Chanal, V. & Mothe, C. (2005). Concilier innovations d'exploitation et d'exploration – Le cas du secteur automobile, *Revue française de gestion, 154*, 173-191.

Chaudhary, N., & Sharma, B. (2012). Impact of employee motivation on performance (productivity) private organization. *International Journal of Business Trends and Technology, 2*, 29–35.

Chiao, B., Lerner, J., & Tirole, J. (2007). The rules of standard-setting organizations: An empirical analysis. *The Rand Journal of Economics, 38*(4), 905–930. doi:10.1111/j.0741-6261.2007.00118.x

Chitura, T., Mupemhi, S., Dube, T., & Bolongkikit, J. (2015). Barriers to electronic commerce adoption in small and medium enterprises: A critical literature review. *Journal of Internet Banking and Commerce.*

Christophers, B. (2018). Risking value theory in the political economy of finance and nature. *Progress in Human Geography, 42*(3), 330–349. doi:10.1177/0309132516679268

Ciravegna Martins da Fonseca, L. M. (2015). ISO 14001:2015: An improved tool for sustainability. *Journal of Industrial Engineering and Management, 8*(1), 37–50. doi:10.3926/jiem.1298

CIVR. (2004). Valutazione triennale della ricerca (VTR): Bando di partecipazione all'esercizio 2001-2003. Retrieved from https://www.unipd.it/sites/unipd.it/files/Bando%20n.35%2016%20 marzo%202004.pdf

Clapp, J. (1998). The Privatization of Global Environmental Governance: ISO 14000 and the Developing World. *Global Governance, 4*(3), 295–316. doi:10.1163/19426720-00403004

Clapp, J., & Dauvergne, P. (2011). *Paths to a Green World – The Political Economy of the Global Environment.* Cambridge, MA: MIT Press.

Cochoy, F., Garel, J. P., & De Terssac, G. (1998). Comment l'écrit travaille l'organisation: Le cas des normes ISO 9000. *Revue Francaise de Sociologie, 39*(4), 673–699. doi:10.2307/3323006

Coen, G., & Smiraglia, R. P. (2019). Toward Better Interoperability of the NARCIS Classification. *Knowledge Organization, 46*(5), 345–353. doi:10.5771/0943-7444-2019-5-345

Cohen, M. D., & Bacdayan, P. (1994). Organizational Routines Are Stored as Procedural Memory: Evidence from a Laboratory Study. *Organization Science, 5*(4), 554–568. doi:10.1287/orsc.5.4.554

Collis, D. J. (1994). How valuable are organizational capabilities? *Strategic Management Journal, 1*(S1), 143–152. doi:10.1002mj.4250150910

Contreras, J. L. (2011). *An empirical study of the effects of ex ante licensing disclosure policies on the development of voluntary technical standards.* National Institute of Standards and Technology, No. GCR (2011): 11-934.

Contreras, J. L. (2014). Divergent patterns of engagement in Internet standardization: Japan, Korea and China. *Telecommunications Policy, 38*(10), 914–932. doi:10.1016/j.telpol.2014.09.005

Cook, S., & Brown, J. S. (1999). Bridging epistemologies: The generative dance between organizational knowledge and organizational knowing. *Organization Science, 10*(4), 381–400. doi:54 doi:10.1287/orsc.10.4.381

Corbett, C. J., Montes-Sancho, M. J., & Kirsch, D. A. (2005). The financial impact of ISO 9000 certification in the United States: An empirical analysis. *Management Science, 51*(7), 1046–1059. doi:10.1287/mnsc.1040.0358

Costanza, R., d'Arge, R., de Groot, R., Farber, S., Grasso, M., Hannon, B., ... van den Belt, M. (1997). The value of the world's ecosystem services and natural capital. *Nature, 387*(6630), 253–260. doi:10.1038/387253a0

Costanza, R., de Groot, R., Braat, L., Kubiszewski, I., Fioramonti, L., Sutton, P., ... Grasso, M. (2017). Twenty years of ecosystem services: How far have we come and how far do we still need to go? *Ecosystem Services, 28*, 1–16. doi:10.1016/j.ecoser.2017.09.008

Costanza, R., de Groot, R., Sutton, P., van der Ploeg, S., Anderson, S. J., Kubiszewski, I., ... Turner, R. K. (2014). Changes in the global value of ecosystem services. *Global Environmental Change, 26*, 152–158. doi:10.1016/j.gloenvcha.2014.04.002

Craig, P., & De Burca, G. (2011). *EU Law: Text, Cases and Materials*. Oxford, UK: Oxford University Press. doi:10.1093/he/9780199576999.001.0001

Cutler, A. C. (2010). The legitimacy of private transnational governance: Experts and the transnational market for force. *Socio-economic Review*, *8*(1), 157–185. doi:10.1093er/mwp027

Da Costa Araujo Sampaio, P. A., de Andrade Saraiva, P. M. T. L., & Gomes, A. C. R. (2014). ISO 9001 European Scoreboard: An instrument to measure Macroquality. *Total Quality Management*, *25*(4), 309–318. doi:10.1080/14783363.2013.807683

Danezis, G. (2015). *Privacy and Data Protection by Design – from policy to engineering*. Retrieved from https://arxiv.org/pdf/1501.03726

Dauvergne, P. (2018). *Will Big Business Destroy Our Planet?* Cambridge, UK: Polity.

De Boer, H., Jongbloed, B. W., & Benneworth, P. S. (2015). *Performance-based funding and performance agreements in fourteen higher education systems. Center for Higher Education Policy Studies*. CHEPS.

de Hert, P., Papakonstantinou, V., & Kamara, I. (2016). The cloud computing standard ISO/IEC 27018 through the lens of the EU legislation on data protection. *Computer Law & Security Review*, *32*(1), 16–30. doi:10.1016/j.clsr.2015.12.005

De Hert, P., Papakonstantinou, V., Malgieri, G., Beslay, L., & Sanchez, I. (2018). The right to data portability in the GDPR: Towards user-centric interoperability of digital services. *Computer Law & Security Review*, *34*(2), 193–203. doi:10.1016/j.clsr.2017.10.003

de Jong, S. P. L., Smit, J., & van Drooge, L. (2015). Scientists' response to societal impact policies: A policy paradox. *Science & Public Policy*, *43*(1), 102–114. doi:10.1093/scipol/scv023

de Villiers, C., & Maroun, W. (Eds.). (2018). *Sustainability Accounting and Integrated Reporting*. London: Routledge.

De Vries, H. J. (2006). IT standards typology. In K. Jakobs (Ed.), Advanced Topics in Information Technology Standards and Standardization Research (Vol. 1, pp. 1–26). IGI Global; doi:10.4018/978-1-59140-938-0.ch001.

de Vries, H. J. (2006). Standards for business - How companies benefit from participation in international standards setting. In A. L. Bement, T. Standage, T. Sugano, & K. Wucherer (Eds.), *International Standardization as a strategic tool - Commended papers from the IEC Centenary Challenge 2006* (pp. 130–141). Geneva, Switzerland: IEC.

De Vries, H. J. (2013). *Standardization: A business approach to the role of national standardization organizations*. Springer Science & Business Media.

De Vries, H. J., Jakobs, K., Egyedi, T. M., Eto, M., Fertig, S., Kanevskaia, O., ... Mirtsch, M. (2018). Standardization: Towards an agenda for research. *International Journal of Standardization Research*, *16*(1), 52–59. doi:10.4018/IJSR.2018010104

Deci, E. L., Connel, J. P., & Ryan, R. M. (1989). Self-determination in a work organization. *The Journal of Applied Psychology*, *74*(4), 580–590. doi:10.1037/0021-9010.74.4.580

Decker, S., Melnik, S., Van Harmelen, F., Fensel, D., Klein, M., Broekstra, J., ... Horrocks, I. (2000). The semantic web: The roles of XML and RDF. *IEEE Internet Computing*, *4*(5), 63–73. doi:10.1109/4236.877487

DeLacey, B. J. (2006). *Strategic behavior in standard-setting organizations*. Academic Press.

Delcamp, H., & Leiponen, A. (2014). Innovating standards through informal consortia: The case of wireless telecommunications. *International Journal of Industrial Organization*, *36*, 36–47. doi:10.1016/j.ijindorg.2013.07.004

Delic, M., Radlovacki, V., Kamberovic, B., Maksimovic, R., & Pecujlija, M. (2014). Examining relationships between quality management and organisational performance in transitional economies. *Total Quality Management*, *25*(4), 367–382. doi:10.1080/14783363.2013.799331

Deloitte. (2013). Redesigning the higher education data and information landscape. Strand 1 project report.

Dempsey, J. (2016). *Enterprising Nature: Economics, Markets, and Finance in Global Biodiversity Politics*. Chichester, UK: Wiley. doi:10.1002/9781118640517

Deschamps, J. P., & Nayak, P. R. (1997). *Les maîtres de l'innovation totale, traduit de Product juggernauts*. Paris: Éditions d'Organisation.

DeVries, H. J. & Van Delden, M. (2006). *How to integrate standardization in knowledge management*. ISO Focus.

Dijstelbloem, H., Huisman, F., Miedema, F., & Mijnhardt, W. (2013). Why science does not work as it should. And what to do about it. Science in Transition Position Paper. Retrieved from http://www.scienceintransition.nl/app/uploads/2013/10/Science-in-Transition-Position-Paper-final.pdf

DIN. (2000). *Economic Benefits of Standardization: Summary of Results*. Berlin: Beuth Verlag GmbH and Deutsches Institut für Normung.

Disterer, G. (2013). ISO/IEC 27000, 27001 and 27002 for Information Security Management. *Journal of Information Security*, *04*(02), 92–100. doi:10.4236/jis.2013.42011

Dobbins, M. (2016). Convergent or divergent Europeanization? An analysis of higher education governance reforms in France and Italy. *International Review of Administrative Sciences*, *83*(1), 177–199. doi:10.1177/0020852315580498

Dokko, G., & Rosenkopf, L. (2010). Mobility of Technical Professionals and Firm Influence in Wireless Standards Committees. *Organization Science*, *21*(3), 677–695. doi:10.1287/orsc.1090.0470

Donate, M. J., & Sanchez de Pablo, J. D. (2015). The role of knowledge-oriented leadership in knowledge management practices and innovation. *Journal of Business Research, 68*(2), 360–370. doi:10.1016/j.jbusres.2014.06.022

Donina, D., Meoli, M., & Paleari, S. (2015). Higher Education Reform in Italy: Tightening Regulation Instead of Steering at a Distance. *Higher Education Policy, 28*(2), 215–234. doi:10.1057/hep.2014.6

Dupuy, M.-P., & Vinuales, J. E. (2018). *International Environmental Law*. Cambridge, UK: Cambridge University Press. doi:10.1017/9781108399821

Edmondson, A. C., Moingeon, B., Dessain, V., & Jensen, A. D. (2008, Apr.). Global Knowledge Management at Danone. *Harvard Business School Review.*

Egyedi, T. M., & Ortt, J. R. (2017). Towards a functional classification of standards for innovation research. In R. Hawkins, K. Blind, & R. Page (Eds.), Handbook of innovation and standards (pp. 105–132). Cheltenham, Northampton, MA: Edward Elgar Publishing; doi:10.4337/97817 83470082.00013.

Egyedi, T. M. (2000). The Standardised Container: Gateway Technologies in Cargo Transport. *Homo Oeconomicus, 17*, 231–262.

Egyedi, T. M., & Blind, K. (2008). *The Dynamics of Standards*. Cheltenham, UK: Edward Elgar.

Engeström, Y. (2001). Expansive learning at work: Toward an activity theoretical reconceptualization. *Journal of Education and Work, 14*(1), 133–156. doi:10.1080/13639080020028747

Engeström, Y. (2015). *Learning by expanding, an activity theoretical approach to developmental research* (2nd ed.). Cambridge University Press.

Erlach, K. (2013). *Value Stream Design*. Springer Berlin Heidelberg. doi:10.1007/978-3-642-12569-0

Ernst & Young, International Federation of Accountants, & Natural Capital Coalition. (2014). *Accounting for Natural Capital – The elephant in the boardroom*. Retrieved from Chartered Institute of Management Accountants website: https://www.ey.com/Publication/vwLUAssets/Accounting-for-natural-capital/$File/EY-Accounting-for-natural-capital.pdf

Ervine, K. (2018). *Carbon*. Cambridge, MA: Polity.

Espeland, W. N., & Stevens, M. L. (1998). Commensuration as a Social Process. *Annual Review of Sociology, 24*(1), 313–343. doi:10.1146/annurev.soc.24.1.313

European Commission. (2015a). *Communication from the Commission to the European Parliament, the Council, the European Economic and Social Committee and the Committee of the Regions: Digital Single Market Strategy for Europe*. Brussels: European Commission. Available at: http://eur-lex.europa.eu/legal-content/EN/TXT/?uri=celex:52015DC0192

European Commission. (2015b). *Flash Eurobarometer 413 (Companies Engaged in Online Activities)*. TNS Political & Social [producer]. GESIS Data Archive, Cologne. ZA6284 Data file Version 1.0.0, doi:10.4232/1.12353

European Commission. (2017). *Communication from the Commission to the European Parliament, the Council, the European Economic and Social Committee and the Committee of the Regions on the Mid-Term Review on the implementation of the Digital Single Market Strategy - A Connected Digital Single Market for All*. COM(2017). Brussels: European Commission. Available at: http://eur-lex.europa.eu/legal-content/EN/TXT/?uri=COM:2017:228:FIN

European Commission. (2017a). DJ Growth. European Innovation Scoreboard. Retrieved from http://ec.europa.eu/growth/industry/innovation/facts-figures/scoreboards_en

European Commission. (2017b). Annual Report on European SMEs 2016/2017. Retrieved from http://ec.europa.eu/docsroom/documents/26563/

European Commission. (2019). *Data protection in the European Union. The General Data Protection Regulation (GDPR)*. Brussels: European Commission. Available at: https://ec.europa.eu/info/law/law-topic/data-protection/data-protection-eu_en

European Commission. (Ed.). (2013). *Options for Strengthening Responsible Research and Innovation*. Report of the Expert Group on the State of Art in Europe on Responsible Research and Innovation. Retrieved from https://ec.europa.eu/research/science-society/document_library/pdf_06/options-for-strengthening_en.pdf

European Commission. (Ed.). (2015). *Internet of Things – IoT Governance, Privacy and Security Issues*. Retrieved from https://www.researchgate.net/profile/Christine_Hennebert/publication/275540220_IoT_Governance_Privacy_and_Security_Issues/links/553f4f390cf24c6a05d1fd2a/IoT-Governance-Privacy-and-Security-Issues.pdf

European Data Protection Board (EPDB). (2019). *Guidelines 4/2018 on the accreditation of certification bodies under Article 43 of the General Data Protection Regulation (2016/679)*. Author.

European Parliament. (Ed.). (2016). *Ethical Aspects of Cyber-Physical Systems – Scientific Foresight study*. Retrieved from http://www.europarl.europa.eu/RegData/etudes/STUD/2016/563501/EPRS_STU(2016)563501_EN.pdf

European Union, Publications Office & ELI Task Force. (2015). *ELI: A technical implementation guide*. Luxembourg: Publications Office.

European Union. (2007). *Directive 2007/2/EC of the European Parliament and of the Council of 14 March 2007 establishing an Infrastructure for Spatial Information in the European Community (INSPIRE)*. Brussels, Belgium: European Union.

EuroPriSe. (2019). Retrieved 11 August 2019, from European Privacy Seal (EuroPriSe) website: https://www.european-privacy-seal.eu/EPS-en/Home

Evangelos, L. P., Pantouvakis, A., & Kafetzopoulos, D. P. (2013). The impact of ISO 9001 effectiveness on the performance of service companies. *Managing Service Quality: An International Journal*, *23*(2), 149–164. doi:10.1108/09604521311303426

Feldman, M. S., & Pentland, B. T. (2003). Reconceptualizing Organizational Routines as a Source of Flexibility and Change. *Administrative Science Quarterly*, *28*(1), 94–118. doi:10.2307/3556620

Felli, R. (2015). Environment, not planning: The neoliberal depoliticisation of environmental policy by means of emissions trading. *Environmental Politics*, *24*(5), 641–660. doi:10.1080/09644016.2015.1051323

Fensel, D., Ding, Y., Omelayenko, B., Schulten, E., Botquin, G., Brown, M., & Flett, A. (2001). Product data integration in B2B e-commerce. *IEEE Intelligent Systems*, *16*(4), 54–59. doi:10.1109/5254.941358

FlexSim Software Products Inc. (2017). *FlexSimVSM*. Retrieved January 26, 2017, from https://www.flexsim.com/value-stream-mapping/

Follett, M. P. (1925). Constructive conflict. In P. Graham (Ed.), Mary parker Follett: Prophet of management. Boston: Harvard Business School Press.

Fondermann, P., & van der Togt, P. L. (2017). How Wageningen University and Research Centre managed to influence researchers publishing behaviour towards more quality, impact and visibility. *Procedia Computer Science*, *106*, 204–211. doi:10.1016/j.procs.2017.03.017

Foray, D. (2000). *L'économie de la connaissance*. Paris: La Découverte.

Franceschini, F., & Maisano, D. (2017). Critical remarks on the Italian research assessment exercise VQR 2011–2014. *Journal of Informetrics*, *11*(2), 337–357. doi:10.1016/j.joi.2017.02.005

Fransen, L., & LeBaron, G. (2019). Big audit firms as regulatory intermediaries in transnational labor governance. *Regulation & Governance*, *13*(2), 260–279. doi:10.1111/rego.12224

Friedman, B., Kahn, P. H., & Borning, A. (2008). Value sensitive design and information systems. The Handbook of Information and Computer Ethics, 69–101.

Fura, B., & Wang, Q. (2017). The level of socioeconomic development of EU countries and the state of ISO 14001 certification. *Quality & Quantity*, *51*(1), 103–119. doi:10.1007/s11135-015-0297-7 PubMed

Gagné, M., & Deci, E. L. (2005). Self determination theory and work motivation. *Journal of Organizational Behavior*, *26*(4), 331–362. doi:10.1002/job.322

Galia, F., & Pekovic, S. (2008). From Quality to Innovation: Evidence from Two French Employer Surveys. Proposal for the 1st DIME Scientific Conference "Knowledge in space and time: Economic and policy implications of the Knowledge-based economy" BETA, University Louis Pasteur, Strasbourg, France.

Galimberti, P., & Mornati, S. (2017). The Italian Model of Distributed Research Information Management Systems: A Case Study. *Procedia Computer Science*, *106*, 183–195. doi:10.1016/j.procs.2017.03.015

Gandal, Gantman, & Genesove. (2004). *Intellectual property and standardization committee participation in the US modem industry*. Academic Press.

Gao, R., Wang, L., Teti, R., Dornfeld, D., Kumara, S., Mori, M., & Helu, M. (2015). Cloud-enabled prognosis for manufacturing. *CIRP Annals - Manufacturing Technology*, *64*(2), 749–772.

Genschel, P., & Werle, R. (1993). From National Hierarchies to International Standardization: Modal Changes in the Governance of Telecommunications. *Journal of Public Policy*, *13*(3), 203–225. doi:10.1017/S0143814X00001045

Giroux, H. (2006). It was such a handy term: Management fashions and pragmatic ambiguity. *Journal of Management Studies*, *43*(6), 1227–1260. doi:10.1111/j.1467-6486.2006.00623.x

Gläser, J., & Laudel, G. (2007). The social construction of bibliometric evaluations. In R. Whitley & J. Gläser (Eds.), Sociology of the Sciences Yearbook: Vol. 26. The Changing Governance of the Sciences: The Advent of Research Evaluation Systems (pp. 101-123). Dordrecht: Springer Netherlands. doi:10.1007/978-1-4020-6746-4_5

Gläser, J. (2006). *Wissenschaftliche Produktionsgemeinschaften: Die soziale Ordnung der Forschung*. Frankfurt am Main: Campus-Verl.

Gläser, J., Lange, S., Laudel, G., & Schimank, U. (2010). Informed authority? The limited use of research evaluation systems for managerial control in universities. In R. Whitley, J. Gläser, & L. Engwall (Eds.), *Reconfiguring Knowledge Production: Changing Authority Relationships in the Sciences and their Consequences for Intellectual Innovation* (pp. 149–183). Oxford, UK: Oxford University Press.

Godwin, U. J. (2001). Privacy and security concerns as major barriers for e-commerce: A survey study. *Information Management & Computer Security*, *9*(4), 165–174. doi:10.1108/EUM0000000005808

Gómez-Baggethun, E., & Ruiz-Pérez, M. (2011). Economic valuation and the commodification of ecosystem services. *Progress in Physical Geography*, *35*(5), 613–628. doi:10.1177/0309133311421708

Good, N., Rubinstein, I., & Maslin, J. (2019). *'When the Dust Doesn't Settle' – GDPR Compliance One Year In*. Retrieved from https://www.ssrn.com/abstract=3378874

Gould, R. (2018, May 8). *The secret to unlocking green finance*. Retrieved 16 April 2019, from ISO website: http://www.iso.org/cms/render/live/en/sites/isoorg/contents/news/2018/05/Ref2287.html

Governatori, G., Hashmi, M., Lam, H.-P., Villata, S., & Palmirani, M. (2016). Semantic Business Process Regulatory Compliance Checking Using LegalRuleML. In E. Blomqvist, P. Ciancarini, F. Poggi, & F. Vitali (Eds.), *Knowledge Engineering and Knowledge Management* (pp. 746–761). Springer International Publishing. doi:10.1007/978-3-319-49004-5_48

Granjou, C. (2003). L'expertise scientifique à destination politique. *Cahiers Internationaux de Sociologie, 1*(114), 175–183. doi:10.3917/cis.114.0175

Grant, R. M. (1996). Towards a knowledge-based view of the firm. *Strategic Management Journal, 17*, 109–122.

Graz, J.-C. (2019). *The Power of Standards: Hybrid Authority and the Globalisation of Services.* Cambridge, UK: Cambridge University Press. doi:10.1017/9781108759038

Graz, J.-C., & Hauert, C. (2019). Translating Technical Diplomacy: The Participation of Civil Society Organisations in International Standardisation. *Global Society, 33*(2), 163–183. doi:10.1080/13600826.2019.1567476

Grimand, A. (2006). *L'appropriation des outils de gestion, vers de nouvelles perspectives théoriques?* Publications de l'Université de Saint-Etienne.

Grosse, R. (1996). International Technology Transfer in Services. *Journal of International Business Studies, 27.* doi:10.1057/palgrave.jibs.8490153

Grunwald, A. (2015). Technology assessment. In *Encyclopaedia of Information Science and Technology* (3rd ed.; pp. 3998–4006). IGI Global. doi:10.4018/978-1-4666-5888-2.ch394

Guasch, J. L., Racine, J.-L., Sánchez, I., & Diop, M. (2007). Quality systems and standards for a competitive edge (Directions in Development). Washington, DC: World Bank Publications; doi:10.1596/978-0-8213-6894-7.

Gupta & Effraimidis. (2018). *IEEE Patent Policy Revisions: An Empirical Examination of Impact.* Available at SSRN 3173799

Hadziselimovic, E., Fatema, K., Pandit, H. J., & Lewis, D. (2017). Linked Data Contracts to Support Data Protection and Data Ethics in the Sharing of Scientific Data. *Proceedings of the First Workshop on Enabling Open Semantic Science (SemSci)*, 55–62. Retrieved from http://ceur-ws.org/Vol-1931/paper-08.pdf

Hahn, R., & Weidtmann, C. (2016). Transnational Governance, Deliberative Democracy, and the Legitimacy of ISO 26000: Analyzing the Case of a Global Multistakeholder Process. *Business & Society, 55*(1), 90–129. doi:10.1177/0007650312462666

Halaweh, M. (2011). Adoption of E-commerce: Understanding of Security Challenge. *The Electronic Journal on Information Systems in Developing Countries, 47.*

Hall, P., Nilsson, T., & Löfgren, K. (2011). *Bureaucratic autonomy revisited: Informal aspects of agency autonomy in Sweden.* Paper presented at the Permanent Study Group VI on Governance of Public Sector organizations, Annual Conference of EGPA, Bucharest, Romania.

Hallström, K. T. (1996). The Production of Management Standards. Revue d'économie industrielle, 61-76.

Hallström, K. T. (2005). *Organizing the process of standardization. In A world of standards* (2nd ed.; pp. 85–99). Oxford University Press.

Hamann, J. (2016). The visible hand of research performance assessment. *Higher Education, 72*(6), 761–779. doi:10.1007/s10734-015-9974-7

Hamdoun, M., Jabbour, Ch. J. Ch., & Ben Othman, H. (2018). Knowledge transfer and organizational innovation: Impacts of quality and environmental management. *Journal of Cleaner Production, 193*, 759–770. doi:10.1016/j.jclepro.2018.05.031

Hamel, G. (2006). The why, what and how of management innovation. *Harvard Business Review, 84*(2), 72–84. PMID:16485806

Hamilton, K. (2016). Measuring Sustainability in the UN System of Environmental-Economic Accounting. *Environmental and Resource Economics, 64*(1), 25–36. doi:10.100710640-015-9924-y

Hampden-Turner, Ch. (1994). *Corporate Culture*. London: Hutchinson.

Hancock, A. (2013). Best practice guidelines for Developing International Statistical Classifications. Expert Group Meeting on International Statistical Classifications.

Handy, C. (1994). *The age of paradox*. Cambridge, MA: Harvard Business School Press.

Handy, C. (1995). *The empty raincoat: Making sense of the future*. Random House Business.

Hanseth, O., Jacucci, E., Grisot, M., & Aanestad, M. (2006). Reflexive standardization: Side effects and complexity in standard making. *Management Information Systems Quarterly, 30*, 563–581. doi:10.2307/25148773

Hansson, F. (2010). Dialogue in or with the peer review? Evaluating research organizations in order to promote organizational learning. *Science & Public Policy, 37*(4), 239–251. doi:10.3152/030234210X496600

Hatch, M. J., & Ehrlich, S. B. (1993). Spontaneous humor as an indicator of paradox and ambiguity in organizations. *Organization Studies, 14*(4), 505–526. doi:10.1177/017084069301400403

Hatchuel, A. (2005). *Entre connaissances et organisation: l'activité collective, Pour une épistémologie de l'action, l'expérience des sciences de gestion*. La découverte.

Hatchuel, A., & Weil, B. (1999). *L'expert et le système*. Paris: Economica.

Heimeriks, K. H., Koen, H., Schijven, M., & Gates, S. (2012). Manifestations of higher-order routines: The under-lying mechanisms of deliberate learning in the context of post-acquisition integration. *Academy of Management Journal, 55*(3), 703–726. doi:10.5465/amj.2009.0572

Helfat, C. E., & Martin, J. A. (2015). Dynamic managerial capabilities: Review and assessment of managerial impact on strategic change. *Journal of Management, 41*(5), 1281–1312. doi:10.1177/0149206314561301

Helm, D. (2016). *Natural Capital: Valuing the Planet*. New Haven, CT: Yale University Press.

Henning, F. (2018). A theoretical framework on the determinants of organisational adoption of interoperability standards in Government Information Networks. *Government Information Quarterly, 35*(4), S61–S67.

Heras-Saizarbitoria, I. (Ed.). (2017). *ISO 9001, ISO 14001, and New Management Standards.* New York: Springer.

Hesser, E. J., Feilzer, A. J., & de Vries, H. J. (2007). *Standardisation in Companies and Markets.* Helmut Schmidt University Hamburg.

Hickel, J. (2018). *The Nobel Prize for Climate Catastrophe.* Retrieved from https://foreignpolicy.com/2018/12/06/the-nobel-prize-for-climate-catastrophe/

Hicks, D. (2012). Performance-based university research funding systems. *Research Policy, 41*(2), 251–261. doi:10.1016/j.respol.2011.09.007

Hicks, D., Wouters, P., Waltman, L., de Rijcke, S., & Rafols, I. (2015). The Leiden Manifesto for research metrics. *Nature, 520*(7548), 429–431. doi:10.1038/520429a PubMed

Higginbotham, B. D. (2017). *The Standardization of Standardization: The Search for Order in Complex Systems.* Fairfax, VA: George Mason University; Retrieved from http://jbox.gmu.edu/xmlui/bitstream/handle/1920/11295/Higginbotham_gmu_0883E_11559.pdf?sequence=1&isAllowed=y

Higgins, V., & Larner, W. (Eds.). (2010). *Calculating the Social: Standards and the Reconfiguration of Governing.* New York: Palgrave Macmillan. doi:10.1057/9780230289673

Hines, P., Rich, N., Bicheno, J., Brunt, D., Taylor, D., Butterworth, C., & Sullivan, J. (1998). Value Stream Management. *International Journal of Logistics Management, 9*(1), 25–42. doi:10.1108/09574099810805726

Hodgson, G. M. (2013). Understanding organizational evolution: Toward a research agenda using generalized Darwinism. *Organization Studies, 34*(7), 973–992. doi:10.1177/0170840613485855

Houssos, N., Jörg, B., Dvořák, J., Príncipe, P., Rodrigues, E., Manghi, P., & Elbæk, M. K. (2014). OpenAIRE Guidelines for CRIS Managers: Supporting Interoperability of Open Research Information through Established Standards. *Procedia Computer Science, 33*, 33–38. doi:10.1016/j.procs.2014.06.006

Hsiao, C. (2007). Panel data analysis—Advantages and challenges. *Test, 16*(1), 1–22. doi:10.1007/s11749-007-0046-x

Hunt, S., & Boliver, V. (2019). Private providers of higher education in the UK: mapping the terrain. Centre for Global Higher Education working paper series No. 47. Retrieved from https://www.researchcghe.org/perch/resources/publications/to-publishwp47.pdf

Husain, Prasad, Kunz, Papageorgiou, & Song. (2014). Recent Trends in Standards Related to the Internet of Things and Machine-to-Machine Communications. *Journal of Information Communication Convergence Engineering, 12*(4), 228-236.

Iannella, R., & Villata, S. (2018, February 15). *ODRL Information Model 2.2*. Retrieved 19 September 2018, from ODRL Information Model 2.2 website: https://www.w3.org/TR/odrl-model/

IEC. (2016). *Guide to the IEC Affiliate Country Programme*. Geneva: IEC.

IEC. (2019a). International Partners - DCMAS Network. Geneva: IEC.

IEC. (2019b). Renewable Energies. Geneva: IEC.

IEC. (2019c). IEC Affiliates – IEC Programme for developing countries. Geneva: IEC.

IEC. (2019d). List of IEC Affiliate Country Programme Participants. Geneva: IEC.

IEC. (2019e). Affiliate Country Programme – Affiliate Plus Status. Geneva: IEC.

IEC. (2019f). Electropedia: The World Online Electrotechnical Vocabulary. Geneva: IEC.

IEEE. (Ed.). (2019). *The IEEE Global Initiative on Ethics of Autonomous and Intelligent Systems. Ethically Aligned Design: A Vision for Prioritizing Human Well-being with Autonomous and Intelligent Systems, First Edition*. IEEE. Retrieved from https://standards.ieee.org/content/ieee-standards/en/industry-connections/ec/ autonomous-systems.html

Igartua, J. I., Garrigós, J. A., & Hervas-Oliver, J. L. (2010). How innovation management techniques support an open innovation strategy. *Research Technology Management*, *53*(3), 41–52. doi:10.1080/08956308.2010.11657630

International Organization for Standardization. (2001). *International Classification for Standards*. Geneva, Switzerland: ICS.

International Organization for Standardization. (2014). *ISO 19115-1:2014 Geographic information - Metadata - Part 1 - Fundamentals*. Geneva, Switzerland: International Organization for Standardization, ISO.

International, W. W. F. (2014). *Accounting for Natural Capital in EU Policy Decision-Making: A WWF background paper on policy developments*. Retrieved from http://wwf.panda.org/?uNewsID=222134

Isaak, J. (2006). The role of individuals and social capital in POSIX standardization. *International Journal of IT Standards and Standardization Research*, *4*(1), 1–23. doi:10.4018/jitsr.2006010101

ISO 2018. ISO in brief - Great things happen when the world agrees. (n.d.). Retrieved from https://www.iso.org/files/live/sites/isoorg/files/store/en/PUB100007.pdf

ISO 2019-1. Benefits of ISO standards. (n.d.). Retrieved July 10, 2019, from https://www.iso.org/benefits-of-standards.html

ISO 2019-2. Developing ISO standards. (n.d.). Retrieved July 10, 2019, from https://www.iso.org/stages-and-resources-for-standards-development.html

ISO 2019-3. ISO forms, model agendas, standard letters. (n.d.). Retrieved July 10, 2019, from https://www.iso.org/iso-forms-model-agendas-standard-letters.html

ISO 2019-4. All about ISO. (n.d.). Retrieved July 10, 2019, from https://www.iso.org/about-us. html https://www.iso.org/about-us.html

ISO 2019-5. International harmonized stage codes. (n.d.). Retrieved July 10, 2019, from https:// www.iso.org/members.html

ISO 2019-6. Who develops standards? (n.d.). Retrieved July 10, 2019, from https://www.iso.org/ who-develops-standards.html

ISO. (2013). ISO Survey of Management System Standard Certifications. ISO 9001. Quality Management System. International Organisation for Standardization. Retrieved from www.iso.org

ISO. (2015). *ISO Strategy 2016-2020*. Geneva: ISO.

ISO. (2018a). *ISO 14000 Environmental management*. Retrieved from ISO website: http:// www.iso.org/cms/render/live/en/sites/isoorg/home/standards/popular-standards/iso-14000-environmental-manageme.html

ISO. (2018a). ISO/TC 238, Solid Biofuels. Geneva: ISO.

ISO. (2018b). *ISO 14008—Monetary Valuation of environmental impacts and related environmental aspects*. Retrieved from https://committee.iso.org/sites/tc207sc1/home/projects/ongoing/iso-14008.html

ISO. (2018b). ISO Action Plan for developing countries 2016-2020. Geneva: ISO.

ISO. (2019). *ISO 14008:2019 has now been published!* Retrieved from ISO/TC 207/SC 1 website: https://committee.iso.org/sites/tc207sc1/home/news/content-left-area/news-and-updates/iso-140082019-has-now-been-publi.html

ISO. (Ed.). (2016). Standards related to the Internet of Things. Unpublished ISO document.

ISO/IEC 2015. ISO membership manual. (n.d.). Retrieved from https://www.iso.org/files/live/ sites/isoorg/files/archive/pdf/en/iso_membership_manual.pdf

ISO/IEC 2019. Directives, Part 1 Consolidated ISO Supplement — Procedures specific to ISO. (n.d.). Retrieved from https://www.iso.org/sites/directives/current/consolidated/index.xhtml

ISO/IEC 2382-1:1993. (1993). Retrieved from http://www.iso.org/cms/render/live/en/sites/isoorg/ contents/data/standard/00/72/7229.html

ISO/IEC. (2016). *ISO/IEC Directives, Part 1*. Geneva: ISO/IEC.

Jakobs, K. (2018b). *'Smart' Standardisation*. Presented at the 82nd IEC General Meeting.

Jakobs, K. (2005). The Role of the 'Third Estate' in ICT Standardisation. In S. Bolin (Ed.), *The Standards Edge: Future Generation*. The Bolin Group.

Jakobs, K. (2006). ICT standards research-Quo Vadis. *Homo Oeconomicus, 23*(1), 79–107.

Jakobs, K. (2018a). Jakobs, K. (2018). On Standardizing the Internet of Things and Its Applications. In *Internet of Things A to Z: Technologies and Applications* (pp. 191–218). IEEE. doi:10.1002/9781119456735.ch7

Jakobs, K., Procter, R., & Williams, R. (1996). Users and standardization - Worlds apart? The Example of electronic mail. *StandardView*, *4*(4), 183–191. doi:10.1145/243492.243495

Jakobs, K., Procter, R., & Williams, R. (2001). The making of standards: Looking inside the work groups. *IEEE Communications Magazine*, (April): 2–7.

Jakobs, K., Procter, R., & Williams, R. (2001, May). The Making of Standards: Looking Inside the Working Groups. *IEEE Communications Magazine*, *39*(4), 102–107. doi:10.1109/35.917511

Jashapara, A. (2004). *Knowledge Management, an integrated approach*. Prentice Hall, Financial Times.

Jay, J. (2013). Navigating paradox as a mechanism of change and innovation in hybrid organizations. *Academy of Management Journal*, *56*(1), 137–159. doi:10.5465/amj.2010.0772

Jennex, M. E., Amoroso, D., & Adelakun, O. (2004). E-commerce infrastructure success factors for small companies in developing economies. *Electronic Commerce Research*, *4*(3), 263–286. doi:10.1023/B:ELEC.0000027983.36409.d4

Jones, P., & Sizer, J. (1990). The universities funding council's 1989 research selectivity exercise. *Beiträge Zur Hochschulforschung*, *4*, 309–348.

Jongbloed, B. (2018). Overview of the Dutch science system. CHEPS Working Papers 201804, University of Twente, Center for Higher Education Policy Studies (CHEPS). Retrieved from https://ideas.repec.org/p/chs/wpachs/201804.html

Jörg, B., Waddington, S., Jones, R., & Trowell, S. (2014). Harmonising Research Reporting in the UK – Experiences and Outputs from UKRISS. *Procedia Computer Science*, *33*, 207–214. doi:10.1016/j.procs.2014.06.034

Josserand, E., & Perret, V. (2003). Pratiques organisationnelles du paradoxe. Le paradoxe: penser et gérer autrement les organisations, 165-187.

JSON-LD. (2014, January 16). Retrieved 11 August 2019, from JSON-LD 1.0 A JSON-based Serialization for Linked Data website: https://www.w3.org/TR/json-ld/

Juran, J. (1998). *Juran's Quality handbook* (5th ed.). McGraw Hill.

Kaltenbrunner, W., & de Rijcke, S. (2017). Quantifying 'output' for evaluation: Administrative knowledge politics and changing epistemic cultures in Dutch law faculties. *Science & Public Policy*, *44*(2), 284–293. doi:10.1093cipolcw064

Kang, B., & Motohashi, K. (2015). Essential intellectual property rights and inventors' involvement in standardization. *Research Policy*, *44*(2), 483–492. doi:10.1016/j.respol.2014.10.012

Kaplan, R. S., & Mikes, A. (2012). Managing Risks: A New Framework. *Harvard Business Review*.

Kasemsap, K. (2018). *The importance of electronic commerce in modern business. In Encyclopedia of Information Science and Technology* (4th ed.; pp. 2791–2801). IGI Global.

Katznelson, R. D. (2016). *The IEEE controversial policy on Standard Essential Patents–the empirical record since adoption.* Presentation to the Symposium on Antitrust, Standard Essential Patents, and the Fallacy of the Anticommons Tragedy.

Katz-Rosene, R., & Paterson, M. (2018). *Thinking Ecologically About the Global Political Economy.* New York: Routledge. doi:10.4324/9781315677835

Kawa, A. (2017). Supply chains of cross-border e-commerce. In Advanced Topics in Intelligent Information and Database Systems (pp. 173-183). Springer. doi:10.1007/978-3-319-56660-3_16

Keyte, B., & Locher, D. A. (2004). *The Complete Lean Enterprise: Value Stream Mapping for Administrative and Office Processes.* CRC Press. doi:10.1201/b16650

Khan, M. A., & Salah, K. (2018). IoT security: Review, blockchain solutions, and open challenges. *Future Generation Computer Systems, 82*, 395–411. doi:10.1016/j.future.2017.11.022

Khojasteh, Y. (2016). *Production Control Systems - A Guide to Enhance Performance of Pull Systems.* Springer.

Kim, D. H. (1993). The Link between Individual and Organizational Learning. *Sloan Management Review, 35*(1), 37–50.

Kirrane, S., Fernández, J. D., Dullaert, W., Milosevic, U., Polleres, A., Bonatti, P., ... Raschke, P. (2018). A Scalable Consent, Transparency and Compliance Architecture. *Proceedings of the Posters and Demos Track of the Extended Semantic Web Conference (ESWC 2018).*

Klabbers, J. (2018). *International Law.* Cambridge, UK: Cambridge University Press.

Klevers, T. (2007). *Wertstrom-Mapping und Wertstrom-Design.* mi-Fachverlag.

KNAW. (2005). Judging research on its merits. An advisory report by the Council for the Humanities and the Social Sciences Council. KNAW. Retrieved from https://www.knaw.nl/en/news/publications/judging-research-on-its-merits

KNAW. NWO, & VSNU. (2001). Kwaliteit verplicht. Naar een nieuw stelsel van kwaliteitszorg voor het wetenschappelijk onderzoek: Rapport van de werkgroep Kwaliteitszorg, Wetenschappelijk Onderzoek en standpuntbepaling KNAW, NWO en VSNU. Amsterdam: Author.

Knublauch, H., & Kontokostas, D. (2017, July). *Shapes Constraint Language (SHACL).* Retrieved 19 September 2018, from Shapes Constraint Language (SHACL) website: https://www.w3.org/TR/shacl/

Korff, D., & Georges, M. (2019, July 30). *The Data Protection Officer Handbook.* Retrieved from https://ssrn.com/abstract=3428957

Kotsemir, M., Abroskin, A., & Meissner, D. (2013). Innovation concepts and typology – an evolutionary discussion. HSE Working papers with number WP BRP 05/STI/2013.

KPMG International Cooperative. (2014). *A New Vision of Value. Connecting corporate and societal value creation.* Amstelveen: KPMG.

KPMG. (2015). The blueprint for a new HE data landscape: Final report.

Kuhlang, P., Hempen, S., Edtmayr, T., Deuse, J., & Sihn, W. (2013). Systematic and Continuous Improvement of Value Streams. *7th IFAC Conference on Manufacturing Modelling, Management, and Control* 10.3182/20130619-3-RU-3018.00257

Kulvatunyou Oh, H., Ivezic, N., & Nieman, S. T. (2019). Standards-based semantic integration of manufacturing information: Past, present, and future. *Journal of Manufacturing Systems, 52,* 184–197. doi:10.1016/j.jmsy.2019.07.003

Kurihara, S. (2008). Foundations and Future Prospects of Standards Studies: Multidisciplinary Approach. *International Journal of IT Standards and Standardization Research, 6*(2), 1–20. doi:10.4018/jitsr.2008070101

Kurnia, S., Choudrie, J., Mahbubur, R. M., & Alzougool, B. (2015). E-commerce technology adoption: A Malaysian grocery SME retail sector study. *Journal of Business Research, 68*(9), 1906–1918. doi:10.1016/j.jbusres.2014.12.010

Lambert, G. & Ouedraogo, N. (2009). Rôles des normes de management de la qualité sur l'apprentissage organisationnel selon les raisons de leur mise en œuvre. *Congrès annuel de l'Administrative Sciences Association of Canada.*

Lambert, G., & Loos-Baroin, J. (2004). Certification ISO 9000 et création de connaissances opérationnelles et conceptuelles: Une étude de cas. *Finance Contrôle Stratégie, 7*(1), 53–79.

Lantmäteriet. (2016). *The national geodata strategy 2016-2020.* Report no. 2016/7. Gävle, Sweden: Lantmäteriet.

Larouche, P., & Schuett, F. (2019). Repeated interaction in standard setting. *Journal of Economics & Management Strategy, 28*(3), 488–509. doi:10.1111/jems.12287

Lawrence, J. E., & Tar, U. A. (2010). Barriers to e-commerce in developing countries. *Information, Society and Justice Journal, 3*(1), 23-35.

LEANPILOT GmbH. (2017). *LEANPILOT.* Retrieved January 26, 2017, from http://www.leanpilot.com/index.html

Leavengood, S., Anderson, T. R., & Daim, T. U. (2014). Exploring linkage of quality management to innovation. *Total Quality Management, 25*(10), 1126–1140. doi:10.1080/14783363.2012.738492

Lebo, T., Sahoo, S., McGuinness, D., Belhajjame, K., Cheney, J., Corsar, D., … Zhao, J. (2013). *PROV-O: The PROV Ontology.* Academic Press.

Lee, C. Y., Ibrahim, H., Othman, M., & Yaakob, R. (2010, July). Resolving semantic interoperability challenges in XML schema matching. In *International Conference on Networked Digital Technologies* (pp. 151-162). Springer. 10.1007/978-3-642-14292-5_17

Leidner, D. E., Alavi, M., & Kayworth, T. (2006). The role of culture in knowledge management: A case study of two global firms. *International Journal of e-Collaboration*, *2*(1), 17–40. doi:10.4018/jec.2006010102

Leiponen, A. (2008). Competing through cooperation: The organization of standard setting in wireless telecommunications. *Management Science*, *54*(11), 1904–1919. doi:10.1287/mnsc.1080.0912

Leone, V., Di Caro, L., & Villata, S. (2019). Taking stock of legal ontologies: A feature-based comparative analysis. *Artificial Intelligence and Law*.

Leont'ev, A. (1981). *Problems of the Development of the Mind*. Moscow: Progress Publishers.

Leontiev, A. N. (1978). *Activity, consciousness, and personality*. Englewood Cliffs, NJ: Prentice-Hall.

Lepori, B., Reale, E., & Spinello, A. O. (2018). Conceptualizing and measuring performance orientation of research funding systems. *Research Evaluation*, *27*(3), 171–183. doi:10.1093/reseval/rvy007

Lerner, J., & Tirole, J. (2006). A model of forum shopping. *The American Economic Review*, *96*(4), 1091–1113. doi:10.1257/aer.96.4.1091

Lerner, J., & Tirole, J. (2015). Standard-essential patents. *Journal of Political Economy*, *123*(3), 547–586. doi:10.1086/680995

Levrel, H., & Missemer, A. (2018). La mise en économie de la nature, contrepoints historiques et contemporains. *Revue Economique*, *69*, 120–146.

Levy, D. L., & Newell, P. (2005). *The Business of Global Environmental Governance*. Cambridge, MA: MIT Press.

Levy, J. (2005). *Freaks of Fortune: The Emerging World of Capitalism and Risk in America*. Cambridge, MA: Harvard University Press.

Lewis, M. W. (2000). Exploring Paradox: Toward a More Comprehensive Guide. *Academy of Management Review*, *25*(4), 760–776. doi:10.5465/amr.2000.3707712

Lewis, M. W., & Smith, W. K. (2014). Paradox as a Metatheoretical Perspective. *The Journal of Applied Behavioral Science*, *50*(2), 127–149. doi:10.1177/0021886314522322

Lickert, R. (2012). Management systems and styles. In *Jean Michel Plane, Théorie et Management des Organisations, Management, Ressources Humaines*. Dunod.

Littoz-Monnet, A. (2017). Production and uses of expertise by international bureaucracies. In A. *Littoz-Monnet, The Politics of Expertise in International Organizations: How International Bureaucracies Produce and Mobilize Knowledge* (pp. 1–18). New York: Routledge. doi:10.4324/9781315542386-1

Lizar, M., & Turner, D. (2017). *Consent Receipt Specification v1.1.0*. Retrieved from Kantara Initiative website: https://docs.kantarainitiative.org/cis/consent-receipt-specification-v1-1-0.pdf

Lodder, A. R., & Murray, A. D. (2017). *EU regulation of E-commerce: A commentary*. Edward Elgar Publishing. doi:10.4337/9781785369346

Lööw, J., Abrahamsson, L., & Johansson, J. (2019). Mining 4.0—The Impact of New Technology from a Work Place Perspective. Mining. *Metallurgy & Exploration, 36*(4), 701–707. doi:10.100742461-019-00104-9

Lopes, I. M., Guarda, T., & Oliveira, P. (2019). How ISO 27001 can help achieve GDPR compliance. *2019 14th Iberian Conference on Information Systems and Technologies (CISTI)*, 1–6.

López-Mielgo, N., Montes-Peón, J., & Vázquez-Ordá, C. J. (2009). Are quality and innovation management conflicting activities? *Technovation, 29*(8), 537–545. doi:10.1016/j.technovation.2009.02.005

Los Reyes, E., Vega, J., & Martínez, A. (2006). ISO 9000 in SMEs. The mediating role of quality systems in the innovation performance. CINet.

Lundsten & Paasch, J. M. (2019, Feb.). Why do people participate in standardization of GI? *Coordinates*, 36-39.

Lundsten, J., & Paasch, J. (2017). Motives for Participation in Formal Standardization Processes for Geographic Information - An Empirical Study in Sweden. *International Journal of Standardization Research, 15*(1), 16–28. doi:10.4018/IJSR.2017010102

Lundsten, J., & Paasch, J. M. (2018). Individual's Motivation in Standardization of Geographic Information. *Proceedings of FIG Congress 2018.*

MacGregor, R. C., & Vrazalic, L. (2009). E-commerce adoption barriers in small businesses and the differential effects of gender. *Journal of Electronic Commerce in Organizations, 4*(2), 1–24. doi:10.4018/jeco.2006040101

MacKenzie, D. (2009). Making things the same: Gases, emission rights and the politics of carbon markets. *Accounting, Organizations and Society, 34*(3), 440–455. doi:10.1016/j.aos.2008.02.004

Maechler, S., Furrer, E., Lunghi, E., Monthoux, M., Yousefzai, C., & Graz, J.-C. (2019). Substituting risk for uncertainty. Where are the limits and how to face them? *Les Cahiers de l'IEP*, (73), 1–28.

Mahieu, B., Arnold, E., & Kolarz, P. (2014). *Measuring scientific performance for improved policy making. Science and Technology Options Assessment (STOA) Study, European Parliamentary Research Service (EPRS)*. Brussels: European Union; Retrieved from https://www.europarl.europa.eu/stoa/en/document/IPOL-JOIN_ET(2014)527383

Mangelsdorf, A. (2009). *Driving factors of service companies to participate in formal standardization processes: An empirical analysis*. doi:10.2139srn.1469512

Mangiarotti, G., & Riillo, A. F. (2010). ISO 9000 Certification and Innovation: an Empirical Analysis for Luxembourg. Economie et Statistiques working paper du STATEC, No 46.

Martin, B. R., & Whitley, R. (2010). The UK Research Assessment Exercise: A Case of Regulatory Capture? In R. Whitley, J. Gläser, & L. Engwall (Eds.), Reconfiguring Knowledge Production: Changing Authority Relationships in the Sciences and their Consequences for Intellectual Innovation (pp. 51–80). Oxford, UK: Oxford University Press; doi:10.1093/acprof:oso/9780199590193.003.0002.

Martinez-Alier, J. (2002). *The Environmentalism of the Poor: A Study of Ecological Conflicts and Valuation.* Cheltenham, UK: Edward Elgar Publishing. doi:10.4337/9781843765486

Martinez, M. G., & Poole, N. (2004). The development of private fresh produce safety standards: Implications for developing Mediterranean exporting countries. *Food Policy, 29*(3), 229–255. doi:10.1016/j.foodpol.2004.04.002

Mattli, W., & Buthe, T. (2011). *The New Global Rulers.* Princeton, NJ: Princeton University Press.

Mazower, M. (2013). *Governing the World: The History of an Idea, 1815 to the Present.* New York: Penguin Books.

McAdam, R., Armstrong, G., & Kelly, B. (1998). Investigation of the relationship between total quality and innovation: A research study involving small organisations. *European Journal of Innovation Management, 1*(3), 139–147. doi:10.1108/14601069810230216

McGrath, A., & Cox, M. (2014). Research Excellence and Evaluation Using a CRIS: A Cross-institutional Perspective. *Procedia Computer Science, 33*, 301–308. doi:10.1016/j.procs.2014.06.048

Mena, S., & Palazzo, G. (2012). Input and Output Legitimacy of Multi-Stakeholder Initiatives. *Business Ethics Quarterly, 22*(3), 527–556. doi:10.5840/beq201222333

Mesoudi, A., Whiten, A., & Laland, K. N. (2006). Towards a unified science of cultural evolution. *Behavioral and Brain Sciences, 29*(4), 329–383. doi:10.1017/S0140525X06009083 PMID:17094820

Miettinen, R. (1998). Object Construction and Networks in Research Work: The Case of Research on Cellulose degrading Enzymes. *Social Studies of Science, 28*(3), 423–463.

Miotti, H. (2009). *The Economic Impact of Standardization.* Technological Change, Standards Growth in France. AFNOR.

Mir, M., Casadesus, M., & Petnji, L. H. (2016). The impact of standardized innovation management systems on innovation capability and business performance: An empirical study. *Journal of Engineering and Technology Management, 41*, 26–44. doi:10.1016/j.jengtecman.2016.06.002

Mittal, S., & Sharma, P. P. (2017). The Role of Consent in Legitimising the Processing of Personal Data Under the Current EU Data Protection Framework. *Asian Journal of Computer Science And Information Technology, 7*, 76–78.

Moed, H. F., & Halevi, G. (2015). Multidimensional assessment of scholarly research impact. *Journal of the Association for Information Science and Technology, 66*(10), 1988–2002. doi:10.1002/asi.23314

Moenius, J. (2004). *Information Versus Product Adaptation: The Role of Standards in Trade (February 2004).* Available at SSRN: https://ssrn.com/abstract=608022

Moisdon, J. C. (1997). *Du mode d'existence des outils de gestion: les instruments de gestion à l'épreuve de l'organisation.* Seli Arslan.

Mougin, F. & Benenati, B. (2005). Danone se raconte des histoires, une version latine du knowledge management. *Séminaire des affaires organisé grâce aux parrains de l'école de Paris.*

Myers, J. P., & Reichert, J. S. (1997). Perspective in nature's services. In G. Daily (Ed.), *Nature's Services: Societal Dependence on Natural Ecosystems* (pp. xvii–xx). Washington, DC: Island Press.

Nacer, H., & Aissani, D. (2014). Semantic web services: Standards, applications, challenges and solutions. *Journal of Network and Computer Applications, 44,* 134–151. doi:10.1016/j.jnca.2014.04.015

Nakatani, K., Chuang, T. T., & Zhou, D. (2006). Data synchronization technology: Standards, business values and implications. *Communications of the Association for Information Systems, 17*(1), 44.

Narin, F. (1976). Evaluative bibliometrics: The use of publication and citation analysis in the evaluation of scientific activity. Report to the National Science Foundation.

Natural Capital Coalition. (2018a). *Natural Capital Coalition | Coalition Organizations.* Retrieved from https://naturalcapitalcoalition.org/who/coalition-organizations/

Natural Capital Coalition. (2018b). *Natural Capital Coalition | Protocol.* Retrieved from https://naturalcapitalcoalition.org/protocol/

Naude, M., & Badenhorst-Weiss, J. (2011). The effect of problems on supply chain wide efficiency. *Journal of Transport and Supply Chain, 5,* 278–298.

Nelson, R. R., & Winter, S. G. (1982). *An Evolutionary Theory of Economic Change.* Cambridge, UK: Belknap Press.

Neves, F. de O., Salgado, E. G., & Beijo, L. A. (2017). Analysis of the Environmental Management System based on ISO 14001 on the American continent. *Journal of Environmental Management, 199,* 251–262. doi:10.1016/j.jenvman.2017.05.049 PMID:28552409

Niklasson, B., & Pierre, J. (2012). Does agency age matter in administrative reform?: Policy autonomy and public management in Swedish agencies. *Policy and Society, 31*(3), 195–210. doi:10.1016/j.polsoc.2012.07.002

Nonaka I., Toyama R., & Hirata., T. (2008). *Managing flow: A process theory of the knowledge-based firm.* doi:10.1057/9780230583702

Nordhaus, W. D. (2007). A Review of the Stern Review on the Economics of Climate Change. *Journal of Economic Literature*, *45*(3), 686–702. doi:10.1257/jel.45.3.686 PMID:17626869

Ntim, C. G., Soobaroyen, T., & Broad, M. J. (2017). Governance structures, voluntary disclosures and public accountability. *Accounting, Auditing & Accountability Journal*, *30*(1), 65–118. doi:10.1108/AAAJ-10-2014-1842

Oberhausen, C. (2018). *Standardisierte Unternehmensübergreifende Wertstrommethode (StreaM)* (Dissertation). Université du Luxembourg.

Oberhausen, C., & Plapper, P. (2016). A Standardized Value Stream Management Method for Supply Chain Networks. In D. Dimitrov & T. Oosthuizen (Eds.), *Proceedings of COMA'16 International Conference on Competitive Manufacturing* (pp. 428–433). COMA'16.

Oberhausen, C., Minoufekr, M., Plapper, P. (2017b). Continuous Improvement of Complex Process Flows by Means of Stream as the "Standardized Cross-Enterprise Value Stream Management Method". *IEEE IEEM*.

Oberhausen, C., Minoufekr, M., Plapper, P. (2018). Application of Value Stream Management to enhance Product and Information Flows in Supply Chain Networks-Based on the example of Web-Based Automotive Retail Business. *Management and Production Engineering Review*, *9*.

Oberhausen, C., Minoufekr, M., & Plapper, P. (2017a). Standardized Value Stream Management Method to Visualize, Analyze and Optimize Cross-Enterprise Value Stream Data. *International Journal of Standardization Research*, *15*.

Oberhausen, C., & Plapper, P. (2015). Value Stream Management in the "Lean Manufacturing Laboratory." *CIRP Conference on Learning Factories*. 10.1016/j.procir.2015.02.087

Oberhausen, C., & Plapper, P. (2017). Cross-Enterprise Value Stream Assessment. *Journal of Advances in Management Research*, *14*(2), 182–193. doi:10.1108/JAMR-05-2016-0038

Oberhausen, C., Weber, D., & Plapper, P. (2015). Value Stream Management in high variability production systems. *SSRG Int. J. Ind. Eng*, *2*(1), 1–4.

OECD. (2004). *Measuring Sustainable Development: Integrated Economic, Environmental and Social Frameworks*. Retrieved from: https://www.oecd-ilibrary.org/environment/measuring-sustainable-development_9789264020139-en

OECD. (2006). *Cost-Benefit Analysis and the Environment: Recent Developments*. Retrieved from http://www.oecd.org/greengrowth/tools-evaluation/cost-benefitanalysisandtheenvironmentrecentdevelopments2006.htm

OECD. (2018). *Cost-Benefit Analysis and the Environment: Further Developments and Policy Use*. Retrieved from https://www.oecd.org/governance/cost-benefit-analysis-and-the-environment-9789264085169-en.htm

Optimat. (2014). Research Study on the Benefits of Linking Innovation and Standardization. Final Report, CEN/CENELEC. Retrieved from https://www.cencenelec.eu/ research/news/publications/ Publications/BRIDGIT-standinno-study.pdf

Orviska, M., & Hunady, J. (2017). Selected Barriers to Online International Trade Within the EU: Could Standards and Common Rules Help? *International Journal of Standardization Research*, *15*(2), 76–93. doi:10.4018/IJSR.2017070105

OWL 2. (2012, December 11). *Retrieved 11 August 2019, from OWL 2 Web Ontology Language Document Overview* (2nd ed.). Retrieved from https://www.w3.org/TR/owl2-overview/

Page, E. S. (1997). Data Collection for the 1996 Research Assessment Exercise: Review (No. M2/97). Retrieved from https://webarchive.nationalarchives.gov.uk/20120118212839/http://www.hefce.ac.uk/pubs/hefce/1997/m2_97.htm

Palattella, M. R., Dohler, M., Grieco, A., Rizzo, G., Torsner, J., Engel, T., & Ladid, L. (2016). Internet of Things in the 5G Era: Enablers, Architecture, and Business Models. *IEEE Journal on Selected Areas in Communications*, *34*(3), 510–527. doi:10.1109/JSAC.2016.2525418

Pandeya, B., Buytaert, W., Zulkafli, Z., Karpouzoglou, T., Mao, F., & Hannah, D. M. (2016). A comparative analysis of ecosystem services valuation approaches for application at the local scale and in data scarce regions. *Ecosystem Services*, *22*, 250–259. doi:10.1016/j.ecoser.2016.10.015

Pandit, H. J., & Lewis, D. (2017). Modelling Provenance for GDPR Compliance using Linked Open Data Vocabularies. *Proceedings of the 5th Workshop on Society, Privacy and the Semantic Web - Policy and Technology (PrivOn2017) (PrivOn)*. Retrieved from http://ceur-ws.org/Vol-1951/PrivOn2017_paper_6.pdf

Pandit, H. J., & Polleres, A. (2019, July 26). *DPV*. Retrieved 11 August 2019, from Data Privacy Vocabulary v0.1 website: https://www.w3.org/ns/dpv

Pandit, H. J., Fatema, K., O'Sullivan, D., & Lewis, D. (2018). GDPRtEXT - GDPR as a Linked Data Resource. *The Semantic Web - European Semantic Web Conference*, 481–495.

Pandit, H. J., Debruyne, C., O'Sullivan, D., & Lewis, D. (2018). An Exploration of Data Interoperability for GDPR. *International Journal of Standardization Research*, *16*(1), 1–21. doi:10.4018/IJSR.2018010101

Pandit, H. J., Debruyne, C., O'Sullivan, D., & Lewis, D. (2019). GConsent—A Consent Ontology Based on the GDPR. In K. Hammar (Ed.), *The Semantic Web*. doi:10.1007/978-3-030-21348-0_18

Pearce, D. W., Markandya, A., & Barbier, E. B. (1989). *Blueprint for a Green Economy*. London: Earthscan.

Pekovic, S., & Galia, F. (2009). From quality to innovation: Evidence from two French Employer Surveys. *Technovation*, *29*, 829–842.

Picciotto, R. (2005). The value of evaluation standards: A comparative assessment. *Journal of Multidisciplinary Evaluation*, *2*(3), 30–59.

Plapper, P., & André, C. (2011). Wertstrommethode – Value Stream Mapping. In Der Qualitätsmanagement-Berater (10th ed.; pp. 1–27). Academic Press.

Pohlmann, T. (2017). *Empirical study on patenting and standardization activities at IEEE.* Available at https://www.iplytics.com/wp-content/uploads/2018/01/IPlytics_2017_Patenting-and-standardization-activities-at-IEEE.pdf

Polanyi, M. (1958). Personal knowledge, towards a post critical philosophy. Chicago Press.

Porter, T. (2005). Private Authority, Technical Authority, and the Globalization of Accounting Standards. *Business and Politics*, *7*(3), 1–30. doi:10.2202/1469-3569.1138

Portugal-Perez, A., Reyes, J. D., & Wilson, J. S. (2010). Beyond the information technology agreement: Harmonisation of standards and trade in electronics. *World Economy*, *33*(12), 1870–1897. doi:10.1111/j.1467-9701.2010.01300.x

Power, M. (2004). *The Risk Management of Everything.* London: Demos. doi:10.1108/eb023001

Power, M. (2015). How accounting begins: Object formation and the accretion of infrastructure. *Accounting, Organizations and Society*, *47*, 43–55. doi:10.1016/j.aos.2015.10.005

Prajogo, D. I., & Sohal, A. S. (2003). The relationship between TQM practices, quality performance, and innovation performance: An empirical examination. *International Journal of Quality & Reliability Management*, *20*(8), 901–918. doi:10.1108/02656710310493625

Prakash, A., & Potoski, M. (2006). *The Voluntary Environmentalists: Green Clubs, ISO 14001, and Voluntary Environmental Regulations.* Cambridge, UK: Cambridge University Press. doi:10.1017/CBO9780511617683

PricewaterhouseCoopers. (2015). *Valuing corporate environmental impacts.* London: PwC.

Profit Surge Consulting. (2017). *Profit Surge VSM Software.* Retrieved January 26, 2017, from http://profit-surge.com/ProfitSurgeVSM.html

Purushothaman, S., Thomas, B., Abraham, R., & Dhar, U. (2013). Beyond money metrics: Alternative approaches to conceptualising and assessing ecosystem services. *Conservation & Society*, *11*(4), 321. doi:10.4103/0972-4923.125739

RAE. (2005). Guidance on submissions (No. 03/2005). RAE.

Ràfols, I. (2019). S&T indicators in the wild: Contextualization and participation for responsible metrics. *Research Evaluation*, *28*(1), 7–22. doi:10.1093/reseval/rvy030

Ramirez, C. (2013). Normalisation des services marchands ou marchandisation des normes. In *J.-C. Graz & N. Niang, Services sans frontières* (pp. 223–252). Paris: Presses de Sciences Po.

Ranganathan, R., Ghosh, A., & Rosenkopf, L. (2018). Competition–cooperation interplay during multifirm technology coordination: The effect of firm heterogeneity on conflict and consensus in a technology standards organization. *Strategic Management Journal*, *39*(12), 3193–3221. doi:10.1002mj.2786

Ranganathan, R., & Rosenkopf, L. (2014). Do ties really bind? The effect of knowledge and commercialization networks on opposition to standards. *Academy of Management Journal, 57*(2), 515–540. doi:10.5465/amj.2011.1064

RDF 1.1 Primer. (2014, June 24). Retrieved 11 August 2019, from RDF 1.1 Primer website: https://www.w3.org/TR/rdf11-primer/

Rebora, G., & Turri, M. (2013). The UK and Italian research assessment exercises face to face. *Research Policy, 42*(9), 1657–1666. doi:10.1016/j.respol.2013.06.009

REF. (2011). Assessment framework and guidance on submissions (No. 02.2011). Retrieved from https://webarchive.nationalarchives.gov.uk/20170302114208/http://www.ref.ac.uk/pubs/2011-02/

REF. (2015). Research Excellence Framework 2014: Manager's report. Retrieved from https://webarchive.nationalarchives.gov.uk/20170302114114/http://www.ref.ac.uk/pubs/refmanagersreport/

REF. (2017). Consultation on the second Research Excellence Framework: Summary of responses (No. 2017/02). Retrieved from https://www.ref.ac.uk/media/1046/ref_2017_02.pdf

REF. (2019a). Guidance on submissions (No. 2019/01). Retrieved from https://www.ref.ac.uk/media/1092/ref-2019_01-guidance-on-submissions.pdf

REF. (2019b). Panel criteria and working methods (No. 2019/02). Retrieved from https://www.ref.ac.uk/media/1084/ref-2019_02-panel-criteria-and-working-methods.pdf

Regulation (EU) 2016/679 of the European Parliament and of the Council of 27 April 2016 on the protection of natural persons with regard to the processing of personal data and on the free movement of such data, and repealing Directive 95/46/EC (General Data Protection Regulation). (2016). *Official Journal of the European Union, L119*, 1–88.

Reinhart, M. (2012). *Soziologie und Epistemologie des Peer Review*. Baden-Baden: Nomos; doi:10.5771/9783845239415

Reuben, J., Martucci, L. A., Fischer-Hübner, S., Packer, H. S., Hedbom, H., & Moreau, L. (2016). Privacy Impact Assessment Template for Provenance. *Availability, Reliability and Security (ARES), 2016 11th International Conference On*, 653–660.

Riboud, F. (2013). *Danone Rapport économique et social*. Academic Press.

Riillo, C. F. A. (2014). *ICT Standardization and use of ICT standards: a firm level analysis*. MPRA Paper No. 63436.

Riillo, C. (2013). Profiles and motivations of Standardization Players. *International Journal of IT Standards and Standardization Research, 11*(2), 17–33. doi:10.4018/jitsr.2013070102

Rodrigues, C. M. de O., Freitas, F. L. G. de, Barreiros, E. F. S., Azevedo, R. R. de, & de Almeida Filho, A. T. (2019). Legal ontologies over time: A systematic mapping study. *Expert Systems with Applications, 130*, 12–30.

Rolland, N. (2012). *L'entreprise 2.0 en France en 2012: Mythe et Réalité*. Etude réalisée par l'Institut de l'Entreprise 2.0 de Grenoble Ecole de Management.

Rother, M., & Shook, J. (1999). *Learning to see: value-stream mapping to create value and eliminate muda (1.2)*. Lean Enterprise Institute.

Ruiz-Mafé, C., Sanz-Blas, S., & Aldás-Manzano, J. (2009). Drivers and barriers to online airline ticket purchasing. *Journal of Air Transport Management, 15*(6), 294–298. doi:10.1016/j.jairtraman.2009.02.001

Russell, R. (2012). Adoption of CERIF in Higher Education Institutions in the UK: A Landscape Study. Version 1.1.

Russell, A. (2006). 'Rough Consensus and Running Code' and the Internet-OSI Standards War. *IEEE Annals of the History of Computing, 28*, 48–61. doi:10.1109/MAHC.2006.42

Russell, A. (2014). *Open Standards and the Digital Age – History, Ideology, and Networks*. Cambridge University Press. doi:10.1017/CBO9781139856553

Ryan, R. M., & Deci, E. L. (2000). Intrinsic and extrinsic motivations: Classic definitions and new directions. *Contemporary Educational Psychology, 25*(1), 54–67. doi:10.1006/ceps.1999.1020 PMID:10620381

Sages, R., & Lundsten, J. (2004). The ambiguous nature of psychology as science and its bearing on methods of inquiry. In M. Lahlou, & R. B. Sages (Eds.), Mèthodes et Terrains de la Psychologie Interculturelle (pp. 189- 220). Lyon, France: L'Interdisciplinaire, Limonest.

Saldaña, J. (2013). *The coding manual for qualitative researchers* (2nd ed.). Thousand Oaks, CA: Sage.

Sampaio, P., Saraiva, P., & Rodrigues, A. G. (2009). ISO 9001 certification research: Questions, answers and approaches. *International Journal of Quality & Reliability Management, 26*(1), 38–58. doi:10.1108/02656710910924161

Sands, P., & Peel, J. (2008). *Principles of International Environmental Law*. Oxford, UK: Oxford University Press.

Sardá, R., & Pogutz, S. (2018). *Corporate Sustainability in the 21st Century: Increasing the Resilience of Social-Ecological Systems*. New York: Routledge. doi:10.4324/9781315180908

Saulais, P., & Ermine, J.-L. (2012). Innovation fondée sur les connaissances: Une expérimentation sur l'innovation technique incrémentale. In GeCSO Gestion des Connaissances dans la Société et les Organisations. Montréal, Canada: Mai.

Schäfermeyer, M., & Rosenkranz, C. (2011). To Standardize or not to Standardize? - Understanding the Effect of Business Process Complexity on Business Process Standardization. *ECIS 2011 Proceedings*.

Schema.org. (n.d.). Retrieved 23 July 2019, from https://schema.org/

Schmitz, V., & Leukel, J. (2005). Findings and Recommendations from a Pan-European Research Project: Comparative Analysis of E-Catalog Standards. *International Journal of IT Standards and Standardization Research*, *3*(2), 51–65. doi:10.4018/jitsr.2005070105

Schneider, K. J. (1990). *The paradoxical self: Toward an understanding of our contradictory nature*. New York: Insight Books, Plenum.

Schweinsberg, K., & Wegner, L. (2017). Advantages of complex SQL types in storing XML documents. *Future Generation Computer Systems*, *68*, 500–507. doi:10.1016/j.future.2016.02.013

Scott, C., & Westbrook, R. (1991). New Strategic Tools for Supply Chain Management. *International Journal of Physical Distribution & Logistics Management*, *21*(1), 23–33. doi:10.1108/09600039110002225

Seawright, J., & Gerring, J. (2008). Case Selection Techniques in Case Study Research: A Menu of Qualitative and Quantitative Options. *Political Research Quarterly*, *61*(2), 294–308. doi:10.1177/1065912907313077

Sengupta, J. (2014). Schumpeterian Innovation. In Theory of Innovation. Cham: Springer; doi:10.1007/978-3-319-02183-6_3.

Serhan, H. (2017). *Pratiques d'appropriation et dynamique des connaissances de la norme ISO 9001: outil de conformation et creuset d'innovation* (Thèse de doctorat). AgroParisTech, Université Paris-Saclay, Paris, France.

Serhan, H. (2018). Creating conformity, facilitating innovation: A practice-based study of implementing ISO 9001 standard. In Congrès RRI – VIII Forum de l'innovation, Les nouveaux modes de l'organisation. IUT Nîmes – Université Montpellier 1.

Sidak, J. G. (2016). Testing for Bias to Suppress Royalties for Standard-Essential Patents. *Criterion J. on Innovation*, *1*, 301.

Siemens PLM Software Inc. (2017). *Tecnomatix*. Retrieved January 26, 2017, from https://www.plm.automation.siemens.com/en_us/products/tecnomatix/manufacturing-simulation/material-flow/plant-simulation.shtml

Sile, L., Guns, R., Vandermoere, F., & Engels, T. (2019). Comparison of classification-related differences in the distribution of journal articles across academic disciplines: the case of social sciences and humanities in Flanders and Norway (2006-2015). In ISSI - the International Society for Informetrics and Scientometrics (Chair), 17 International Conference on Scientometrics & Informetrics. Sapienza University of Rome.

Simcoe, T. (2012). Standard setting committees: Consensus governance for shared technology platforms. *The American Economic Review*, *102*(1), 305–336. doi:10.1257/aer.102.1.305

Sitek, P., Nielsen, I. E., & Wikarek, J. (2014). A hybrid multi-agent approach to the solving supply chain problems. *Procedia Computer Science*, *35*, 1557–1566. doi:10.1016/j.procs.2014.08.239

Sivertsen, G. (2017). Unique, but still best practice? The Research Excellence Framework (REF) from an international perspective. Palgrave Communications, 3(1), 725. doi:10.1057/palcomms.2017.78

Smiraglia, R. P. (2019). Trajectories for Research: Fathoming the Promise of the NARCIS Classification. *Knowledge Organization, 46*(5), 337–344. doi:10.5771/0943-7444-2019-5-337

Smith, W. K., Lewis, M. W., & Tushman, M. L. (2011). Organizational sustainability: Organization design and senior leadership to enable strategic paradox. In K. Cameron, & G. Spreitzer (Eds.), The Oxford handbook of positive organizational scholarship (pp. 798-810). New York, NY: Oxford University Press.

Smith, W. K., Lewis, M. W., Jarzabkowski, P., & Langley, A. (2017). *The oxford handbook of organizational paradox.* OUP. doi:10.1093/oxfordhb/9780198754428.001.0001

Smith, W. K., & Tushman, M. L. (2005). Managing strategic contradictions: A top management model for managing innovation streams. *Organization Science, 16*(5), 522–536. doi:10.1287/orsc.1050.0134

Solaymani, S., Sohaili, K., & Yazdinejad, E. A. (2012). Adoption and use of e-commerce in SMEs. *Electronic Commerce Research, 12*(3), 249–263. doi:10.100710660-012-9096-6

Song, Z., Sun, Y., Wan, J., Huang, L., & Zhu, J. (2019). Smart e-commerce systems: Current status and research challenges. *Electronic Markets, 29*(2), 221–238. doi:10.100712525-017-0272-3

SPARQL 1.1 Query Language. (n.d.). Retrieved 30 April 2019, from SPARQL 1.1 Query Language website: https://www.w3.org/TR/sparql11-query/

Spinuzzi, C. (2011). Losing by expanding: Coralling the runaway object. *Journal of Business and Technical Communication, 25*(4), 449–486. doi:10.1177/1050651911411040

Spinuzzi, C. (2014). How noemployer firms stage-manage ad-hoc collaboration: An activity theory analysis. *Technical Communication Quarterly, 23*(2), 88–114. doi:10.1080/10572252.2013.797334

Stamper, R. (1996). Organisational semiotics. In *Information systems: An emerging discipline?* McGraw-Hill.

Steinfield, C., Wigand, R., Markus, M. L., & Minton, G. (2007). Promoting e-business through vertical information systems standards: Lessons from the US home mortgage industry. In S. Greenstein & V. Stango (Eds.), *Standards and Public Policy* (pp. 160–207). Cambridge, UK: Cambridge University Press.

Stern, N. (2016). Building on success and learning from experience: an independent review of the Research Excellence Framework. Retrieved from Department for Business, Energy & Industrial Strategy website: https://www.gov.uk/government/publications/research-excellence-framework-review

Stern, N. (2006). *Stern Review: The Economics of Climate Change.* London: Stationery Office.

Steyskal, S., & Kirrane, S. (2015). If you can't enforce it, contract it: Enforceability in Policy-Driven (Linked) Data Markets. *SEMANTiCS (Posters & Demos)*, 63–66. Retrieved from https://pdfs.semanticscholar.org/f2c3/cac9b4af913f32dbd5034ed9aa1751a8a337.pdf

Stich, V., Schmidt, C., Meier, C., Cuber, S., & Kompa, S. (2011). Cross-company coordination in Built-to-Order Production Networks in Machinery and Equipment Industry. *4th Int. Conf. Chang. Agil. Reconfigurable Virtual Prod.*, 563-568.

Stockdale, R., & Standing, C. (2006). A classification model to support SME e-commerce adoption initiatives. *Journal of Small Business and Enterprise Development*, *13*(3), 381–394. doi:10.1108/14626000610680262

Stoll, T. P. (2014). Are You Still in?–The Impact of Licensing Requirements on the Composition of Standards Setting Organizations. In *The Impact of Licensing Requirements on the Composition of Standards Setting Organizations*. Max Planck Institute for Innovation & Competition Research Paper 14-18.

Stuurman, K. (2017). The Digitisation Driven Impact of Data Protection Regulation on the Standardisation Process. In *Digitalisation: Challenge and Opportunity for Standardisation. Proc. 22nd EURAS Annual Standardisation Conference*. Mainz Publishers.

Sullivan, S. (2017). Making nature investable: From legibility to leverageability in fabricating 'nature' as 'natural capital'. *Science & Technology Studies*, *20*, 1–30.

Sun, Y. (2014). Fixed-smoothing Asymptotics and Asymptotic F and t Tests in the Presence of Strong Autocorrelation. In *Essays in Honor of Peter C. B. Phillips*. Emerald Group Publishing Limited; doi:10.1108/S0731-905320140000033002

Swann, G. M. P. (2009). The Economics of Metrology and Measurement. Retrieved from http://webarchive.nationalarchives.gov.uk/+/http://www.nmo.bis.gov.uk/fileuploads/NMS/Prof_Swann_report_Econ_Measurement_Revisited_Oct_09.pdf

Swann, G. M. P. (2000). *The economics of standardization. Final report for Standards and Technical Regulations Directorate*. Department of Trade and Industry.

Swann, P., Temple, P., & Shurmer, M. (1996). Standards and trade performance: The UK experience. *Economic Journal (London)*, *106*(438), 1297–1313. doi:10.2307/2235522

Swedish government. (2006). Förordning (2006:1009) om ändring i förordningen (1995:1418) med instruktion för det statliga lantmäteriet [Ordinance (2006:1009) concerning changes in ordinance (1996:1418) for the governmental Lantmäteriet]. Svensk författningssamling 2006:1009. Stockholm, Sweden: Ministry of the Environment.

Swedish government. (2007). *Den osynliga infrastrukturen - om förbättrad samordning av offentlig ITstandardisering. SOU 2007:47* [The invisible infrastructure - concerning improved coordination of public ITstandardization. SOU 2007:47]. Stockholm, Sweden: Ministry of Enterprise and Innovation.

Swedish government. (2009). Förordning (2009:946) med instruktion för Lantmäteriet [Ordinance with instructions for Lantmäteriet]. Svensk författningssamling 2009:946. With later amendments. Stockholm, Sweden: Ministry of Enterprise and Innovation.

Swedish Standards Institute & Lantmäteriet. (2017). *Avtal nr LMV8589* [Agreement no. LMV8589]. Stockholm, Sweden: Swedish Standards Institute and Gävle, Sweden: Lantmäteriet.

Swedish Standards Institute. (2009). *SS 637004:2009. Geografisk information - Väg- och järnvägsnät - Applikationsschema* [Geographic information - Road and railway networks - Application schema]. Stockholm, Sweden: Swedish Standards Institute.

Swedish Standards Institute. (2012). Rapport om förslag till utveckling av Stanlis metodik [Report on suggestions for development of the STANLI methology]. 2012-05-25. Stockholm, Sweden: Swedish Standards Institute, technical committee TK323.

Swedish Standards Institute. (2014). *SS-EN ISO 19115-1:2014. Geografisk information - Metadata - Del 1: Grunder (ISO 19115-1:2014)* [ISO 19115-1:2014 Geographic information -- Metadata -- Part 1: Fundamentals]. Stockholm, Sweden: Swedish Standards Institute.

Swedish Standards Institute. (2016). *SS 637040:2016. Geografisk information - Detaljplan - Applikationsschema för planbestämmelser* [Geographic information - Detail plan- Application schema for planning instructions]. Stockholm, Sweden: Swedish Standards Institute.

Szulanski, G. (1996). Exploring internal stickiness: Impediments to the transfer of best practice within the firm. *Strategic Management Journal, 17*(S2), 27–43. doi:10.1002mj.4250171105

Takeuchi, H., & Osono, E. (2008). The contradictions that drive Toyota's success. *Harvard Business Review, 86*(6), 96. PMID:18411967

Technopolis. (2009). Identification and dissemination of lessons learned by institutions participating in the Research Excellence Framework (REF) bibliometrics pilot: Results of the Round Two Consultation. Retrieved from https://webarchive.nationalarchives.gov.uk/20180103220839/http://www.hefce.ac.uk/data/year/2009/Identification,and,dissemination,of,lessons,learned,by,institutions,participating,in,the,Research,Excellence,Framework,REF,bibliometrics,pilot,Results,of,the,Round,Two,Consultation/

Teece, D. J. (2007). Explicating dynamic capabilities: Nature and microfoundations of sustainable enterprise performance. *Strategic Management Journal, 28*(13), 1319–1350. doi:10.1002mj.640

Teichmann, H. (2016). Plugs and Socket-Outlets: Pet Peeve of International Travelers and Standardizers Alike. *EURAS Proceedings 2016.*

Tennison, J. (2016, February 25). *CSV on the Web*. Retrieved 11 August 2019, from CSV on the Web: A Primer website: https://www.w3.org/TR/tabular-data-primer/

Terlaak, A., & King, A. (2006). The effect of certification with the ISO 9000 Quality Management Standard: A signalling approach. *Journal of Economic Behavior & Organization, 60*(4), 579–602. doi:10.1016/j.jebo.2004.09.012

Terziovski, M., & Guerrero-Cusumano, J.-L. (2009). ISO 9000 Quality Systems Certification and Its Impact on Innovation Performance. *Academy of Management Annual Meeting Proceedings.*

The Association of Chartered Certified Accountants, Fauna & Flora International, & KPMG International Cooperative. (2012). *Is natural capital a material issue? Executive summary.* Retrieved from http://www.acca.ee/content/dam/acca/global/PDF-technical/environmental-publications/natural-capital-summary.pdf

The eVSM Group. (2017). *eVSM.* Retrieved January 26, 2017, from https://evsm.com/

Timmermans, S., & Epstein, S. (2010). A World of Standards but not a Standard World: Toward a Sociology of Standards and Standardization. *Annual Review of Sociology, 36*(1), 69–89. doi:10.1146/annurev.soc.012809.102629

Tobach, E. (1999). Activity theory and the concept of integrative levels. In Y. Engeström, R. Miettinen, & R.-L. Punamäki (Eds.), *Perspectives on activity theory* (pp. 133–146). New York, NY: Cambridge University Press. doi:10.1017/CBO9780511812774.011

Tsai, J., & Wright, J. D. (2015). Standard setting, intellectual property rights, and the role of antitrust in regulating incomplete contracts. *Antitrust Law Journal, 80*(1), 157–188.

Turnhout, E., Neves, K., & de Lijster, E. (2014). 'Measurementality' in Biodiversity Governance: Knowledge, Transparency, and the Intergovernmental Science-Policy Platform on Biodiversity and Ecosystem Services (Ipbes). *Environment and Planning A. Economy and Space, 46*(3), 581–597.

Tushman, M. L., & O'Reilly, C. A. I. III. (1996). Ambidextrous organizations: Managing evolutionary and revolutionary change. *California Management Review, 38*(4), 8–30. doi:10.2307/41165852

Tzolov, T. (2018). One Model For Implementation GDPR Based On ISO Standards. *2018 International Conference on Information Technologies (InfoTech),* 1–3.

UN. (2018). *Criteria For Identification Of LDCs.* New York: United Nations Department of Economic and Social Affairs.

UNCTAD. (2018). *What are the Least Developed Countries.* Geneva: UNCTAD.

United Nations. (Ed.). (2014). *System of environmental-economic accounting 2012: Central framework.* New York: United Nations.

Universities, U. K. (2017). Universities UK response to the UK Funding Councils consultation on the second Research Excellence Framework. Retrieved from https://www.universitiesuk.ac.uk/policy-and-analysis/reports/Documents/2017/second-ref-consultation-response.pdf

Van de Kaa, G. (2013). Responsible innovation and standardization: A new research approach? *International Journal of IT Standards and Standardization Research, 11*(2), 61–65. doi:10.4018/jitsr.2013070105 van de Kaa, G., Janssen, M., & Rezaei, J. (2018). Standards battles for business-to-government data exchange: Identifying success factors for standard dominance using the Best Worst Method. *Technological Forecasting and Social Change, 137*, 182–189. doi:10.1016/j.techfore.2018.07.041

Van der Meulen, B. (2007). Interfering governance and emerging centres of control. In P. Weingart, R. Whitley, & J. Gläser (Eds.), The Changing Governance of the Sciences (Vol. 26, pp. 191–203). Dordrecht: Springer Netherlands; doi:10.1007/978-1-4020-6746-4_9.

Van der Meulen, B., & Rip, A. (1998). Mediation in the Dutch science system. *Research Policy, 27*(8), 757–769. doi:10.1016/S0048-7333(98)00088-2

Van Drooge, L., Jong, S., Faber, M., & Westerheijden, D. F. (2013). *Twenty years of research evaluation.* The Hague, Netherlands: Academic Press.

Van Leeuwen, T. (2004). Descriptive Versus Evaluative Bibliometrics. In H. F. Moed, W. Glänzel, & U. Schmoch (Eds.), Handbook of Quantitative Science and Technology Research: The Use of Publication and Patent Statistics in Studies of S&T Systems (pp. 373–388). Dordrecht: Springer Netherlands; doi:10.1007/1-4020-2755-9_17.

Van Steen, J. (2012). *The science system in the Netherlands: An organisational overview.* Den Haag: Academic Press.

Van Vught, F. A. (1997). Combining planning and the market: An analysis of the Government strategy towards higher education in the Netherlands. *Higher Education Policy, 10*(3-4), 211–224. doi:10.1016/S0952-8733(97)00014-7

Verma, P. K., Verma, R., Prakash, A., Tripathi, R., & Naik, K. (2016). A novel hybrid medium access control protocol for inter-M2M communications. *Journal of Network and Computer Applications, 75*, 77–88. doi:10.1016/j.jnca.2016.08.011

Verona, G., & Ravasi, D. (2003). Unbundling dynamic capabilities: An exploratory study of continuous product innovation. *Industrial and Corporate Change, 12*(3), 577–606. doi:10.1093/icc/12.3.577

Vistawide. (2019). *World Languages and Cultures.* Retrieved from www.vistawide.com/languages/top_30_anguages

Vos, M. D., Kirrane, S., Padget, J., & Satoh, K. (2019). ODRL policy modelling and compliance checking. *3rd International Joint Conference on Rules and Reasoning (RuleML+RR 2019)*, 16.

VSNU. (1994). *Quality Assessment of Research, Protocol 1994.* Utrecht: VSNU.

VSNU. (2009). *NWO, KNAW 2009–2015.* Amsterdam: Standard Evaluation Protocol.

VSNU. (2015). *NWO, KNAW 2015–2021.* Amsterdam: Standard Evaluation Protocol.

VSNU. (2019). *Definitieafspraken Wetenschappelijk Onderzoek: Toelichting bij KUOZ.* Den Haag: VSNU.

VSNU. NWO, & KNAW. (2003). Standard Evaluation Protocol 2003-2009 for public research organisations. Utrecht: Author.

Vygotski, L. (1934). Pensée et langage. la dispute.

Wachter, S. (2018). The GDPR and the Internet of Things: A three-step transparency model. Law. *Innovation and Technology, 10*(2), 266–294.

Waddington, S., Joerg, B., Jones, R., McDonald, D., Gartner, R., Ritchie, M., . . . Trowell, S. (2014). UK Research Information Shared Service (UKRISS) Final Report, July 2014. Technical Report. Retrieved from JISC website: http://bura.brunel.ac.uk/handle/2438/10192

Waddington, S., Sudlow, A., Walshe, K., Scoble, R., Mitchell, L., Jones, R., & Trowell, S. (2013). Feasibility Study Into the Reporting of Research Information at a National Level Within the UK Higher Education Sector. New Review of Information Networking, 18(2), 74–105. doi:10.108 0/13614576.2013.841446

Waguespack, D. M., & Fleming, L. (2009). Scanning the commons? Evidence on the benefits to startups participating in open standards development. *Management Science, 55*(2), 210–223. doi:10.1287/mnsc.1080.0944

Walsh, P. (2007). Models for Standardization Bodies in Small and Developing Countries. *EURAS Proceedings 2007.*

Walsh, P. (2011). Governance and Structure of National Standards Bodies in Developing Countries as They Transition to Developed Status. *EURAS Proceedings 2011.*

Wang, W. Y. C., Heng, M. S. H., & Chau, P. Y. K. (2007). *Supply Chain Management : Issues in the New Era of Collaboration and Competition.* Retrieved from http://www.loc.gov/catdir/toc/ecip0611/2006010099.html

Wang, X. V., & Xu, X. W. (2015). A collaborative product data exchange environment based on STEP. *International Journal of Computer Integrated Manufacturing, 28*(1), 75–86. doi:10.108 0/0951192X.2013.785028

WBCSD. (2011). Guide to corporate ecosystem valuation: A framework for improving corporate decision-making. Geneva: World Business Council for Sustainable Development (WBCSD).

Wenning, R., & Kirrane, S. (2018). Compliance Using Metadata. In T. Hoppe, B. Humm, & A. Reibold (Eds.), *Semantic Applications: Methodology* (pp. 31–45). Technology, Corporate Use. doi:10.1007/978-3-662-55433-3_3

Westerheijden, D. F., de Boer, H., & Enders, J. (2009). Netherlands: An 'Echternach' Procession in Different Directions: Oscillating Steps Towards Reform. In C. Paradeise, E. Reale, I. Bleiklie, & E. Ferlie (Eds.), University Governance: Western European Comparative Perspectives (pp. 103–125). Dordrecht: Springer Netherlands; doi:10.1007/978-1-4020-9515-3_5.

Whitley, R. (2007). Changing Governance of the Public Sciences. In R. Whitley & J. Gläser (Eds.), Sociology of the Sciences Yearbook: Vol. 26. The Changing Governance of the Sciences: The Advent of Research Evaluation Systems (pp. 3–27). Dordrecht: Springer Netherlands. doi:10.1007/978-1-4020-6746-4_1

Whitley, R. (2011). Changing governance and authority relations in the public sciences. *Minerva*, *49*(4), 359–385. doi:10.1007/s11024-011-9182-2

Williams, R., & Edge, D. (1996). The Social Shaping of Technology. *Research Policy*, *25*(6), 856–899. doi:10.1016/0048-7333(96)00885-2

Wilsdon, J., Allen, L., Belfiore, E., Campbell, P., Curry, S., Hill, S., . . . Johnson, B. (2015). The Metric Tide: Report of the Independent Review of the Role of Metrics in Research Assessment and Management. Retrieved from https://responsiblemetrics.org/the-metric-tide/

Womack, J. P., & Jones, D. T. (2011). *Seeing the Whole Value Stream* (2nd ed.). Lean Enterprise Institute.

Wong, J., & Henderson, T. (2018). How Portable is Portable?: Exercising the GDPR's Right to Data Portability. *Proceedings of the 2018 ACM International Joint Conference and 2018 International Symposium on Pervasive and Ubiquitous Computing and Wearable Computers*, 911–920.

Wooldridge, J. M. (2010). *Econometric Analysis of Cross Section and Panel Data* (2nd ed.). Cambridge, MA: MIT Press.

Wurster, S., Egyedi, T. M., & Hommels, A. (2013). *The development of the public safety standard TETRA: lessons and recommendations for research managers and strategists in the security industry*. IEEE.

Xie, Z., Hall, J., McCarthy, I. P., Skitmore, M., & Schen, L. (2016). Standardization efforts: The relationship between knowledge dimensions, search processes and innovation outcomes. *Technovation*, *48*(4), 69–78. doi:10.1016/j.technovation.2015.12.002

XQuery. (2017, March). Retrieved 11 August 2019, from XQuery 3.1: An XML Query Language website: https://www.w3.org/TR/xquery-31/

Yates, J., & Murphy, C. N. (2009). *The International Organization for Standardization*. London: Routledge.

Yates, J., & Murphy, C. N. (2019). *Engineering Rules. Global Standard Setting since 1880*. Baltimore, MD: Johns Hopkins University Press.

Zaied, A. N. H. (2012). Barriers to e-commerce adoption in Egyptian SMEs. International. *Journal of Information Engineering and Electronic Business*, *4*(3), 9. doi:10.5815/ijieeb.2012.03.02

Zairi, M. (1994). Innovation or innovativeness? Results of benchmarking study. *Total Quality Management*, *5*(3), 27–44. doi:10.1080/09544129400000023

Zhao, K., Xia, M., & Shaw, M. (2007). An Integrated Model of Consortium-Based E-Business Standardization: Collaborative Development and Adoption with Network Externalities. *Journal of Management Information Systems*, 23(4), 247–271. doi:10.2753/MIS0742-1222230411

Zi, A., & Blind, K. (2015). Researchers' participation in standardisation: A case study from a public research institute in Germany. *The Journal of Technology Transfer*, 40(2), 346–360. doi:10.100710961-014-9370-y

Ziegler, J. (2013). *Betting on Famine: Why the World still Goes Hungry*. The New Press.

Zingales & Kanevskaia. (2016). The IEEE-SA patent policy update under the lens of EU competition law. *European Competition Journal*, 12(2-3), 195-235.

About the Contributors

Kai Jakobs joined RWTH Aachen University's Computer Science Department as a member of technical staff in 1985. His current research interests and activities focus on various aspects of ICT standards and the underlying standardisation process and he has published quite extensively in this field. Kai is Vice President of the European Academy for Standardisation (EURAS). He is also founder of the 'International Journal on Standardization Research', the 'Advances in Information Technology Standards and Standardization Research' and the 'EURAS Contributions to Standardisation Research' book series. He holds a PhD in Computer Science from the University of Edinburgh and is a Certified Standards Professional.

* * *

Justus Baron is a Senior Research Associate in Economics at Northwestern University Pritzker School of Law. His research focuses on innovation and the role of Intellectual Property Rights in standardization. He is a member of the European Commission expert group on Standard-Essential Patents, and the creator of the Searle Center Database on Technology Standards and Standard-Setting Organizations.

Sophie Biesenbender has been a researcher at the Institute for Research Information and Quality Assurance – iFQ since 2012, which in 2016 merged with the German Centre for Higher Education Research and Science Studies – DZHW. Previously she worked as a postdoctoral researcher at the University of Konstanz (2011-2012) and as a research associate at the European University Institute, Florence, Italy (2008-2011). She has a Master's in Public Affairs and Politics from Rutgers University, New Jersey, USA, and a doctorate in Politics and Public Administration from the University of Konstanz. Her dissertation project dealt with the comparative analysis of innovation in environmental policy. Her current research focus is on qualitative and quantitative research methods, classifications as well as the governance of research and science systems.

Christophe Debruyne is a Research Fellow at Trinity College Dublin (Ireland) and is affiliated with the ADAPT Centre. He received his PhD in Computer Science from the Vrije Universiteit Brussel (Belgium) in 2013. His main research interests are collaborative ontology engineering, data governance, and data integration. Dr. Debruyne has a keen interest in industry collaboration to demonstrate and validate his research, and to tackle problems that industry face. He has applied his research in various domains including HR, B2B, GLAM, and geospatial data.

Jean-Christophe Graz is Professor of international relations at the Institut d'Etudes Politiques (IEP) of the University of Lausanne, Switzerland, and co-founder of the Centre d'Histoire Internationale et d'Etudes Politiques de la Mondialisation (CRHIM). He has worked for the last 15 years on regulation issues in global political economy. His research focuses on transnational private governance, international standards, service offshoring, and more recently on labour and sustainability standards, risk and uncertainty, and the transformations of contemporary capitalism. His most recent book is The Power of Standards: Hybrid authority and the Globalisation of Services (Cambridge University Press, 2019 – Open Access).

Jan Hunady, PhD, is an assistant professor at the Faculty of Economics, Matej Bel University in Banska Bystrica, Slovakia. He received his PhD in public economics and services. He has published a number of papers in journals such as Transportation Research Part A: Policy and Practice, Information Polity and Engineering Economics. His research interests are focused on public finance, institutions, standardization and innovation. He participates in several research projects in the area of research policy and innovation. His expertise is also in econometrics and econometrics programs, particularly panel data and time series analysis.

Doudja Kabèche is assistant professor at Agroparistech. Her research interests concern the management tools and techniques and their relation with management innovation. She contributed to the French standardization organization (AFNOR) working group for the development of ISO innovation management standard.

Dave Lewis is the Deputy Director of the €50 Million SFI/Industry funded ADAPT Centre, leading its research on Digital Content Management and its programme of industry co-funded research projects. His current interests include modelling contextual integrity for personal data management, and the analysis and management of data ethics.

Jonas Lundsten is assistant professor at Malmö University (Sweden), Department of Urban Studies. His main research focus is the relationship between organizational routines and motivation.

Sylvain Maechler is a PhD student and teaching assistant in international relations at the Institut d'Etudes Politiques (IEP) of the University of Lausanne, Switzerland. He is member of the Centre d'Histoire Internationale et d'Etudes Politiques de la Mondialisation (CRHIM). His research focuses on the governance of capitalism in the face of ecological crises, with a special interest on international standards, private regulations, risk policies, corporate reporting and environmental accounting. His most recent publication is "Substituting risk for uncertainty. Where are the limits and how to face them?" (Les Cahiers de l'IEP n°73, 2019 – Open Access).

Jeff Mangers graduated from the Vienna University of Technology (TU Wien) with a bachelor's degree and a master's degree in Mechanical Engineering & Management. In 2019, he started as a doctoral researcher within the Research Unit in Engineering (RUES) at the University of Luxembourg. His research topics are Value Stream Management (VSM) in relation to Operational Excellence and Circular Economy. Since 2019, he has been representing ILNAS (Luxembourg) as an expert member of International Organization for Standardization in the Technical Committee 154 (ISO/ TC/ 154). He is also the project leader of ISO 22468, which handles the standardization of a common and standardized method for Value Stream Management.

Petros Maravelakis is Associate Professor at the Department of Business Administration of the University of Piraeus, Greece. His research interests are Statistical Process Control, Process Capability Indices, Applied Statistics, Reliability theory, indices for questionnaires and applied informatics. He has published more than 30 papers in peer reviewed international journals and he is associate editor of the international journal "Quality Technology and Quantitative Management" (published by Taylor and Francis).He has acted as referee for 34 international journals and 4 conferences. He has been and currently is involved in a variety of projects acting as research collaborator.

Vasileios Mavroeidis is a researcher of quality management at Hellenic Open University.

Meysam Minoufekr is chief engineer of the department of Operational Excellence at Luxembourg University. He has several years of experience in the development computer-aided manufacturing solution, both in industry and academia. He conducted his research activities on process simulations, data analysis and process optimization.

Declan O'Sullivan lectures at TCD's School of Computer Science and Statistics, is the Director of Research in the School, a co-champion of the Trinity Digital Engagement interdisciplinary theme, and a Principal Investigator at the Science Foundation Ireland (SFI) ADAPT Research Centre (http://www.adaptcentre.ie). In ADAPT he leads the research strand 'Transparent Digital Governance", encompassing research in data governance, data protection, data integration, data ethics, data value.

Christof Oberhausen holds a M.Sc. degree in Industrial Engineering from RWTH Aachen University and obtained his PhD degree at the Research Unit in Engineering (RUES) at the University of Luxembourg. His main field of research was Operational Excellence with a special focus on Value Stream Management. Since 2018, he is working as a project manager at Paul Wurth Geprolux S.A. in Luxembourg.

Marta Orviska is a professor of finance, banking and investment at Matej Bel University, Banska Bystrica. She is one of the most cited economists in Slovakia. Her research interest is focused on macroeconomics and public finance, including tax policy and tax evasion, standardisation, wellbeing, voting behaviour and the analysis of attitudes to, for example, NATO and the EU in the new applicant countries and new members of the EU, and to new technologies. She has held several positions in national and international projects in these areas. She has a large number of publications in leading academic journals. She has organized several international conferences and is a member of several professional, national and international boards and committees.

Jesper Paasch is professor (mso) at Aalborg University (Denmark) and associated professor at the University of Gävle (Sweden) in Land Management, and research coordinator at Lantmäteriet, the Swedish mapping cadastral and land registration authority. He has been working with geographic information and standardisation for more than three decades.

Harshvardhan Pandit is currently pursuing his PhD in Computer Science at Trinity College Dublin, Ireland. He works on assessing provenance-based legal obligations, with a specific focus on GDPR.

Sabrina Petersohn has been a researcher at the German Centre for Higher Education Research and Science Studies – DZHW since 2017. She holds a PhD in sociology from the University of Wuppertal and a masters degree in sociology, political sciences and public law from the University of Potsdam. Her dissertation project dealt with the professionalization of bibliometric research evaluation. Previously she worked as a doctoral researcher at the University of Wuppertal (2016-2017) and at the GESIS Leibniz Institute of Social Sciences in Cologne (2012-2016). Her current research interests revolve around the governance of science, science policy, research evaluation, the professionalization of bibliometrics, research information, research administration and management as well as the role of academic libraries and qualitative methods.

Peter Plapper obtained his PhD degree at the Laboratory for Machine Tools and Production Engineering (WZL) from the Technical University of Aachen (RWTH). Since 2010, he is Professor for Tool Machines and Production Technology at the University of Luxembourg. Topics of research are laser welding of dissimilar materials, robotic, and operational excellence. He is fellow of European Academy of Industrial Management, AIM, and member of "Wissenschaftliche Gesellschaft für Arbeits- und Betriebsorganisation", WGAB. This publication results from his service as convener of ISO TC 154 WG 7.

Hiam Serhan is Doctor in Management Sciences at AgroParisTech-Université Paris-Saclay. Her research focuses upon innovation management and how eco-design can be integrated into business models. She has written extensively on the impact of standards on food industry innovation. Her current research is on business model innovation for sustainability in local food industries.

Katarzyna Tarnawska has been a lecturer and researcher in knowledge management and economics in University of Cracow while now acts as a temporary policy officer in European Commission.

Hans Teichmann was employed as an electrical engineer from 1961 to 1981 by Swiss companies and the General Electric Co. in Schenectady, New York. From 1981 to 2000, he worked at the Central Office of the International Electrotechnical Commission (IEC) in Geneva, Switzerland successively as engineer, principal engineer and technical group manager. He holds a Dipl.-Ing. degree in electrical engineering of the Technical University Darmstadt, Germany; an M.Sc. (engineering) degree from Union College, Schenectady, New York; and the "Diploma in Translation" of the University of South Africa (UNISA), Pretoria.

Christoph Thiedig has been a researcher at the German Centre for Higher Education Research and Science Studies (DZHW) since 2017, working on topics of research information standardization, implementation and policy changes (most prominently, the German Research Core Dataset standard) as well as current developments surrounding research information systems in Germany and abroad. He holds a master's degree in science studies from the Humboldt University of Berlin and a bachelor's degree in sociology from the University of Bremen.

Index

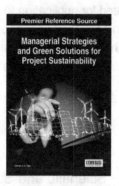

Printed in the United States
By Bookmasters